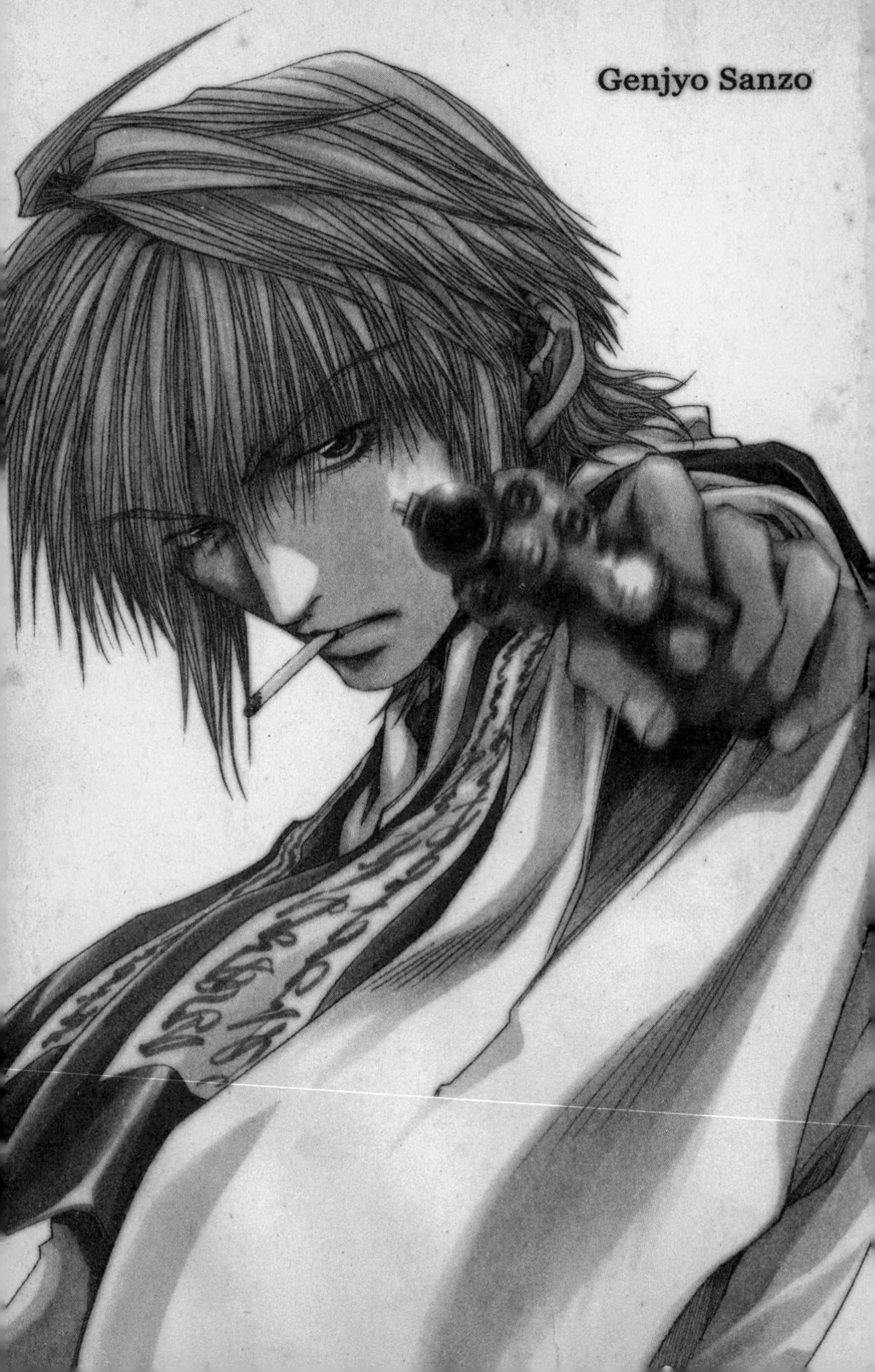
Genjyo Sanzo

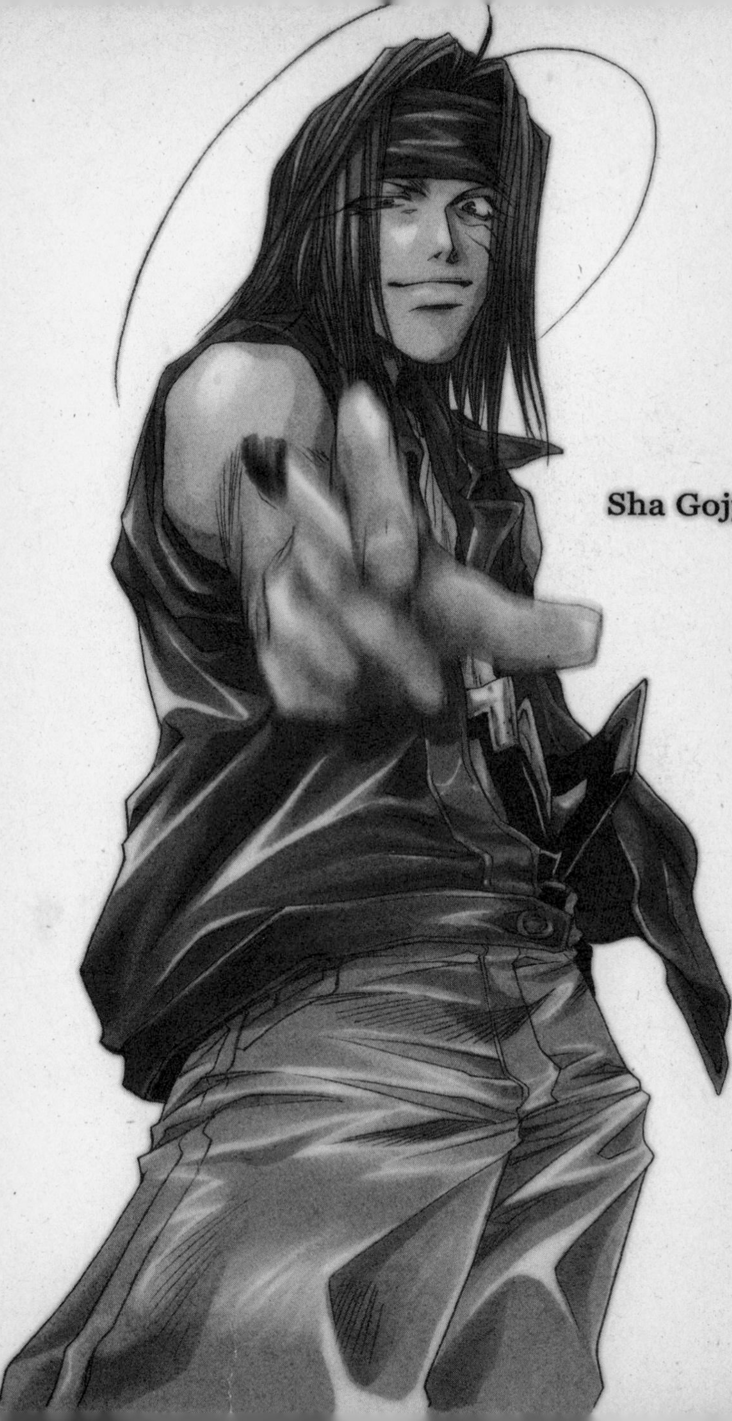

Sha Gojyo

Cho Hakkai

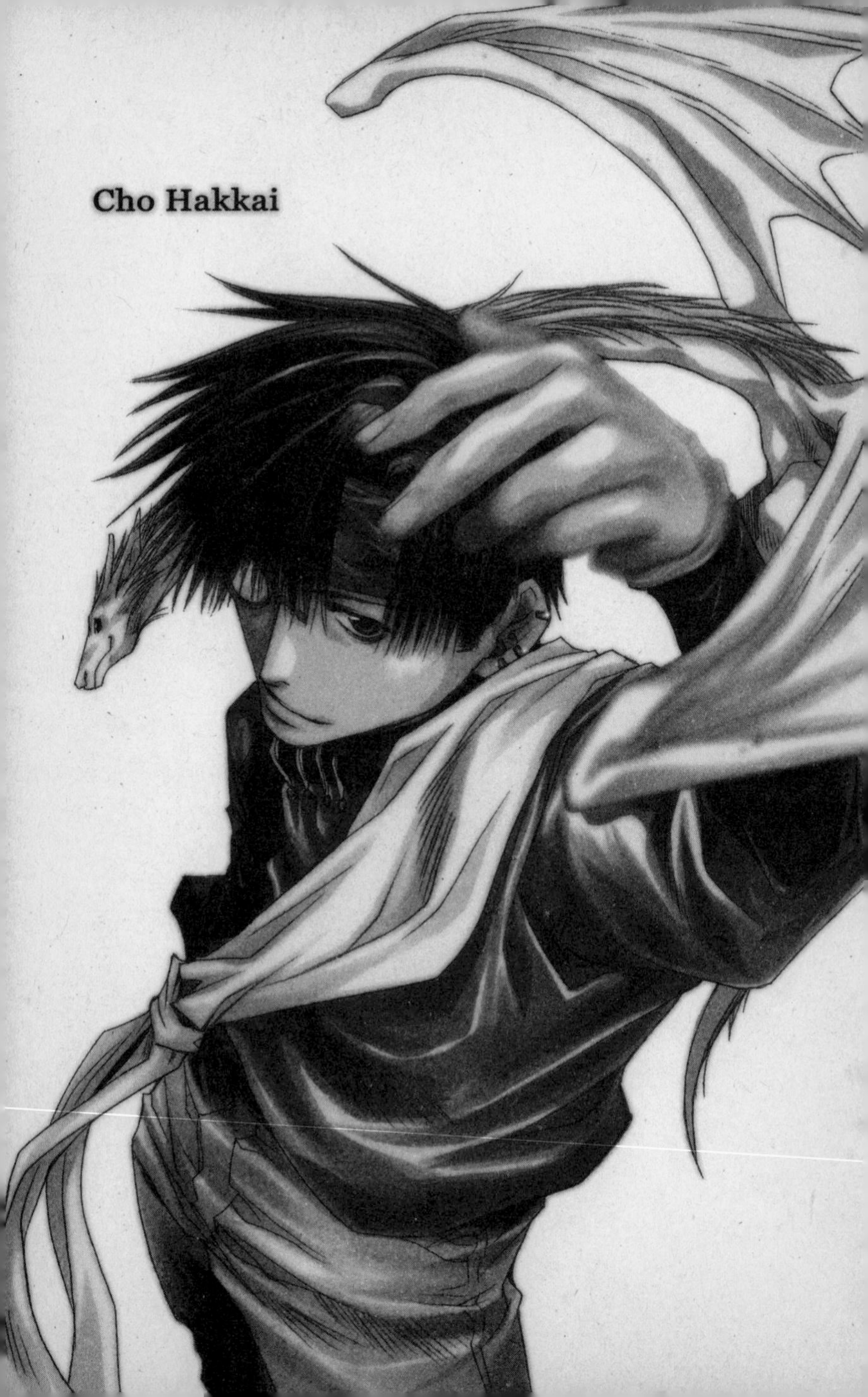

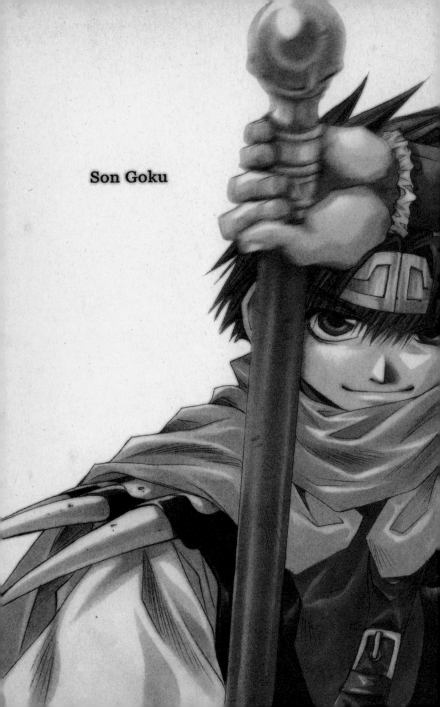

Son Goku

最遊記 SAIYUKI

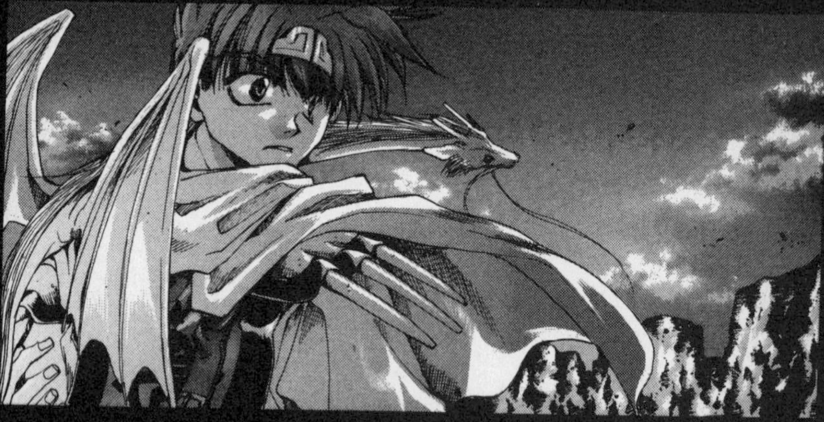

1

KAZUYA MINEKURA

Translator - Alethea Nibley & Athena Nibley
Associate Editor - Lianne Seater
Copy Editors - Carol Fox, Katherine Schilling & Christine Schilling
Retouch and Lettering - James Dashiell
Cover Layout - Anna Kernbaum

Editor - Jake Forbes
Digital Imaging Manager - Chris Buford
Pre-Press Manager - Antonio DePietro
Production Managers - Jennifer Miller, Mutsumi Miyazaki
Art Director - Matt Alford
Managing Editor - Jill Freshney
VP of Production - Ron Klamert
President & C.O.O. - John Parker
Publisher & C.E.O. - Stuart Levy

E-mail: info@TOKYOPOP.com
Come visit us online at www.TOKYOPOP.com

A **TOKYOPOP**® Manga

TOKYOPOP Inc.
5900 Wilshire Blvd. Suite 2000
Los Angeles, CA 90036

SAIYUKI Vol. 1

SAIYUKI volume 1 ©2002 by KAZUYA MINEKURA
All rights reserved.
First published in Japan in 2002 BY ISSAISHA, Tokyo. English translation rights arranged with
ISSAISHA through Tuttle-Mori Agency, Inc., Tokyo.

English text copyright ©2004 TOKYOPOP Inc

ISBN: 1-59182-651-9

First TOKYOPOP printing: March 2004

10 9 8 7 6

Printed in the USA

THIS AIN'T YOUR FATHER'S SAIYUKI.

Kazuya Minekura's *Saiyuki* is a rather unconventional adaptation of the Chinese "Xi-You-Ji" legend. Appropriately, the title of her modern update of the legend is a play on words, sounding like the classic title "Journey to the West," but being written with Kanji which say "Journey to the Extreme." The four heroes—Sanzo, Goku, Gojyo and Hakkai—are "extreme" upgrades to their traditional counterparts, both with their bad boy personalities and their *bishonen* good looks. This isn't the first time the legend was adapted for manga (Toriyama's *Dragonball* is another; Tezuka did it too), but Sanzo and Co. have never been so sexy.

The *Saiyuki* manga you are reading, which began its run in 1997, is the first series in what's become an ongoing saga. Completed at volume nine, the series became a surprise hit (especially with female fans), spawning an anime series (now available in English) and character goods. Minekura began (but as of now, has not completed) a prequel series called *Saiyuki Gaiden*. Currently, Minekura is hard at work on the sequel to *Saiyuki*, *Saiyuki Reloaded*, which runs in the monthly anthology *Zero Sum*.

For the English edition of *Saiyuki*, TOKYOPOP is proud to be using the original wraparound covers from the *Zero-Sum* edition, published in Japan in 2002. In order to leave the interior art as close to the original as possible, sound effects are left in Japanese, However a glossary is included at the back of the book to help you understand them. You'll also find a glossary of translator notes which are intended to give you a deeper understanding of the text, but are not necessary for its enjoyment (any notes which are crucial for a scene are noted on the page itself).

Now, hop on the jeep with the Sanzo team for the journey to the West. It's gonna be a wild ride.

Editor
January 2004

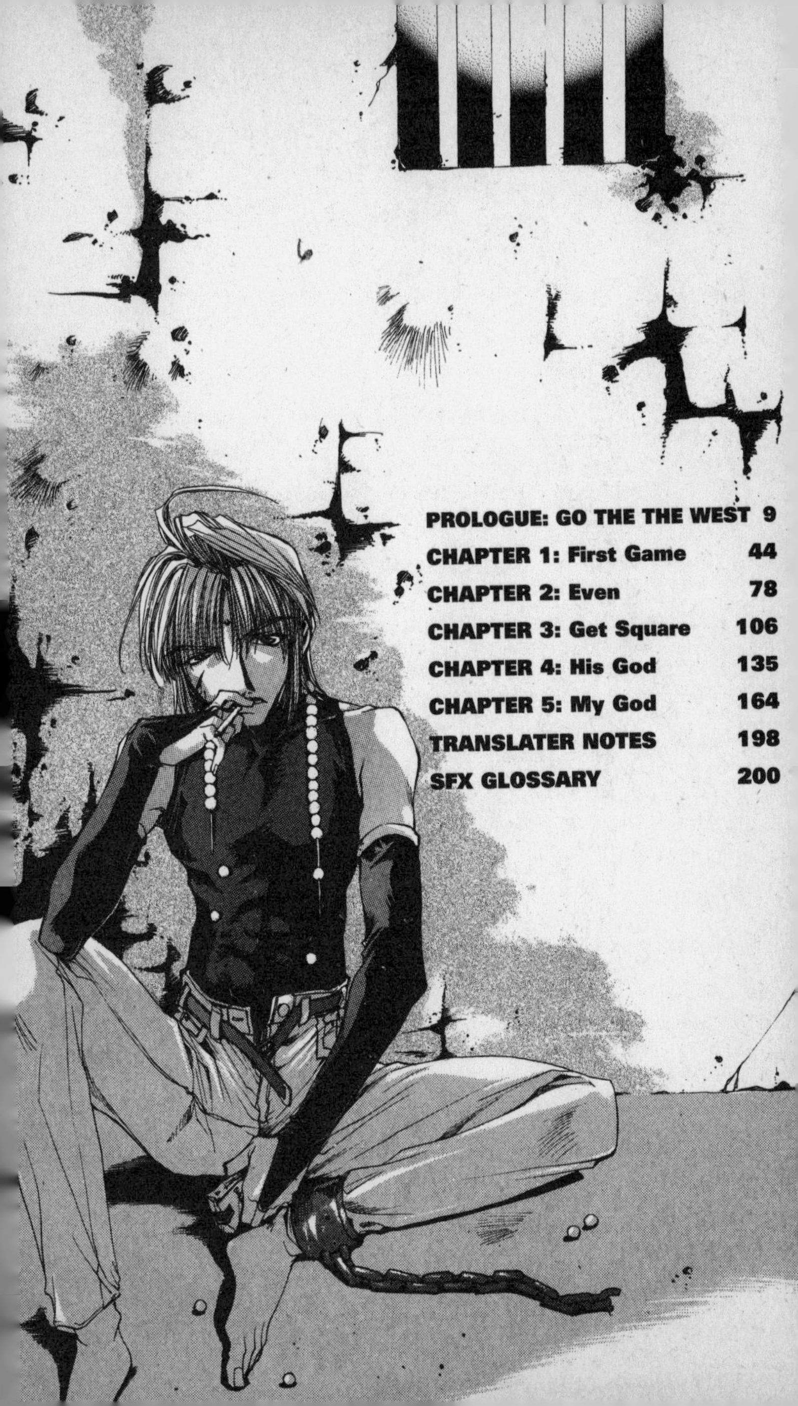

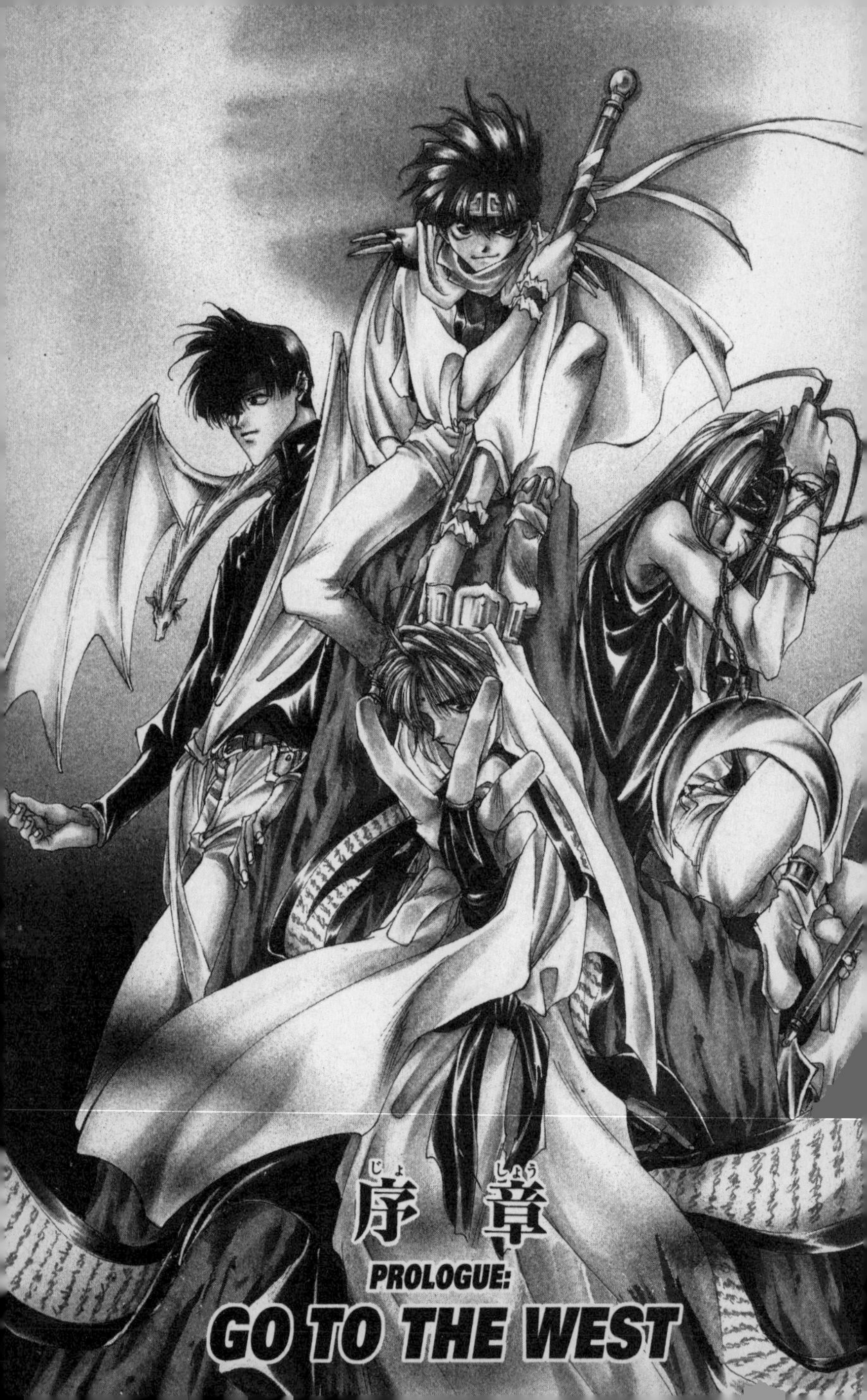

序章
じょしょう
PROLOGUE:
GO TO THE WEST

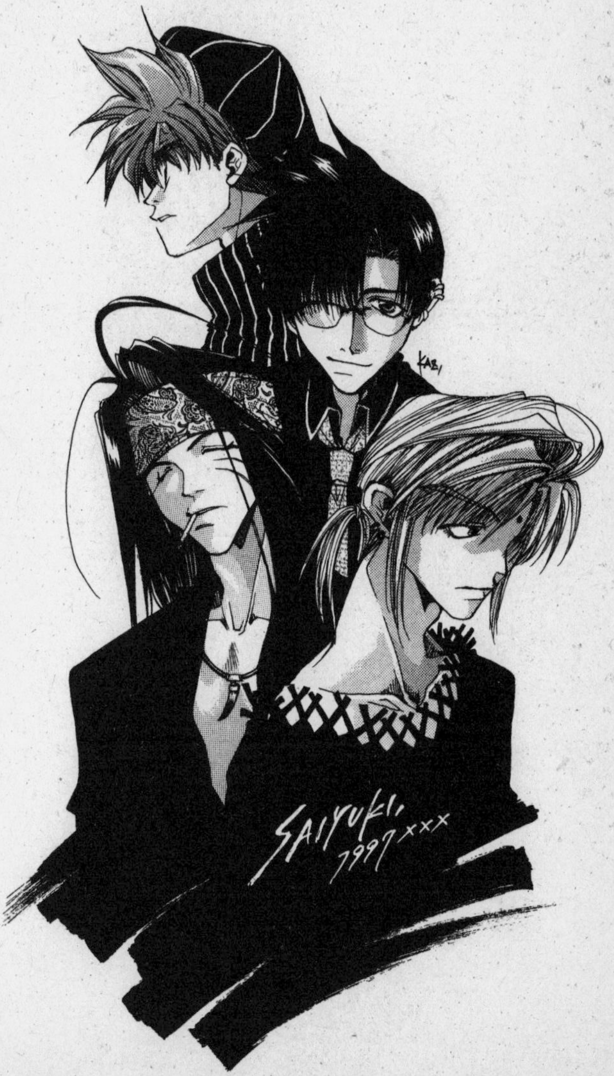
KABI
SAIYUKI
1997 ×××

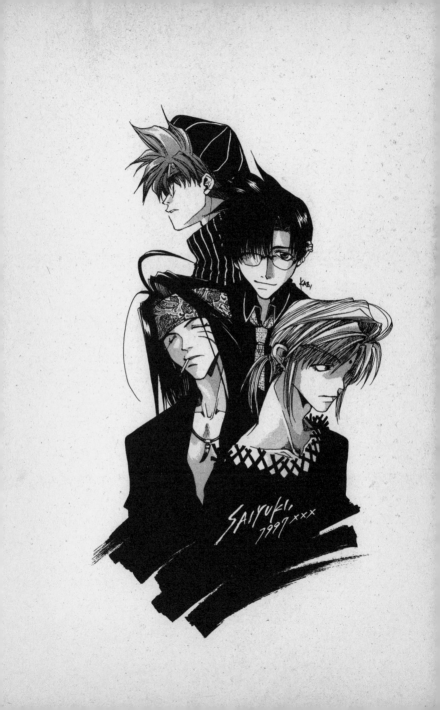

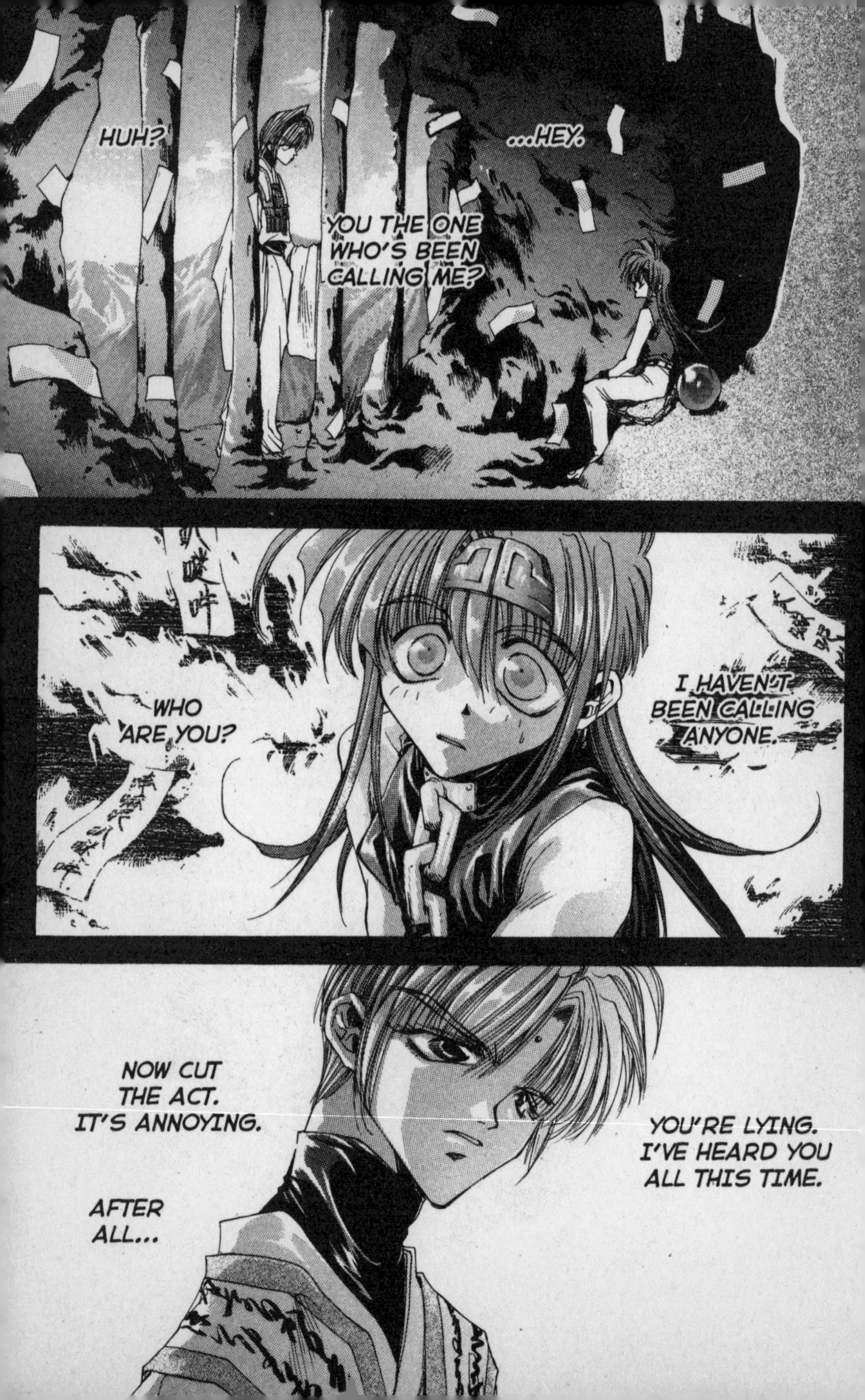
...HEY.
HUH?
YOU THE ONE WHO'S BEEN CALLING ME?
I HAVEN'T BEEN CALLING ANYONE.
WHO ARE YOU?
YOU'RE LYING. I'VE HEARD YOU ALL THIS TIME.
NOW CUT THE ACT. IT'S ANNOYING.
AFTER ALL...

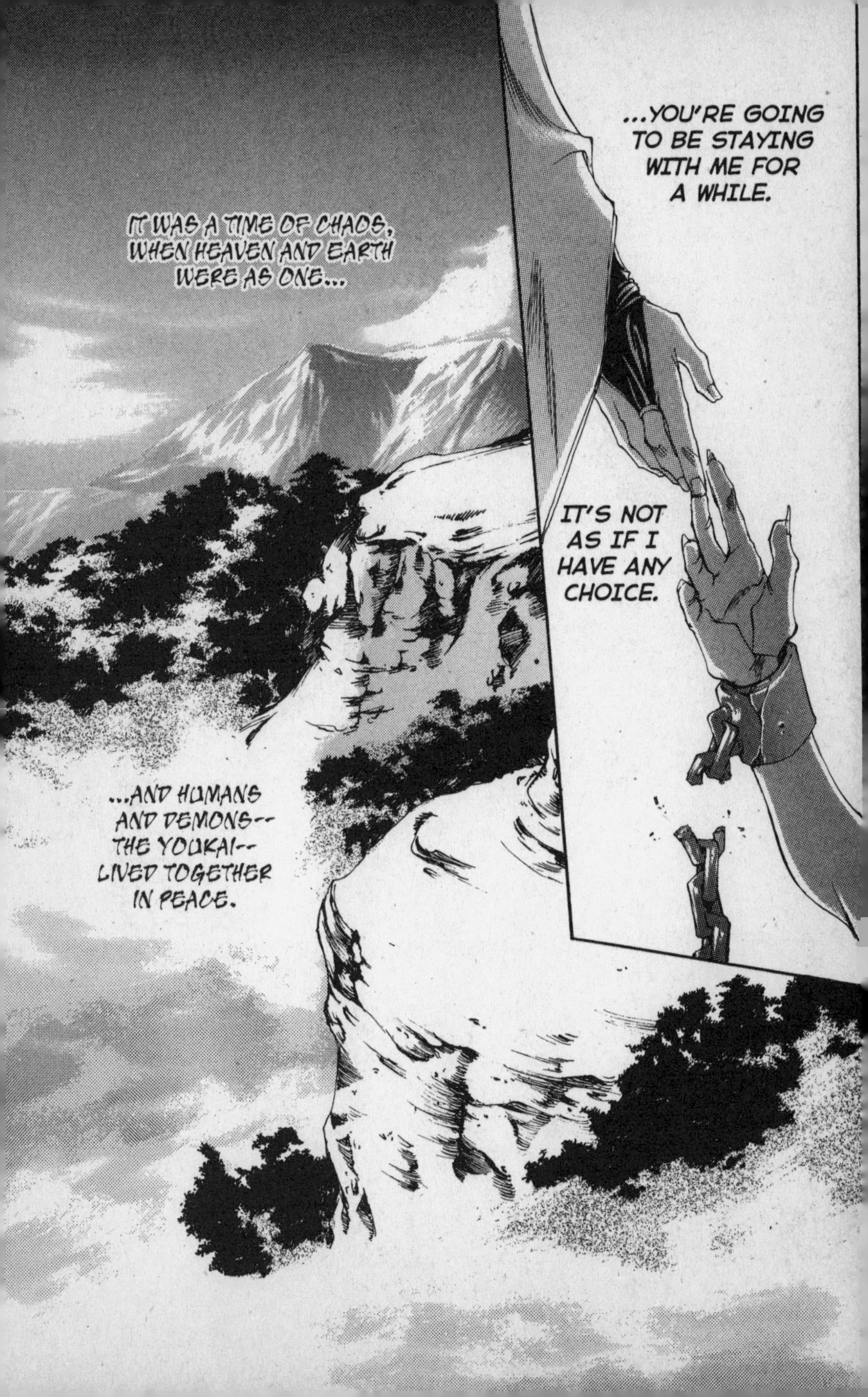
...YOU'RE GOING TO BE STAYING WITH ME FOR A WHILE.
IT WAS A TIME OF CHAOS, WHEN HEAVEN AND EARTH WERE AS ONE...
IT'S NOT AS IF I HAVE ANY CHOICE.
...AND HUMANS AND DEMONS--THE YOUKAI--LIVED TOGETHER IN PEACE.

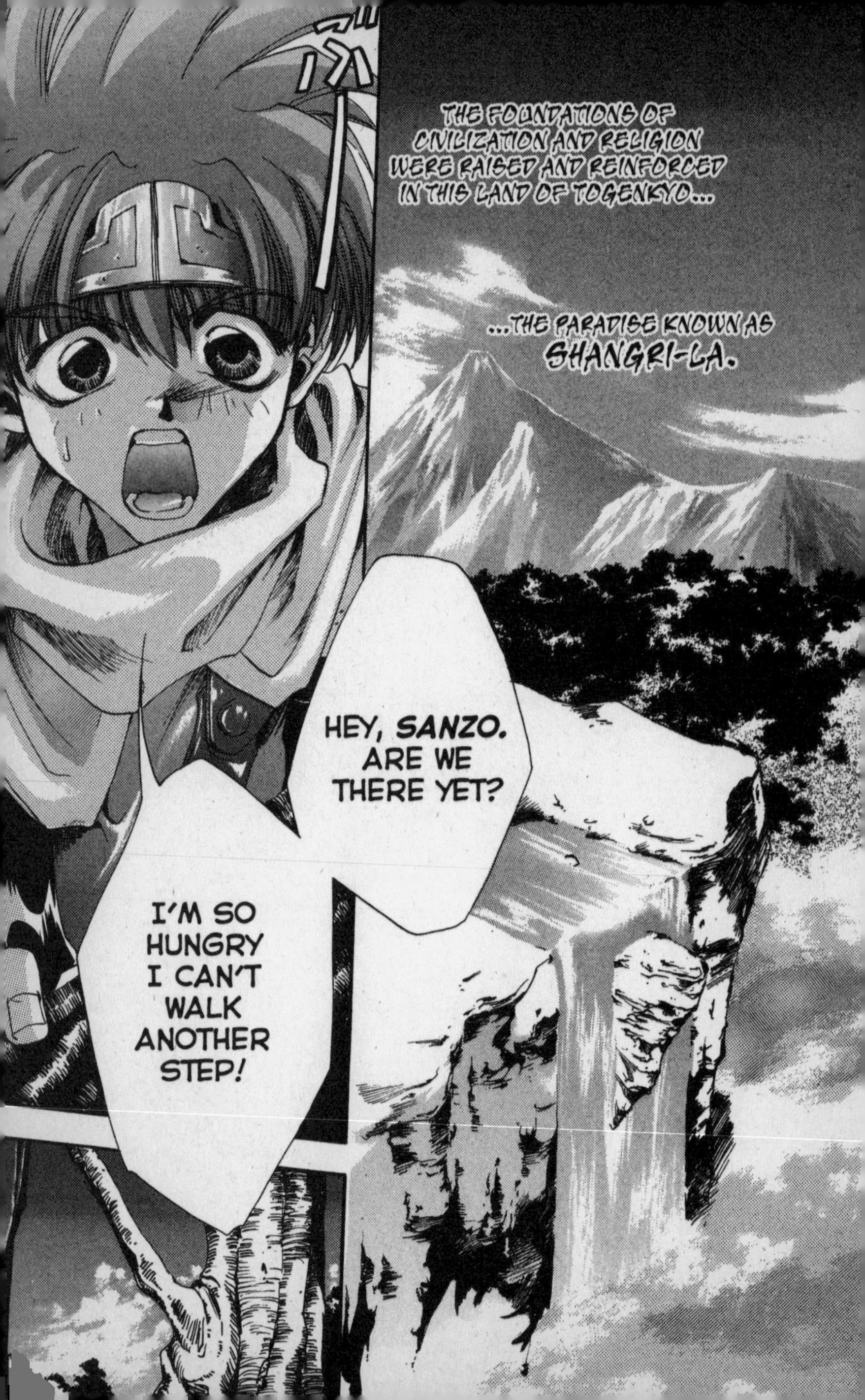
THE FOUNDATIONS OF CIVILIZATION AND RELIGION WERE RAISED AND REINFORCED IN THIS LAND OF TOGENKYO...
...THE PARADISE KNOWN AS SHANGRI-LA.
HEY, SANZO. ARE WE THERE YET?
I'M SO HUNGRY I CAN'T WALK ANOTHER STEP!

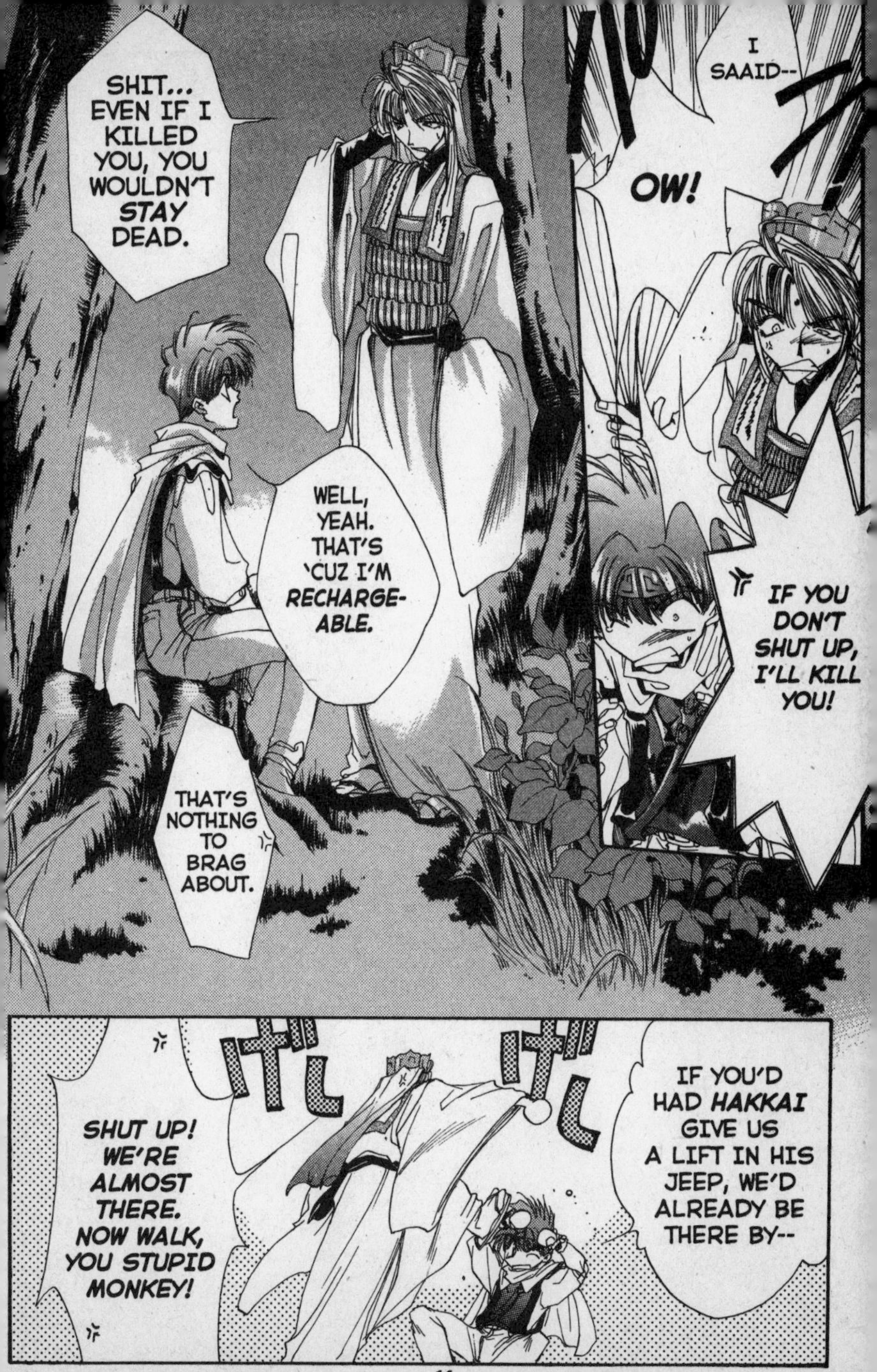
I SAAID--
OW!
IF YOU DON'T SHUT UP, I'LL KILL YOU!
SHIT... EVEN IF I KILLED YOU, YOU WOULDN'T STAY DEAD.
WELL, YEAH. THAT'S 'CUZ I'M RECHARGE-ABLE.
THAT'S NOTHING TO BRAG ABOUT.
IF YOU'D HAD HAKKAI GIVE US A LIFT IN HIS JEEP, WE'D ALREADY BE THERE BY--
ゲシ
ゲシ
SHUT UP! WE'RE ALMOST THERE. NOW WALK, YOU STUPID MONKEY!

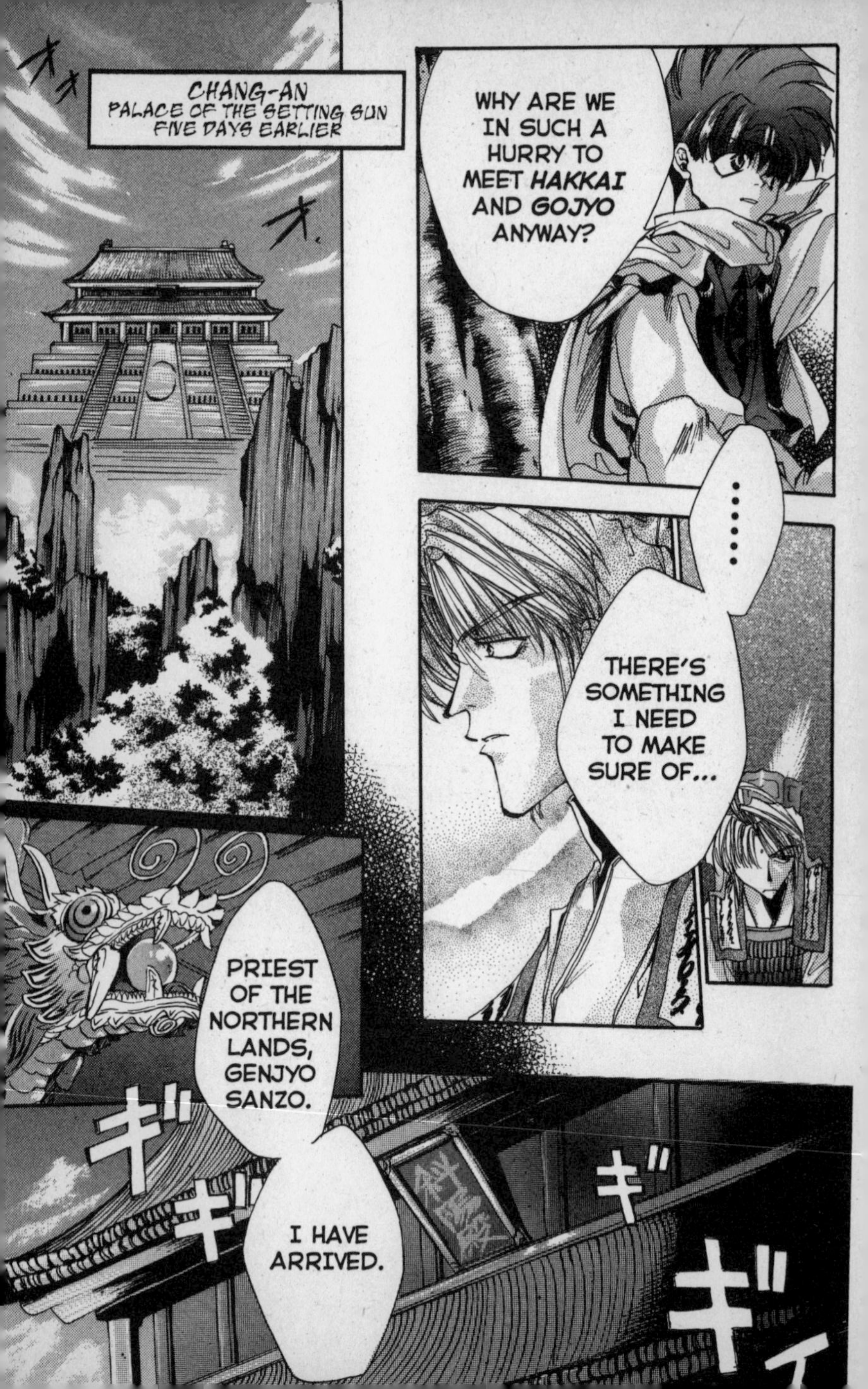
WHY ARE WE IN SUCH A HURRY TO MEET ***HAKKAI*** AND ***GOJYO*** ANYWAY?
......
THERE'S SOMETHING I NEED TO MAKE SURE OF...
オオ
CHANG-AN
PALACE OF THE SETTING SUN
FIVE DAYS EARLIER
オ.
PRIEST OF THE NORTHERN LANDS, GENJYO SANZO.
I HAVE ARRIVED.
ギ
ギ
ギ
ギ
ギィ

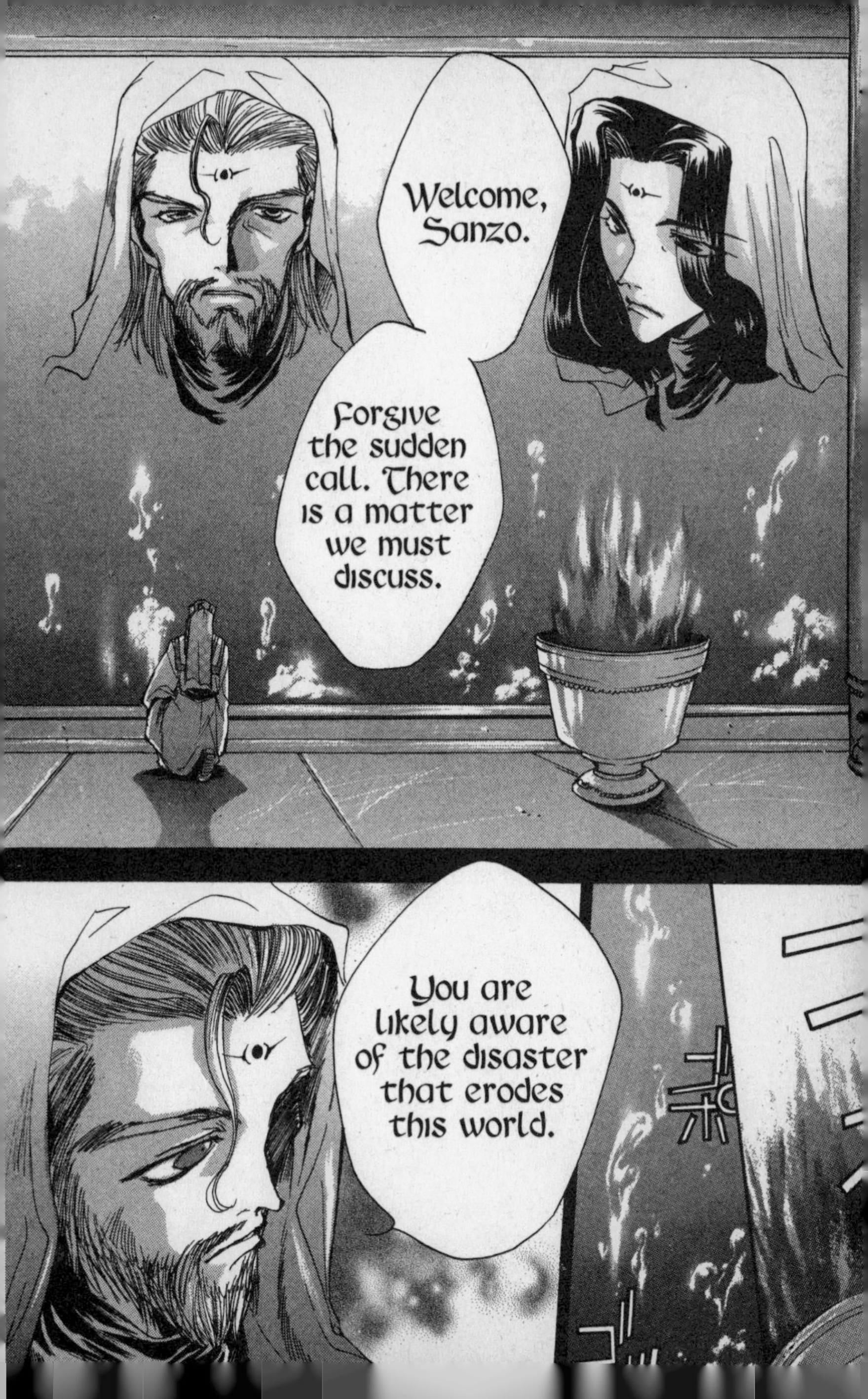
Welcome, Sanzo.
Forgive the sudden call. There is a matter we must discuss.
You are likely aware of the disaster that erodes this world.

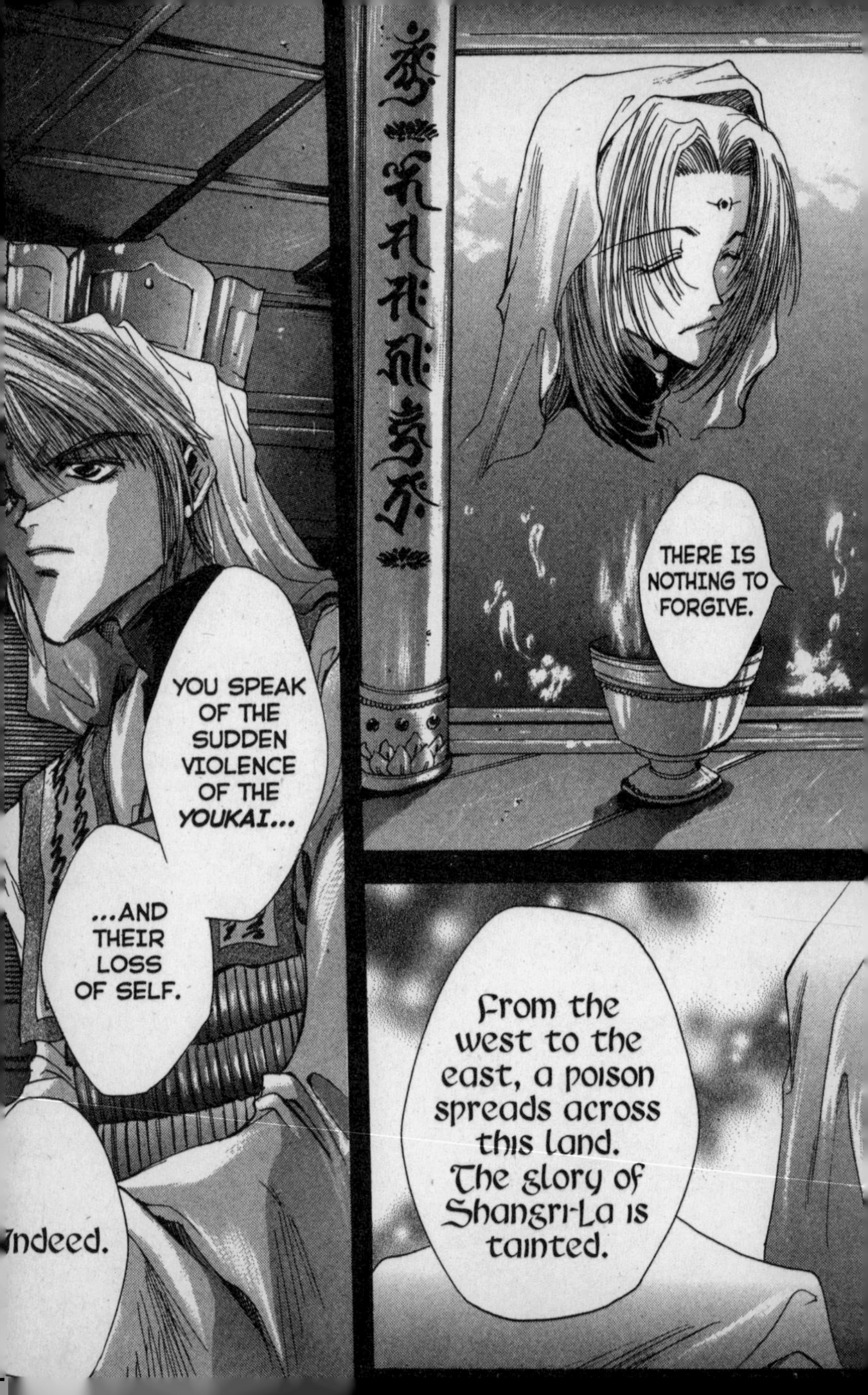
THERE IS NOTHING TO FORGIVE.
From the west to the east, a poison spreads across this land. The glory of Shangri-La is tainted.
YOU SPEAK OF THE SUDDEN VIOLENCE OF THE *YOUKAI*...
...AND THEIR LOSS OF SELF.
Indeed.

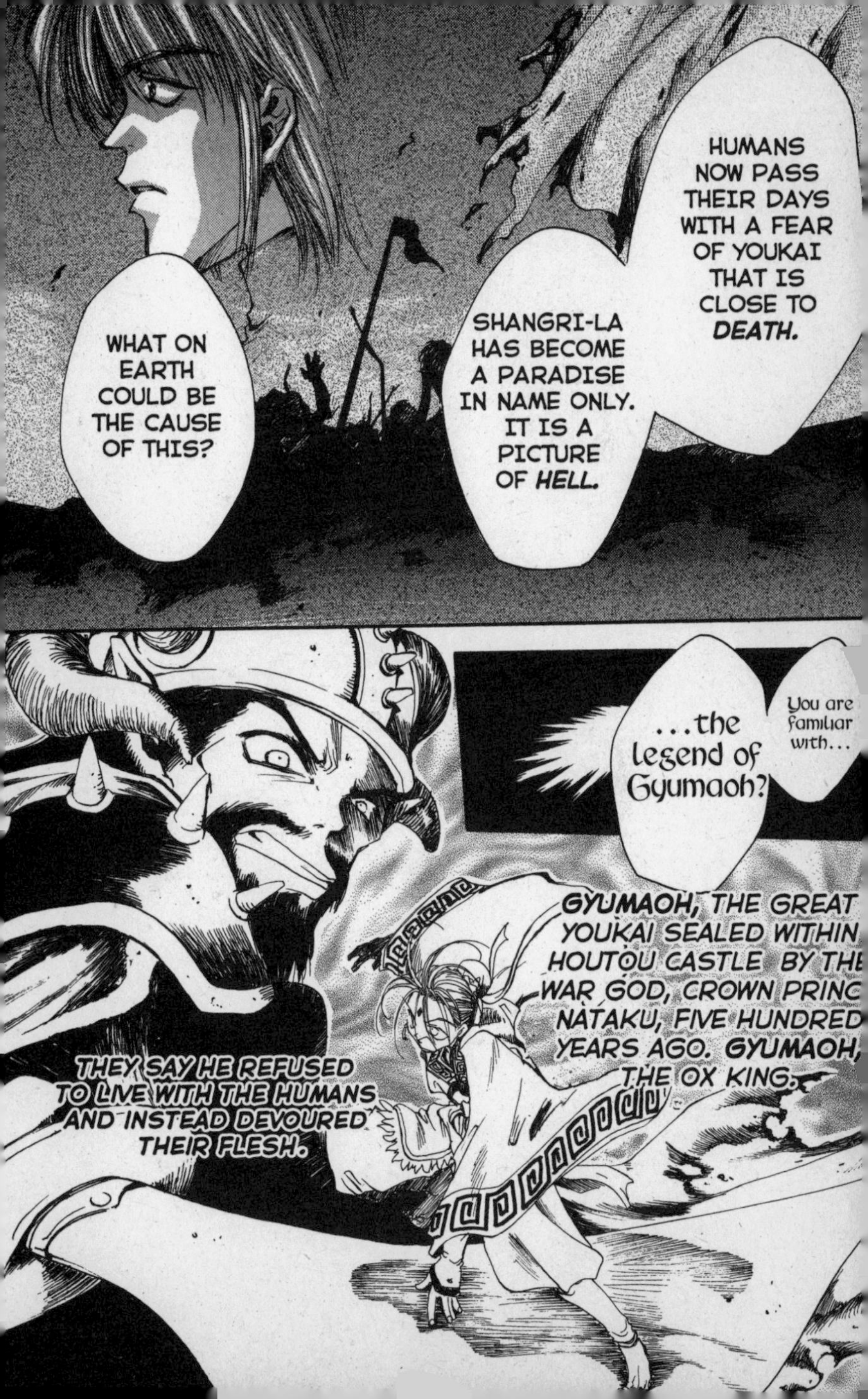
HUMANS NOW PASS THEIR DAYS WITH A FEAR OF YOUKAI THAT IS CLOSE TO *DEATH.*
SHANGRI-LA HAS BECOME A PARADISE IN NAME ONLY. IT IS A PICTURE OF *HELL.*
WHAT ON EARTH COULD BE THE CAUSE OF THIS?
You are familiar with...
...the legend of Gyumaoh?
GYUMAOH, THE GREAT YOUKAI SEALED WITHIN HOUTOU CASTLE BY THE WAR GOD, CROWN PRINC NATAKU, FIVE HUNDRED YEARS AGO. GYUMAOH, THE OX KING.
THEY SAY HE REFUSED TO LIVE WITH THE HUMANS AND INSTEAD DEVOURED THEIR FLESH.

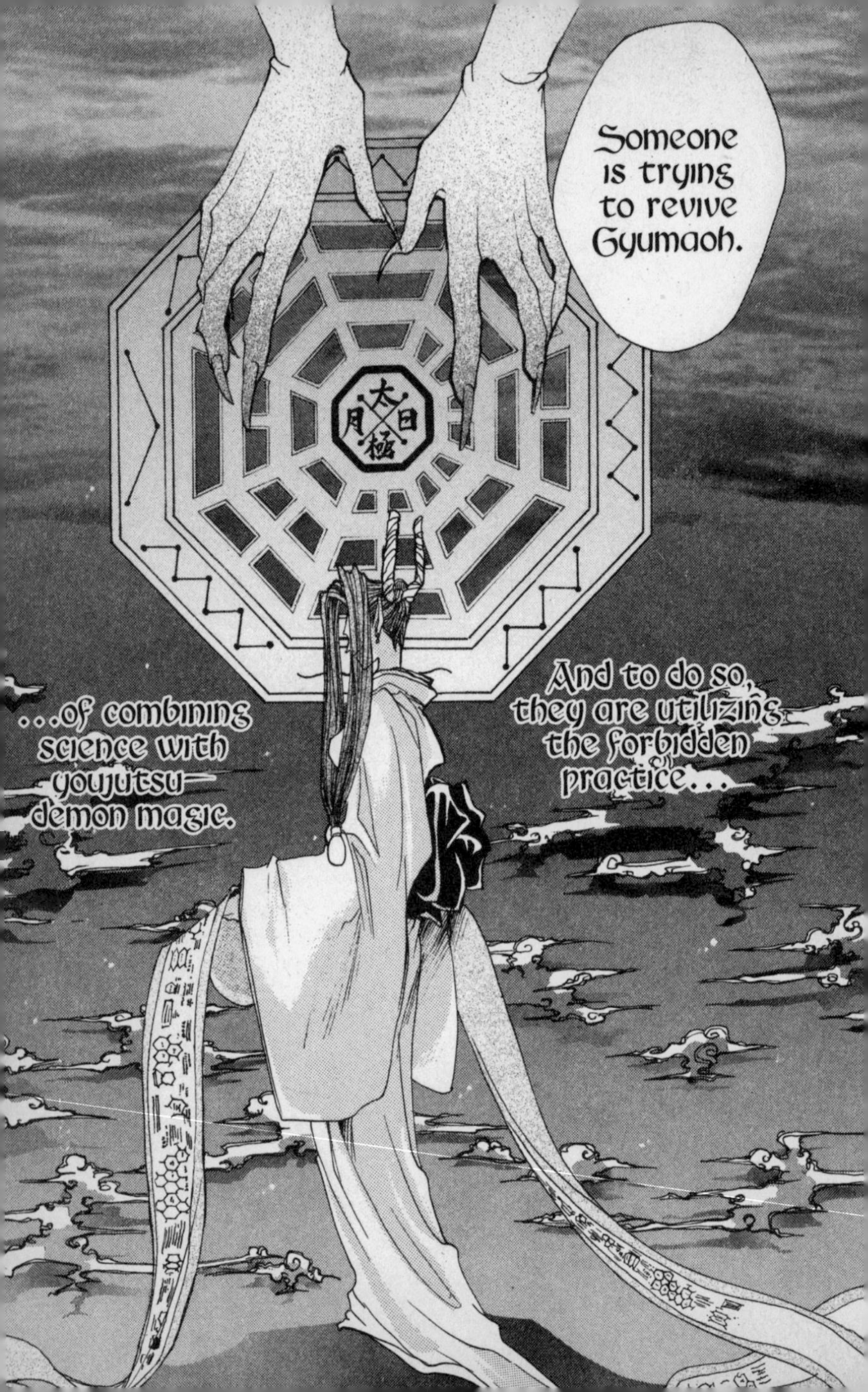
Someone is trying to revive Gyumaoh.
And to do so, they are utilizing the forbidden practice...
...of combining science with youjutsu—demon magic.

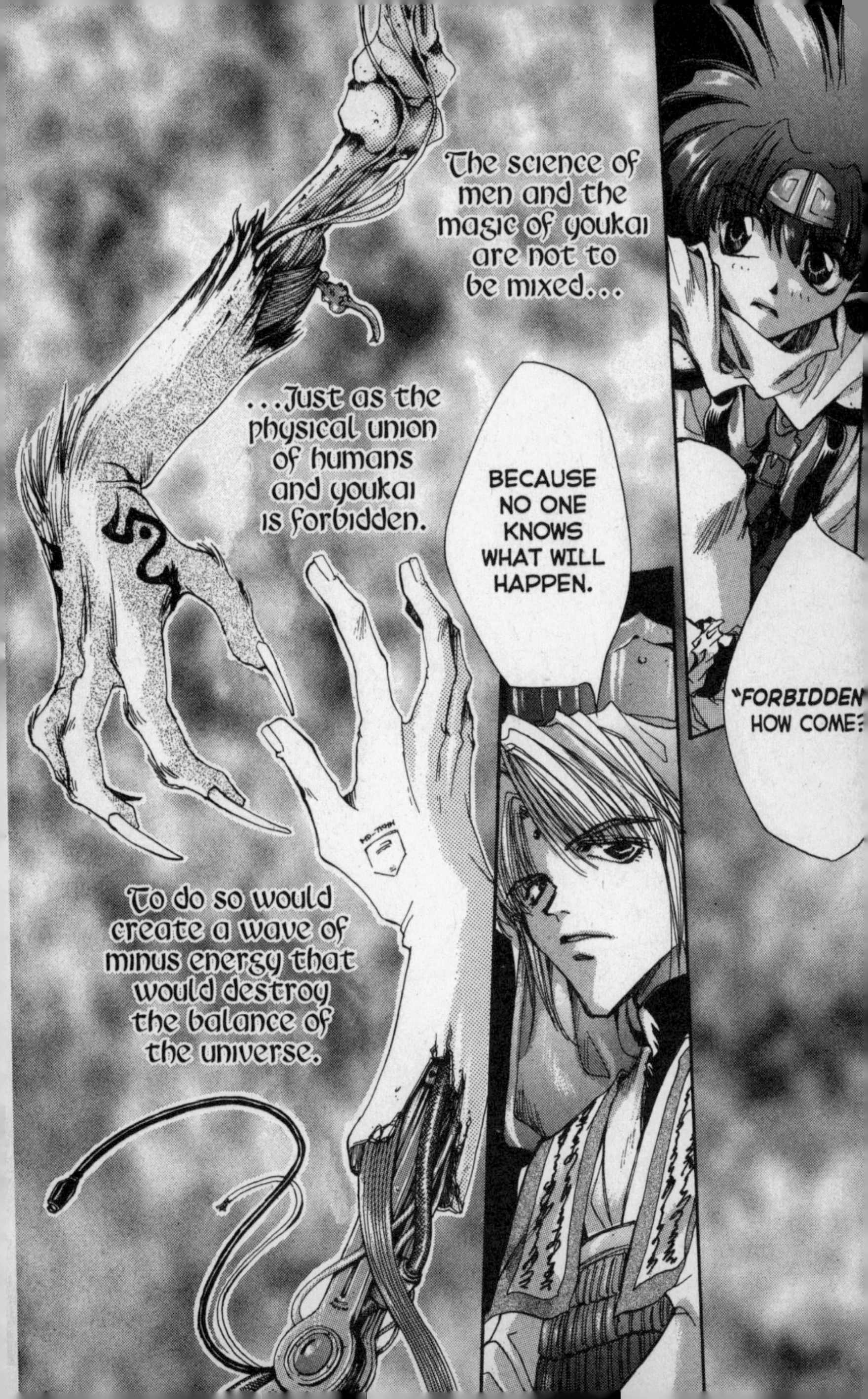
"FORBIDDEN
HOW COME?
BECAUSE NO ONE KNOWS WHAT WILL HAPPEN.
The science of men and the magic of youkai are not to be mixed...
...Just as the physical union of humans and youkai is forbidden.
To do so would create a wave of minus energy that would destroy the balance of the universe.

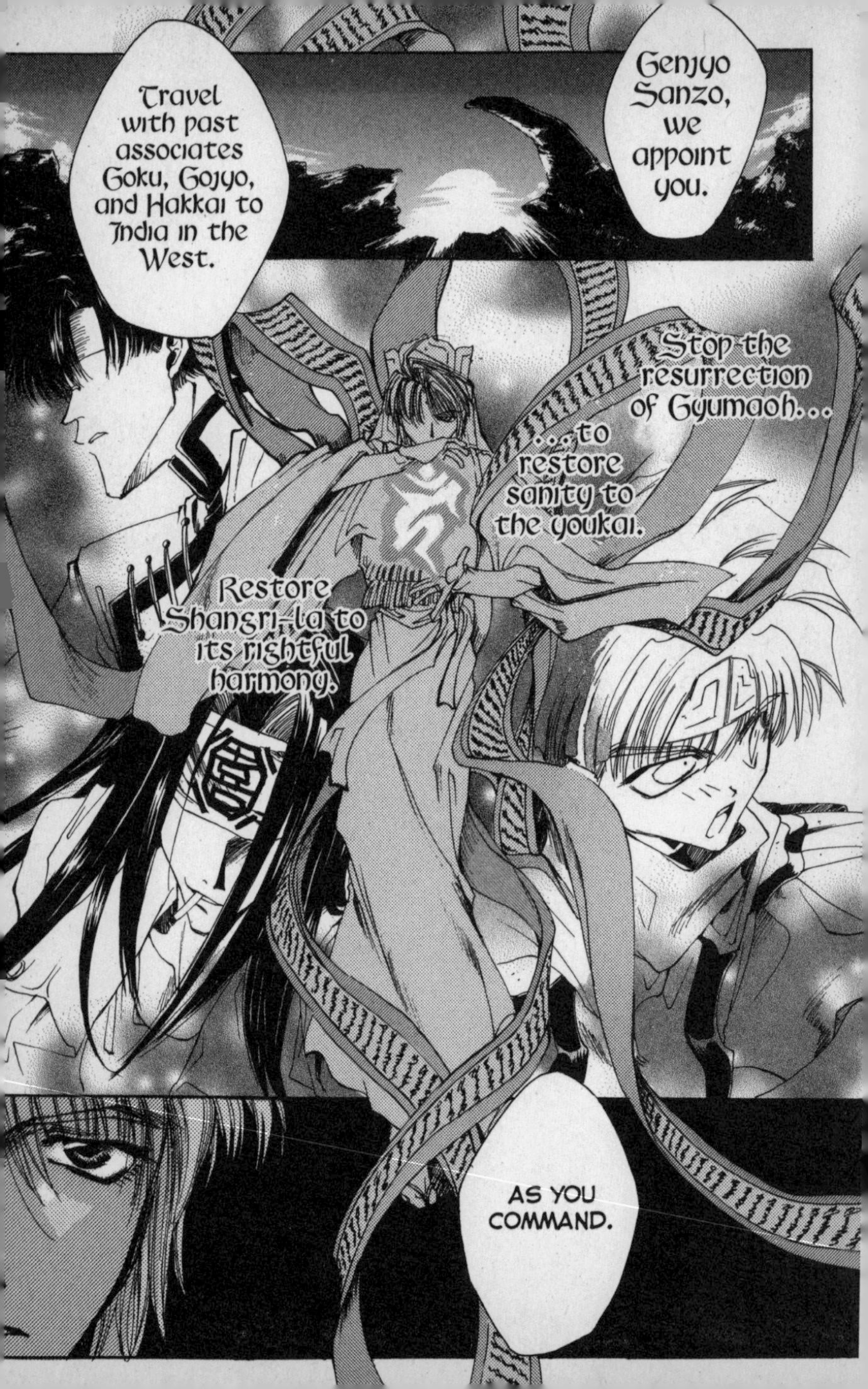
Genjyo Sanzo, we appoint you.
Travel with past associates Goku, Gojyo, and Hakkai to India in the West.
Stop the resurrection of Gyumaoh...
...to restore sanity to the youkai.
Restore Shangri-la to its rightful harmony.
AS YOU COMMAND.

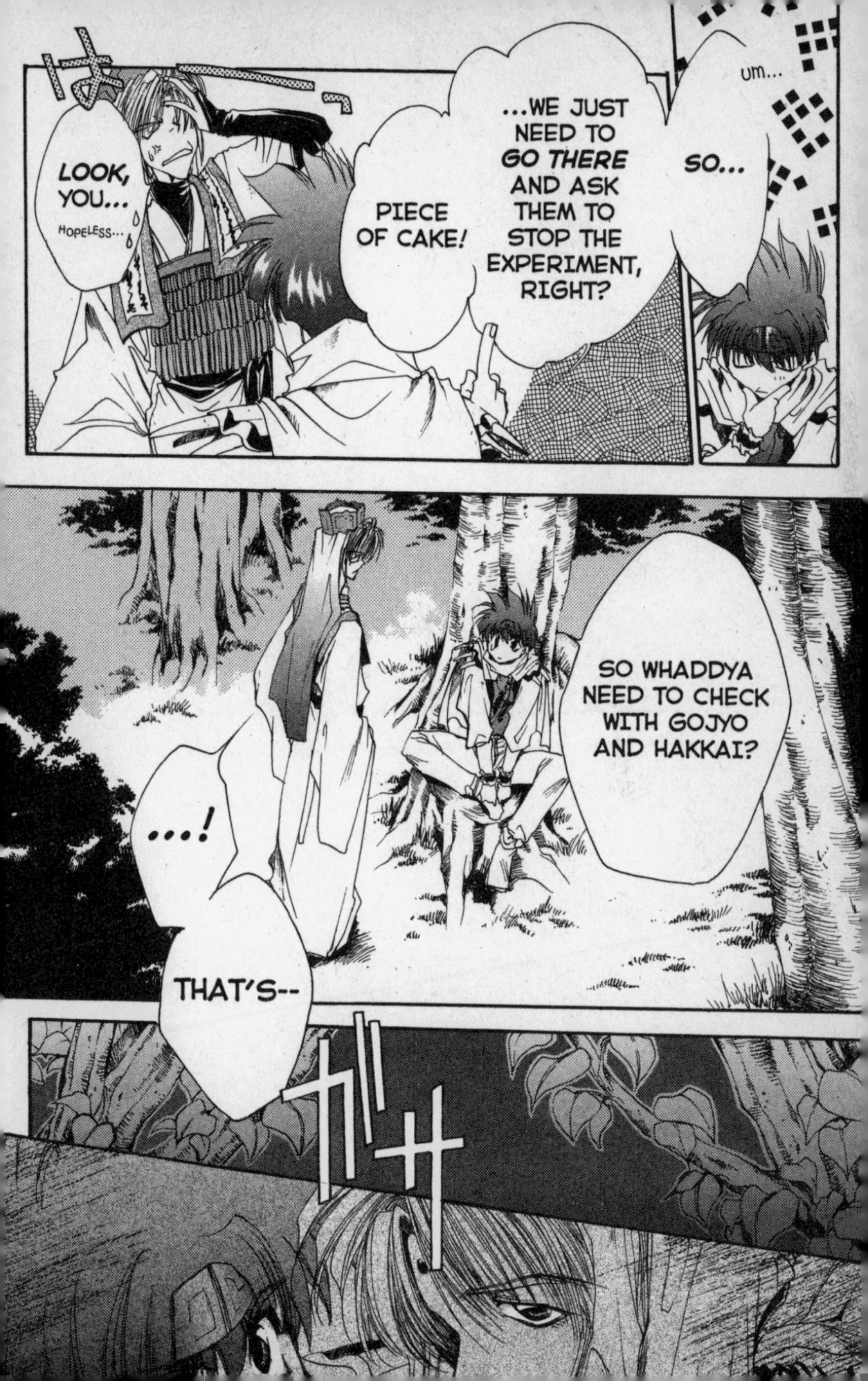
um...
SO...
...WE JUST NEED TO *GO THERE* AND ASK THEM TO STOP THE EXPERIMENT, RIGHT?
PIECE OF CAKE!
LOOK, YOU...
HOPELESS...
SO WHADDYA NEED TO CHECK WITH GOJYO AND HAKKAI?
...!
THAT'S--
ガサ

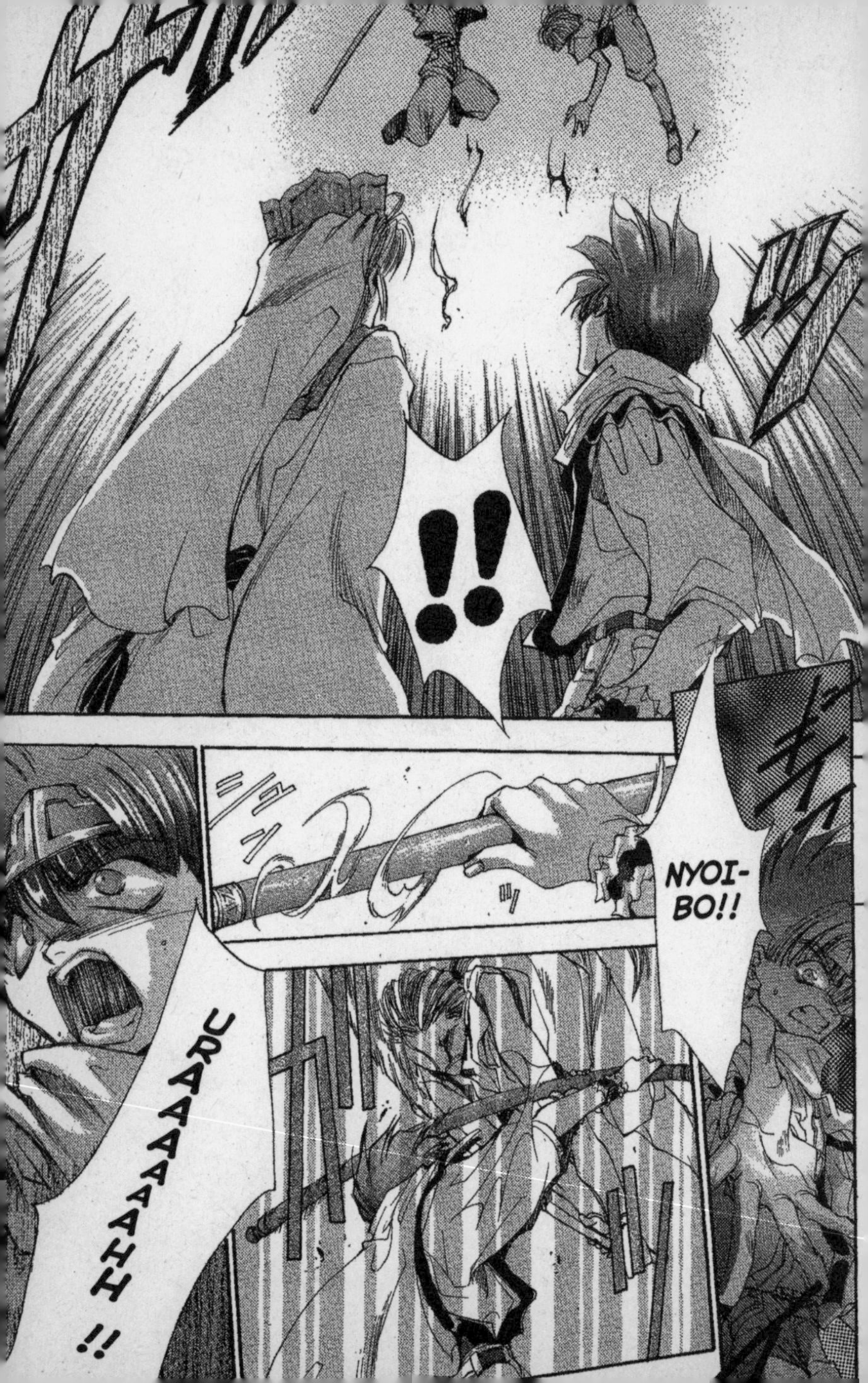
!!
NYOI-BO!!
URAAAAAAAAH!!

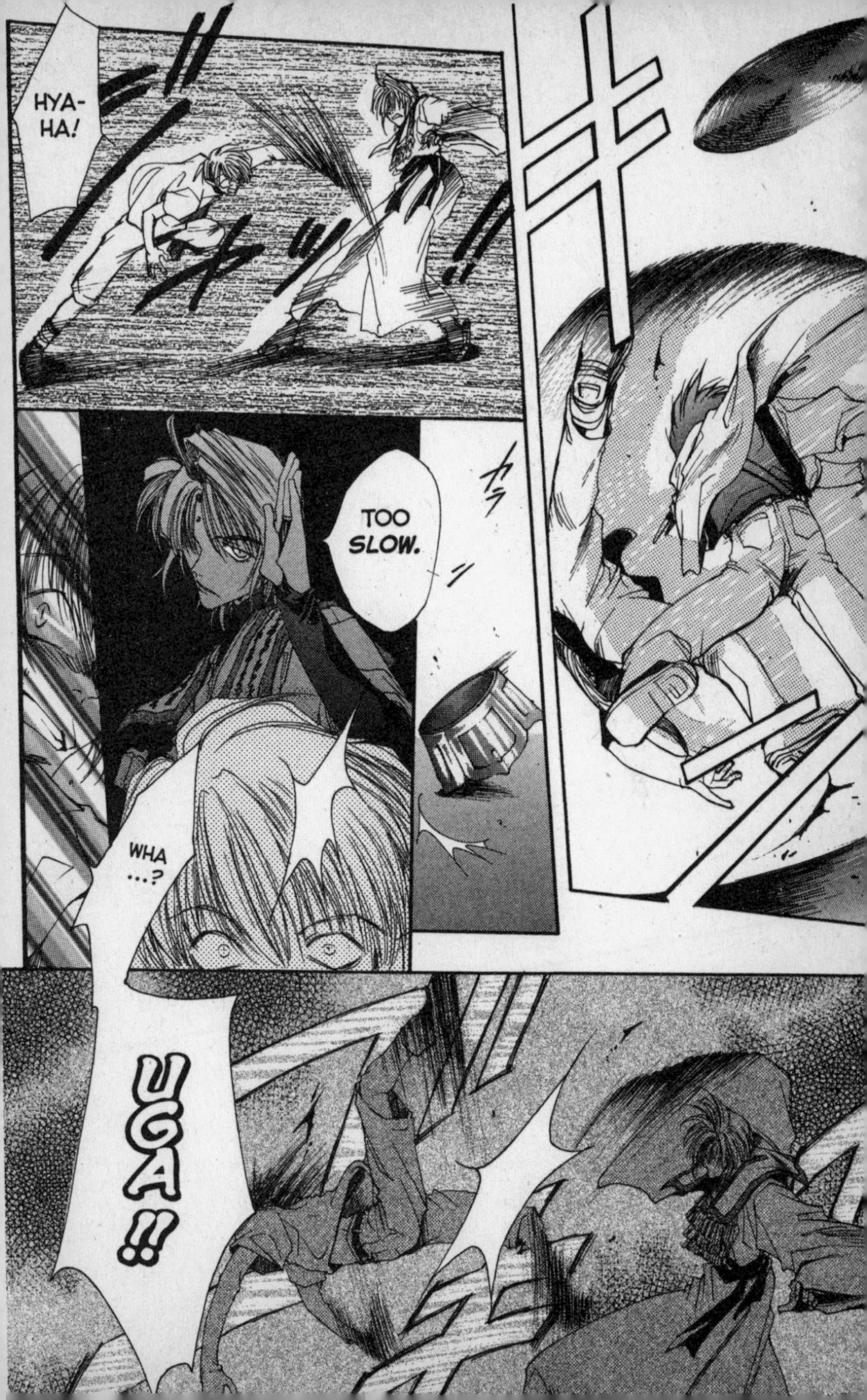
HYA-HA!
TOO SLOW.
WHA ...?
UGA!!

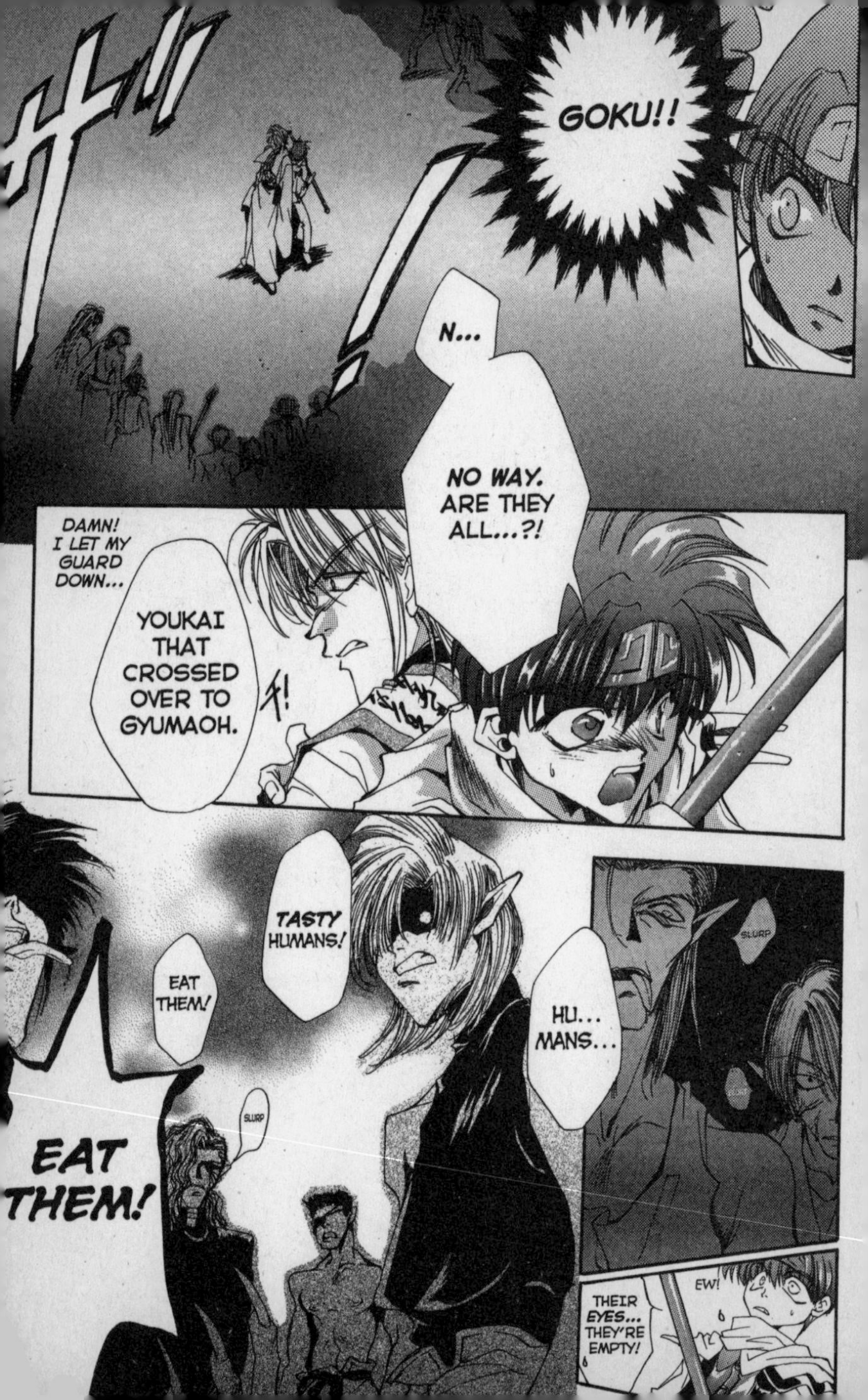
GOKU!!
N...
NO WAY. ARE THEY ALL...?!
DAMN! I LET MY GUARD DOWN...
YOUKAI THAT CROSSED OVER TO GYUMAOH.
SLURP
HU... MANS...
TASTY HUMANS!
EAT THEM!
SLURP
EAT THEM!
EW!
THEIR EYES... THEY'RE EMPTY!

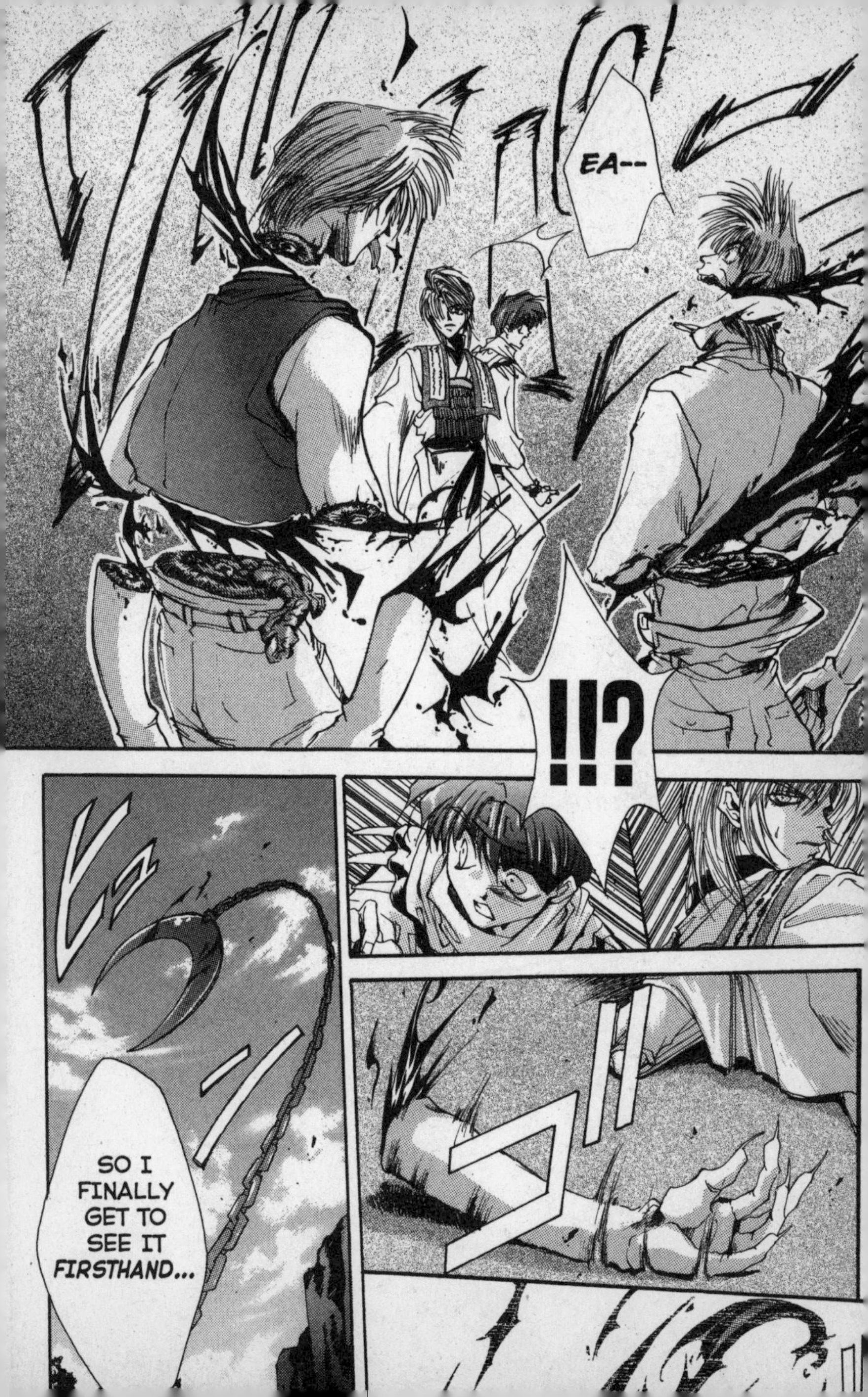
EA--
!!?
SO I FINALLY GET TO SEE IT *FIRSTHAND...*

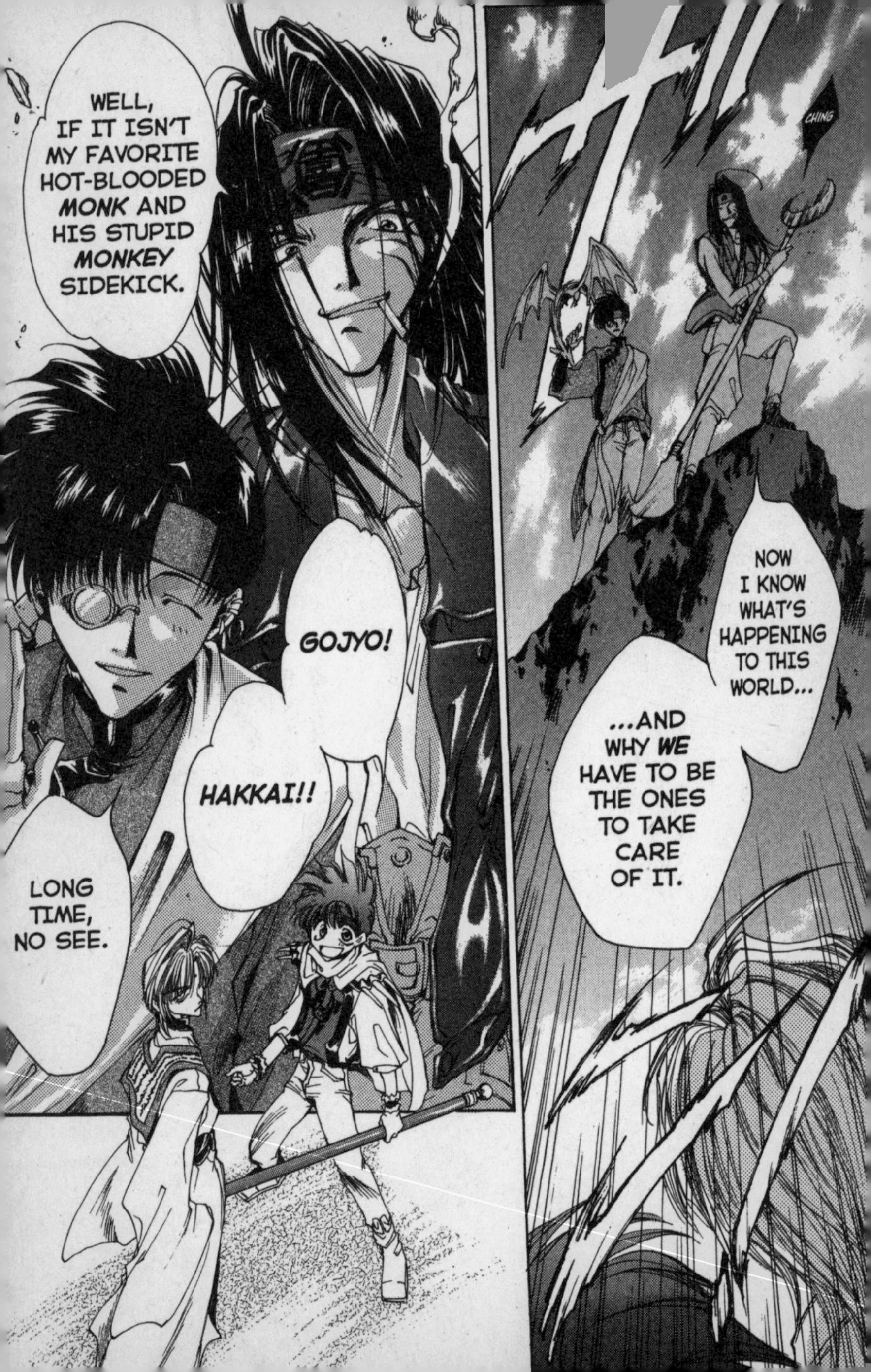
CHING
NOW I KNOW WHAT'S HAPPENING TO THIS WORLD...
...AND WHY *WE* HAVE TO BE THE ONES TO TAKE CARE OF IT.
WELL, IF IT ISN'T MY FAVORITE HOT-BLOODED *MONK* AND HIS STUPID *MONKEY* SIDEKICK.
GOJYO!
HAKKAI!!
LONG TIME, NO SEE.

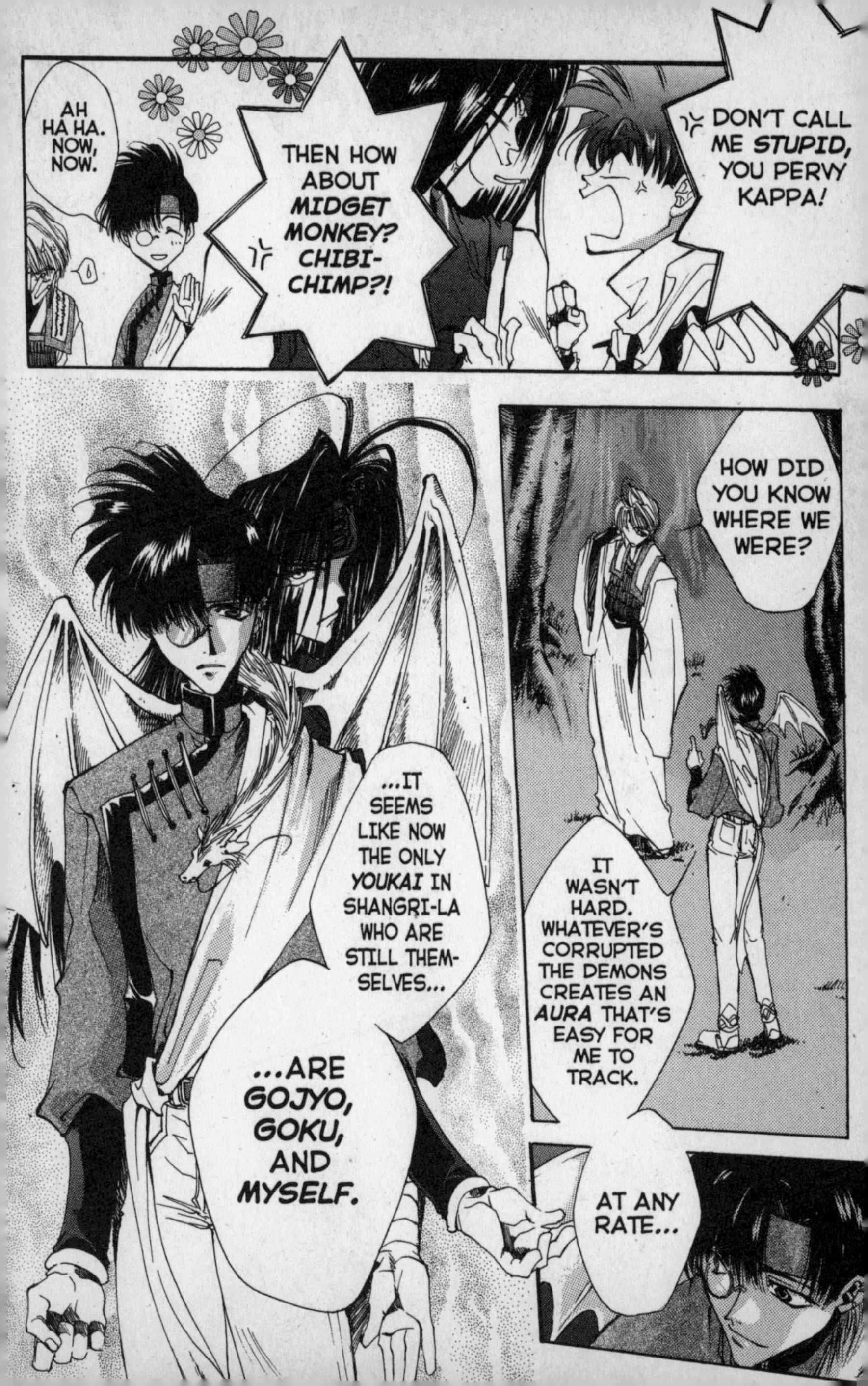
DON'T CALL ME STUPID, YOU PERVY KAPPA!
THEN HOW ABOUT MIDGET MONKEY? CHIBI-CHIMP?!
AH HA HA. NOW, NOW.
HOW DID YOU KNOW WHERE WE WERE?
IT WASN'T HARD. WHATEVER'S CORRUPTED THE DEMONS CREATES AN AURA THAT'S EASY FOR ME TO TRACK.
AT ANY RATE...
...IT SEEMS LIKE NOW THE ONLY YOUKAI IN SHANGRI-LA WHO ARE STILL THEM-SELVES...
...ARE GOJYO, GOKU, AND MYSELF.

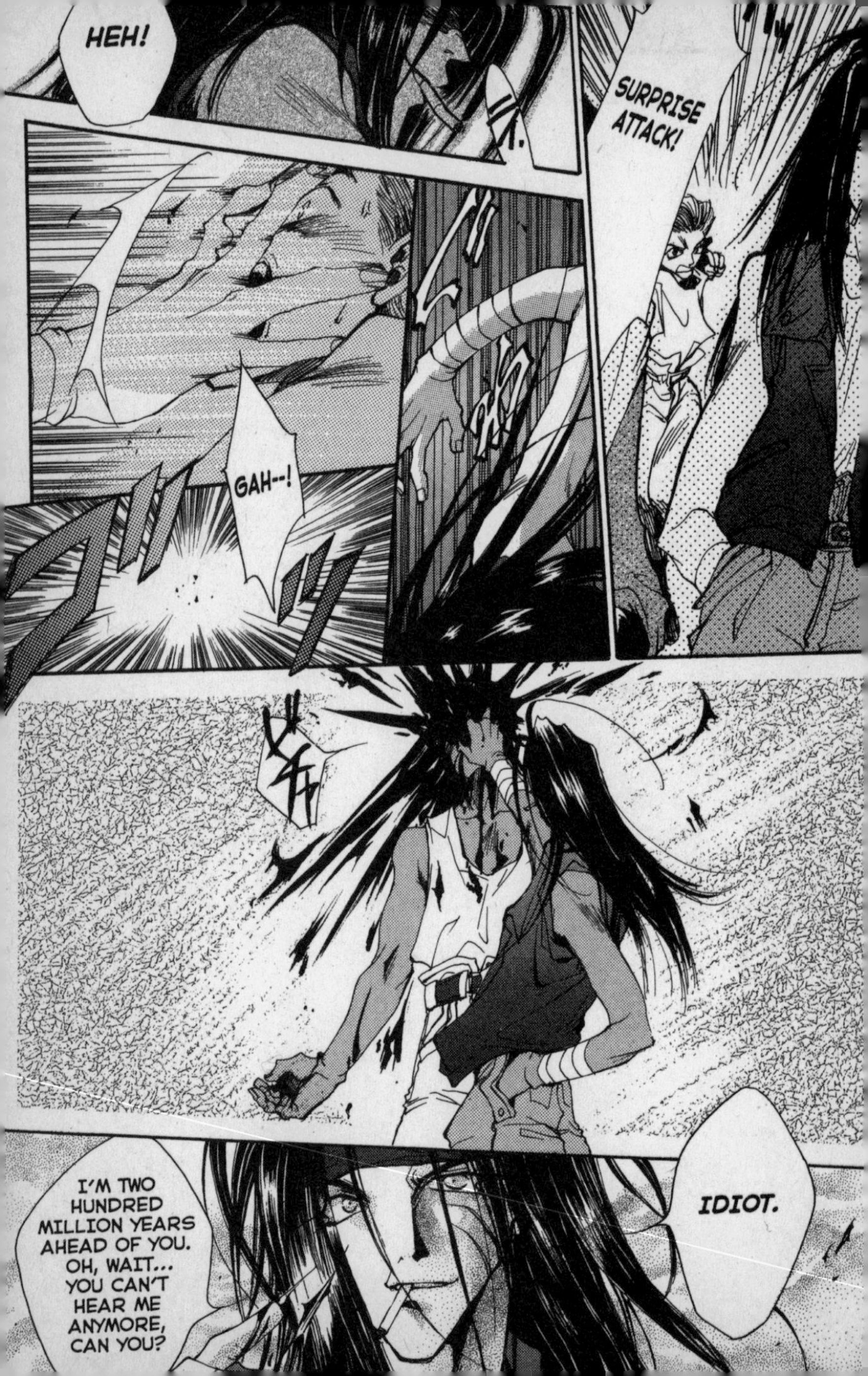
SURPRISE ATTACK!
HEH!
GAH--!
IDIOT.
I'M TWO HUNDRED MILLION YEARS AHEAD OF YOU. OH, WAIT... YOU CAN'T HEAR ME ANYMORE, CAN YOU?

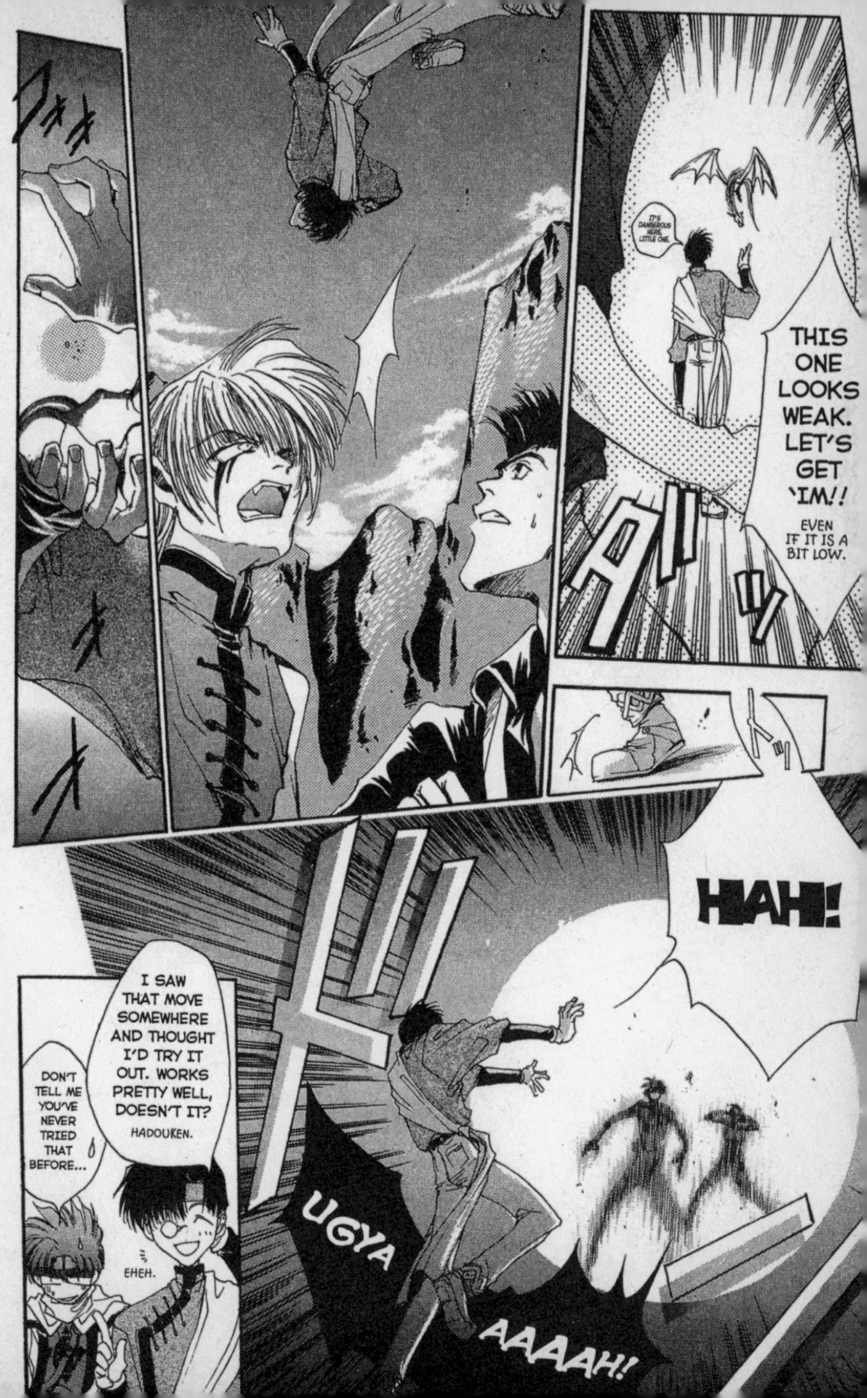
IT'S DANGEROUS HERE, LITTLE ONE.
THIS ONE LOOKS WEAK. LET'S GET 'IM!!
EVEN IF IT IS A BIT LOW.
HIAH!
UGYA
AAAAH!
I SAW THAT MOVE SOMEWHERE AND THOUGHT I'D TRY IT OUT. WORKS PRETTY WELL, DOESN'T IT?
HADOUKEN.
DON'T TELL ME YOU'VE NEVER TRIED THAT BEFORE...
EHEH.

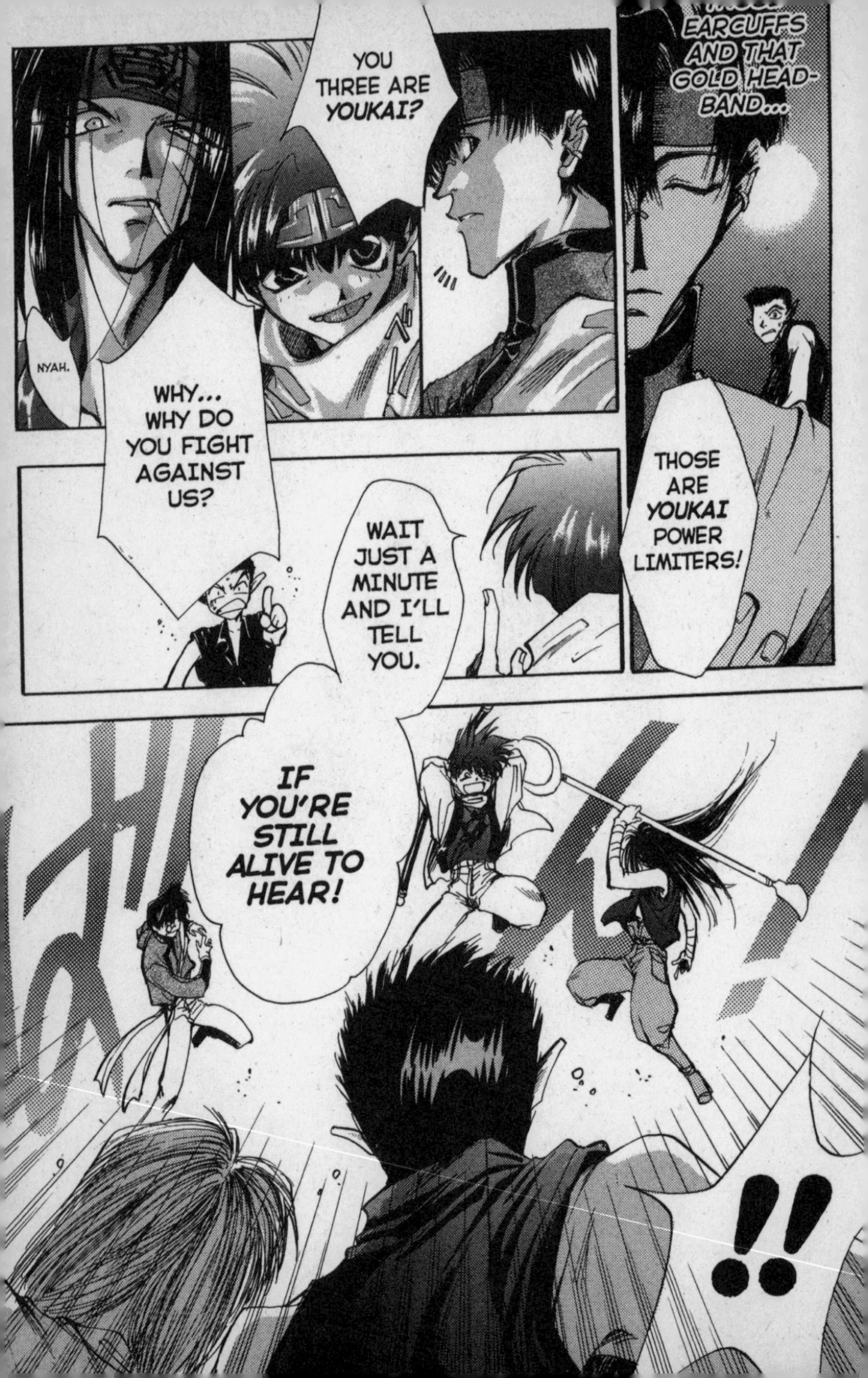
EARCUFFS AND THAT GOLD HEAD-BAND...
THOSE ARE YOUKAI POWER LIMITERS!
YOU THREE ARE YOUKAI?
NYAH.
WHY... WHY DO YOU FIGHT AGAINST US?
WAIT JUST A MINUTE AND I'LL TELL YOU.
IF YOU'RE STILL ALIVE TO HEAR!
!!

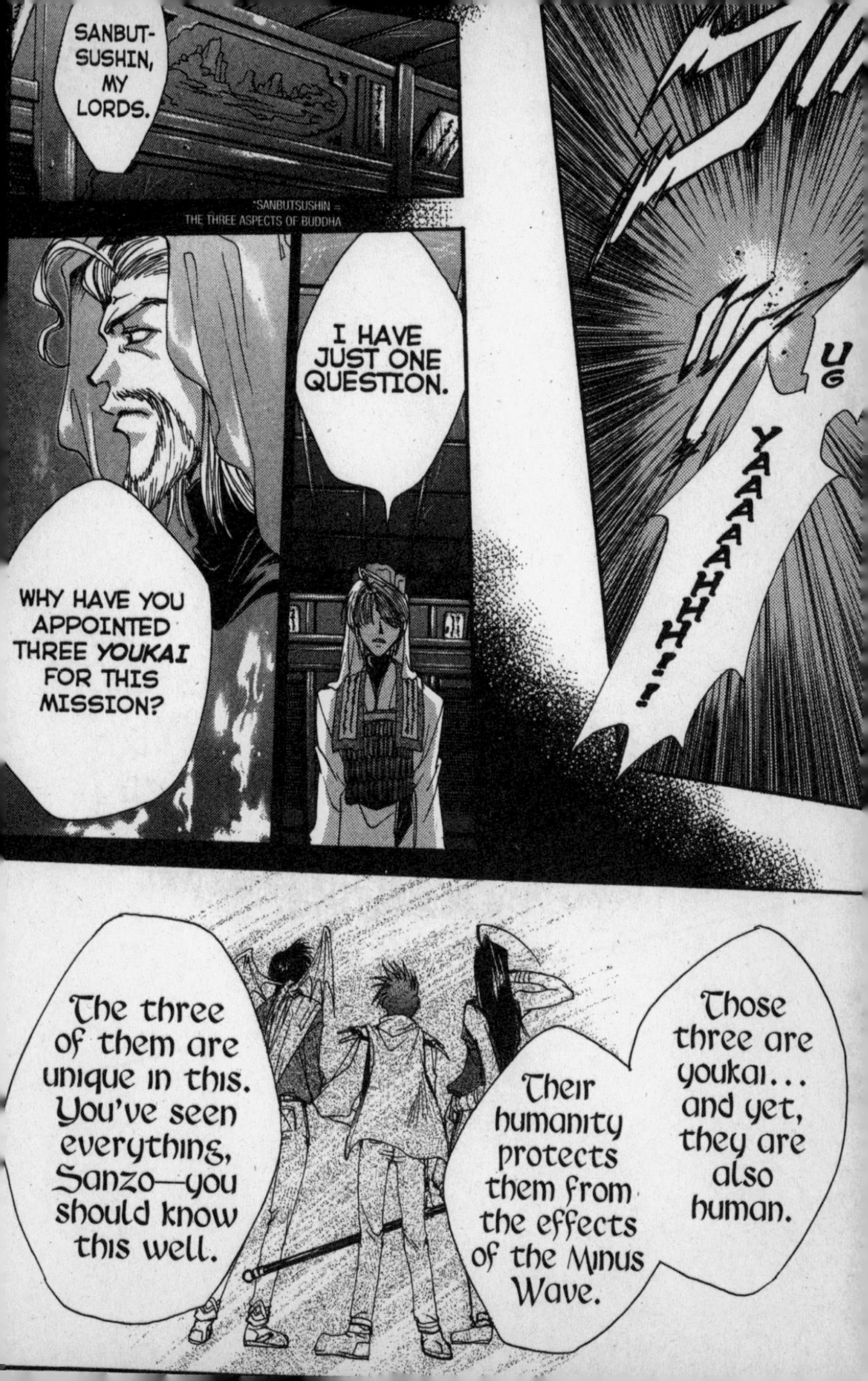
UGYAAAAHHH!!!
SANBUT-SUSHIN, MY LORDS.
*SANBUTSUSHIN = THE THREE ASPECTS OF BUDDHA
I HAVE JUST ONE QUESTION.
WHY HAVE YOU APPOINTED THREE *YOUKAI* FOR THIS MISSION?
Those three are youkai... and yet, they are also human.
Their humanity protects them from the effects of the Minus Wave.
The three of them are unique in this. You've seen everything, Sanzo—you should know this well.

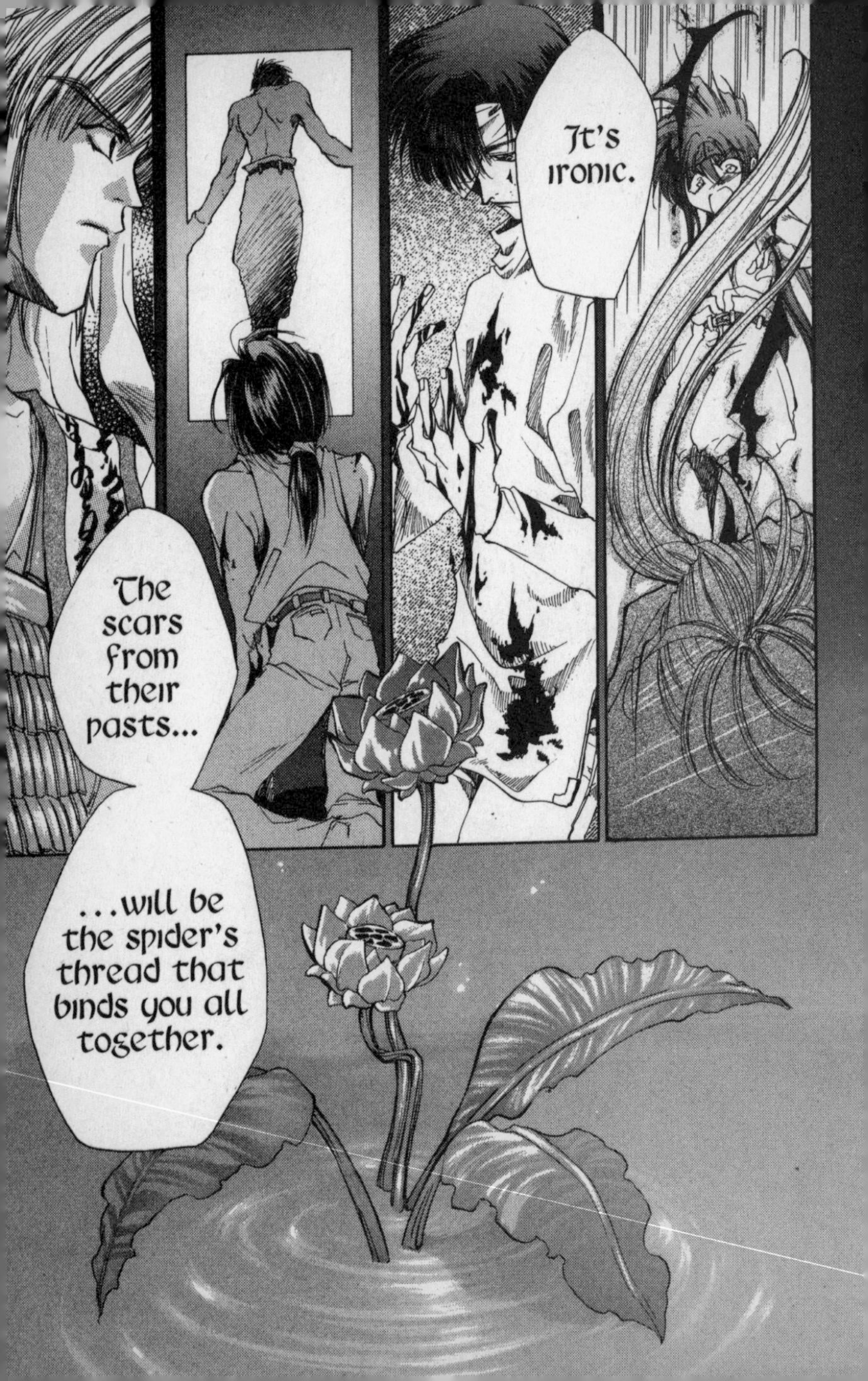
It's ironic.
The scars from their pasts...
...will be the spider's thread that binds you all together.

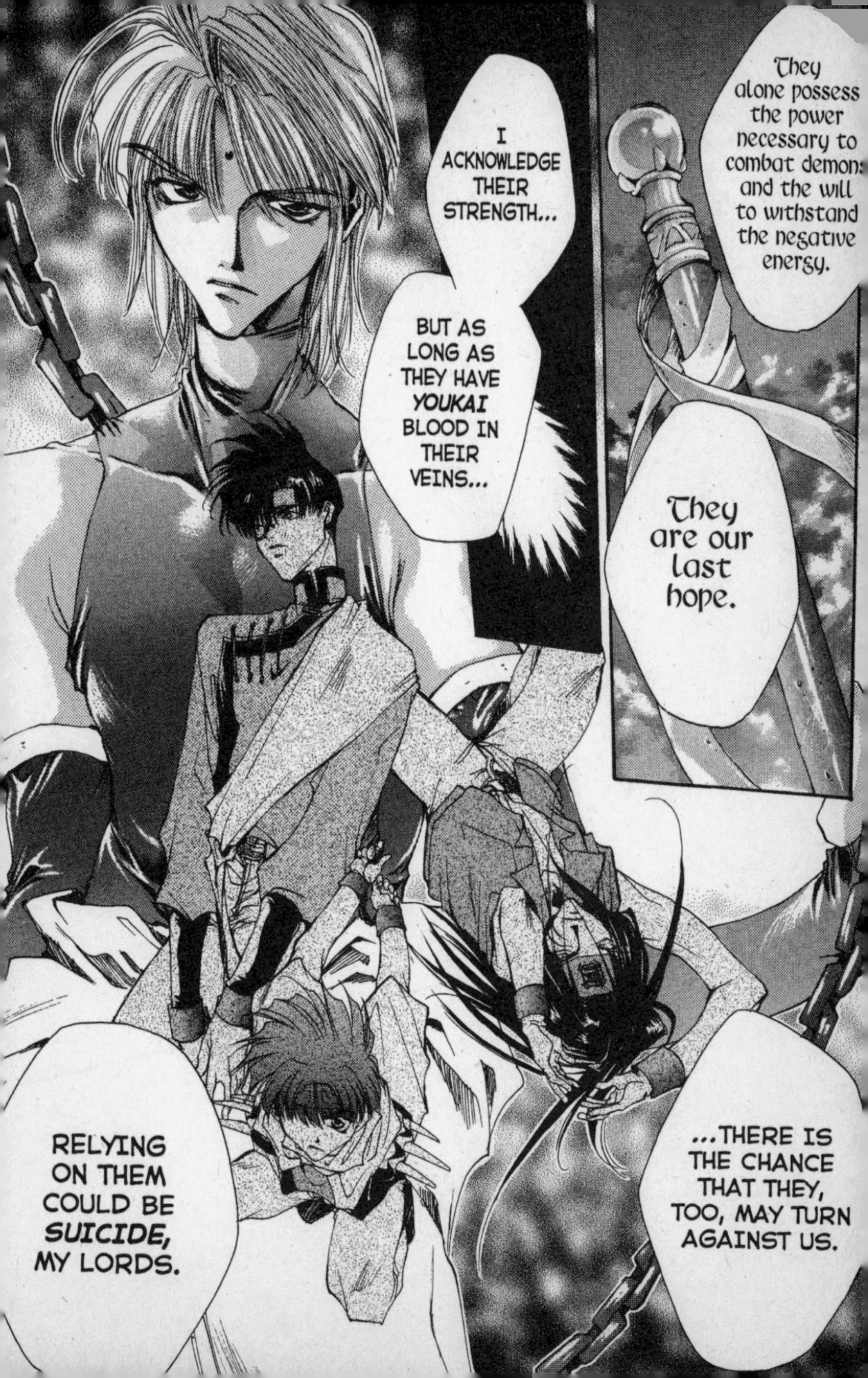
They alone possess the power necessary to combat demons and the will to withstand the negative energy.
They are our last hope.
I ACKNOWLEDGE THEIR STRENGTH...
BUT AS LONG AS THEY HAVE *YOUKAI* BLOOD IN THEIR VEINS...
...THERE IS THE CHANCE THAT THEY, TOO, MAY TURN AGAINST US.
RELYING ON THEM COULD BE *SUICIDE,* MY LORDS.

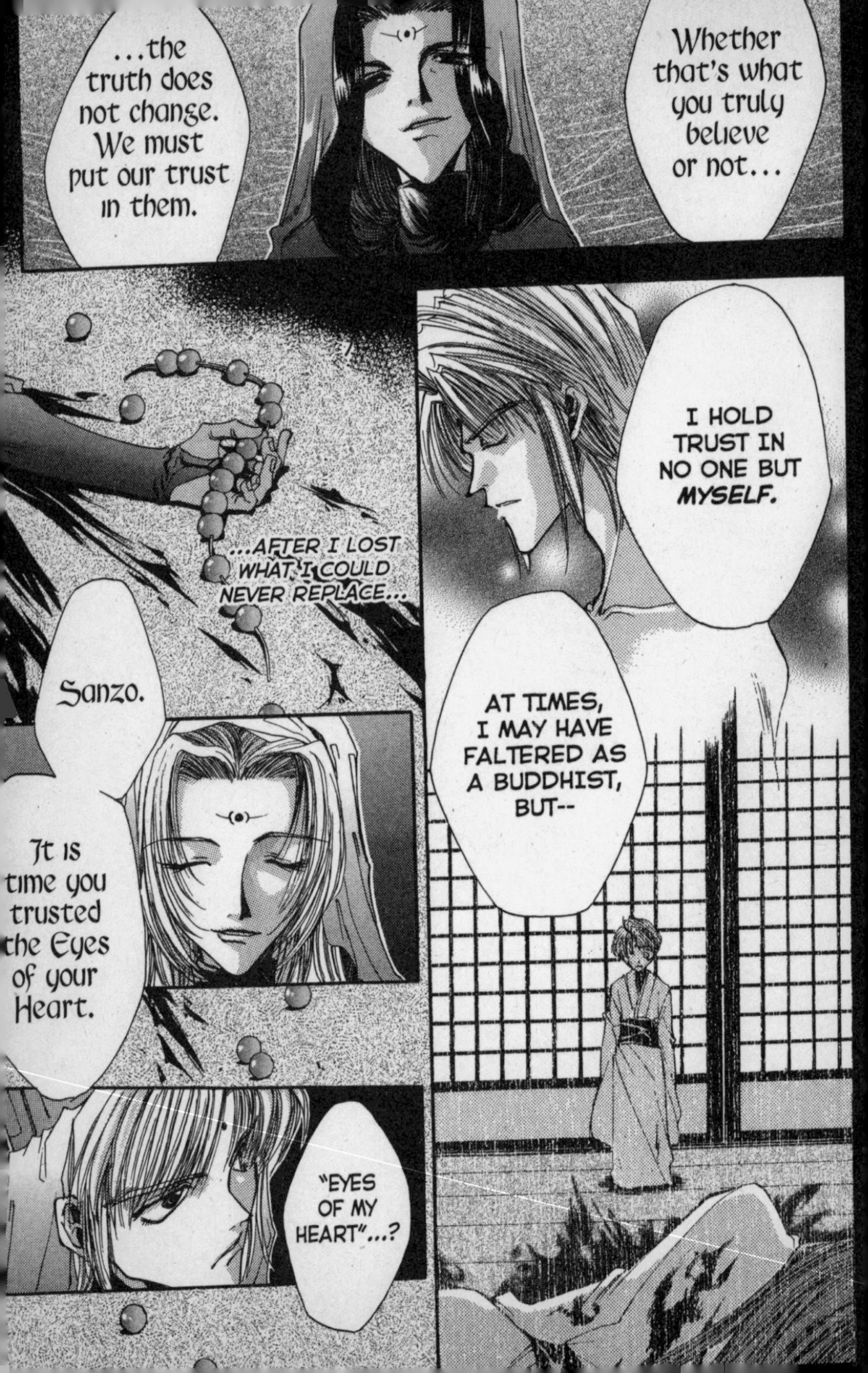
Whether that's what you truly believe or not...
...the truth does not change. We must put our trust in them.
I HOLD TRUST IN NO ONE BUT *MYSELF.*
AT TIMES, I MAY HAVE FALTERED AS A BUDDHIST, BUT--
...AFTER I LOST WHAT I COULD NEVER REPLACE...
Sanzo.
It is time you trusted the Eyes of your Heart.
"EYES OF MY HEART"...?

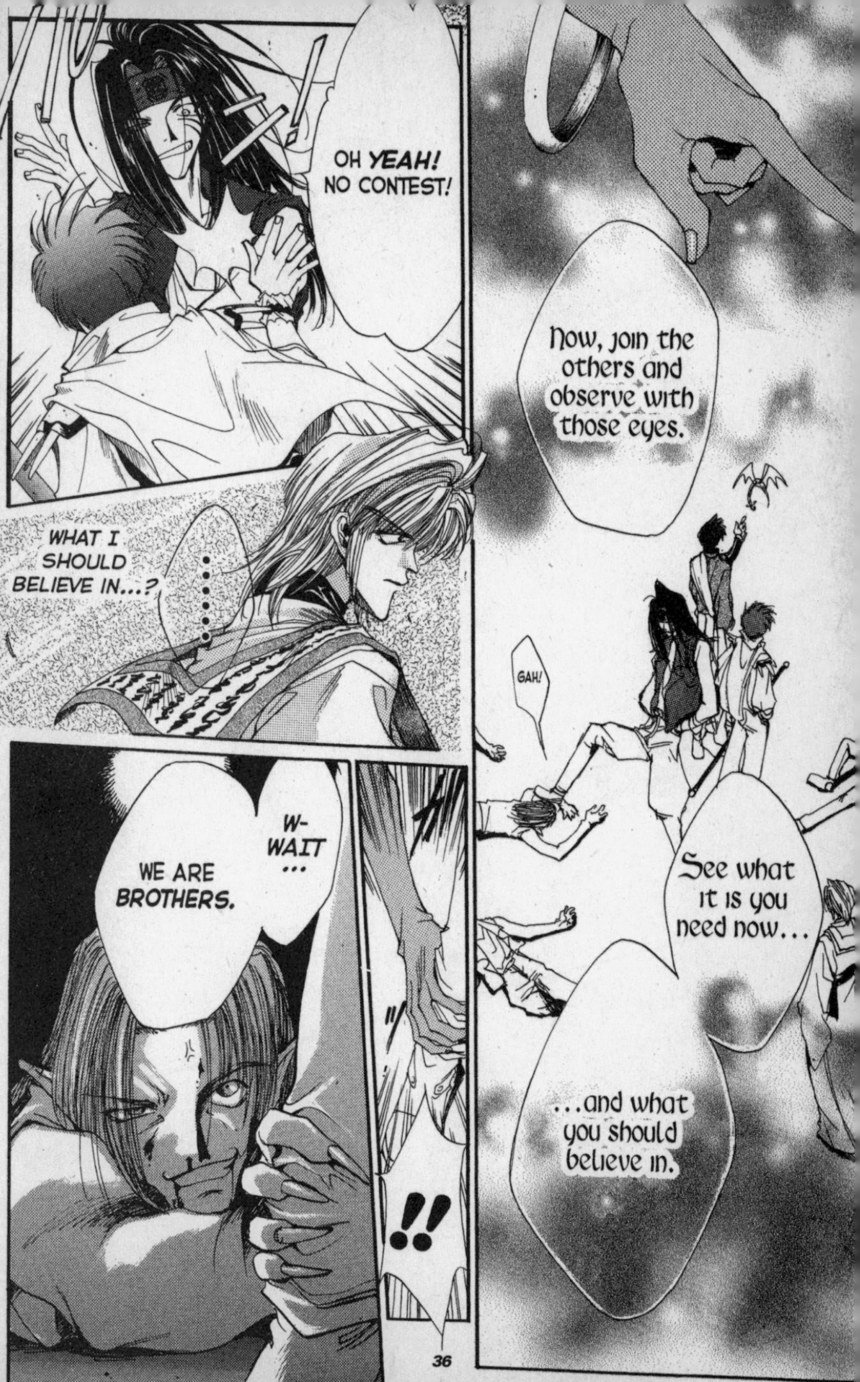
Now, join the others and observe with those eyes.
GAH!
See what it is you need now...
...and what you should believe in.
OH YEAH! NO CONTEST!
WHAT I SHOULD BELIEVE IN...?
......
!!
W-WAIT...
WE ARE BROTHERS.

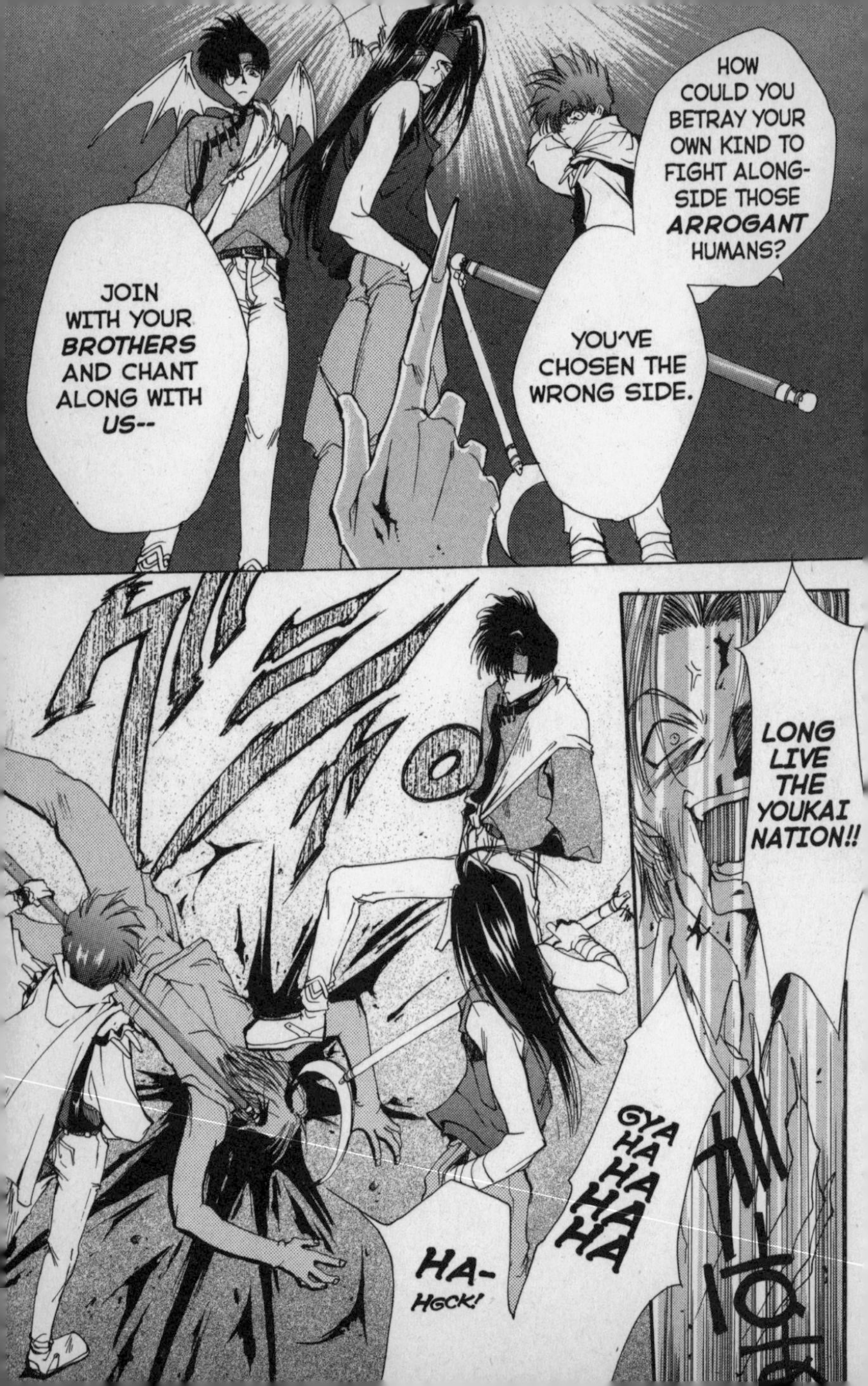
HOW COULD YOU BETRAY YOUR OWN KIND TO FIGHT ALONG-SIDE THOSE **ARROGANT** HUMANS?
YOU'VE CHOSEN THE WRONG SIDE.
JOIN WITH YOUR **BROTHERS** AND CHANT ALONG WITH **US--**
LONG LIVE THE YOUKAI NATION!!
GYA HA HA HA HA HA
HA-
HGCK!

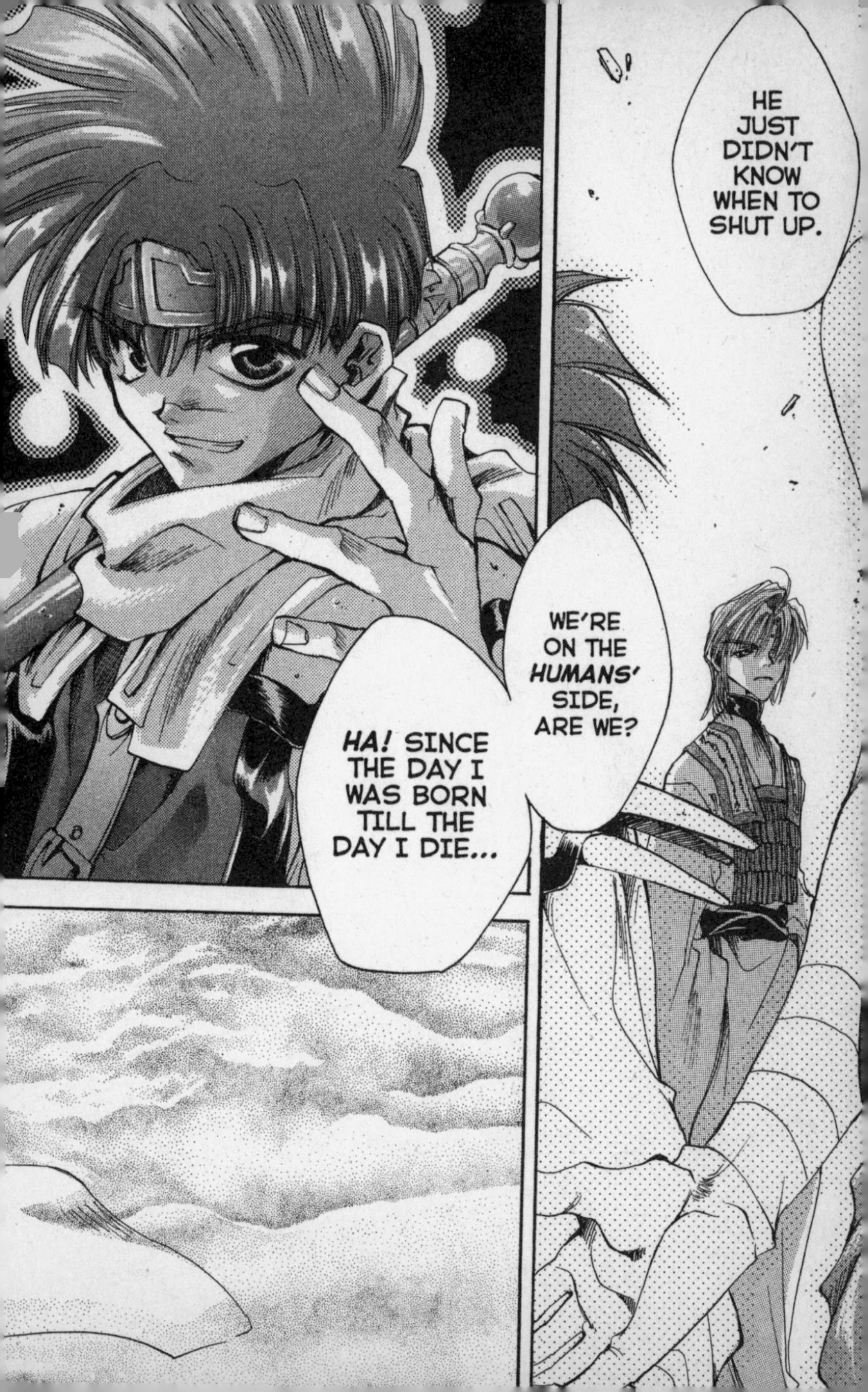
HE JUST DIDN'T KNOW WHEN TO SHUT UP.
WE'RE ON THE *HUMANS'* SIDE, ARE WE?
HA! SINCE THE DAY I WAS BORN TILL THE DAY I DIE...

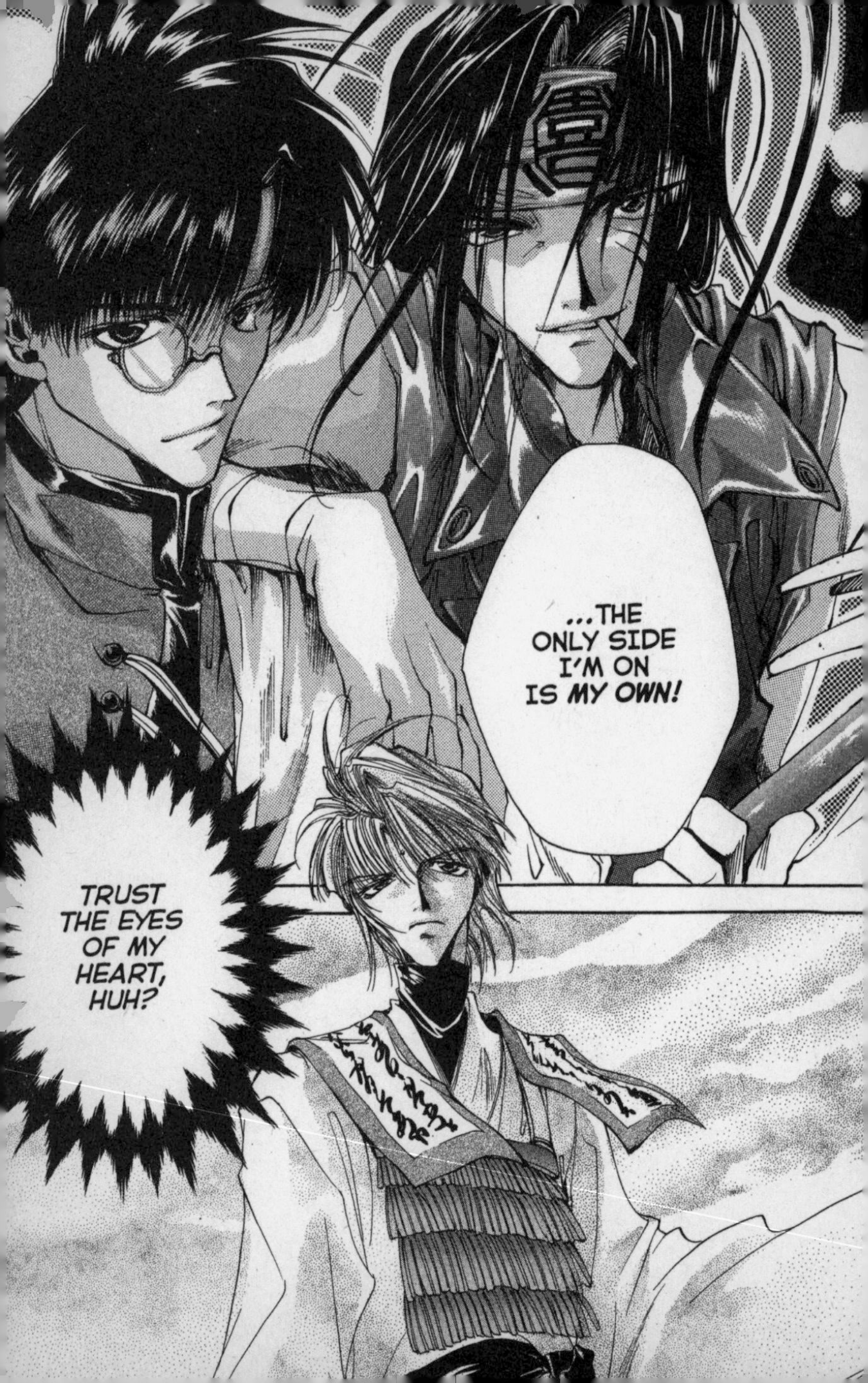
...THE ONLY SIDE I'M ON IS MY OWN!
TRUST THE EYES OF MY HEART, HUH?

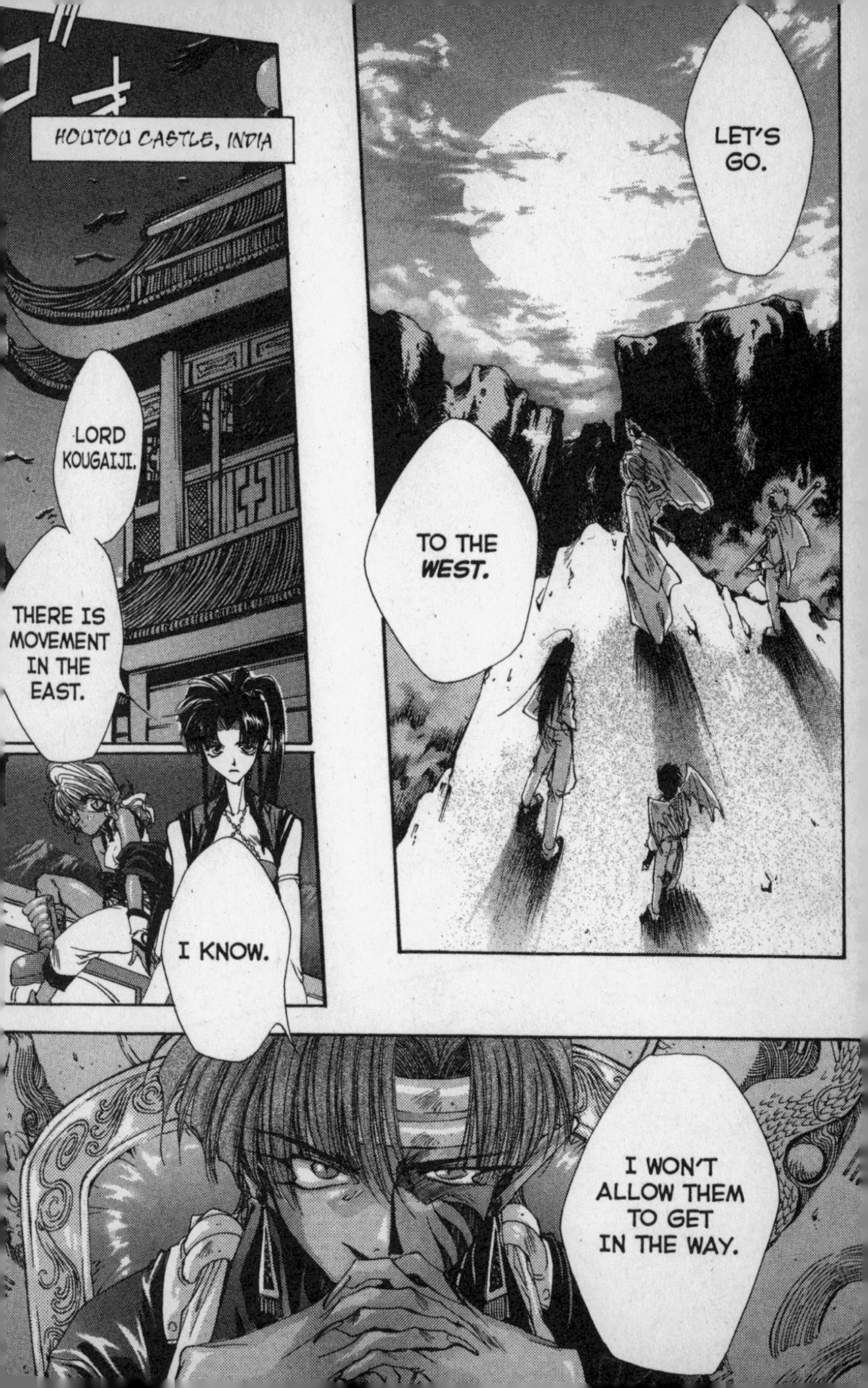
LET'S GO.
TO THE WEST.
HOUTOU CASTLE, INDIA
LORD KOUGAIJI.
THERE IS MOVEMENT IN THE EAST.
I KNOW.
I WON'T ALLOW THEM TO GET IN THE WAY.

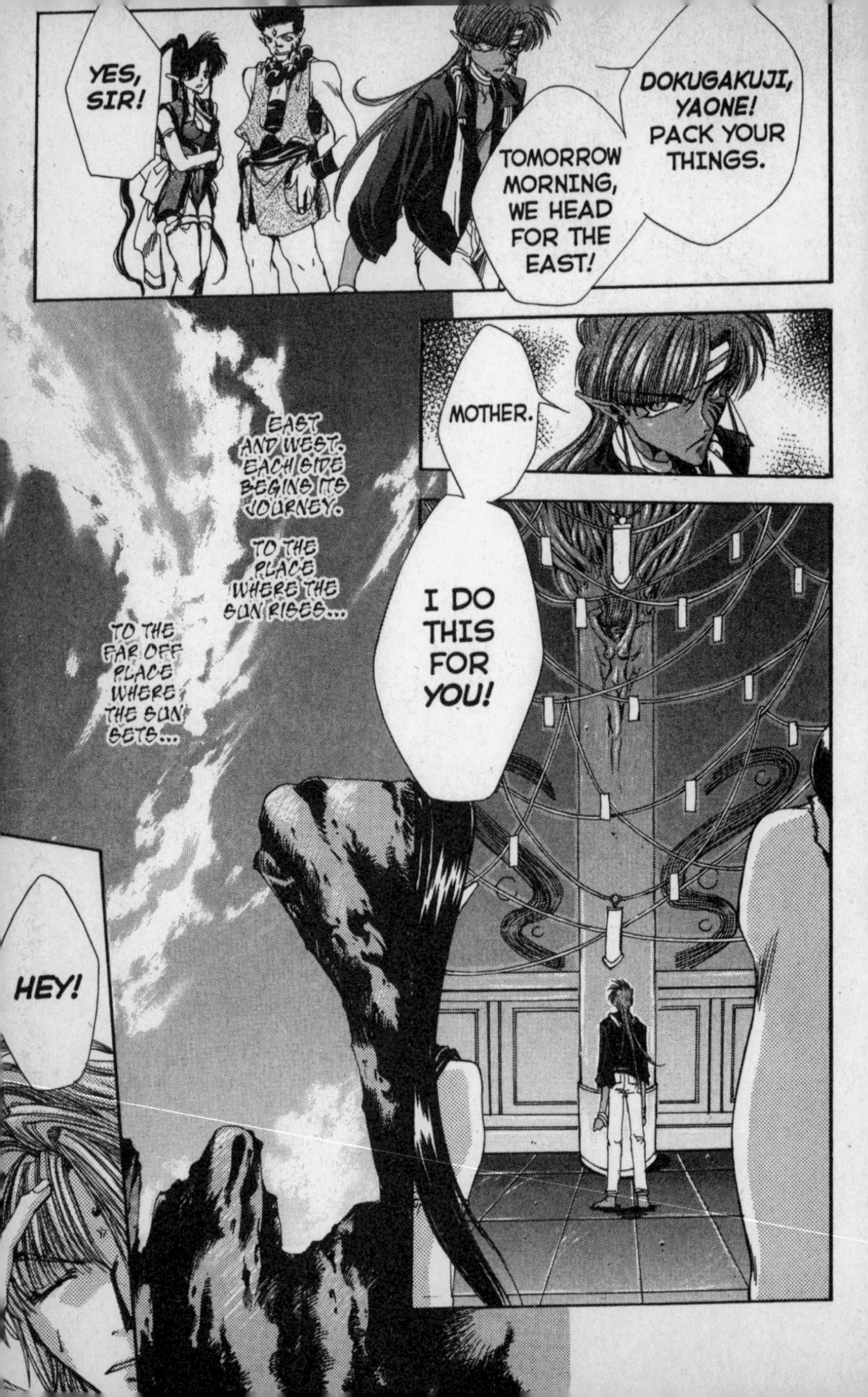
DOKUGAKUJI, YAONE! PACK YOUR THINGS.
TOMORROW MORNING, WE HEAD FOR THE EAST!
YES, SIR!
MOTHER.
I DO THIS FOR YOU!
EAST AND WEST. EACH SIDE BEGINS ITS JOURNEY.
TO THE PLACE WHERE THE SUN RISES...
TO THE FAR OFF PLACE WHERE THE SUN SETS...
HEY!

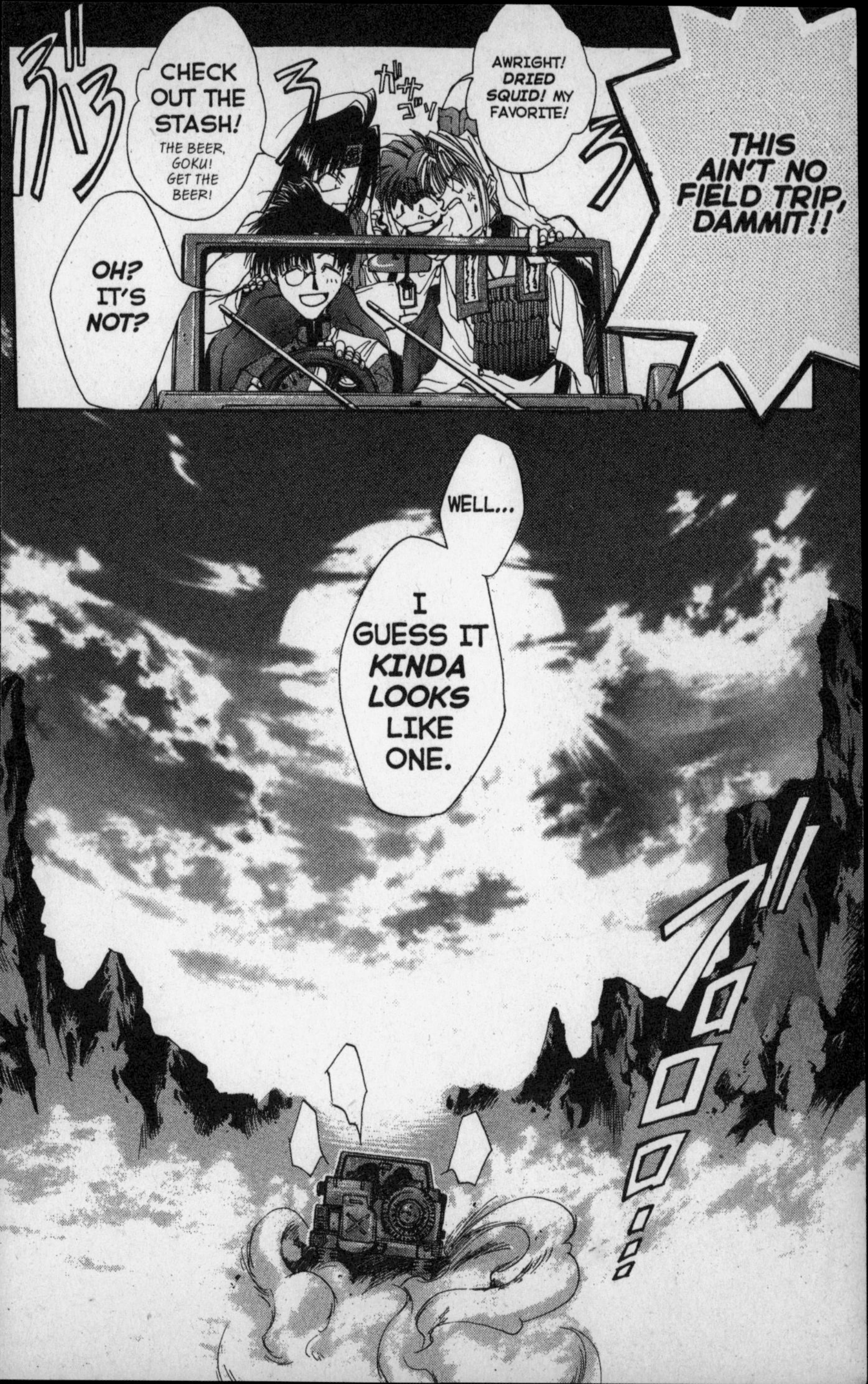
CHECK OUT THE STASH!
THE BEER, GOKU! GET THE BEER!
AWRIGHT! DRIED SQUID! MY FAVORITE!
THIS AIN'T NO FIELD TRIP, DAMMIT!!
OH? IT'S NOT?
WELL...
I GUESS IT KINDA LOOKS LIKE ONE.

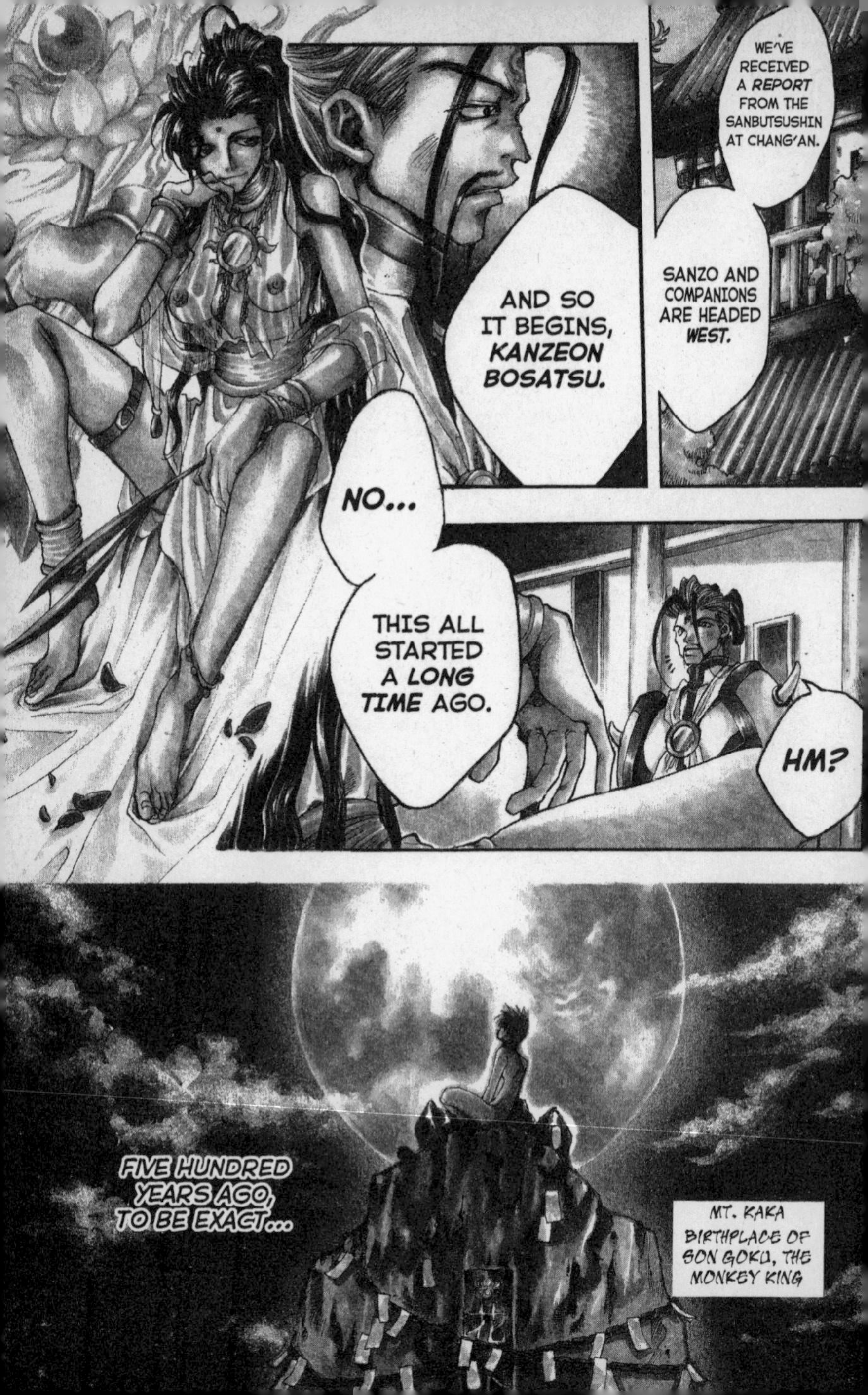
WE'VE RECEIVED A REPORT FROM THE SANBUTSUSHIN AT CHANG'AN.
SANZO AND COMPANIONS ARE HEADED WEST.
AND SO IT BEGINS, KANZEON BOSATSU.
NO...
THIS ALL STARTED A LONG TIME AGO.
HM?
MT. KAKA BIRTHPLACE OF SON GOKU, THE MONKEY KING
FIVE HUNDRED YEARS AGO, TO BE EXACT...

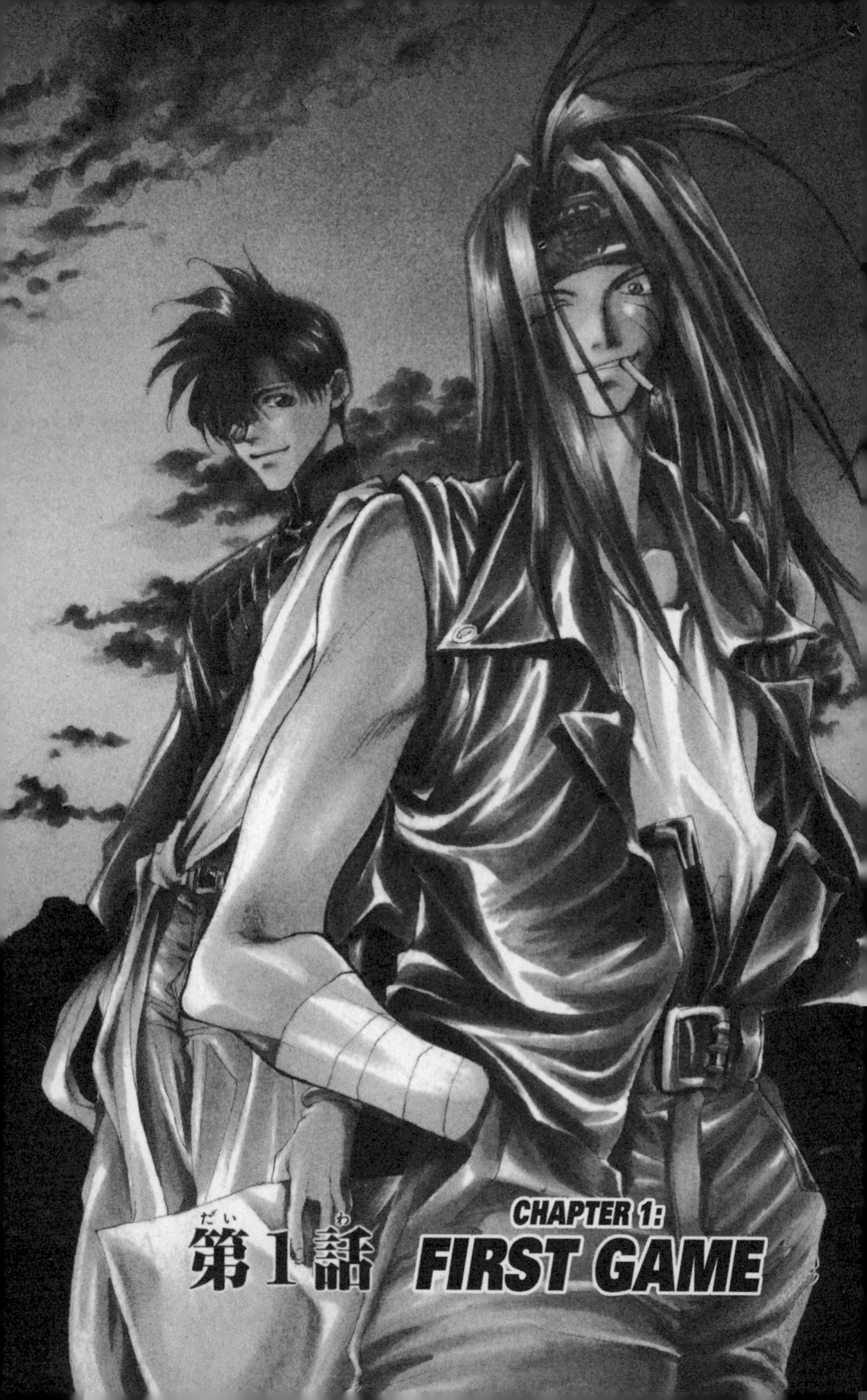
第1話
CHAPTER 1:
FIRST GAME

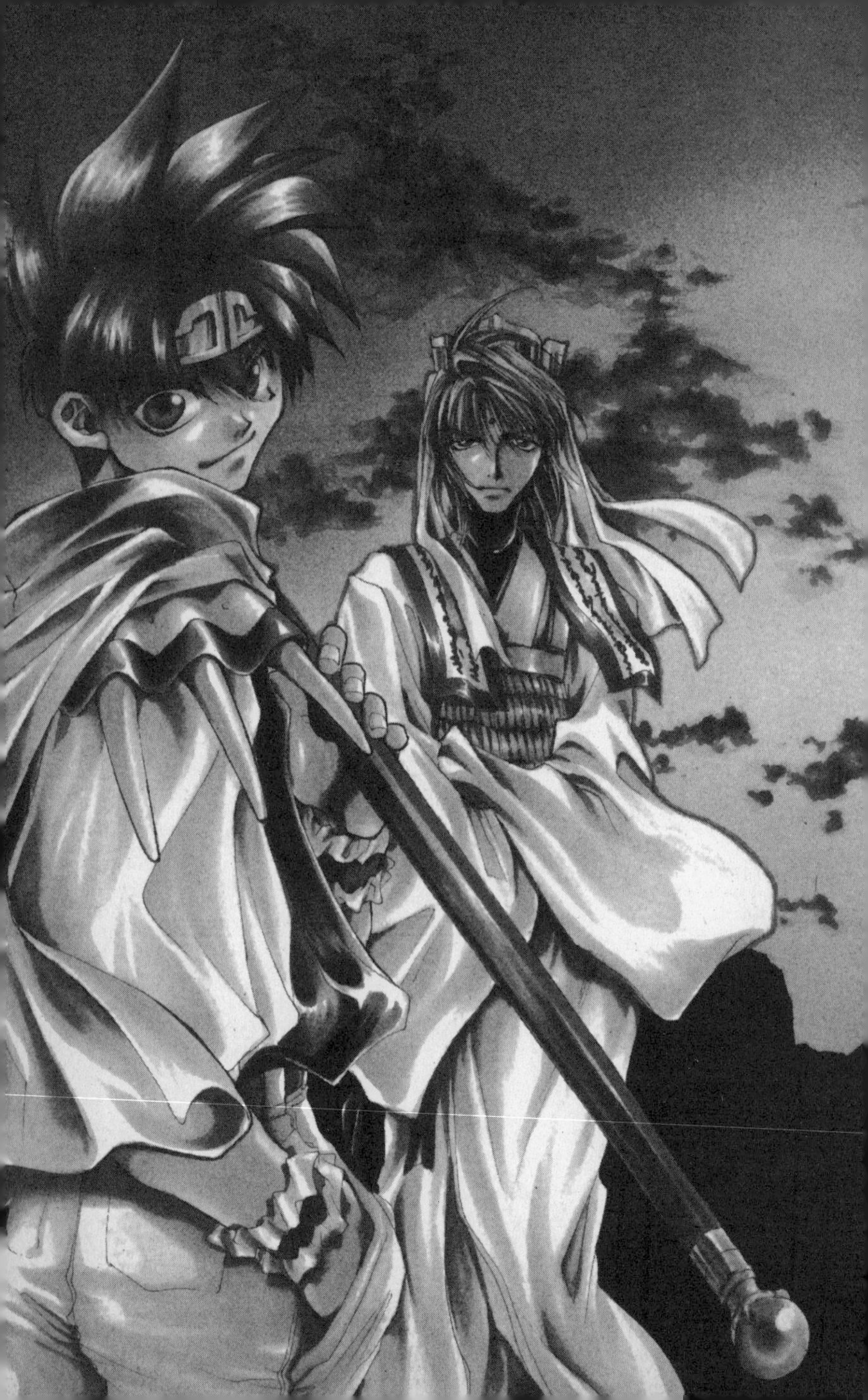

KANZEON BOSATSU

HERMAPHRODITE

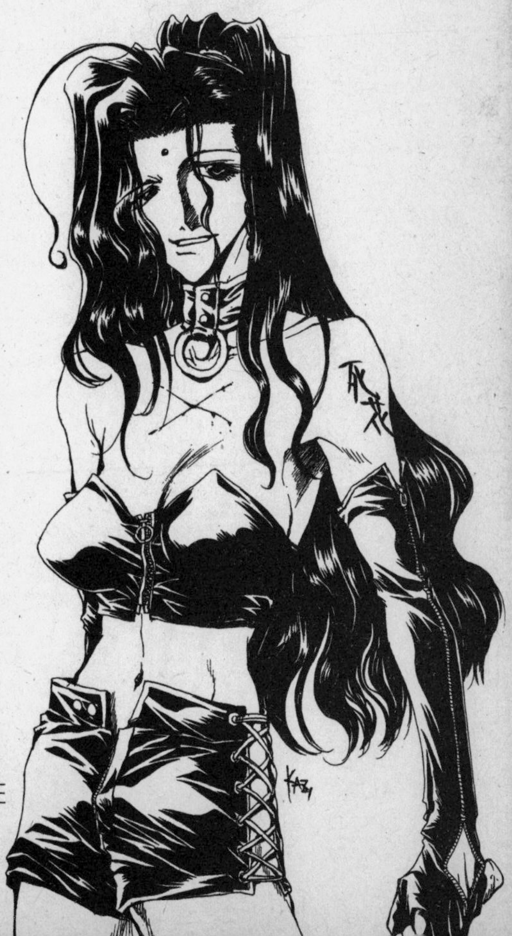

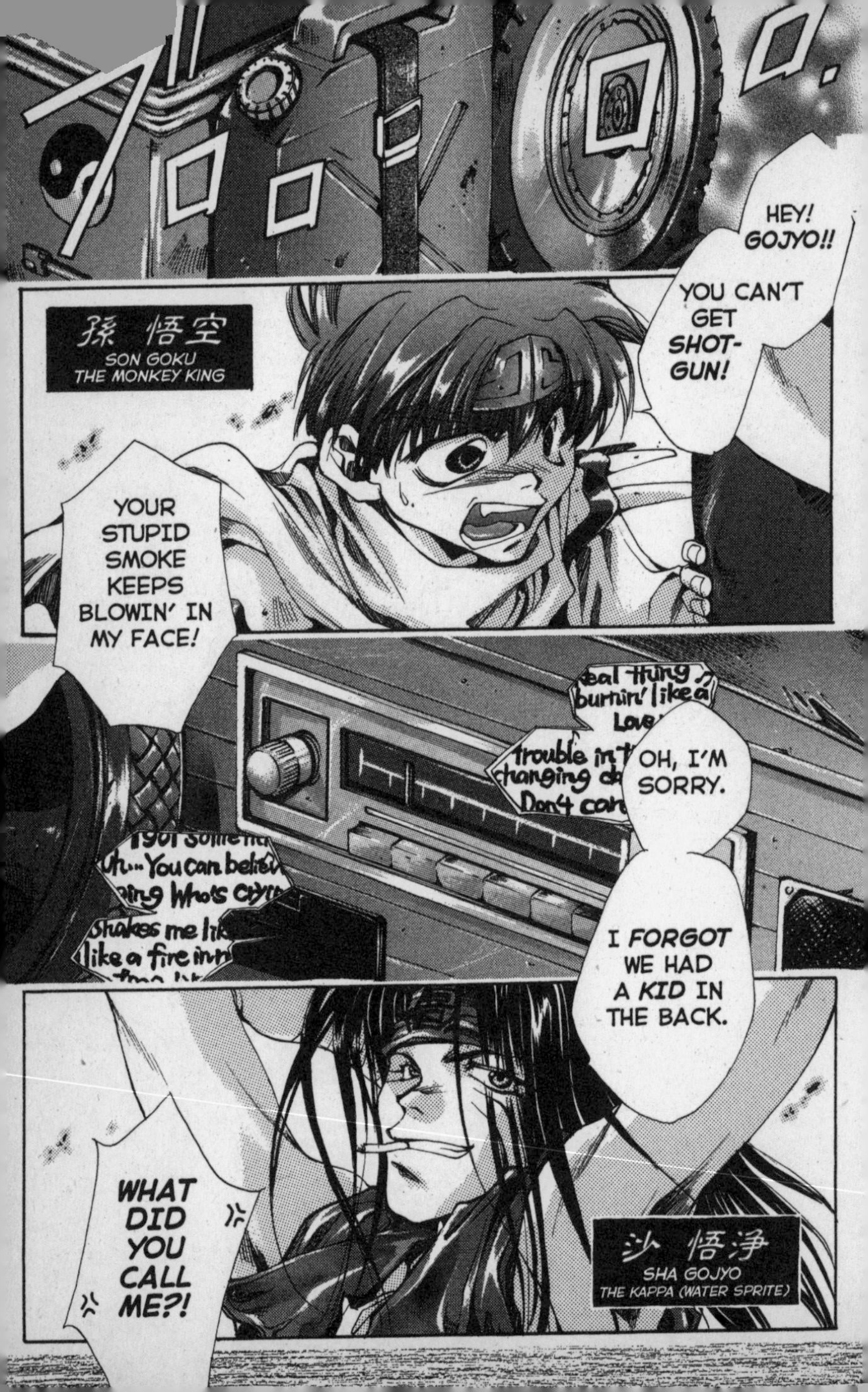
HEY! GOJYO!!
YOU CAN'T GET SHOT-GUN!
孫悟空
SON GOKU
THE MONKEY KING
YOUR STUPID SMOKE KEEPS BLOWIN' IN MY FACE!
OH, I'M SORRY.
I FORGOT WE HAD A KID IN THE BACK.
沙悟浄
SHA GOJYO
THE KAPPA (WATER SPRITE)
WHAT DID YOU CALL ME?!

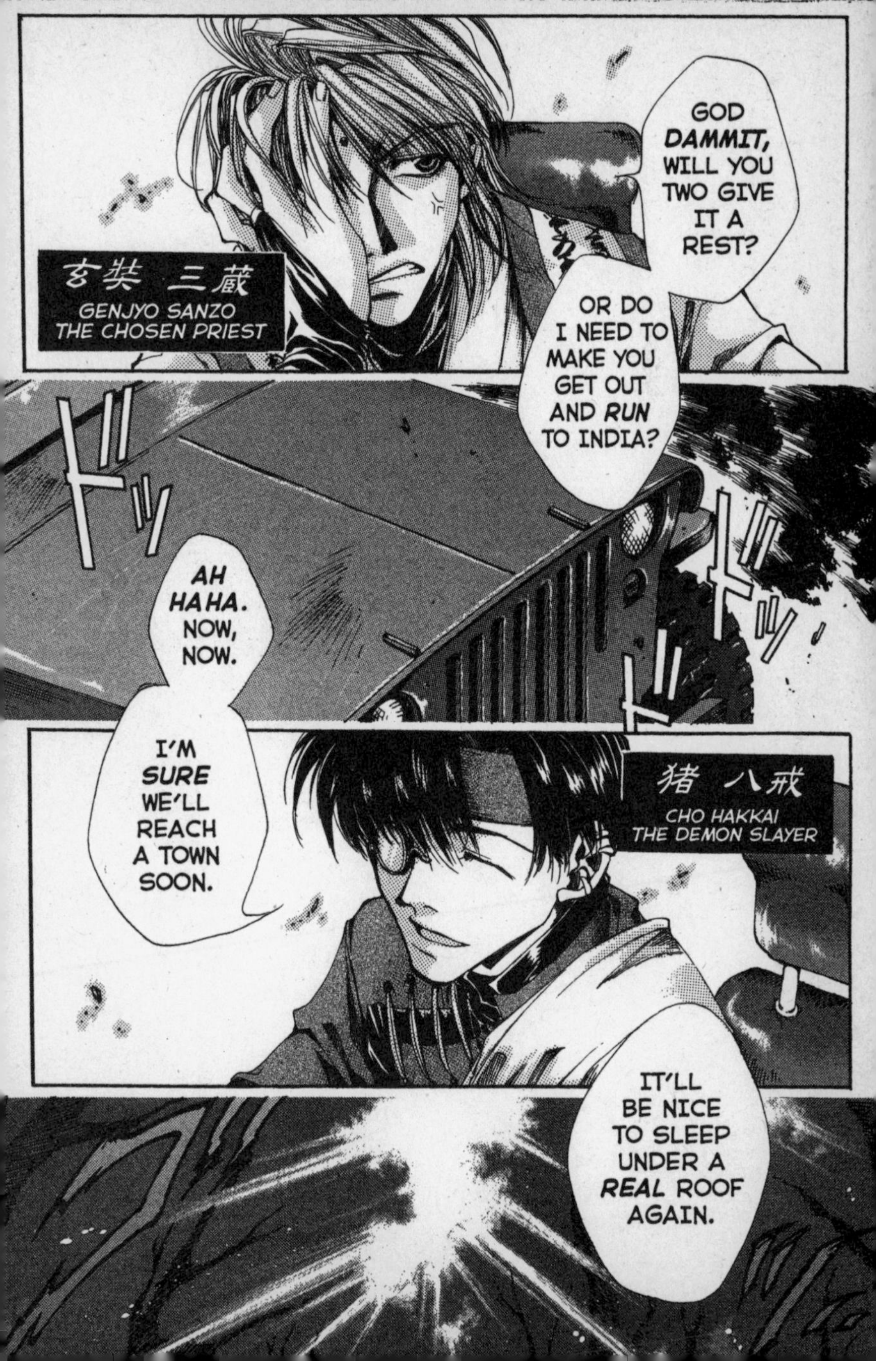
玄奘 三蔵
GENJYO SANZO
THE CHOSEN PRIEST
GOD *DAMMIT,* WILL YOU TWO GIVE IT A REST?
OR DO I NEED TO MAKE YOU GET OUT AND *RUN* TO INDIA?
ドドッ
ドッ
AH HAHA. NOW, NOW.
猪 八戒
CHO HAKKAI
THE DEMON SLAYER
I'M *SURE* WE'LL REACH A TOWN SOON.
IT'LL BE NICE TO SLEEP UNDER A *REAL* ROOF AGAIN.

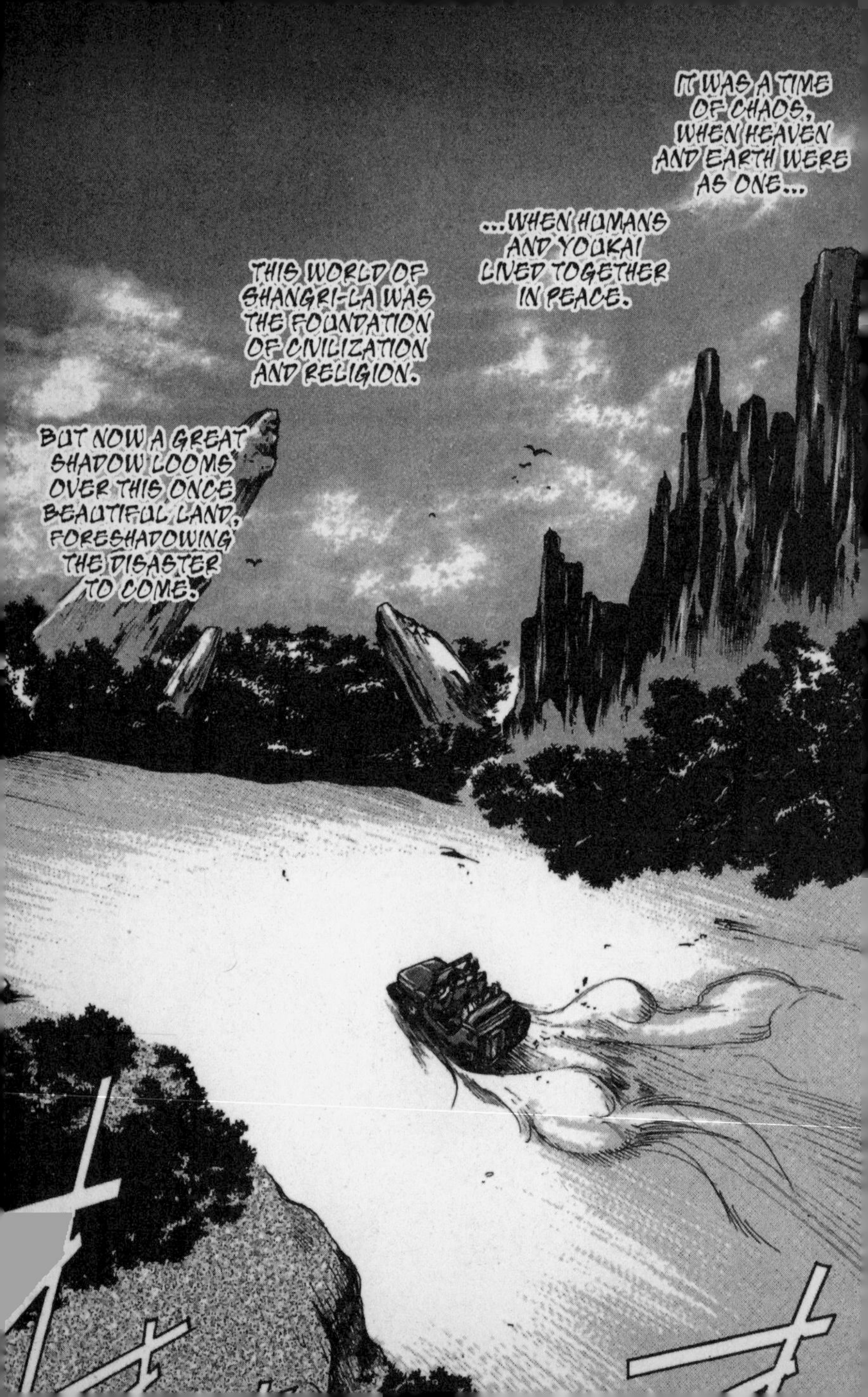
IT WAS A TIME OF CHAOS, WHEN HEAVEN AND EARTH WERE AS ONE...
...WHEN HUMANS AND YOUKAI LIVED TOGETHER IN PEACE.
THIS WORLD OF SHANGRI-LA WAS THE FOUNDATION OF CIVILIZATION AND RELIGION.
BUT NOW A GREAT SHADOW LOOMS OVER THIS ONCE BEAUTIFUL LAND, FORESHADOWING THE DISASTER TO COME.

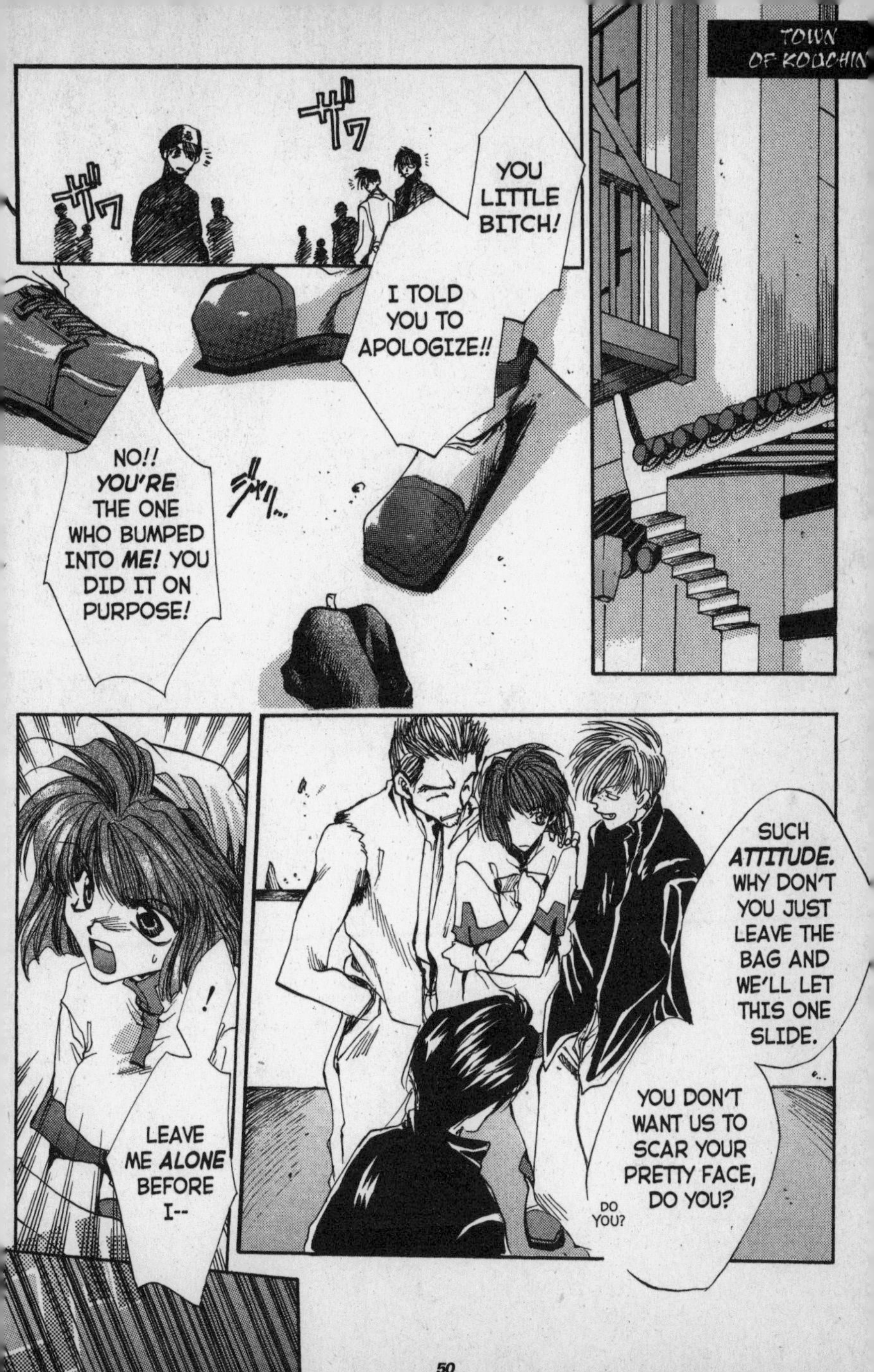
TOWN OF KOUCHIN
ザワ
ザワ
YOU LITTLE BITCH!
I TOLD YOU TO APOLOGIZE!!
ジャリ…
NO!! *YOU'RE* THE ONE WHO BUMPED INTO *ME!* YOU DID IT ON PURPOSE!
SUCH *ATTITUDE.* WHY DON'T YOU JUST LEAVE THE BAG AND WE'LL LET THIS ONE SLIDE.
YOU DON'T WANT US TO SCAR YOUR PRETTY FACE, DO YOU?
DO YOU?
!
LEAVE ME *ALONE* BEFORE I--

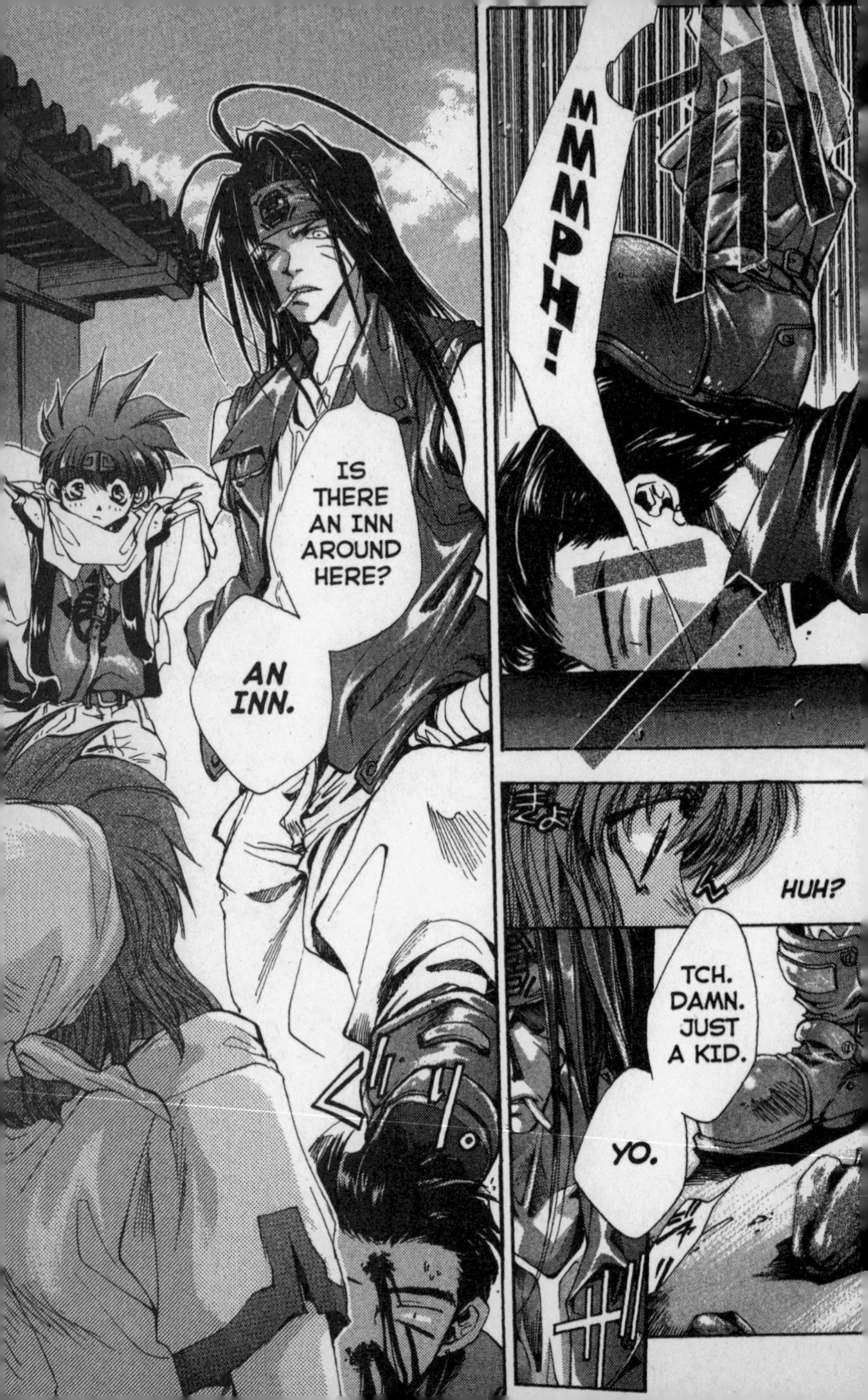
MMMPH!
HUH?
TCH. DAMN. JUST A KID.
YO.
IS THERE AN INN AROUND HERE?
AN INN.

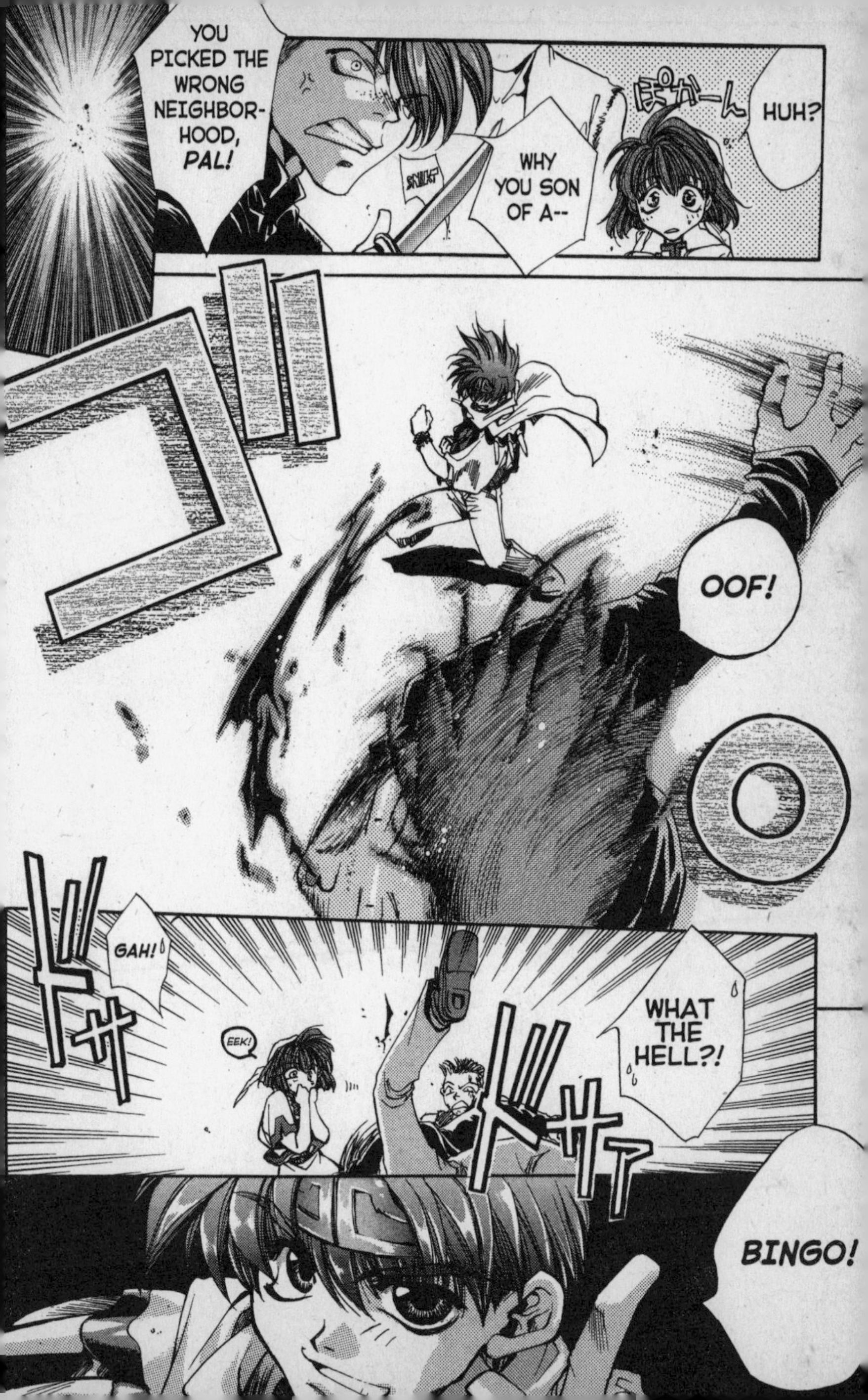
ぽかーん
HUH?
WHY YOU SON OF A--
YOU PICKED THE WRONG NEIGHBOR-HOOD, PAL!
OOF!
WHAT THE HELL?!
EEK!
GAH!
BINGO!

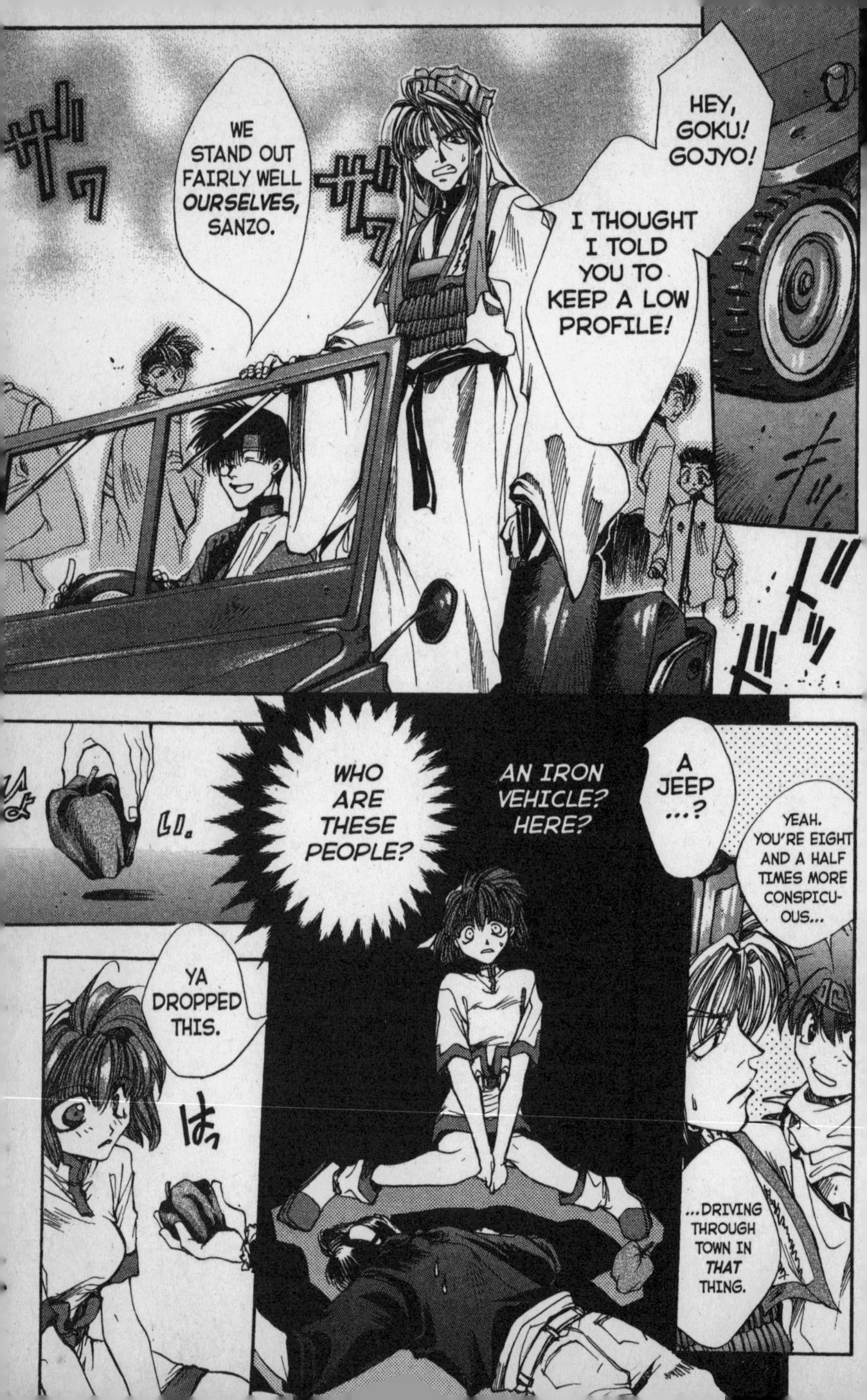
HEY, GOKU! GOJYO!
I THOUGHT I TOLD YOU TO KEEP A LOW PROFILE!
ザワ
ザワ
WE STAND OUT FAIRLY WELL *OURSELVES*, SANZO.
ドドッ
A JEEP ...?
YEAH. YOU'RE EIGHT AND A HALF TIMES MORE CONSPICU-OUS...
...DRIVING THROUGH TOWN IN *THAT* THING.
AN IRON VEHICLE? HERE?
WHO ARE THESE PEOPLE?
YA DROPPED THIS.
はっ

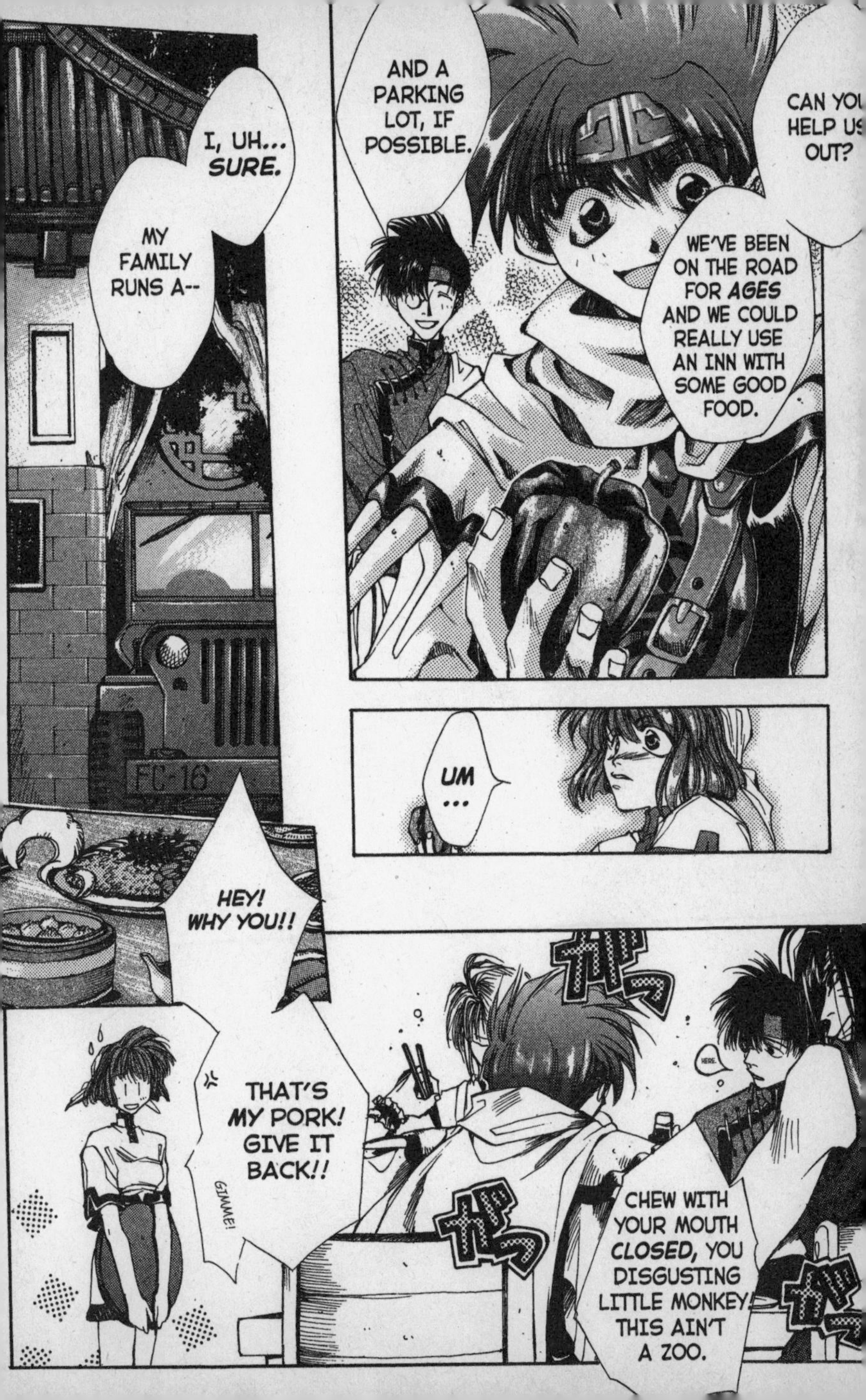

CAN YOU HELP US OUT?
WE'VE BEEN ON THE ROAD FOR AGES AND WE COULD REALLY USE AN INN WITH SOME GOOD FOOD.
AND A PARKING LOT, IF POSSIBLE.
UM ...
I, UH... SURE.
MY FAMILY RUNS A--
FC-16
HERE.
HEY! WHY YOU!!
THAT'S MY PORK! GIVE IT BACK!!
GIMME!
CHEW WITH YOUR MOUTH CLOSED, YOU DISGUSTING LITTLE MONKEY! THIS AIN'T A ZOO.

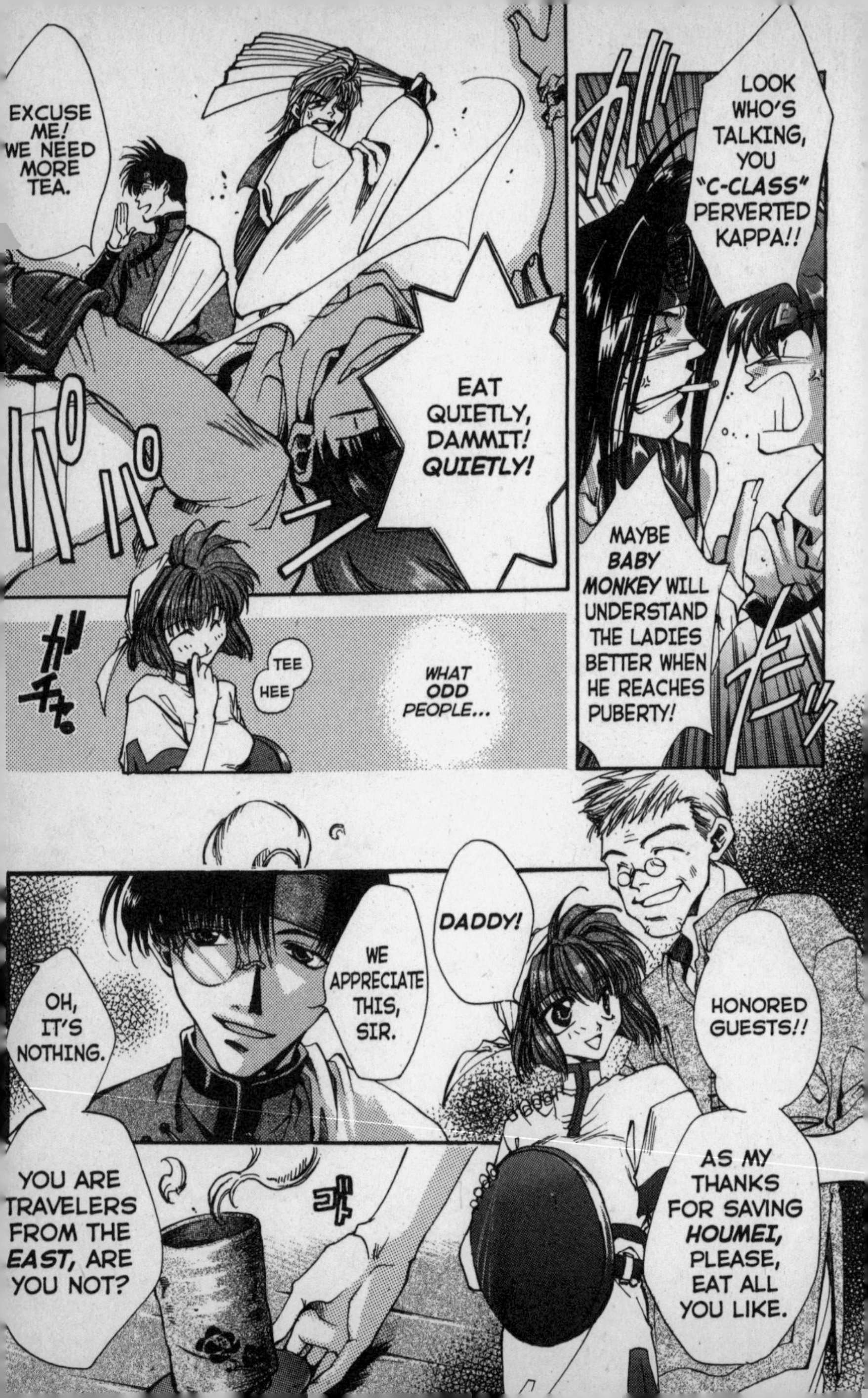

LOOK WHO'S TALKING, YOU "C-CLASS" PERVERTED KAPPA!!
MAYBE *BABY MONKEY* WILL UNDERSTAND THE LADIES BETTER WHEN HE REACHES PUBERTY!
EAT QUIETLY, DAMMIT! *QUIETLY!*
EXCUSE ME! WE NEED MORE TEA.
TEE HEE
WHAT ODD PEOPLE...
DADDY!
HONORED GUESTS!!
WE APPRECIATE THIS, SIR.
OH, IT'S NOTHING.
AS MY THANKS FOR SAVING *HOUMEI,* PLEASE, EAT ALL YOU LIKE.
YOU ARE TRAVELERS FROM THE *EAST,* ARE YOU NOT?

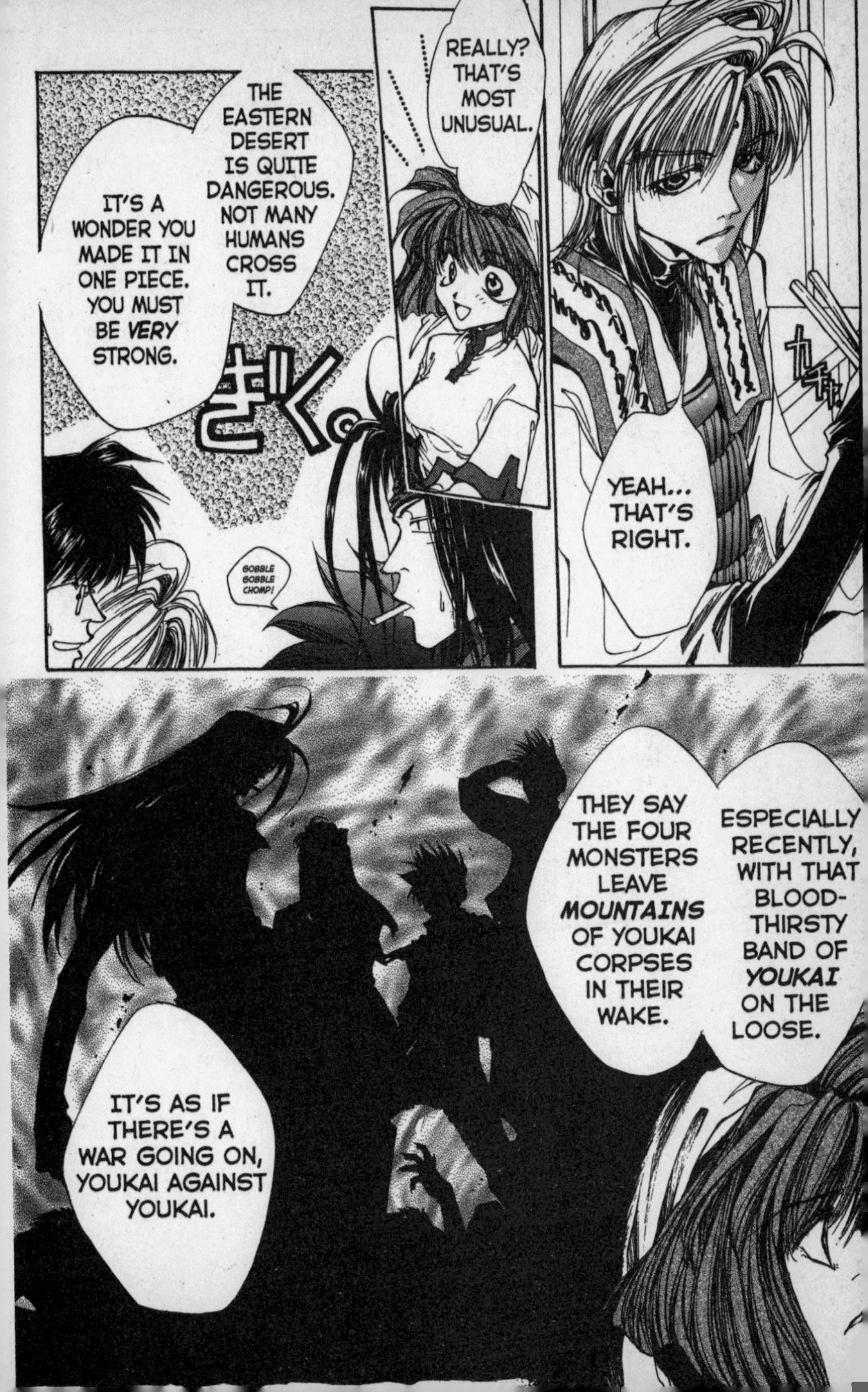
YEAH... THAT'S RIGHT.
カチャ
REALLY? THAT'S MOST UNUSUAL.
THE EASTERN DESERT IS QUITE DANGEROUS. NOT MANY HUMANS CROSS IT.
IT'S A WONDER YOU MADE IT IN ONE PIECE. YOU MUST BE *VERY* STRONG.
ぎく。
GOBBLE GOBBLE CHOMP!
ESPECIALLY RECENTLY, WITH THAT BLOOD-THIRSTY BAND OF *YOUKAI* ON THE LOOSE.
THEY SAY THE FOUR MONSTERS LEAVE *MOUNTAINS* OF YOUKAI CORPSES IN THEIR WAKE.
IT'S AS IF THERE'S A WAR GOING ON, YOUKAI AGAINST YOUKAI.

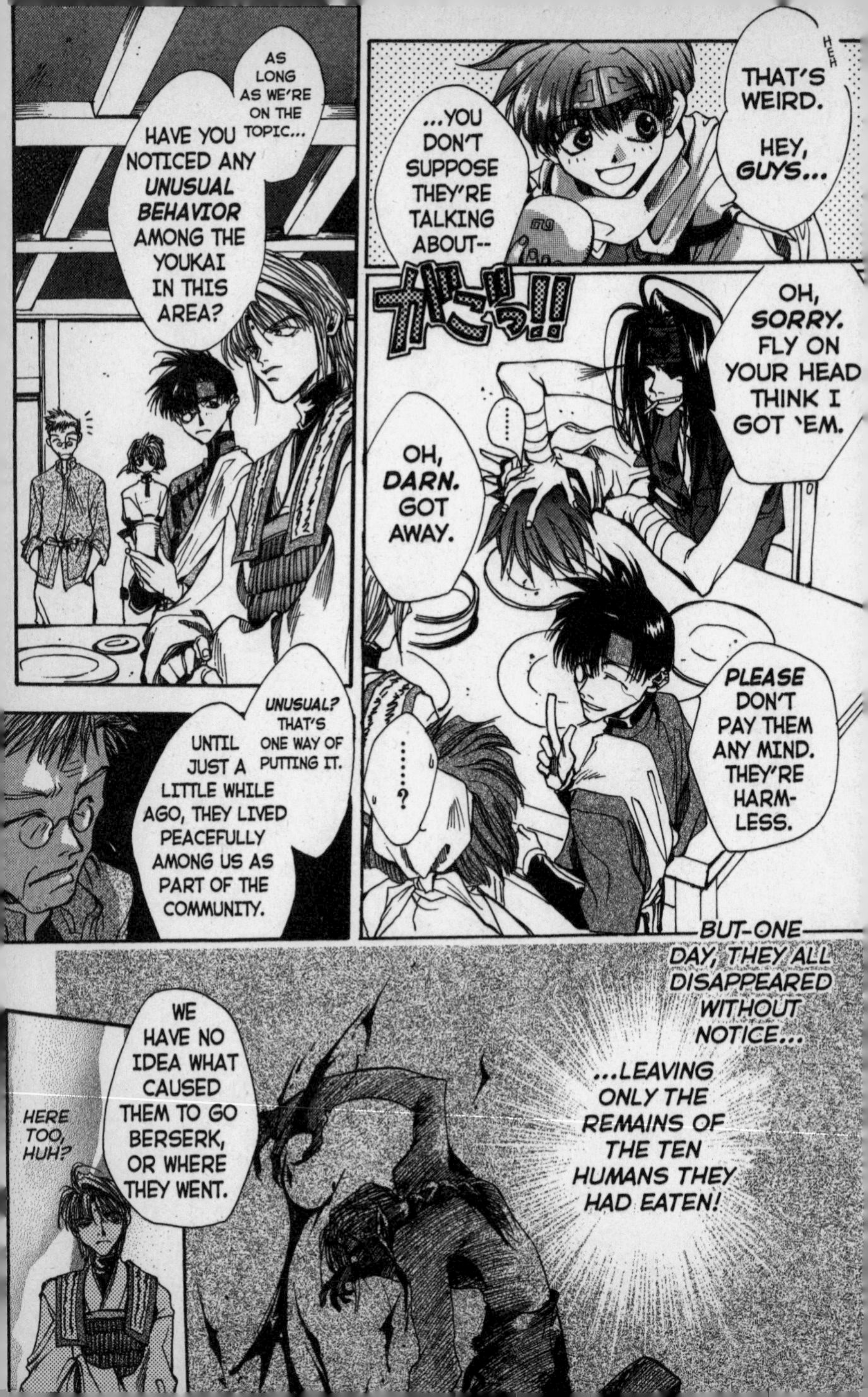
HEH
THAT'S WEIRD. HEY, GUYS...
...YOU DON'T SUPPOSE THEY'RE TALKING ABOUT--
OH, SORRY. FLY ON YOUR HEAD THINK I GOT 'EM.
OH, DARN. GOT AWAY.
......
PLEASE DON'T PAY THEM ANY MIND. THEY'RE HARMLESS.
......?
AS LONG AS WE'RE ON THE TOPIC...
HAVE YOU NOTICED ANY UNUSUAL BEHAVIOR AMONG THE YOUKAI IN THIS AREA?
UNUSUAL? THAT'S ONE WAY OF PUTTING IT.
UNTIL JUST A LITTLE WHILE AGO, THEY LIVED PEACEFULLY AMONG US AS PART OF THE COMMUNITY.
BUT ONE DAY, THEY ALL DISAPPEARED WITHOUT NOTICE...
...LEAVING ONLY THE REMAINS OF THE TEN HUMANS THEY HAD EATEN!
WE HAVE NO IDEA WHAT CAUSED THEM TO GO BERSERK, OR WHERE THEY WENT.
HERE TOO, HUH?

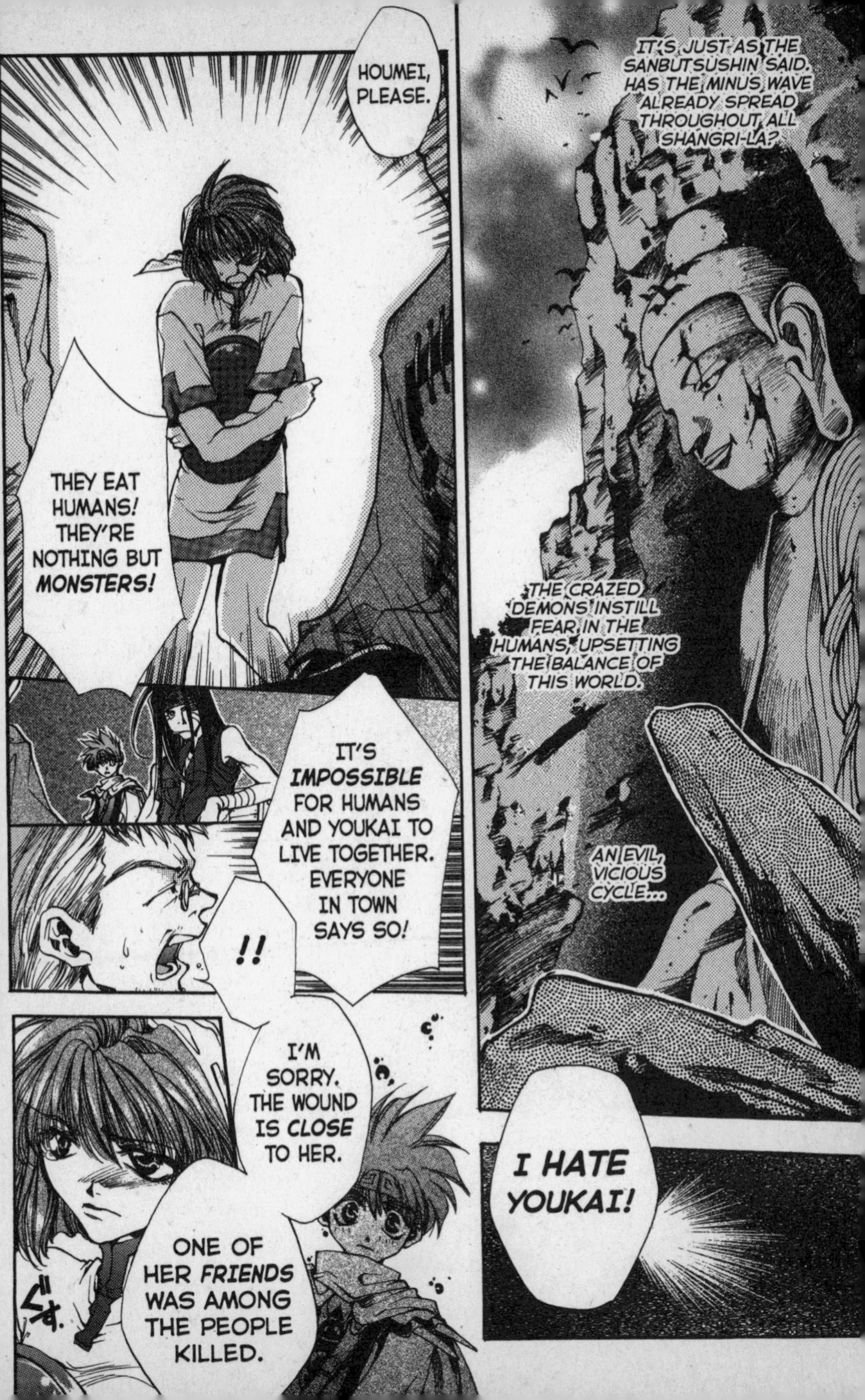
IT'S JUST AS THE SANBUTSUSHIN SAID. HAS THE MINUS WAVE ALREADY SPREAD THROUGHOUT ALL SHANGRI-LA?
THE CRAZED DEMONS INSTILL FEAR IN THE HUMANS, UPSETTING THE BALANCE OF THIS WORLD.
AN EVIL, VICIOUS CYCLE...
I HATE YOUKAI!
HOUMEI, PLEASE.
THEY EAT HUMANS! THEY'RE NOTHING BUT MONSTERS!
IT'S IMPOSSIBLE FOR HUMANS AND YOUKAI TO LIVE TOGETHER. EVERYONE IN TOWN SAYS SO!
!!
I'M SORRY. THE WOUND IS CLOSE TO HER.
ONE OF HER FRIENDS WAS AMONG THE PEOPLE KILLED.

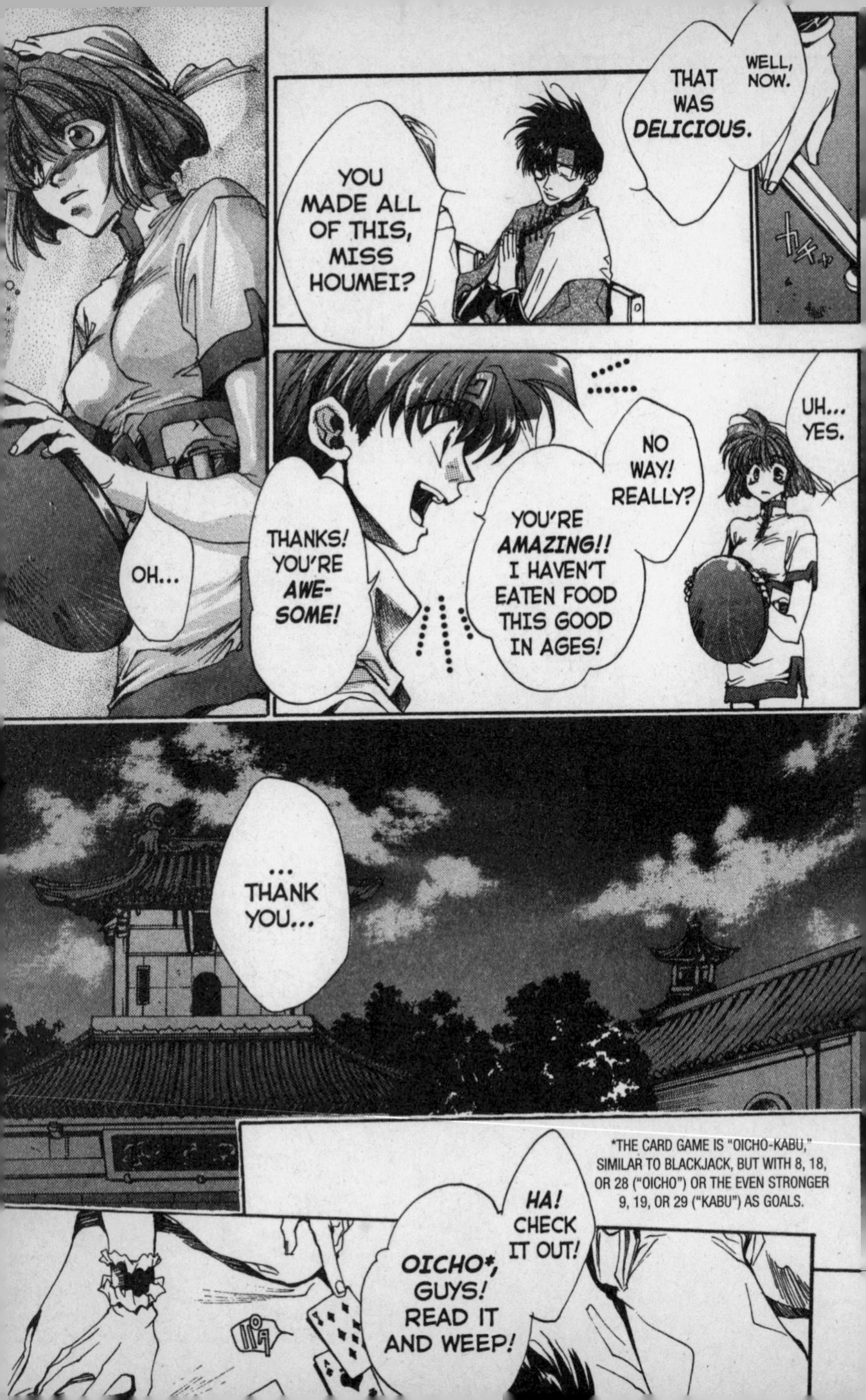
WELL, NOW.
THAT WAS DELICIOUS.
YOU MADE ALL OF THIS, MISS HOUMEI?
UH... YES.
......
NO WAY! REALLY?
YOU'RE AMAZING!! I HAVEN'T EATEN FOOD THIS GOOD IN AGES!
THANKS! YOU'RE AWE-SOME!
OH...
...THANK YOU...
*THE CARD GAME IS "OICHO-KABU," SIMILAR TO BLACKJACK, BUT WITH 8, 18, OR 28 ("OICHO") OR THE EVEN STRONGER 9, 19, OR 29 ("KABU") AS GOALS.
HA! CHECK IT OUT!
OICHO*, GUYS! READ IT AND WEEP!

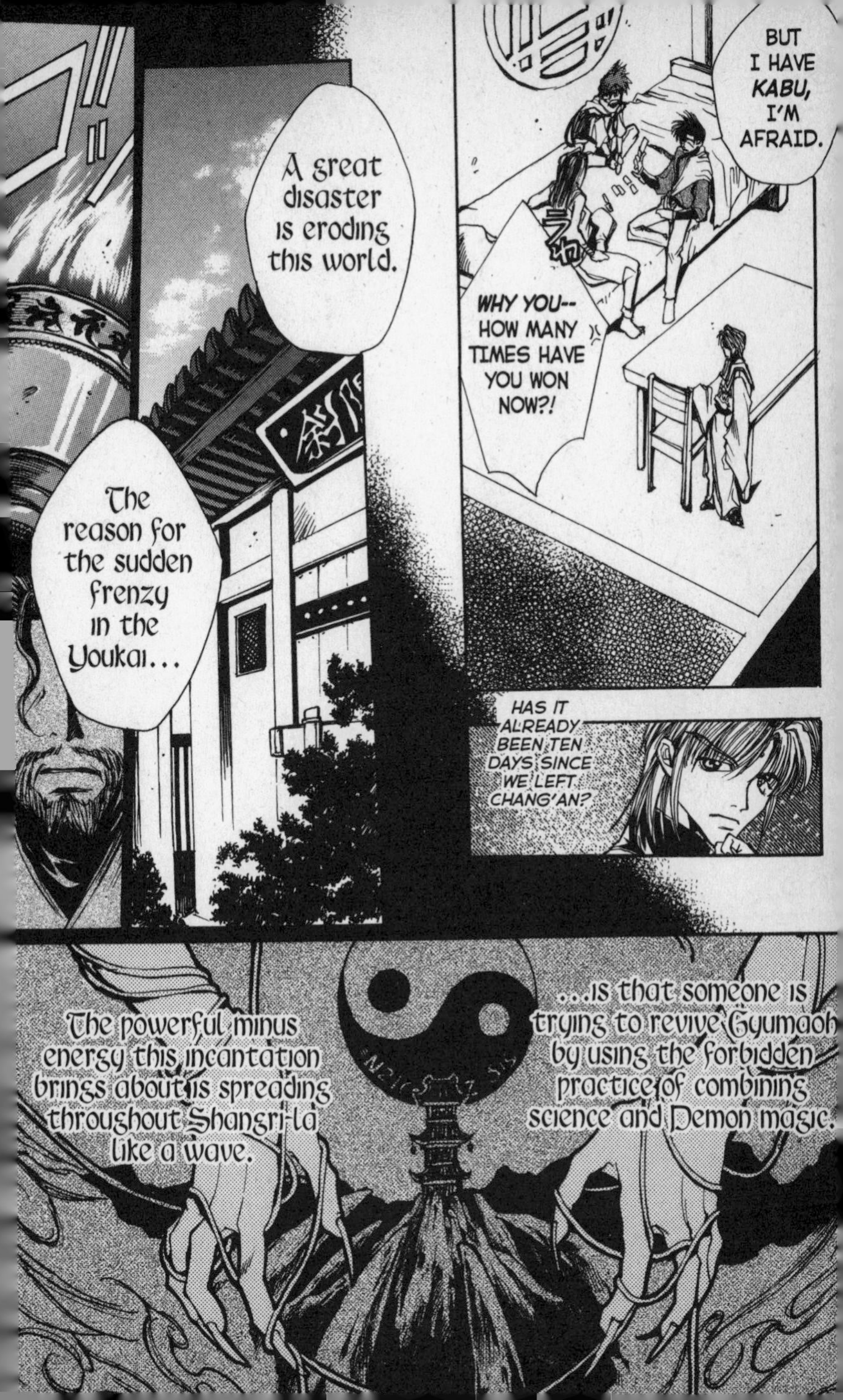

BUT I HAVE KABU, I'M AFRAID.
WHY YOU-- HOW MANY TIMES HAVE YOU WON NOW?!
HAS IT ALREADY BEEN TEN DAYS SINCE WE LEFT CHANG'AN?
A great disaster is eroding this world.
The reason for the sudden frenzy in the Youkai...
...is that someone is trying to revive Gyumaoh by using the forbidden practice of combining science and Demon magic.
The powerful minus energy this incantation brings about is spreading throughout Shangri-la like a wave.

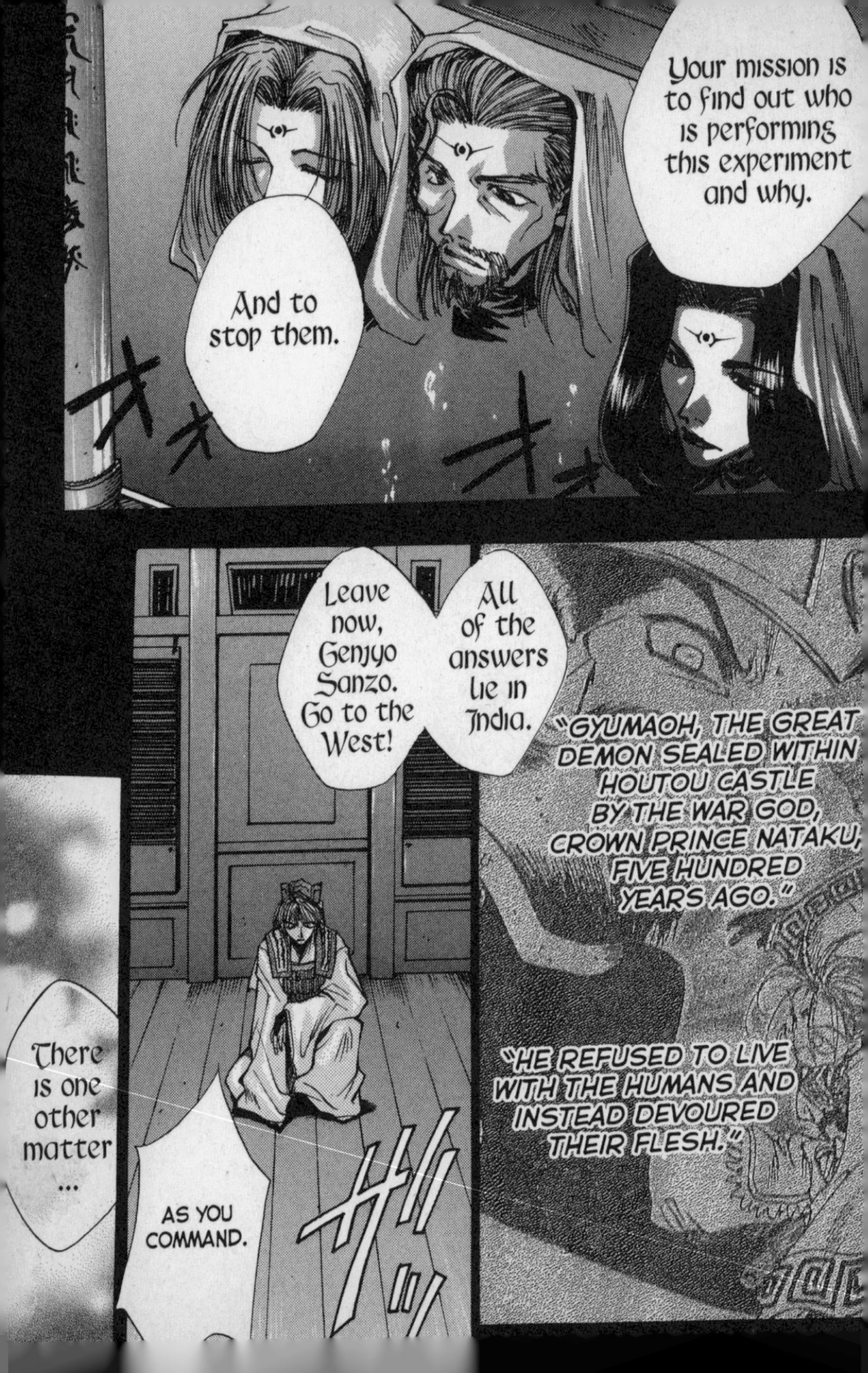
Your mission is to find out who is performing this experiment and why.
And to stop them.
"GYUMAOH, THE GREAT DEMON SEALED WITHIN HOUTOU CASTLE BY THE WAR GOD, CROWN PRINCE NATAKU, FIVE HUNDRED YEARS AGO."
"HE REFUSED TO LIVE WITH THE HUMANS AND INSTEAD DEVOURED THEIR FLESH."
All of the answers lie in India.
Leave now, Genjyo Sanzo. Go to the West!
AS YOU COMMAND.
There is one other matter...

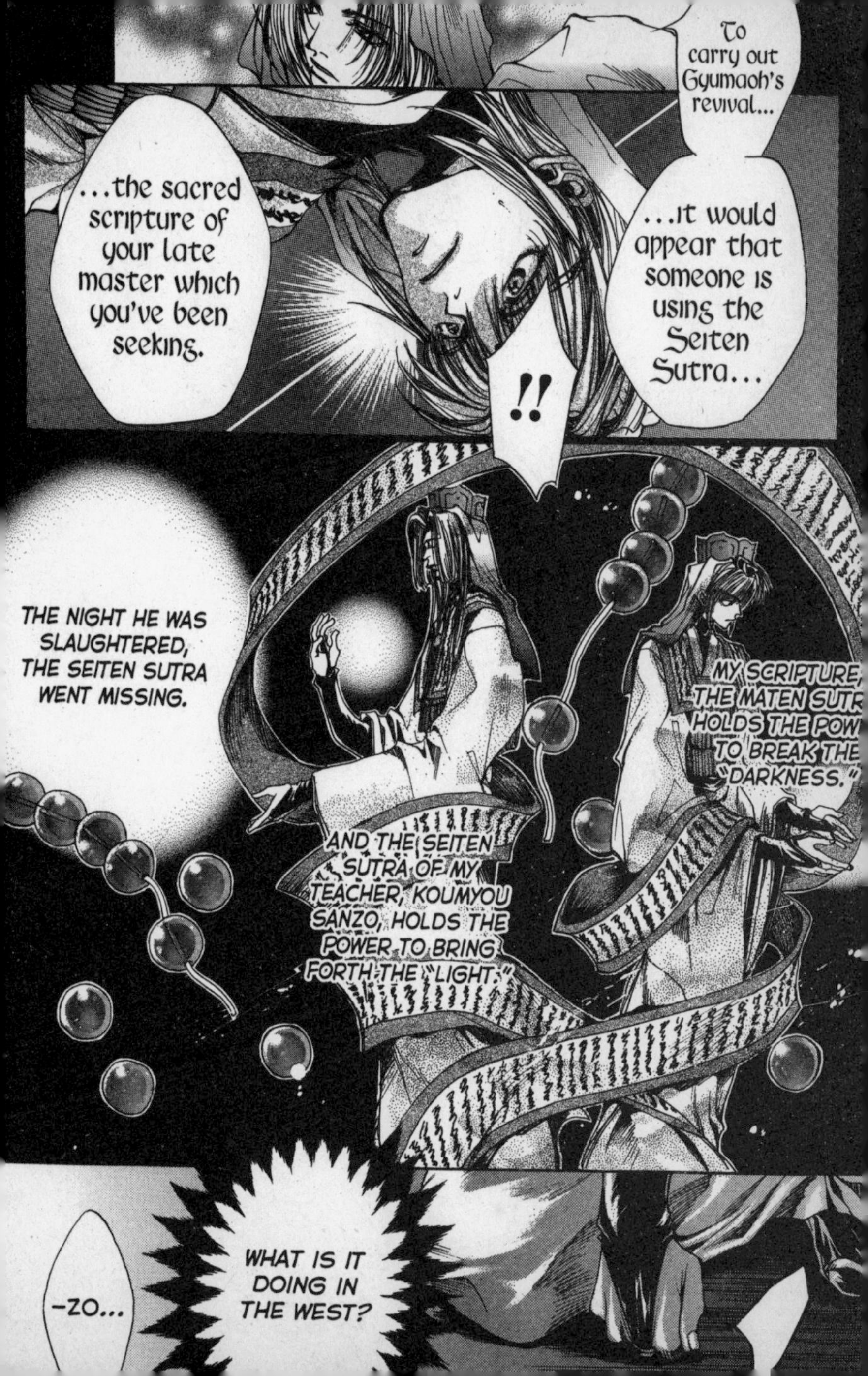
To carry out Gyumaoh's revival...
...it would appear that someone is using the Seiten Sutra...
...the sacred scripture of your late master which you've been seeking.
!!
MY SCRIPTURE, THE MATEN SUTR HOLDS THE POW TO BREAK THE "DARKNESS."
AND THE SEITEN SUTRA OF MY TEACHER, KOUMYOU SANZO, HOLDS THE POWER TO BRING FORTH THE "LIGHT."
THE NIGHT HE WAS SLAUGHTERED, THE SEITEN SUTRA WENT MISSING.
WHAT IS IT DOING IN THE WEST?
-ZO...

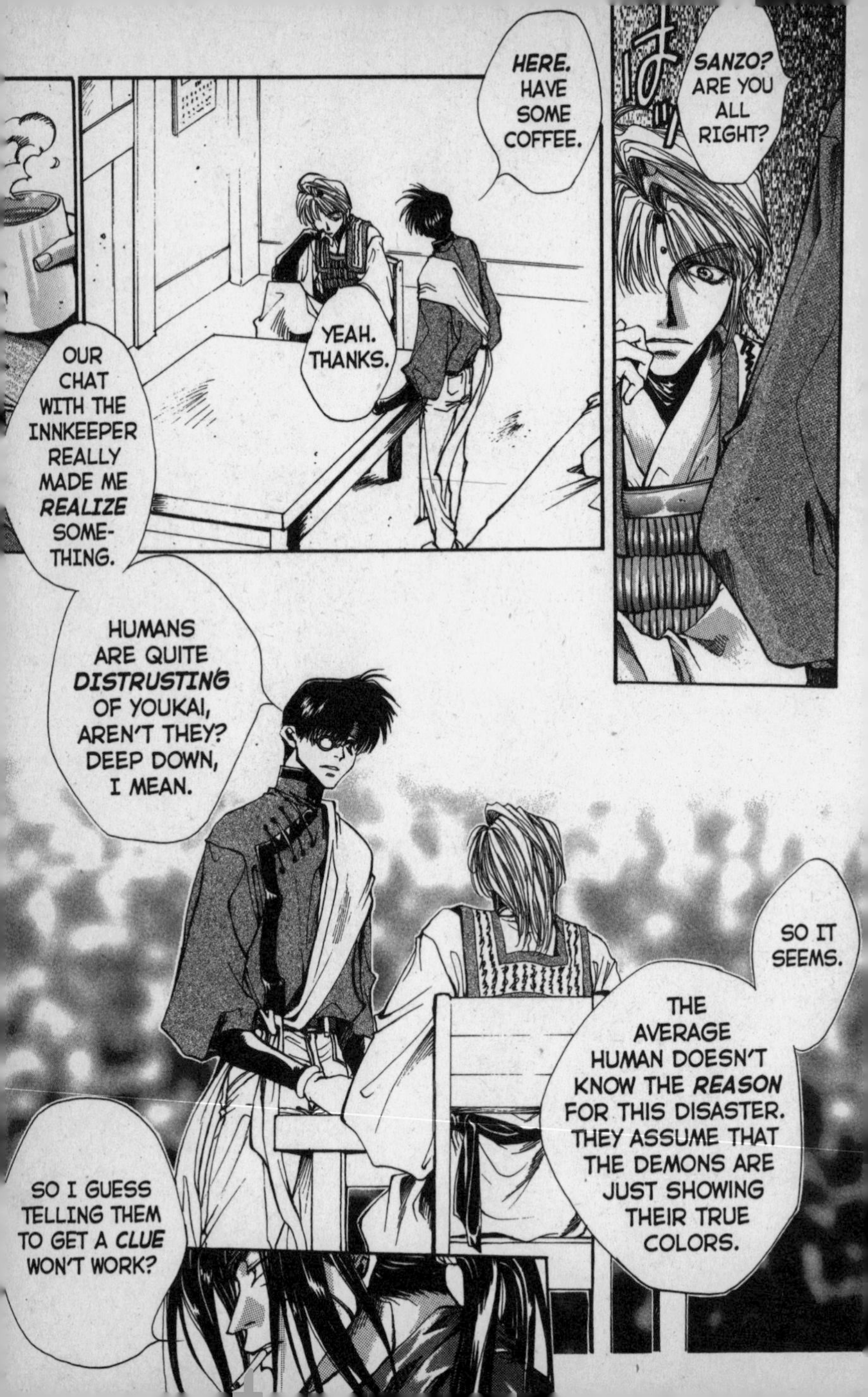
はっ
SANZO? ARE YOU ALL RIGHT?
HERE. HAVE SOME COFFEE.
YEAH. THANKS.
OUR CHAT WITH THE INNKEEPER REALLY MADE ME REALIZE SOME-THING.
HUMANS ARE QUITE DISTRUSTING OF YOUKAI, AREN'T THEY? DEEP DOWN, I MEAN.
SO IT SEEMS.
THE AVERAGE HUMAN DOESN'T KNOW THE REASON FOR THIS DISASTER. THEY ASSUME THAT THE DEMONS ARE JUST SHOWING THEIR TRUE COLORS.
SO I GUESS TELLING THEM TO GET A CLUE WON'T WORK?

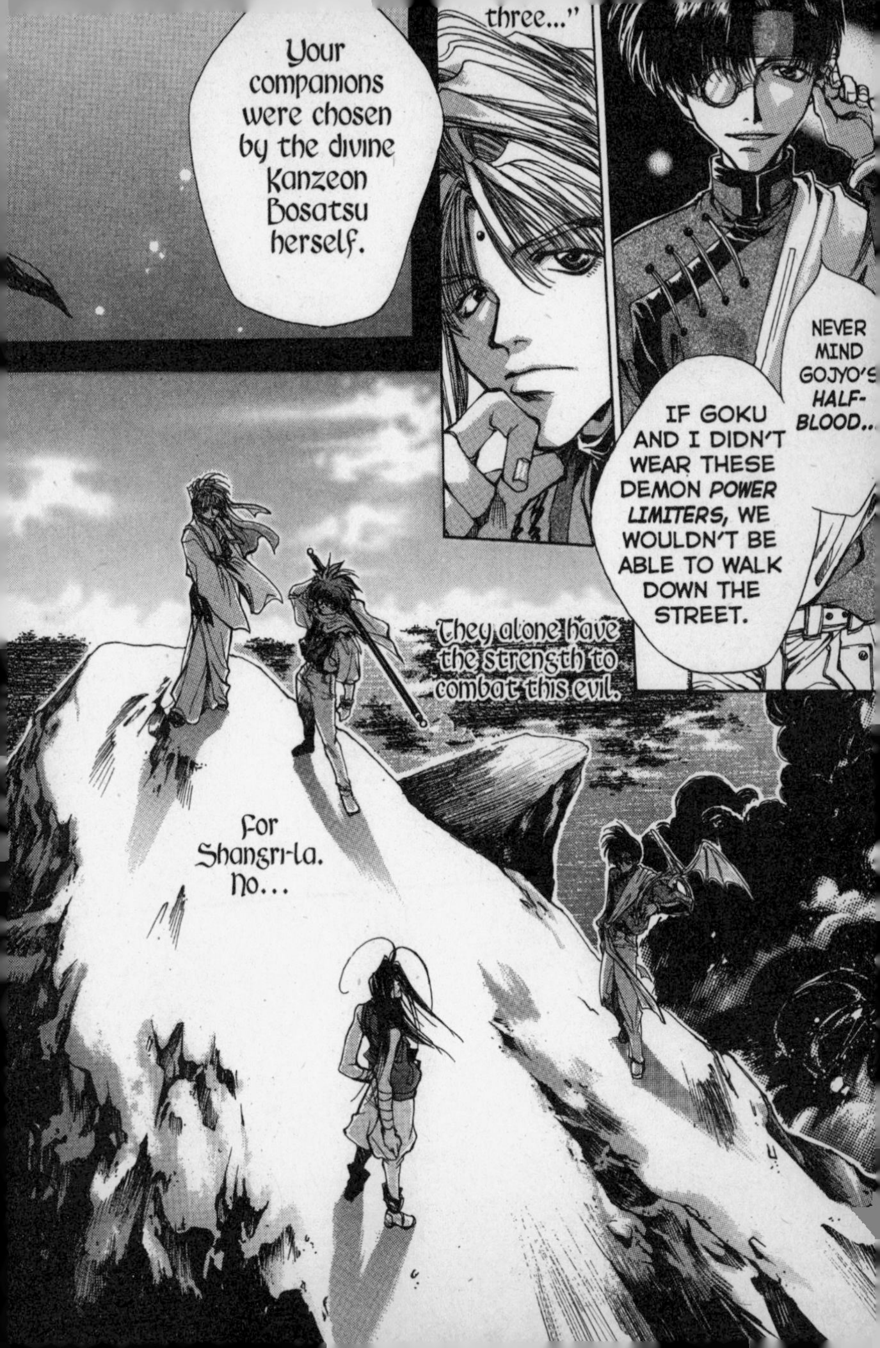

NEVER MIND GOJYO'S HALF-BLOOD...
IF GOKU AND I DIDN'T WEAR THESE DEMON POWER LIMITERS, WE WOULDN'T BE ABLE TO WALK DOWN THE STREET.
three..."
Your companions were chosen by the divine Kanzeon Bosatsu herself.
They alone have the strength to combat this evil.
For Shangri-la. No...

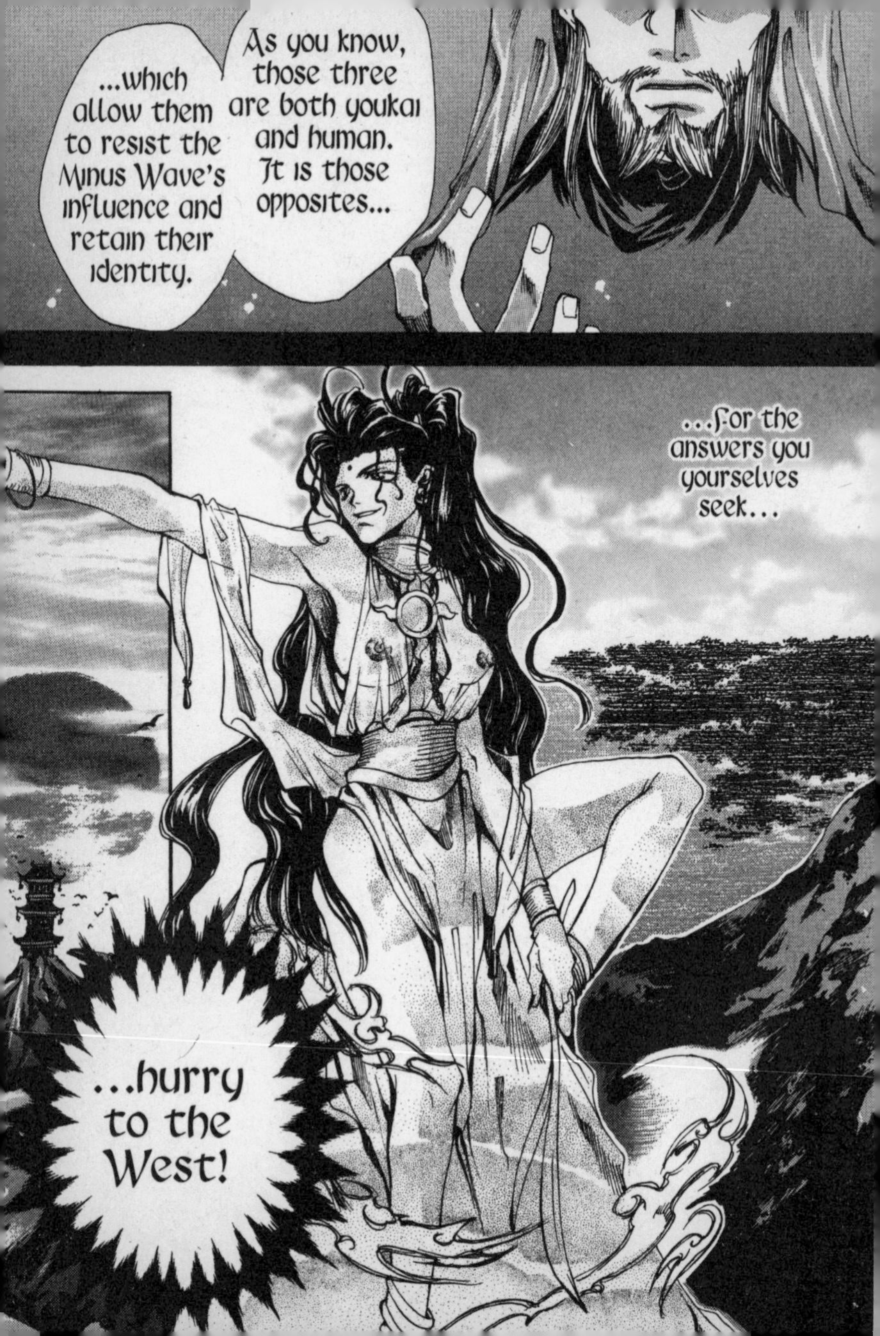
As you know, those three are both youkai and human. It is those opposites...
...which allow them to resist the Minus Wave's influence and retain their identity.
...For the answers you yourselves seek...
...hurry to the West!

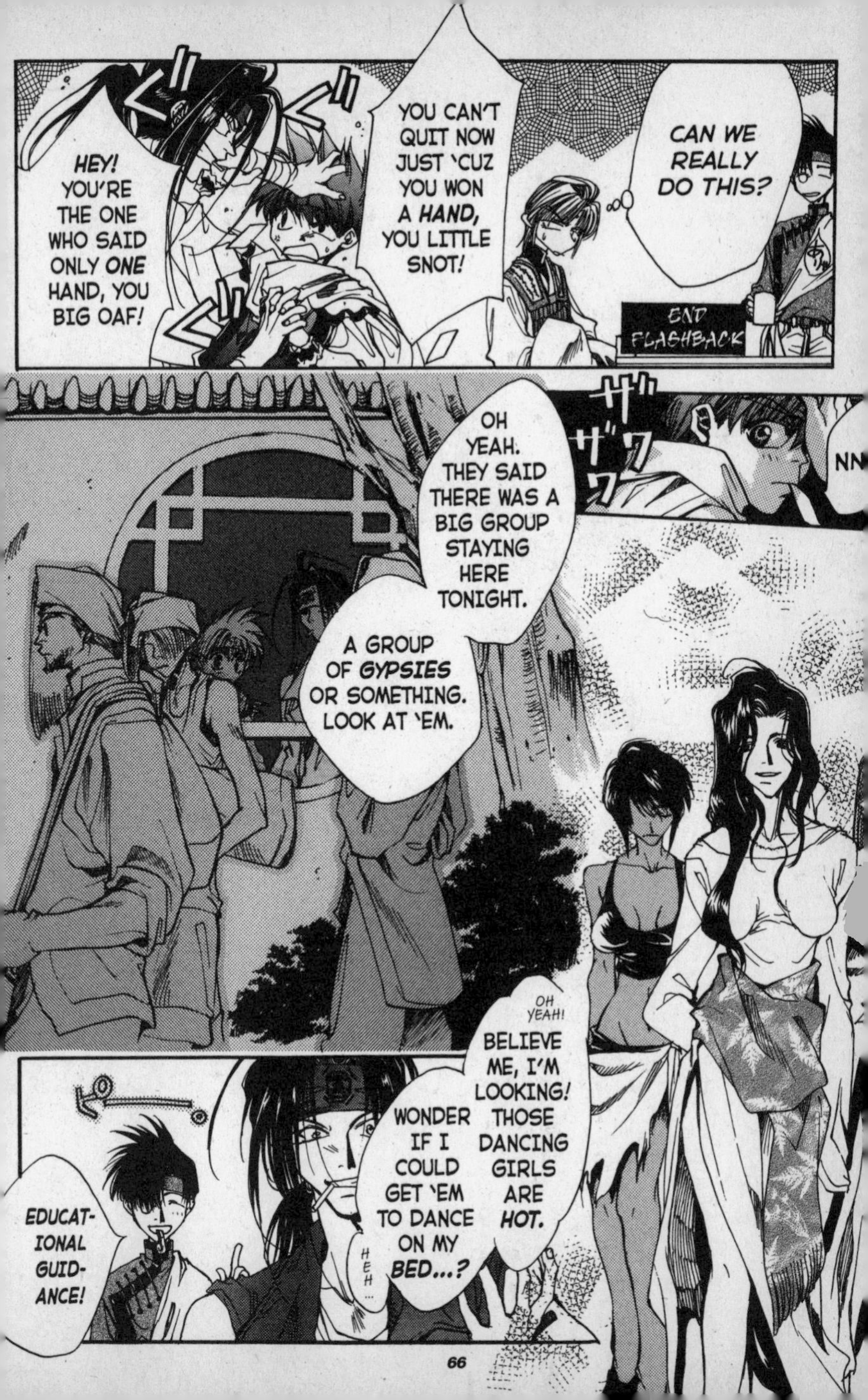
CAN WE REALLY DO THIS?
END FLASHBACK
YOU CAN'T QUIT NOW JUST 'CUZ YOU WON A HAND, YOU LITTLE SNOT!
HEY! YOU'RE THE ONE WHO SAID ONLY ONE HAND, YOU BIG OAF!
NN
OH YEAH. THEY SAID THERE WAS A BIG GROUP STAYING HERE TONIGHT.
A GROUP OF GYPSIES OR SOMETHING. LOOK AT 'EM.
OH YEAH!
BELIEVE ME, I'M LOOKING! THOSE DANCING GIRLS ARE HOT.
WONDER IF I COULD GET 'EM TO DANCE ON MY BED...?
HEH...
EDUCAT-IONAL GUID-ANCE!

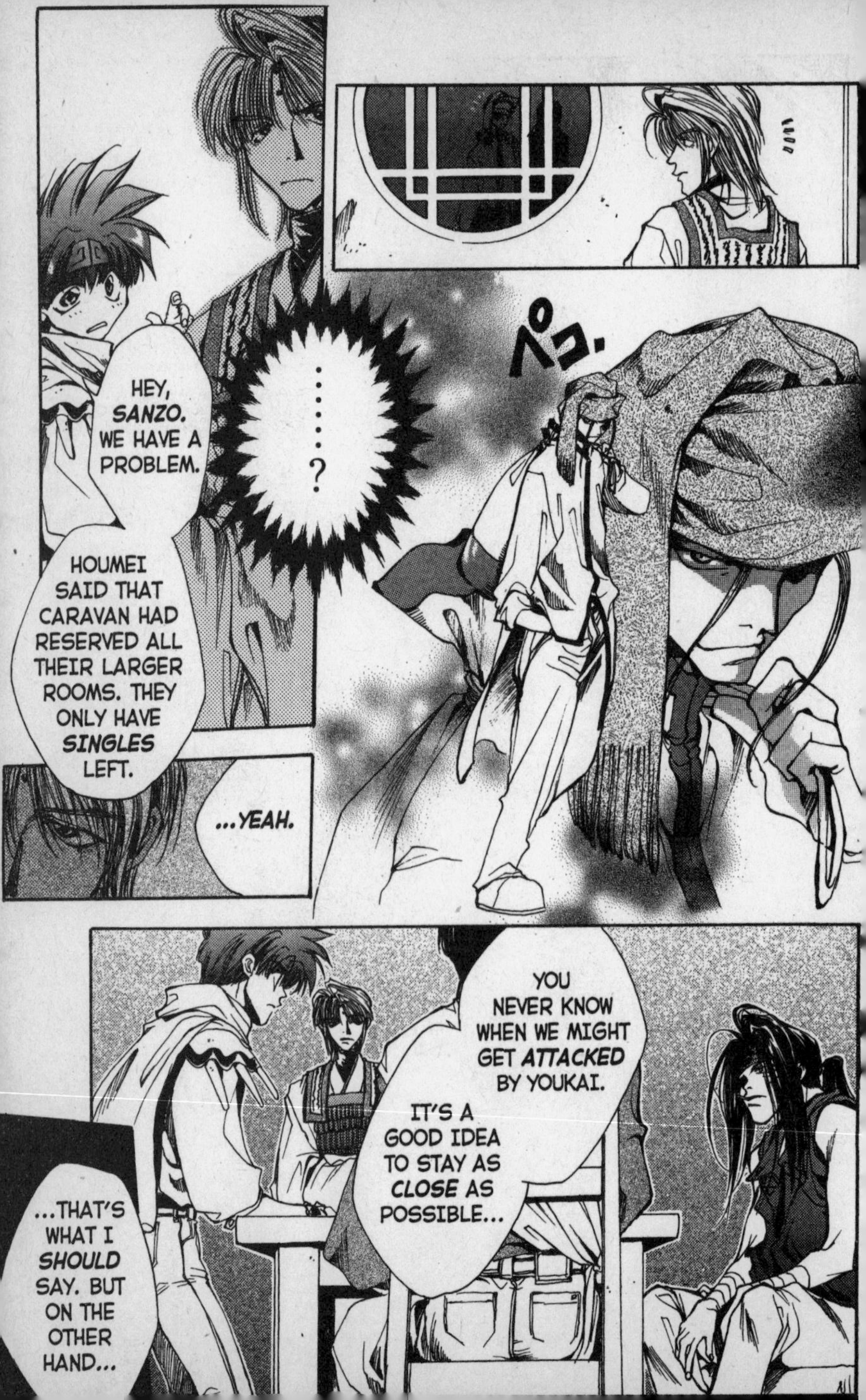
......?
ぺコ.
HEY, SANZO. WE HAVE A PROBLEM.
HOUMEI SAID THAT CARAVAN HAD RESERVED ALL THEIR LARGER ROOMS. THEY ONLY HAVE SINGLES LEFT.
...YEAH.
YOU NEVER KNOW WHEN WE MIGHT GET ATTACKED BY YOUKAI.
IT'S A GOOD IDEA TO STAY AS CLOSE AS POSSIBLE...
...THAT'S WHAT I SHOULD SAY. BUT ON THE OTHER HAND...

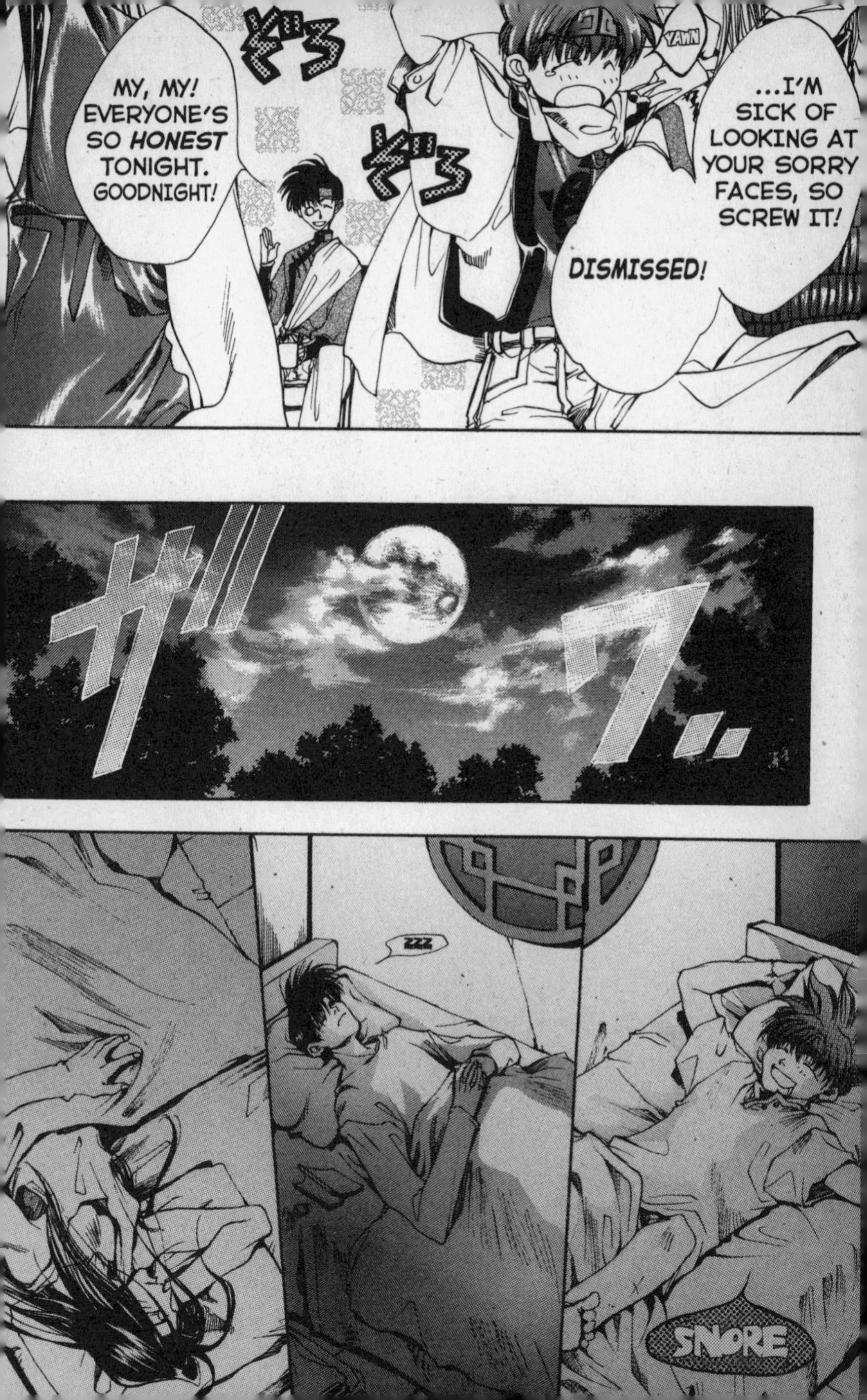
YAWN
...I'M SICK OF LOOKING AT YOUR SORRY FACES, SO SCREW IT!
DISMISSED!
ぞろ
ぞろ
MY, MY! EVERYONE'S SO *HONEST* TONIGHT. GOODNIGHT!
ザワ..
ZZZ
SNORE

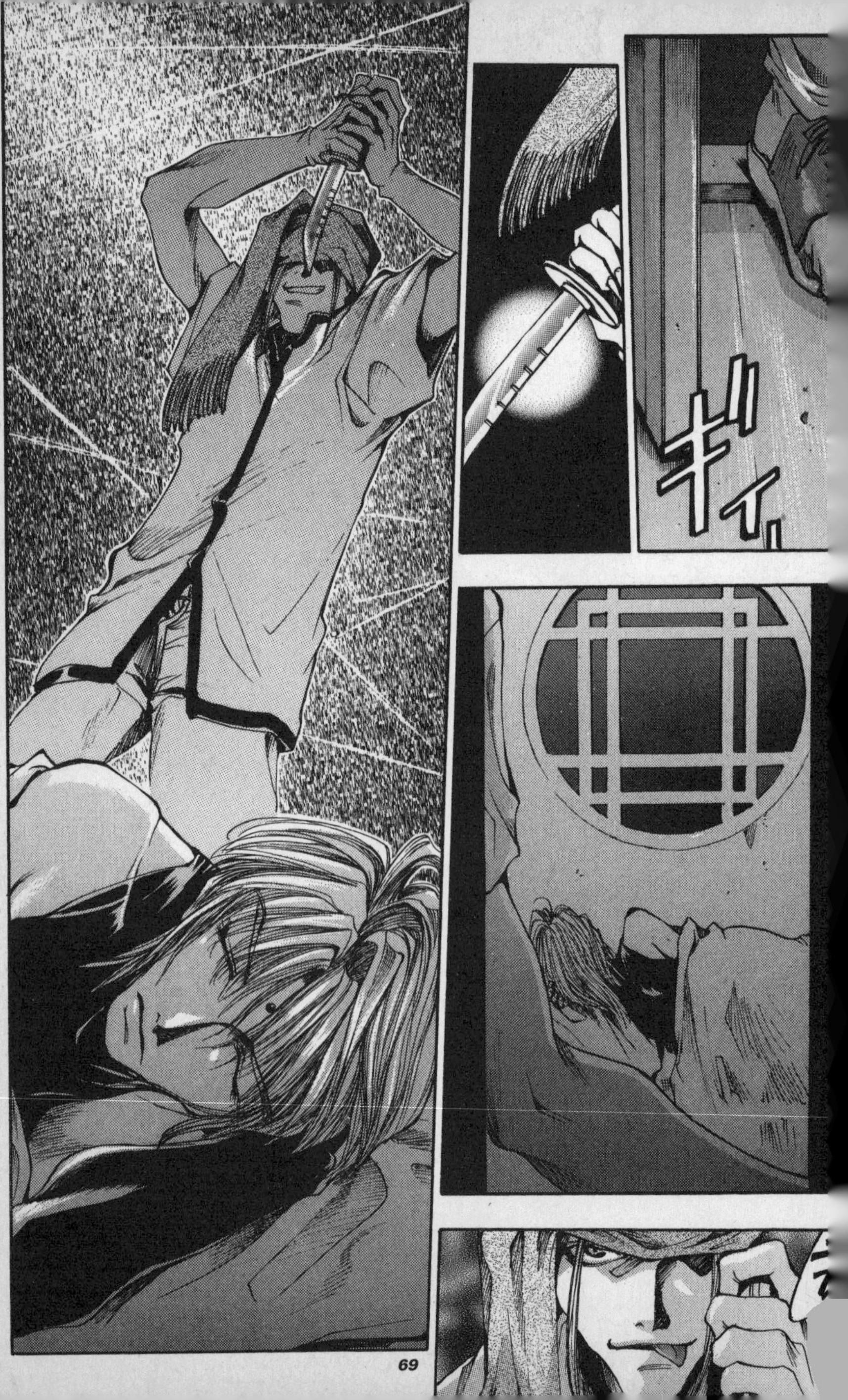
ギィィ

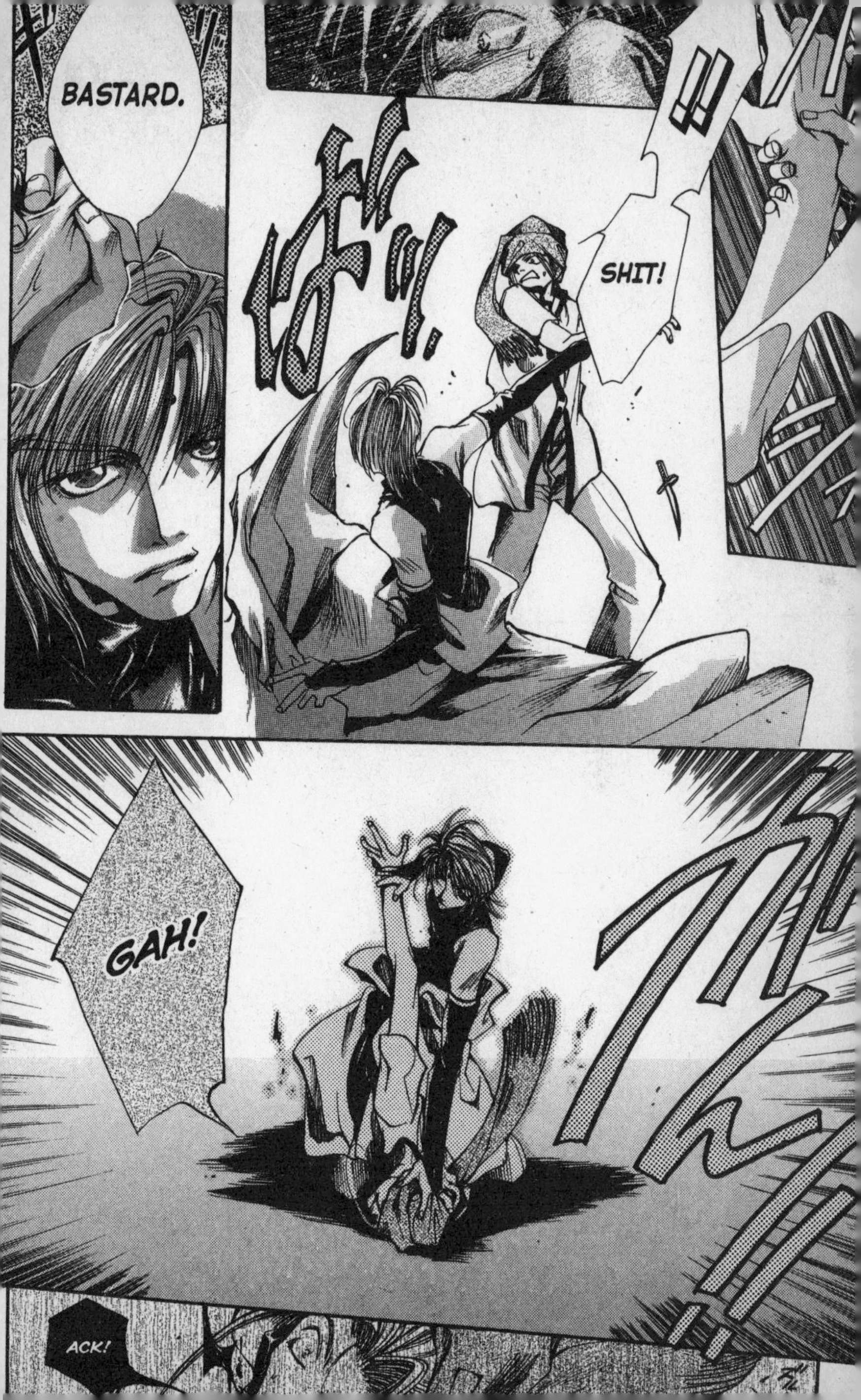
!!
SHIT!
BASTARD.
GAH!
ACK!

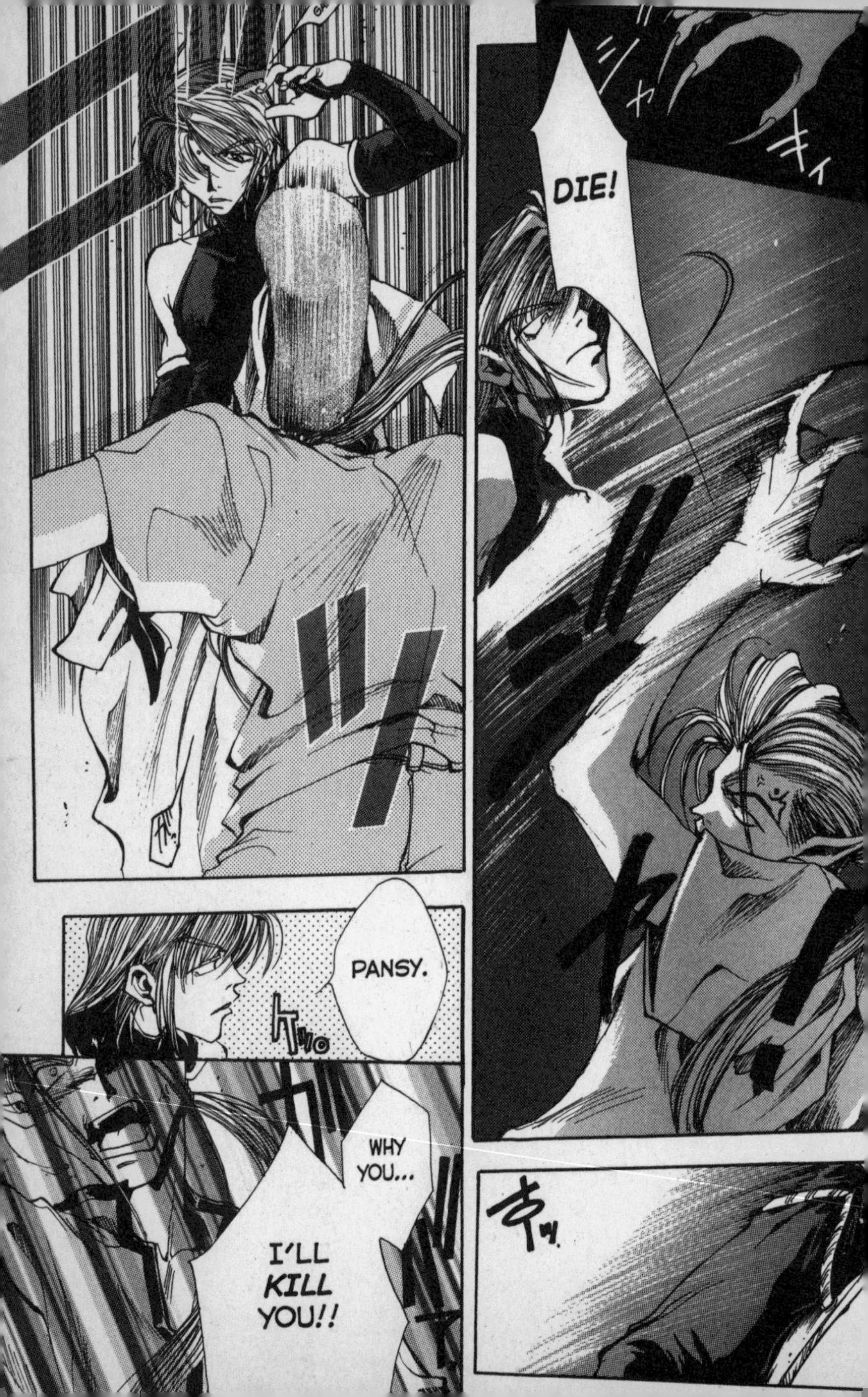
DIE!
PANSY.
WHY YOU...
I'LL KILL YOU!!

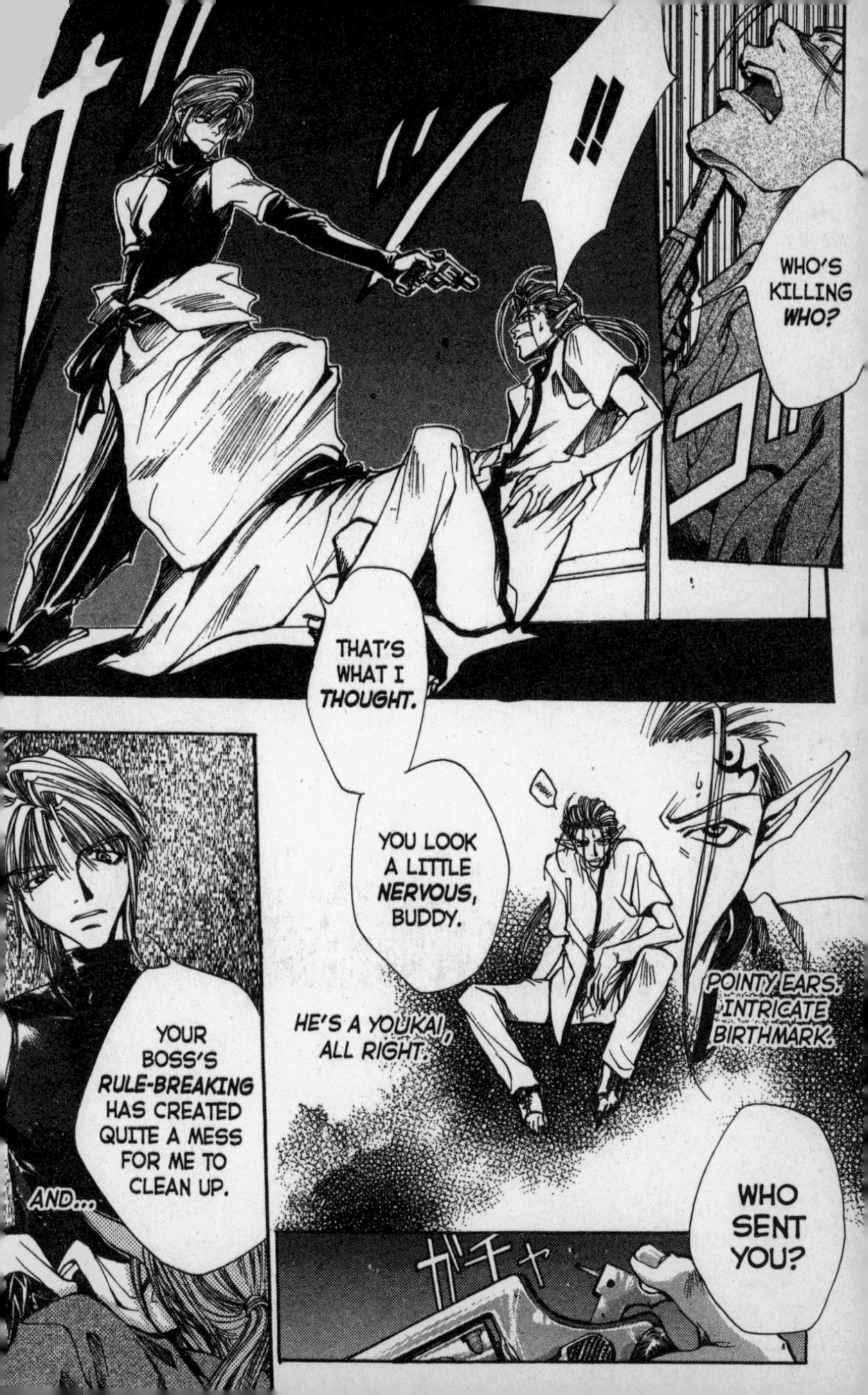
WHO'S KILLING WHO?
THAT'S WHAT I THOUGHT.
YOU LOOK A LITTLE NERVOUS, BUDDY.
RGH!
POINTY EARS. INTRICATE BIRTHMARK.
HE'S A YOUKAI, ALL RIGHT.
WHO SENT YOU?
ガチャ
YOUR BOSS'S RULE-BREAKING HAS CREATED QUITE A MESS FOR ME TO CLEAN UP.
AND...

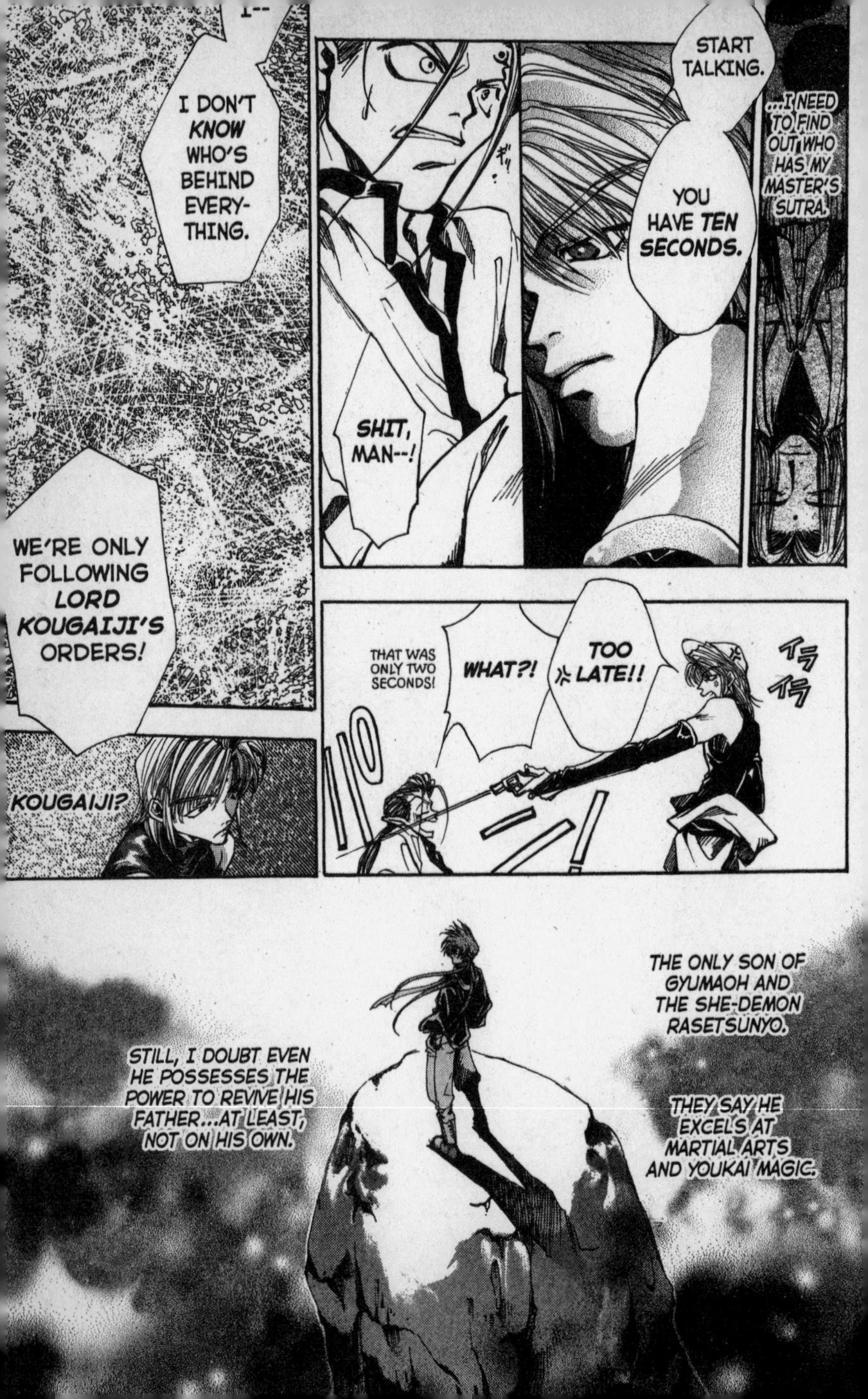

...I NEED TO FIND OUT WHO HAS MY MASTER'S SUTRA.
START TALKING.
YOU HAVE TEN SECONDS.
SHIT, MAN--!
I--
I DON'T KNOW WHO'S BEHIND EVERY-THING.
WE'RE ONLY FOLLOWING LORD KOUGAIJI'S ORDERS!
TOO LATE!!
WHAT?!
THAT WAS ONLY TWO SECONDS!
KOUGAIJI?
THE ONLY SON OF GYUMAOH AND THE SHE-DEMON RASETSUNYO.
THEY SAY HE EXCELS AT MARTIAL ARTS AND YOUKAI MAGIC.
STILL, I DOUBT EVEN HE POSSESSES THE POWER TO REVIVE HIS FATHER...AT LEAST, NOT ON HIS OWN.

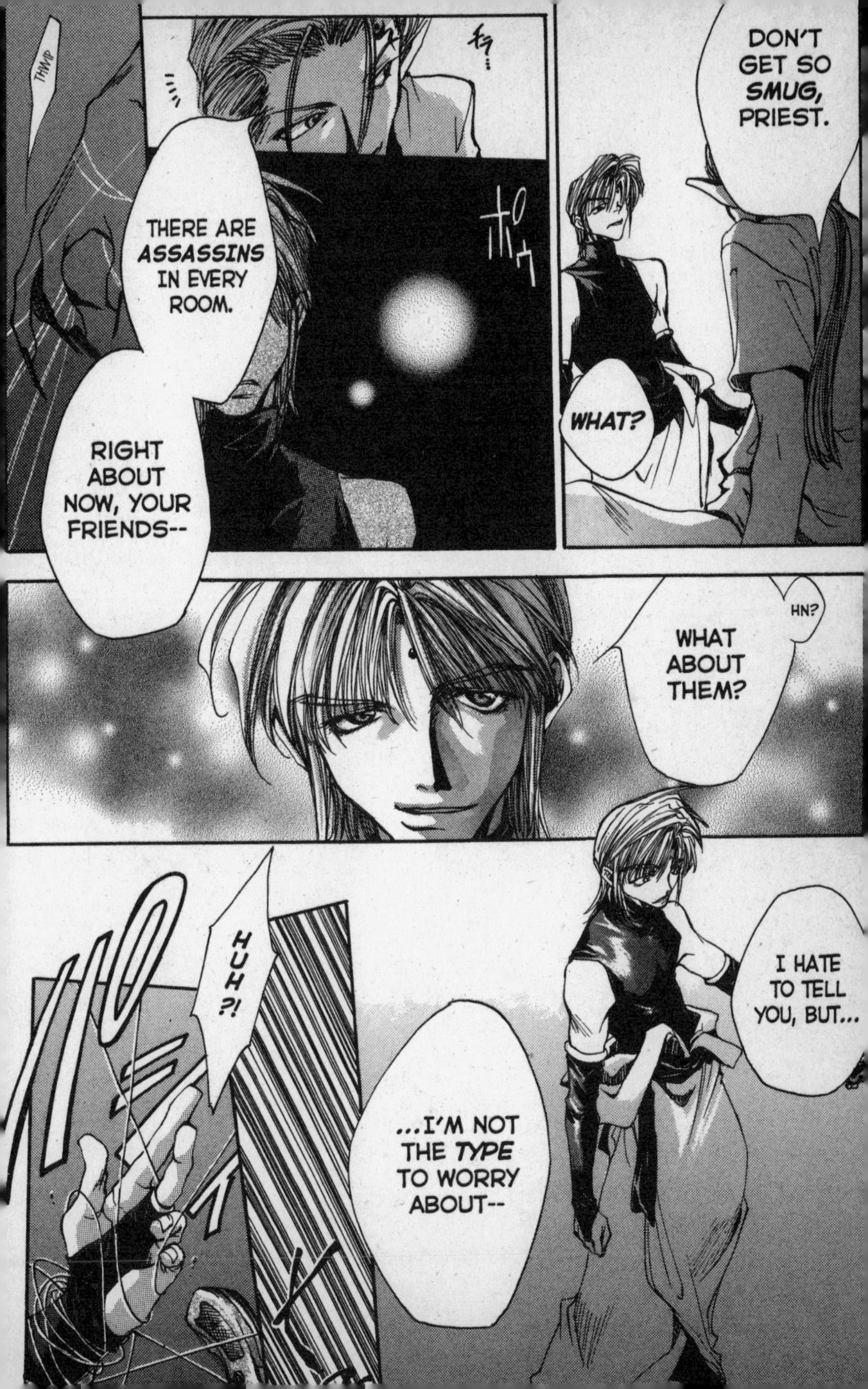
DON'T GET SO SMUG, PRIEST.
WHAT?
THERE ARE ASSASSINS IN EVERY ROOM.
RIGHT ABOUT NOW, YOUR FRIENDS--
THMP
HN?
WHAT ABOUT THEM?
I HATE TO TELL YOU, BUT...
...I'M NOT THE TYPE TO WORRY ABOUT--
HUH?!

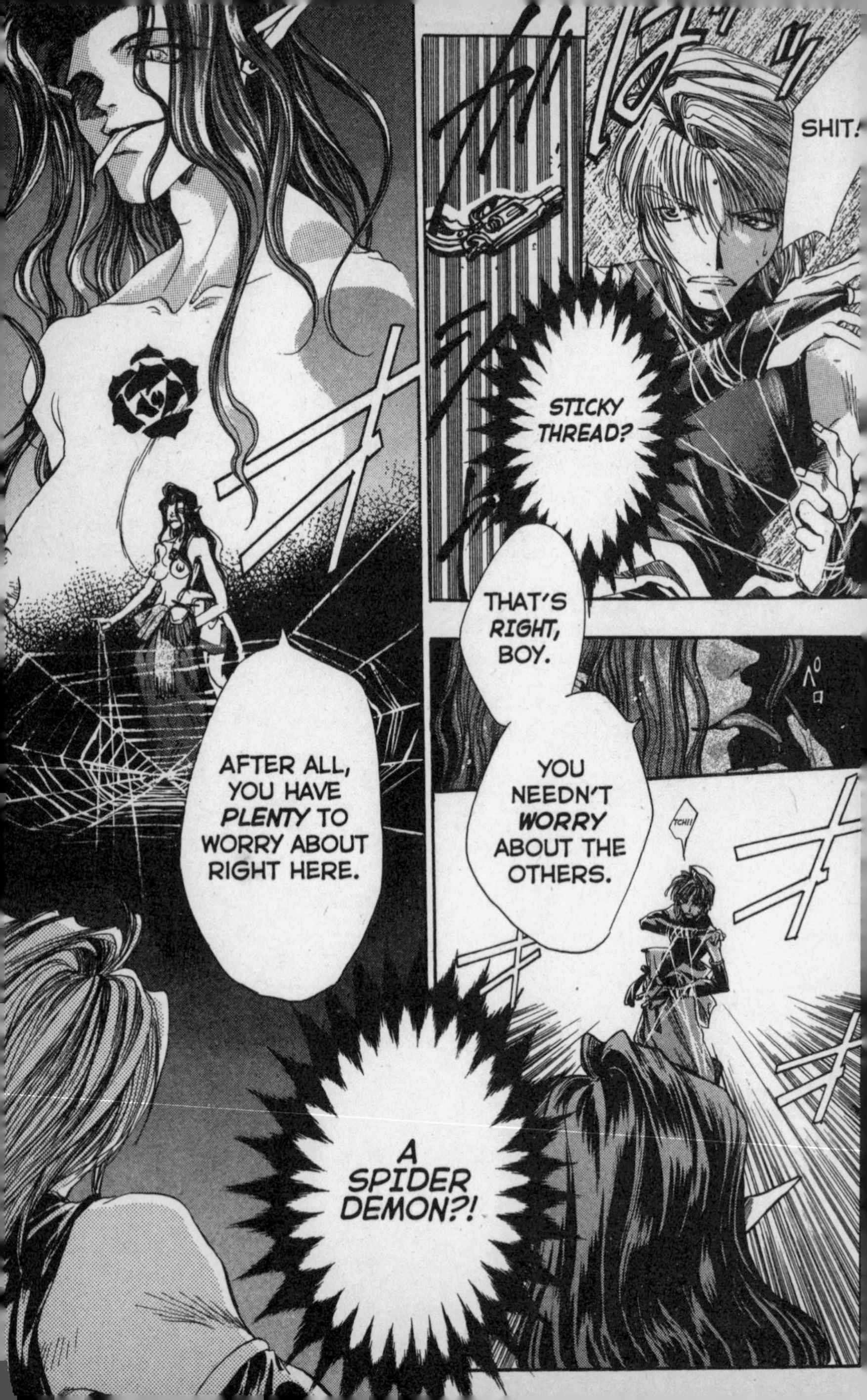
SHIT!
STICKY THREAD?
THAT'S RIGHT, BOY.
YOU NEEDN'T WORRY ABOUT THE OTHERS.
TCH!!
AFTER ALL, YOU HAVE PLENTY TO WORRY ABOUT RIGHT HERE.
A SPIDER DEMON?!

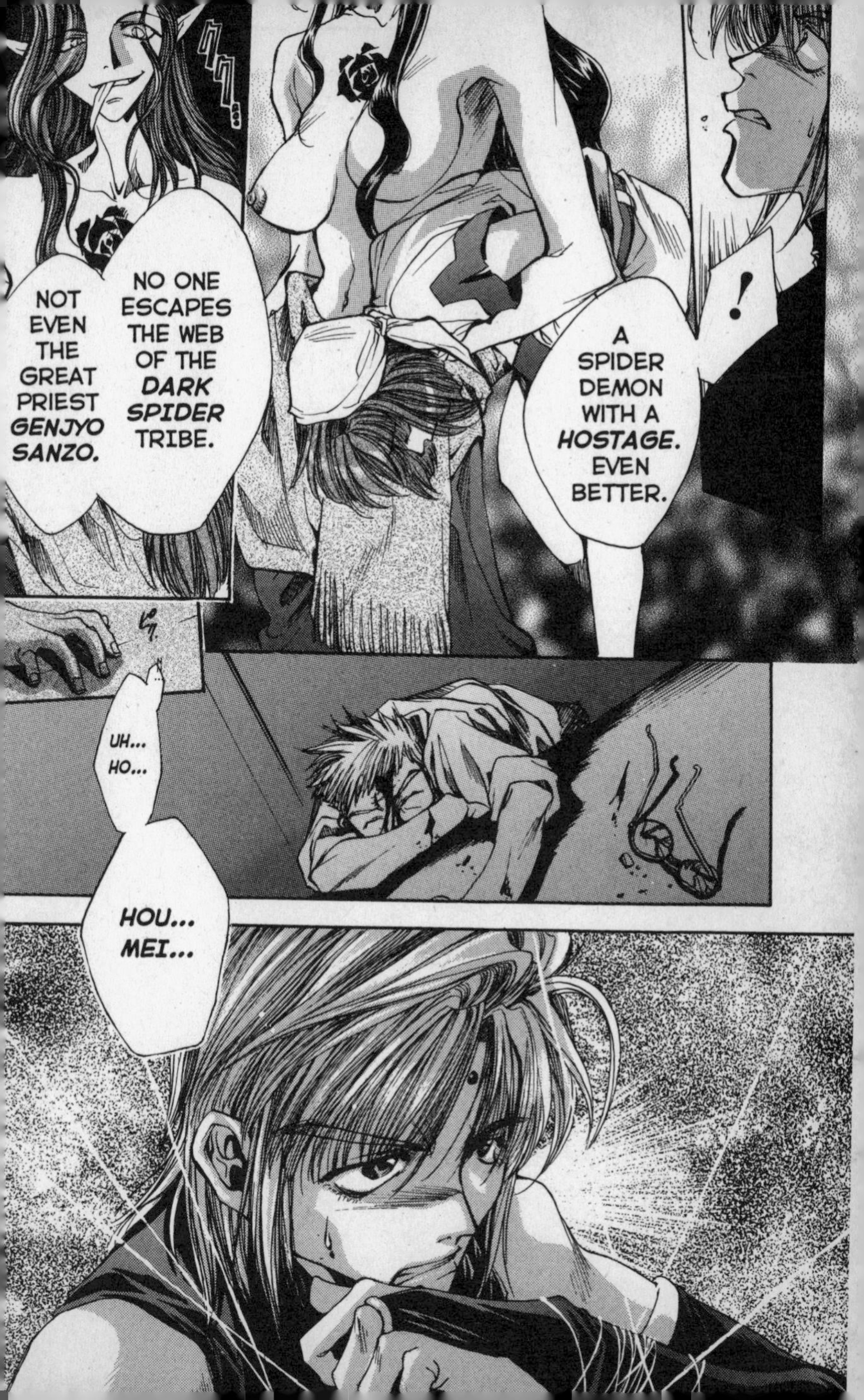
!
A SPIDER DEMON WITH A HOSTAGE. EVEN BETTER.
NO ONE ESCAPES THE WEB OF THE DARK SPIDER TRIBE.
NOT EVEN THE GREAT PRIEST GENJYO SANZO.
UH... HO...
HOU... MEI...

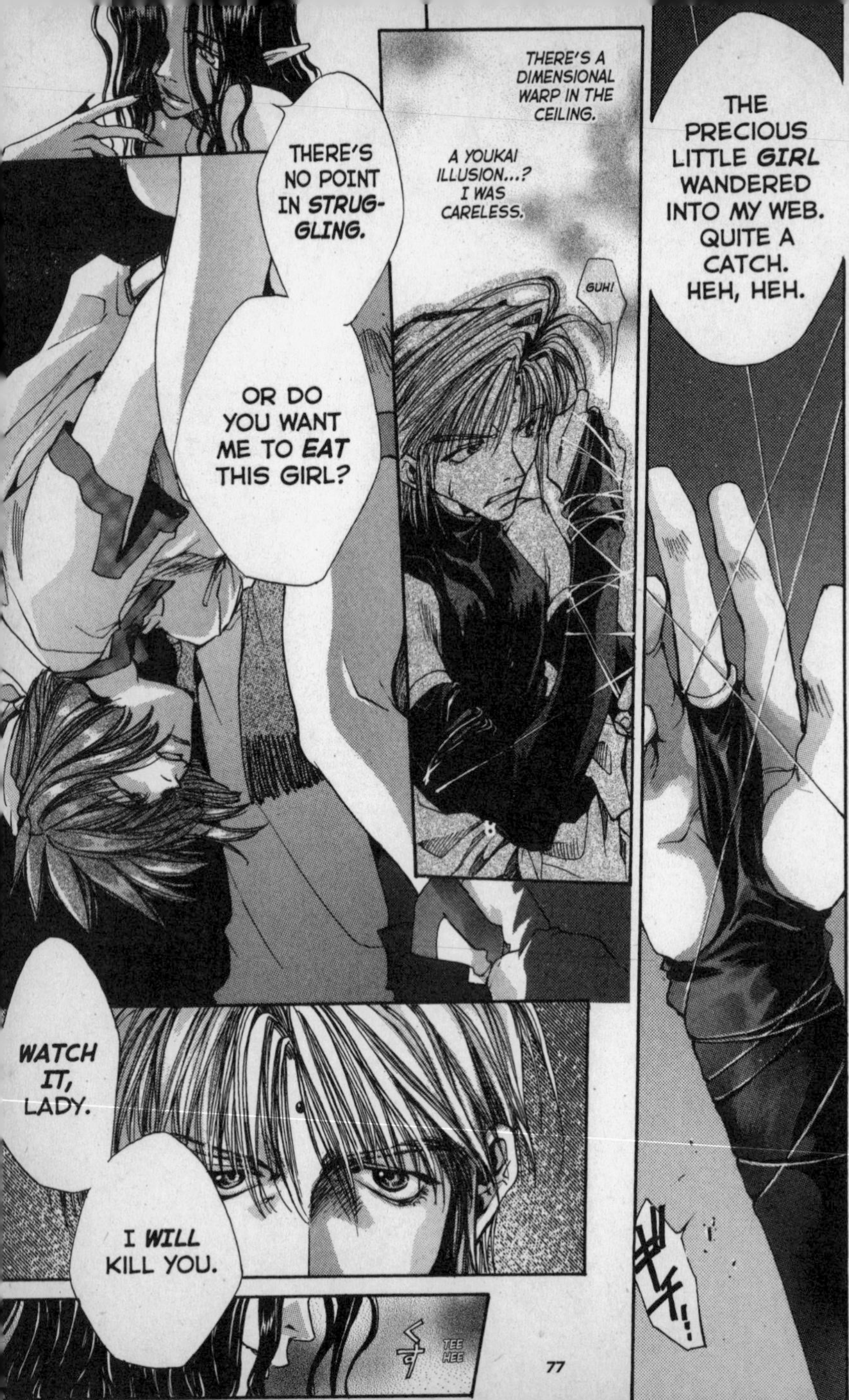
THE PRECIOUS LITTLE GIRL WANDERED INTO MY WEB. QUITE A CATCH. HEH, HEH.
THERE'S A DIMENSIONAL WARP IN THE CEILING.
A YOUKAI ILLUSION...? I WAS CARELESS.
GUH!
THERE'S NO POINT IN STRUG-GLING.
OR DO YOU WANT ME TO EAT THIS GIRL?
WATCH IT, LADY.
I WILL KILL YOU.
くす
TEE HEE

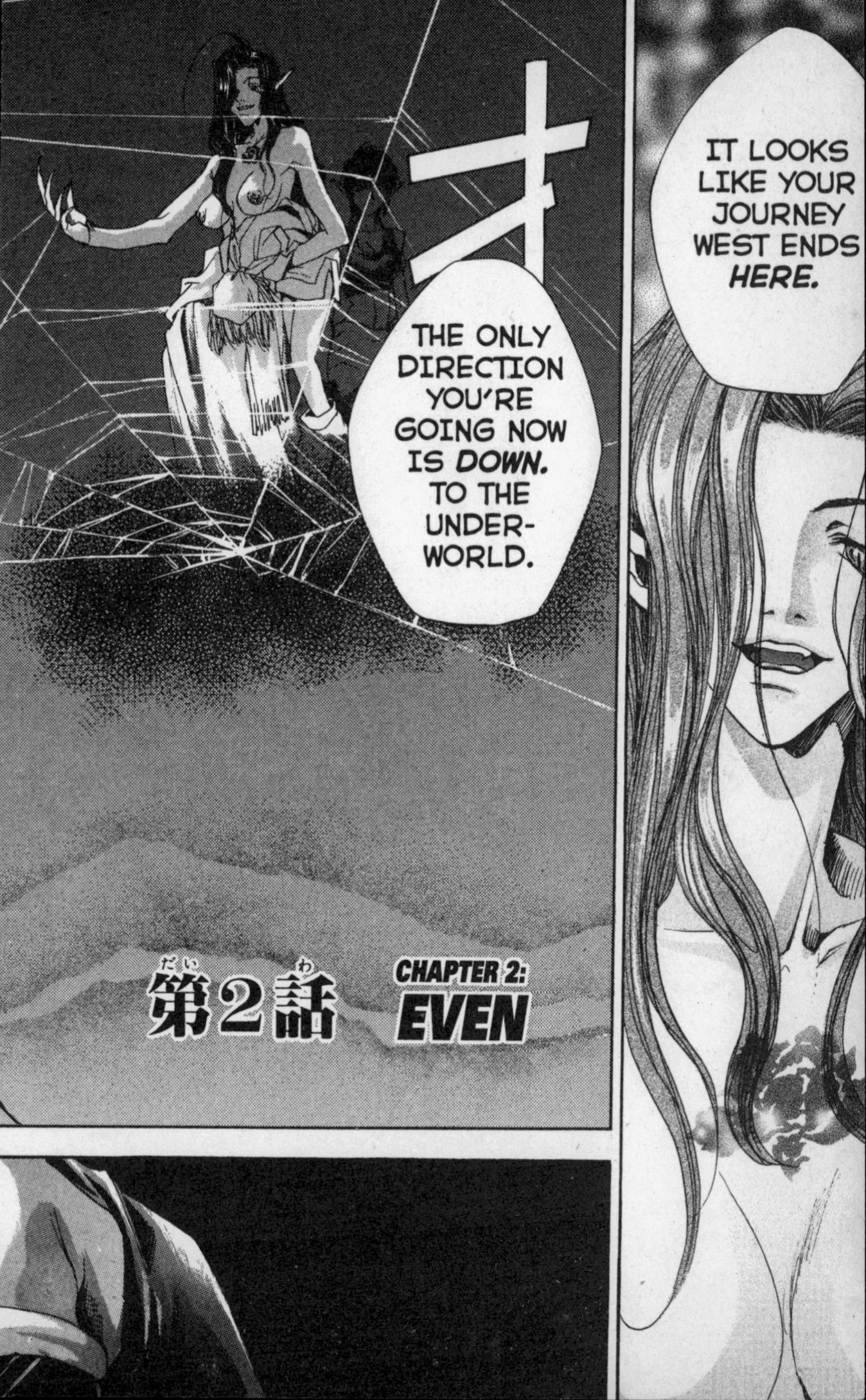
IT LOOKS LIKE YOUR JOURNEY WEST ENDS HERE.
オ
THE ONLY DIRECTION YOU'RE GOING NOW IS DOWN. TO THE UNDER-WORLD.
第2話
CHAPTER 2: EVEN

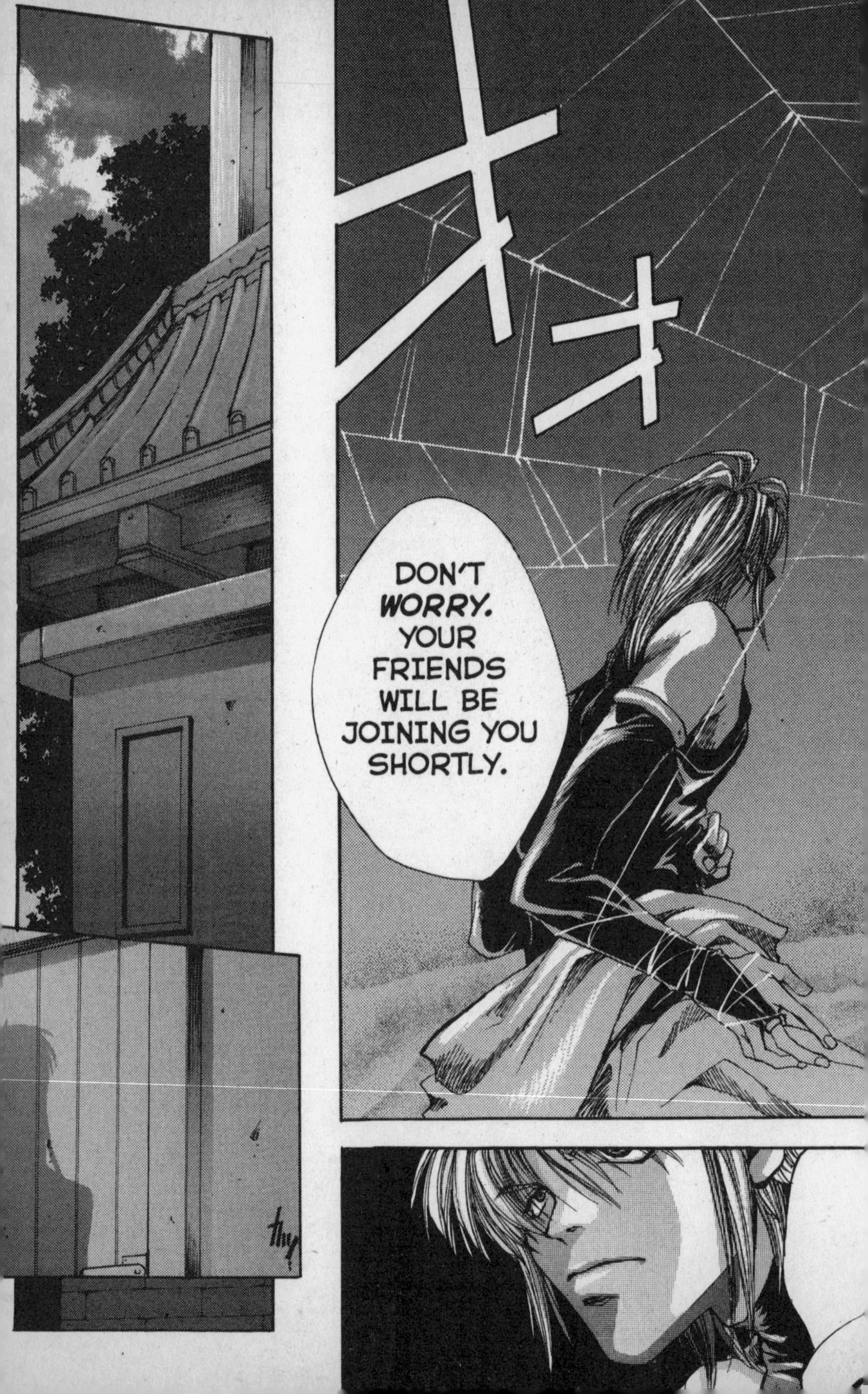
DON'T *WORRY.* YOUR FRIENDS WILL BE JOINING YOU SHORTLY.

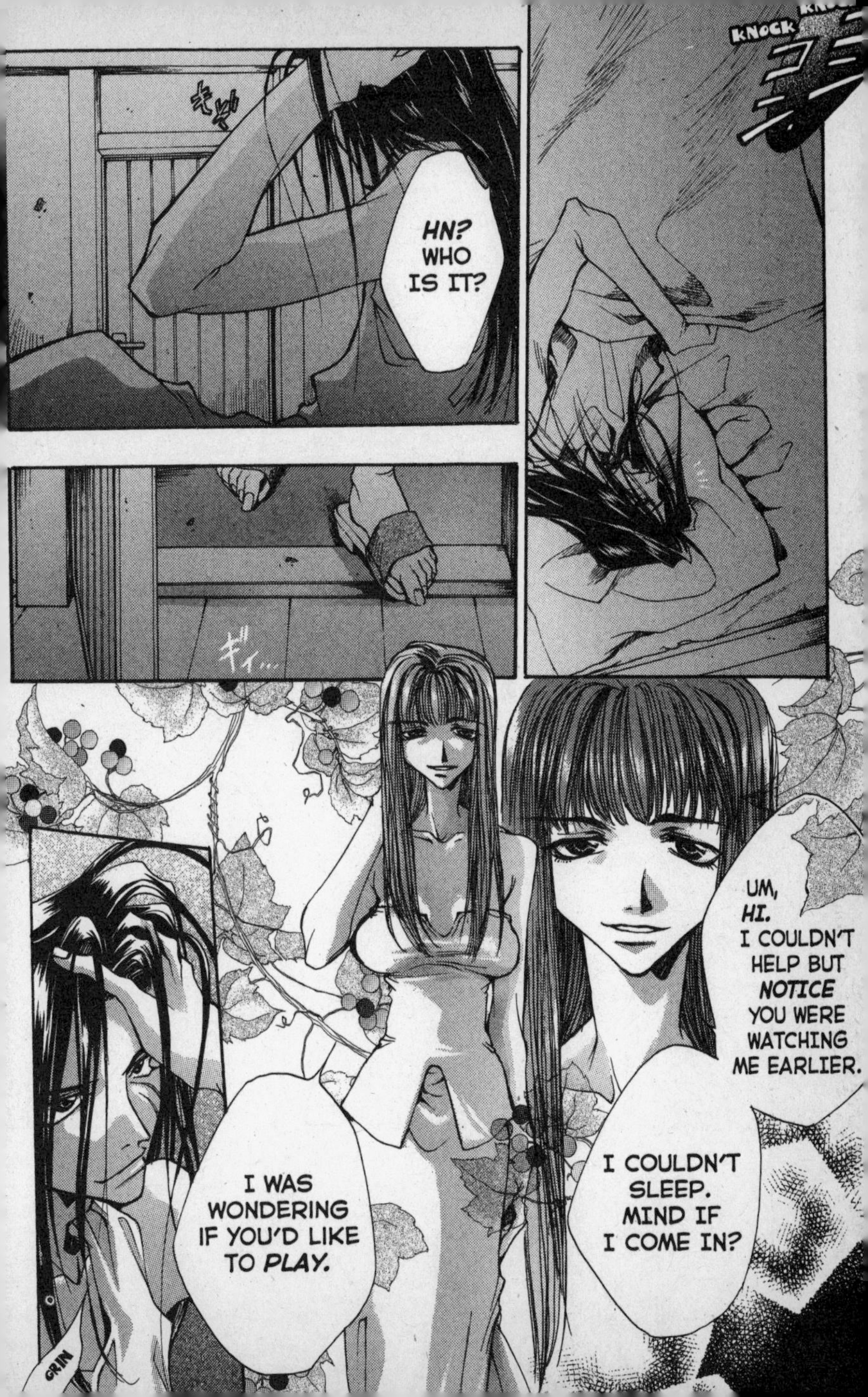

KNOCK
HN? WHO IS IT?
ギィ...
UM, HI. I COULDN'T HELP BUT NOTICE YOU WERE WATCHING ME EARLIER.
I COULDN'T SLEEP. MIND IF I COME IN?
I WAS WONDERING IF YOU'D LIKE TO PLAY.
GRIN

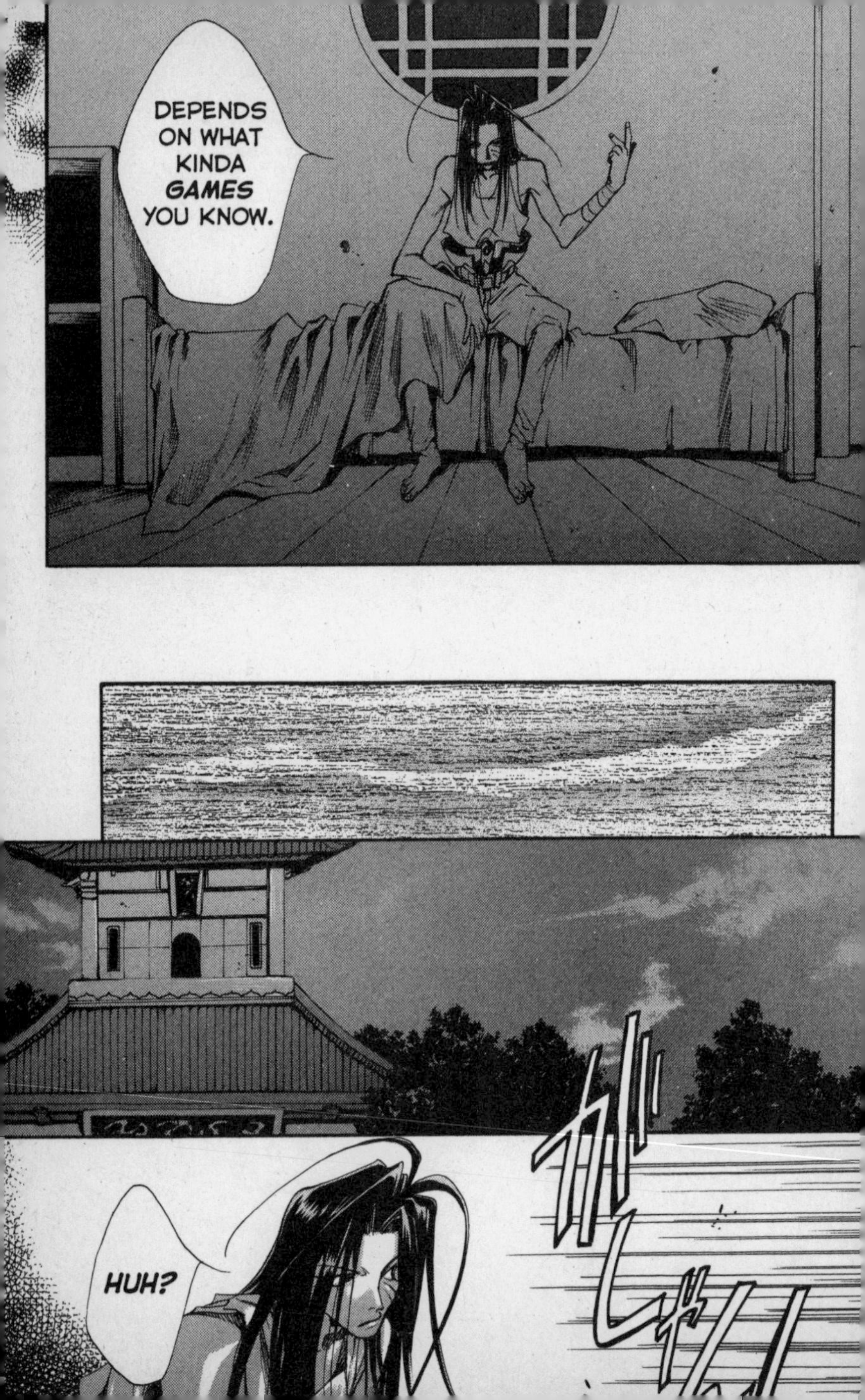
DEPENDS ON WHAT KINDA *GAMES* YOU KNOW.
HUH?

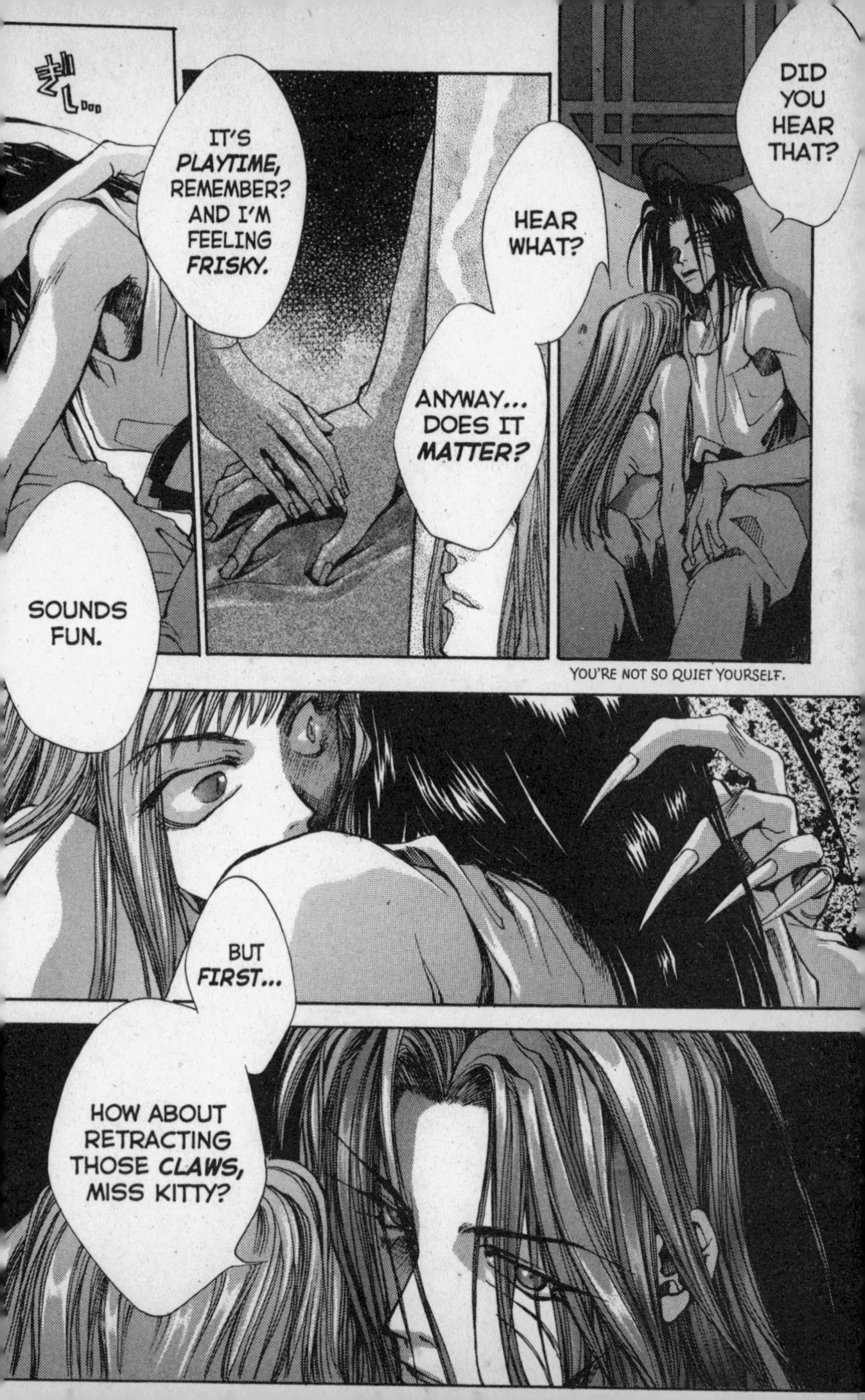
DID YOU HEAR THAT?
HEAR WHAT?
ANYWAY... DOES IT *MATTER?*
YOU'RE NOT SO QUIET YOURSELF.
IT'S *PLAYTIME,* REMEMBER? AND I'M FEELING *FRISKY.*
ぎし...
SOUNDS FUN.
BUT *FIRST...*
HOW ABOUT RETRACTING THOSE *CLAWS,* MISS KITTY?

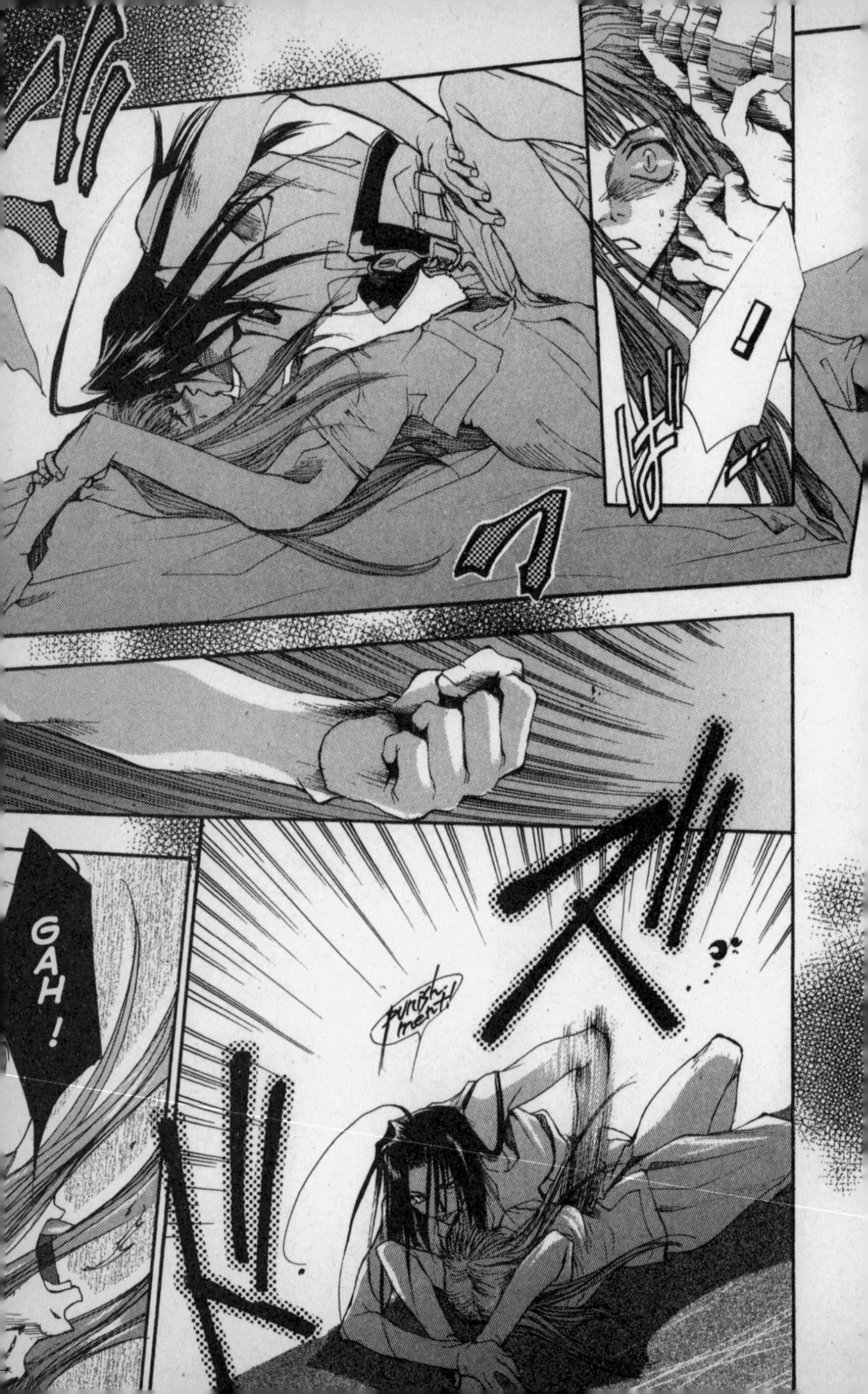
GAH!
punish-ment!

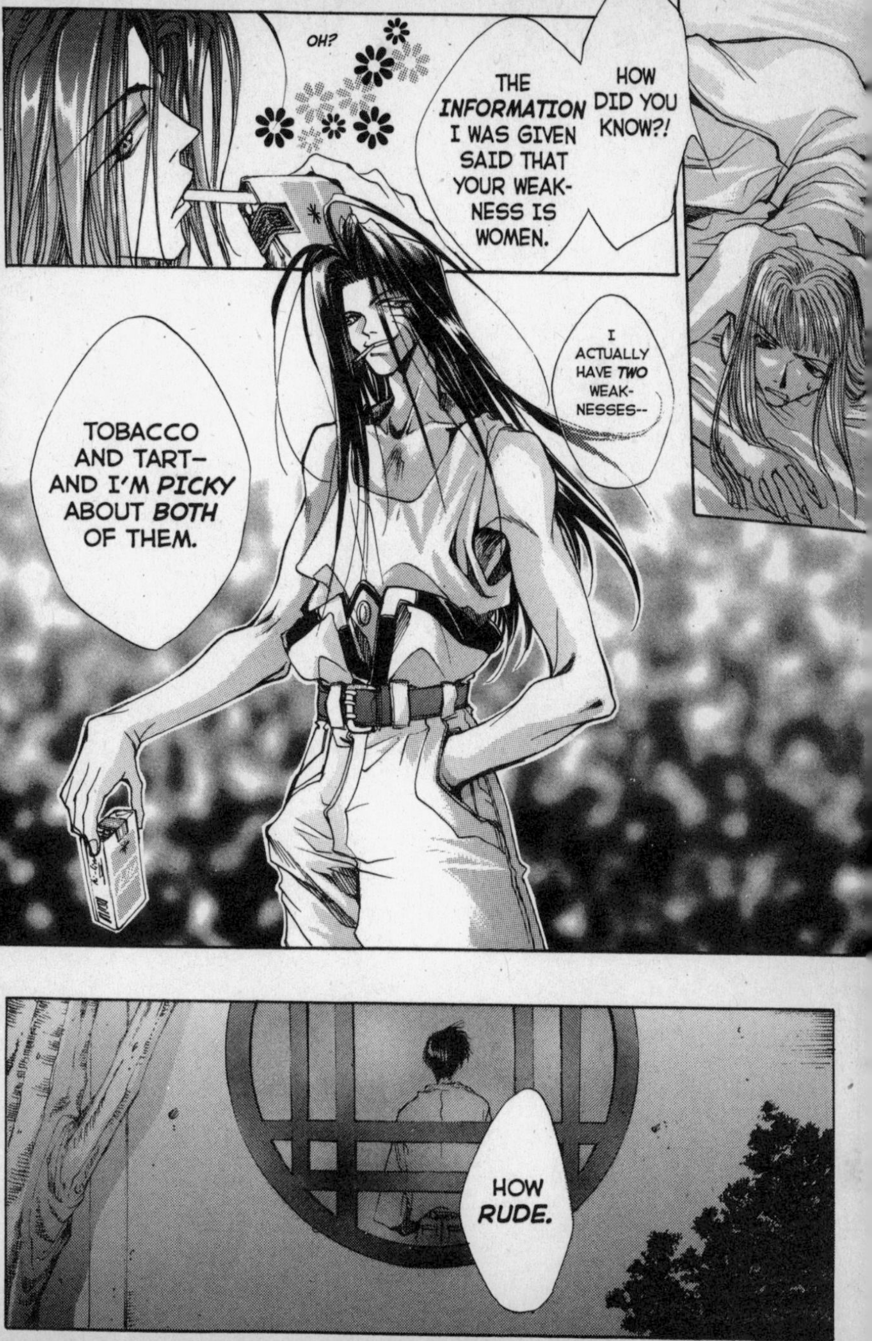
HOW DID YOU KNOW?!
THE INFORMATION I WAS GIVEN SAID THAT YOUR WEAKNESS IS WOMEN.
OH?
I ACTUALLY HAVE TWO WEAKNESSES--
TOBACCO AND TART– AND I'M PICKY ABOUT BOTH OF THEM.
HOW RUDE.

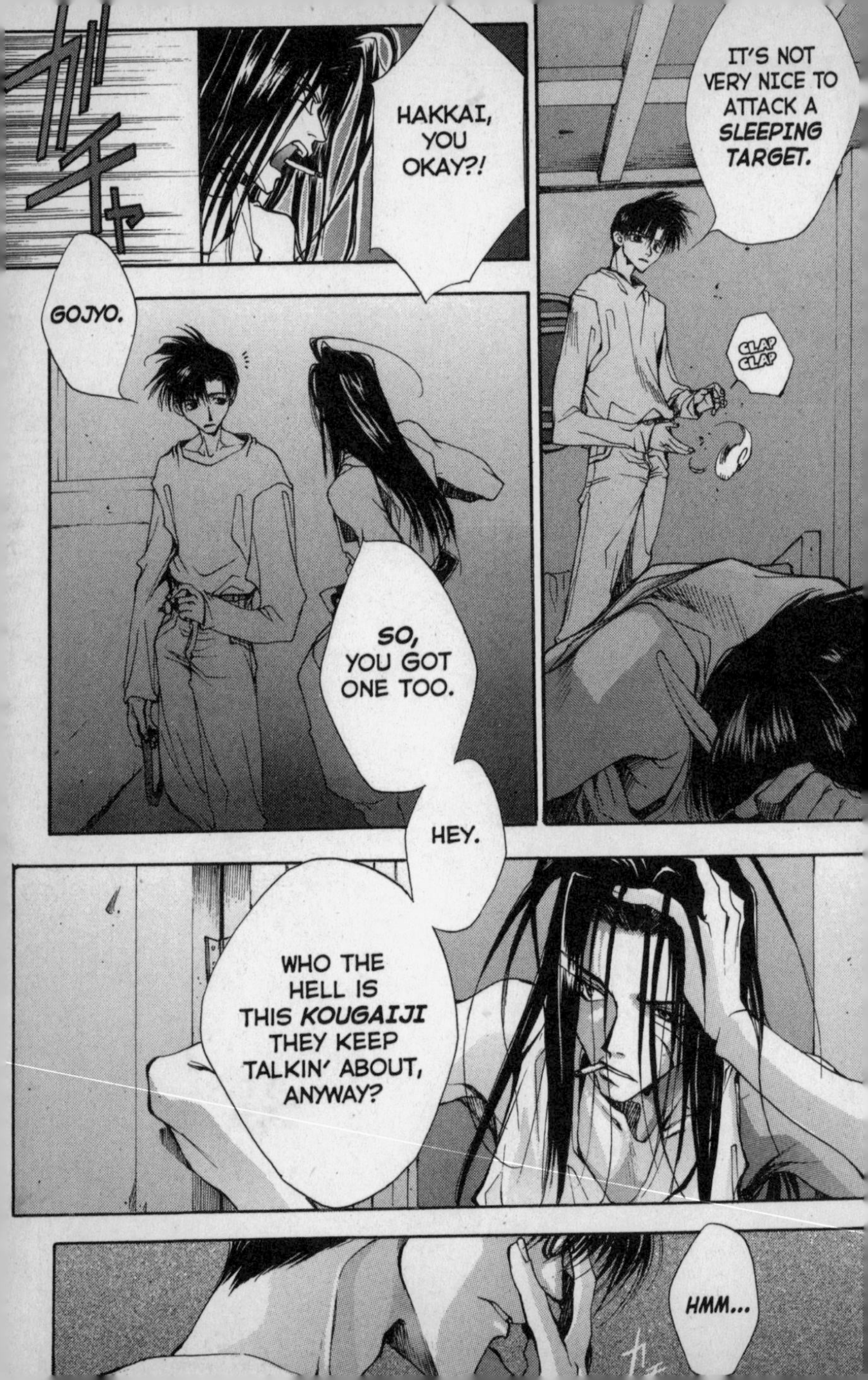
IT'S NOT VERY NICE TO ATTACK A *SLEEPING TARGET*.
CLAP CLAP
ガチャ
HAKKAI, YOU OKAY?!
GOJYO.
SO, YOU GOT ONE TOO.
HEY.
WHO THE HELL IS THIS *KOUGAIJI* THEY KEEP TALKIN' ABOUT, ANYWAY?
HMM...

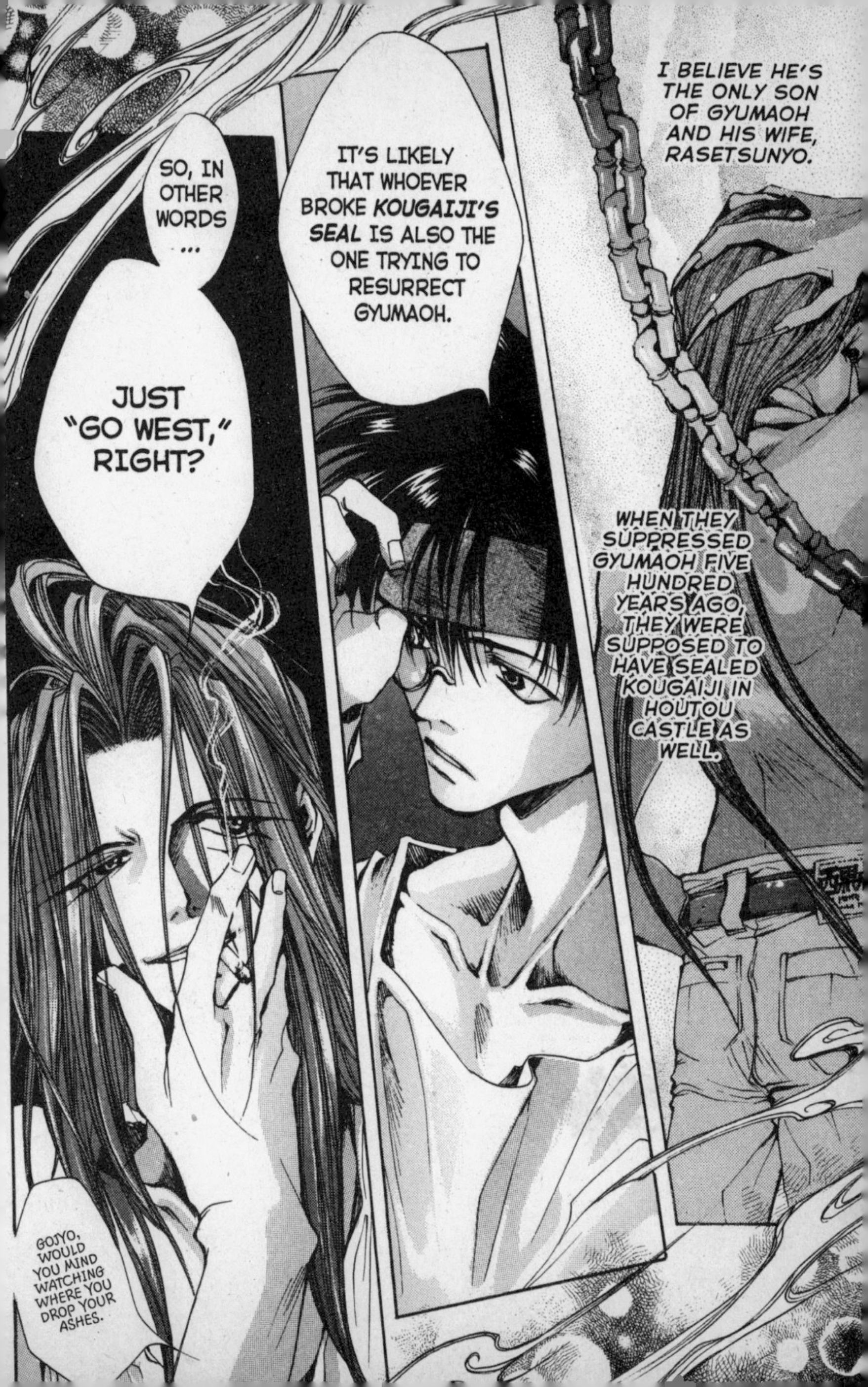
I BELIEVE HE'S THE ONLY SON OF GYUMAOH AND HIS WIFE, RASETSUNYO.
WHEN THEY SUPPRESSED GYUMAOH FIVE HUNDRED YEARS AGO, THEY WERE SUPPOSED TO HAVE SEALED KOUGAIJI IN HOUTOU CASTLE AS WELL.
IT'S LIKELY THAT WHOEVER BROKE *KOUGAIJI'S SEAL* IS ALSO THE ONE TRYING TO RESURRECT GYUMAOH.
SO, IN OTHER WORDS ...
JUST "GO WEST," RIGHT?
GOJYO, WOULD YOU MIND WATCHING WHERE YOU DROP YOUR ASHES.

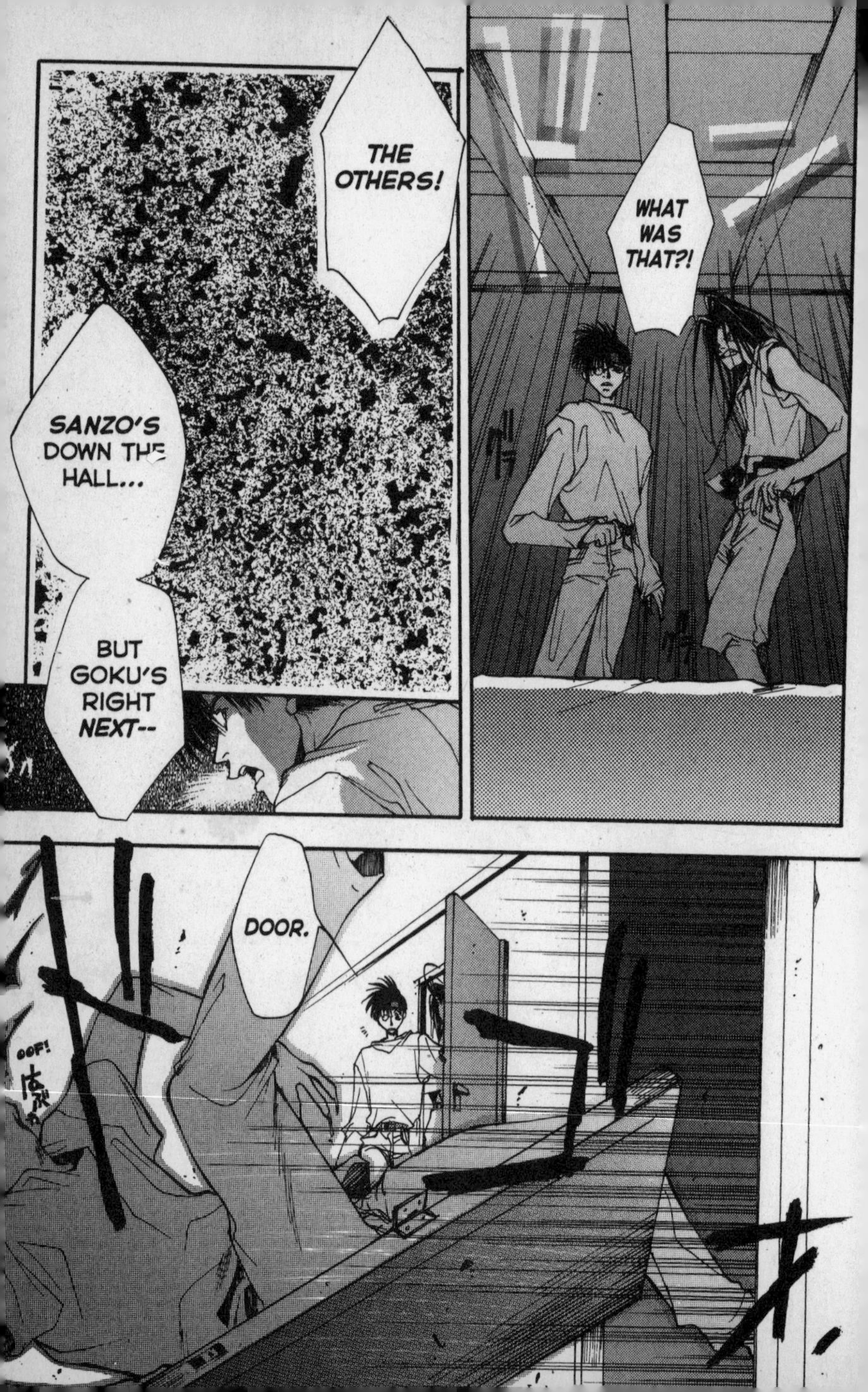
WHAT WAS THAT?!
THE OTHERS!
SANZO'S DOWN THE HALL...
BUT GOKU'S RIGHT *NEXT*--
DOOR.
OOF!

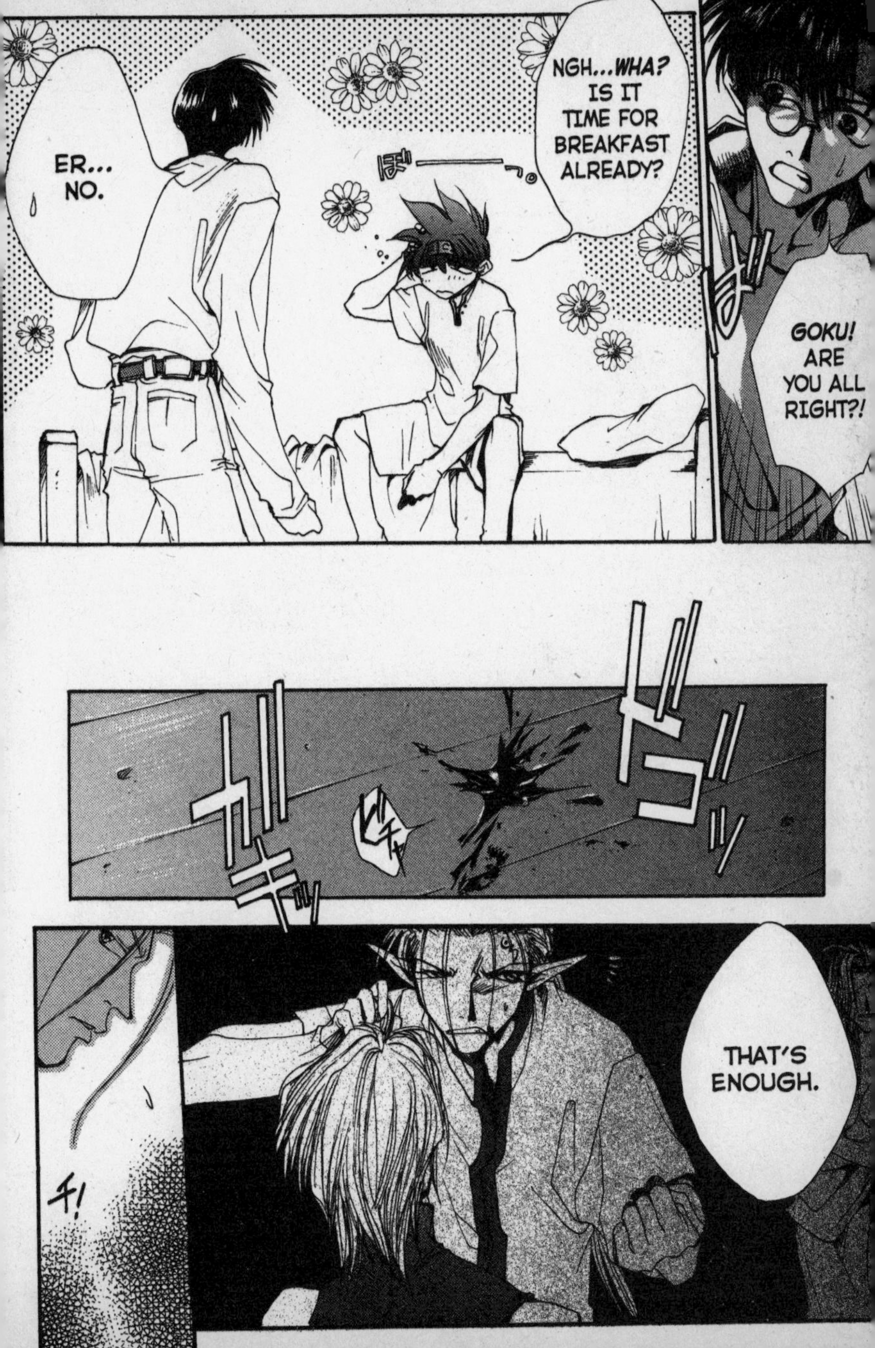
GOKU! ARE YOU ALL RIGHT?!
NGH...WHA? IS IT TIME FOR BREAKFAST ALREADY?
ER... NO.
THAT'S ENOUGH.
チ!

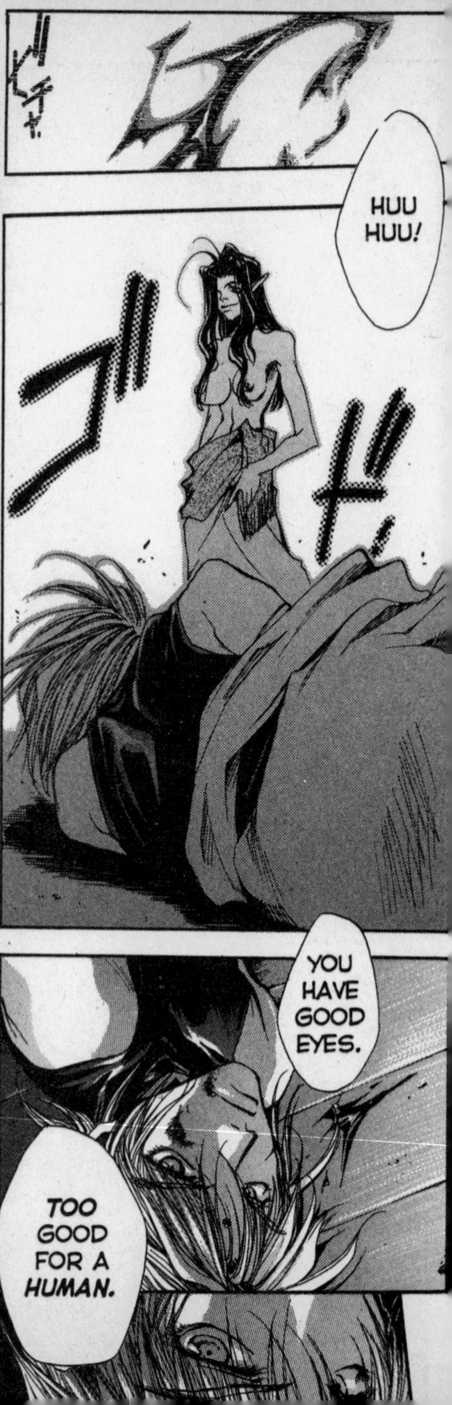
HUU HUU!
YOU HAVE GOOD EYES.
TOO GOOD FOR A *HUMAN.*
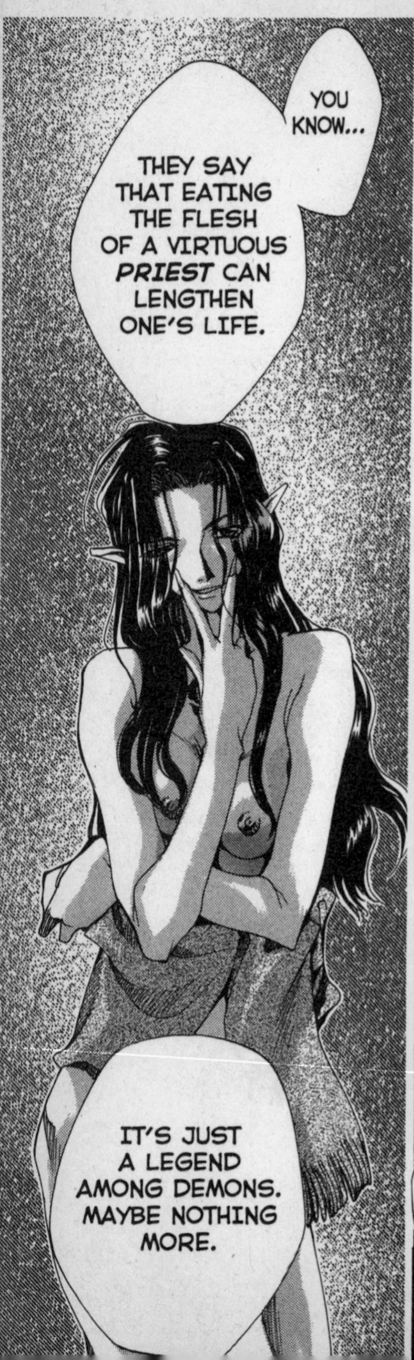
YOU KNOW...
THEY SAY THAT EATING THE FLESH OF A VIRTUOUS *PRIEST* CAN LENGTHEN ONE'S LIFE.
IT'S JUST A LEGEND AMONG DEMONS. MAYBE NOTHING MORE.

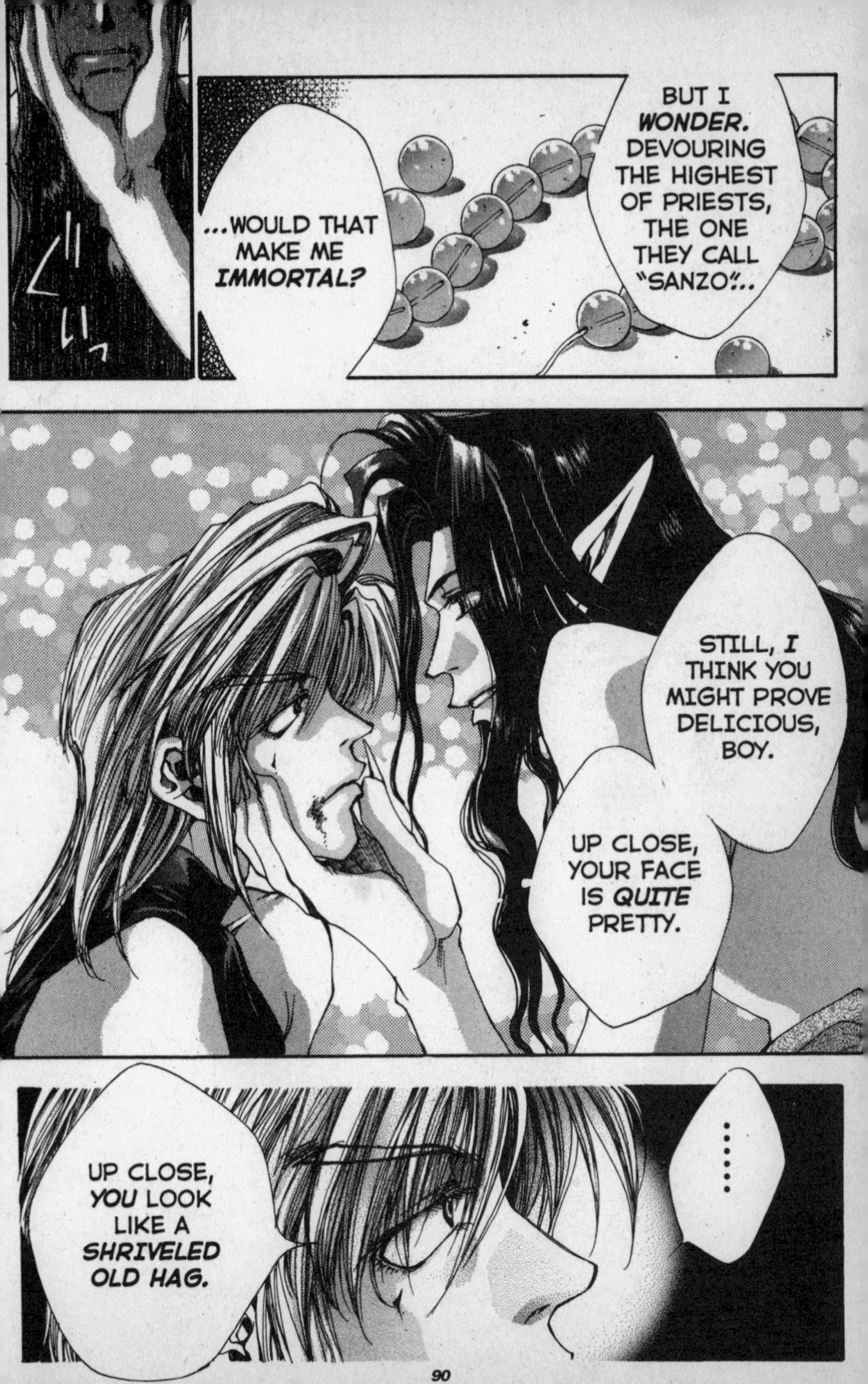
BUT I WONDER. DEVOURING THE HIGHEST OF PRIESTS, THE ONE THEY CALL "SANZO"...
...WOULD THAT MAKE ME IMMORTAL?
STILL, I THINK YOU MIGHT PROVE DELICIOUS, BOY.
UP CLOSE, YOUR FACE IS QUITE PRETTY.
......
UP CLOSE, YOU LOOK LIKE A SHRIVELED OLD HAG.

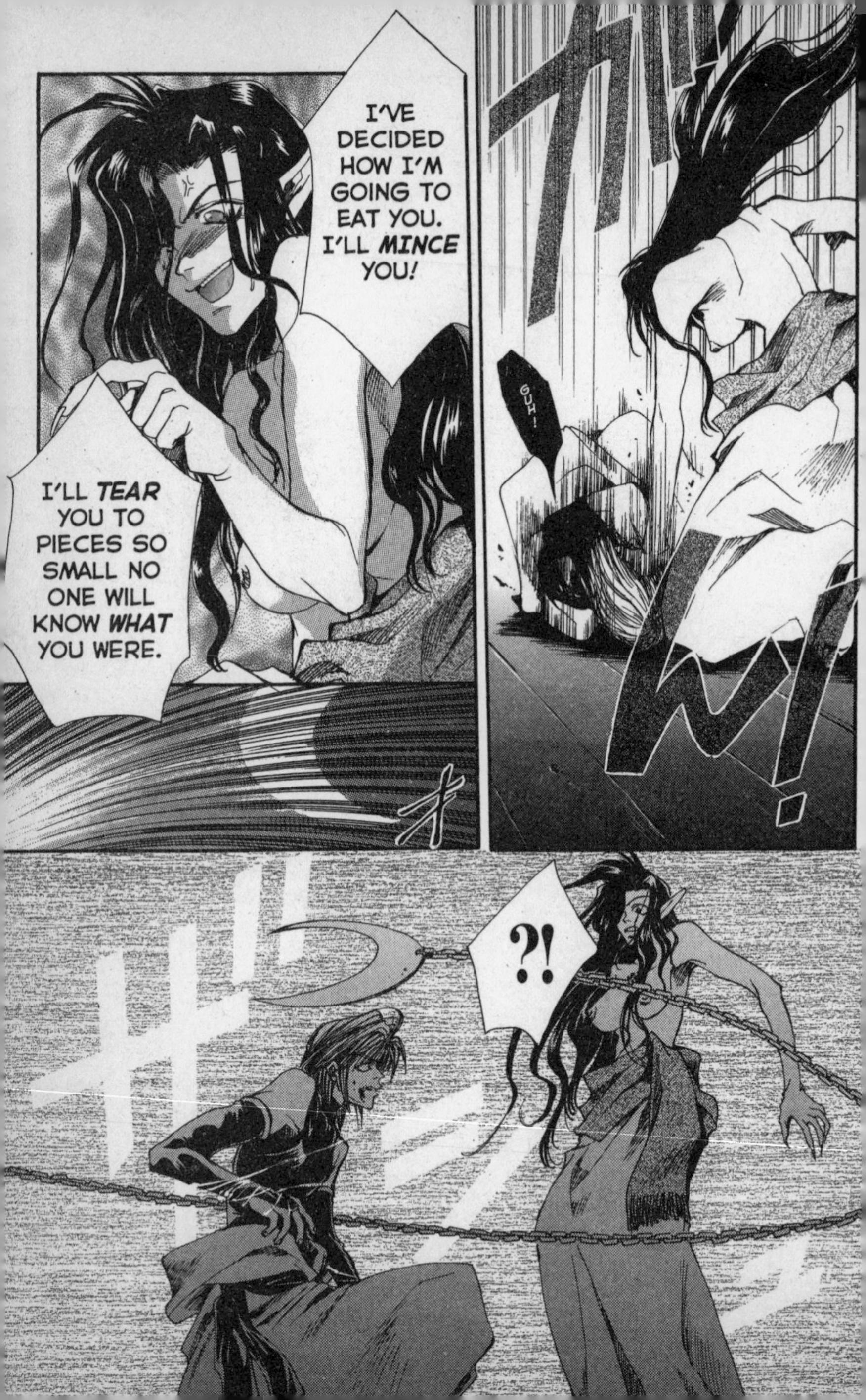
GUH!
I'VE DECIDED HOW I'M GOING TO EAT YOU. I'LL *MINCE* YOU!
I'LL *TEAR* YOU TO PIECES SO SMALL NO ONE WILL KNOW *WHAT* YOU WERE.
?!

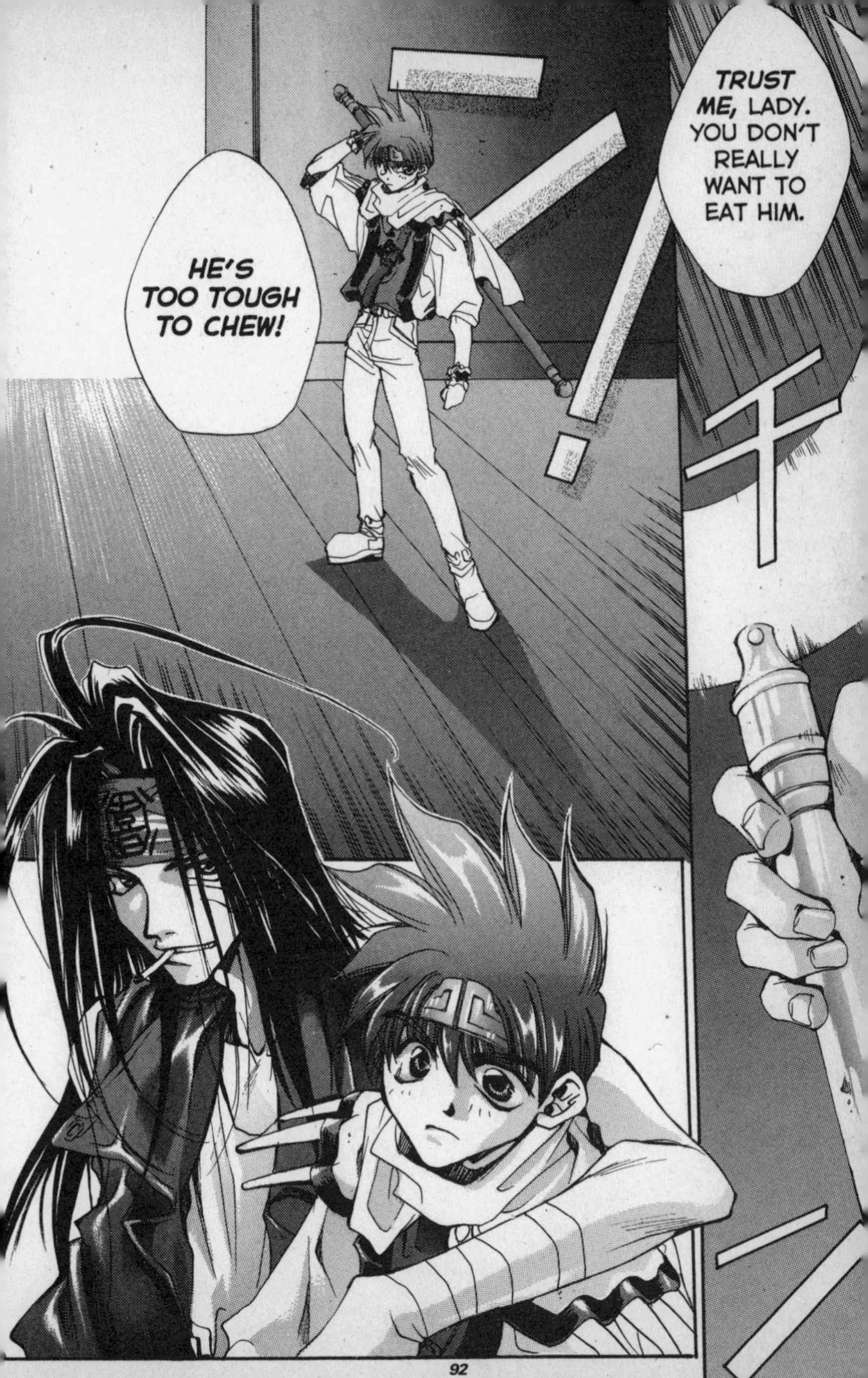
TRUST ME, LADY. YOU DON'T REALLY WANT TO EAT HIM.
HE'S TOO TOUGH TO CHEW!

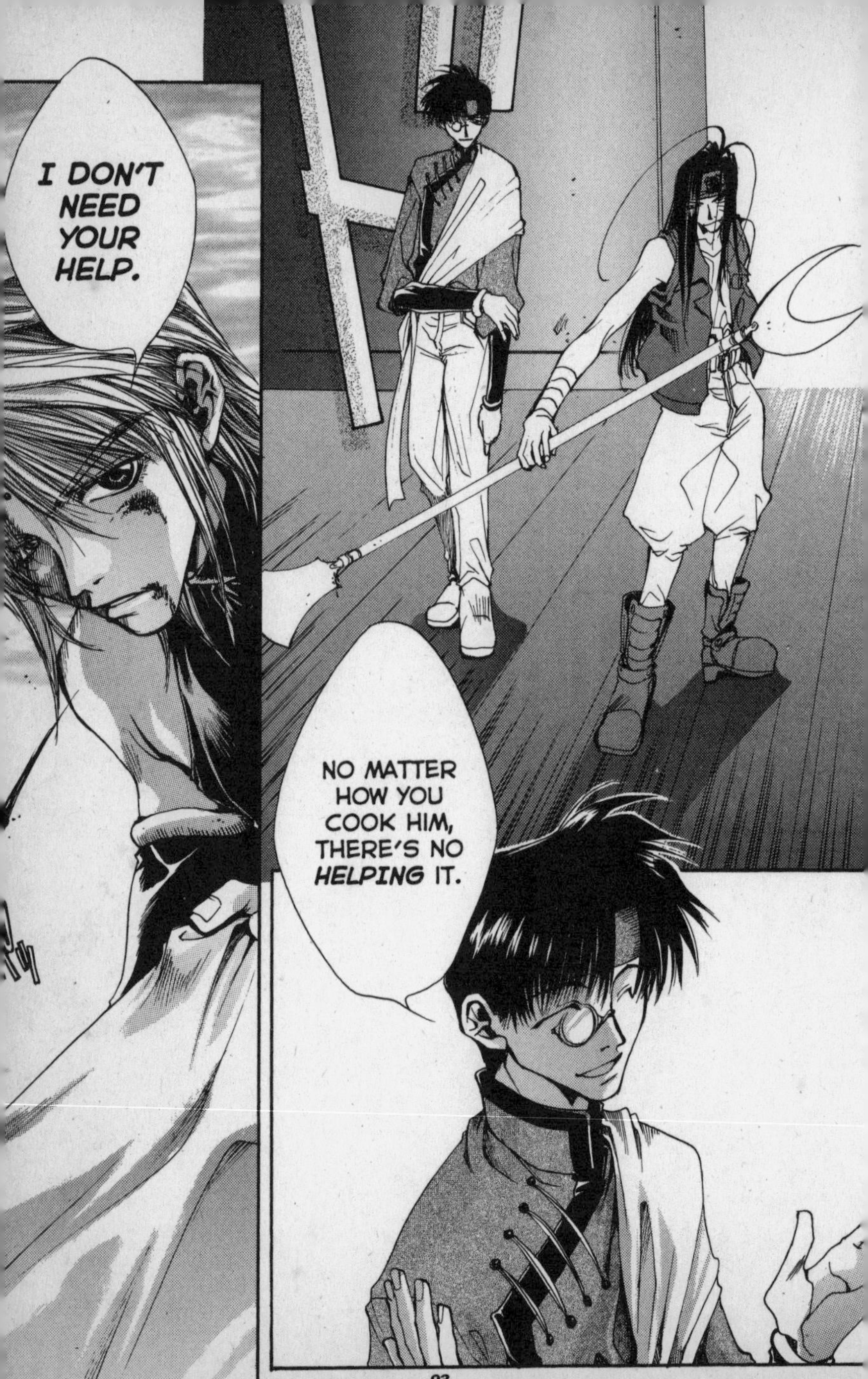
NO MATTER HOW YOU COOK HIM, THERE'S NO *HELPING* IT.
I DON'T NEED YOUR HELP.

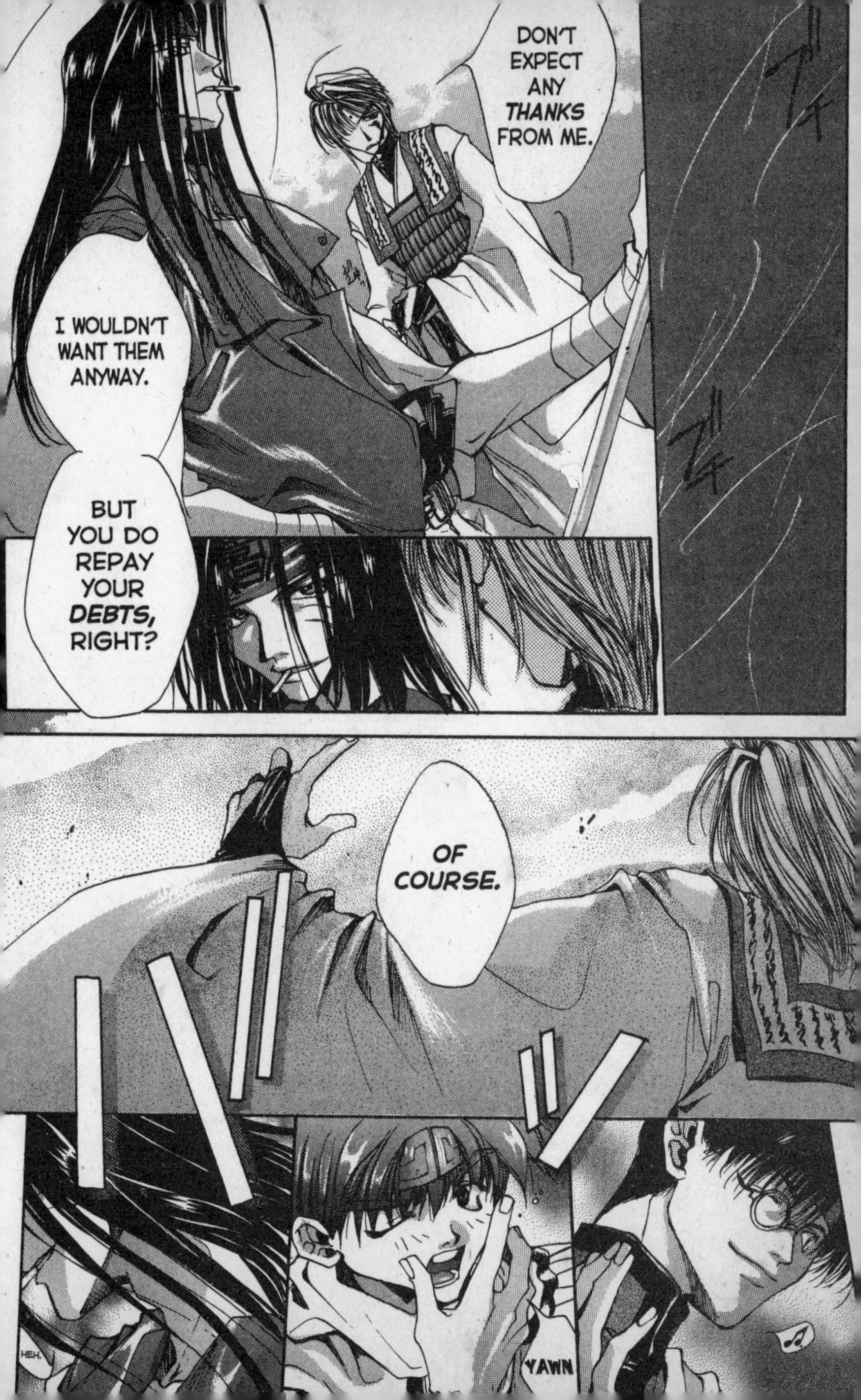
DON'T EXPECT ANY *THANKS* FROM ME.
I WOULDN'T WANT THEM ANYWAY.
BUT YOU DO REPAY YOUR *DEBTS,* RIGHT?
OF COURSE.
YAWN
HEH.

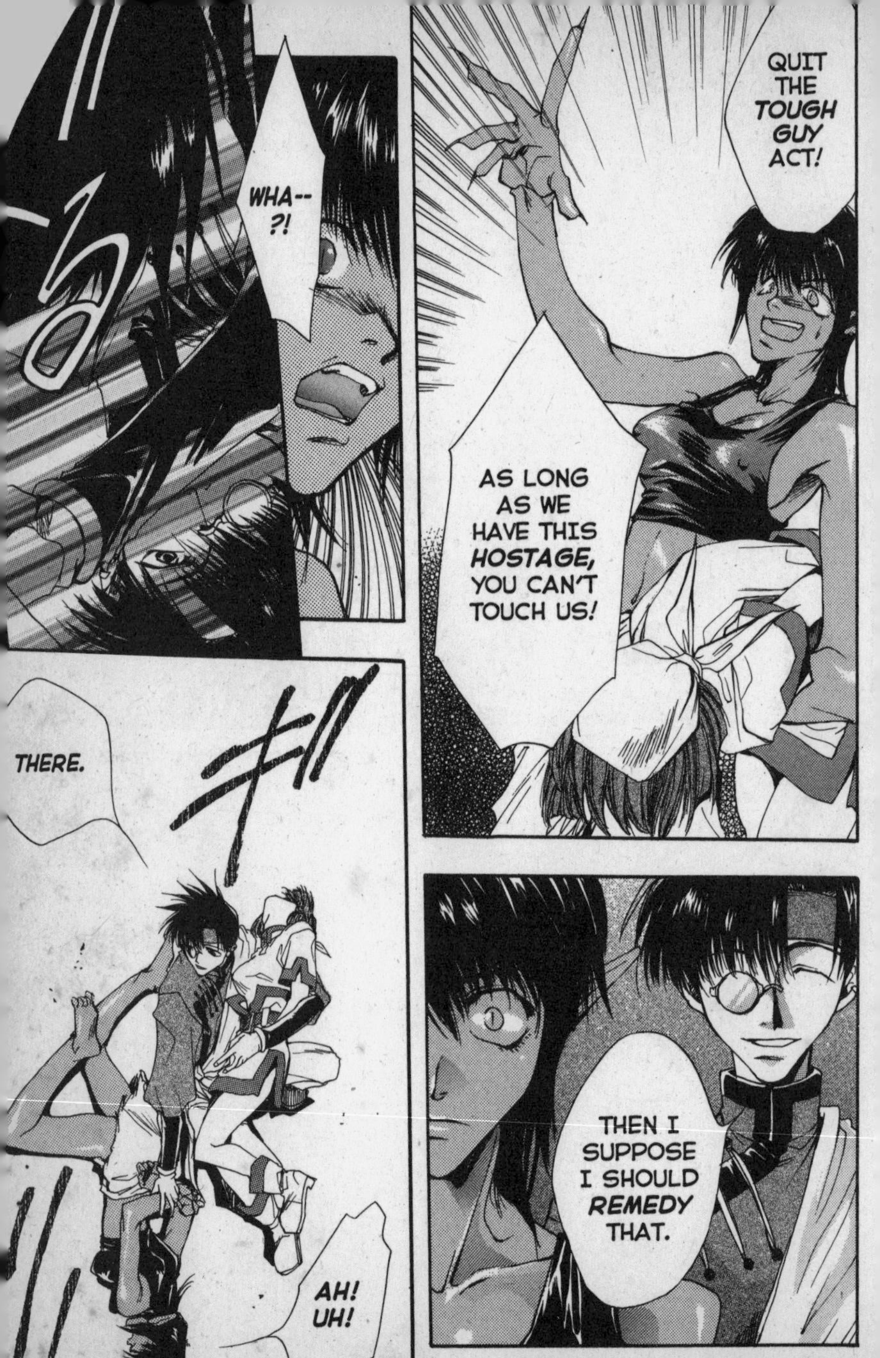
QUIT THE *TOUGH GUY* ACT!
AS LONG AS WE HAVE THIS *HOSTAGE,* YOU CAN'T TOUCH US!
THEN I SUPPOSE I SHOULD *REMEDY* THAT.
WHA-- ?!
THERE.
AH! UH!

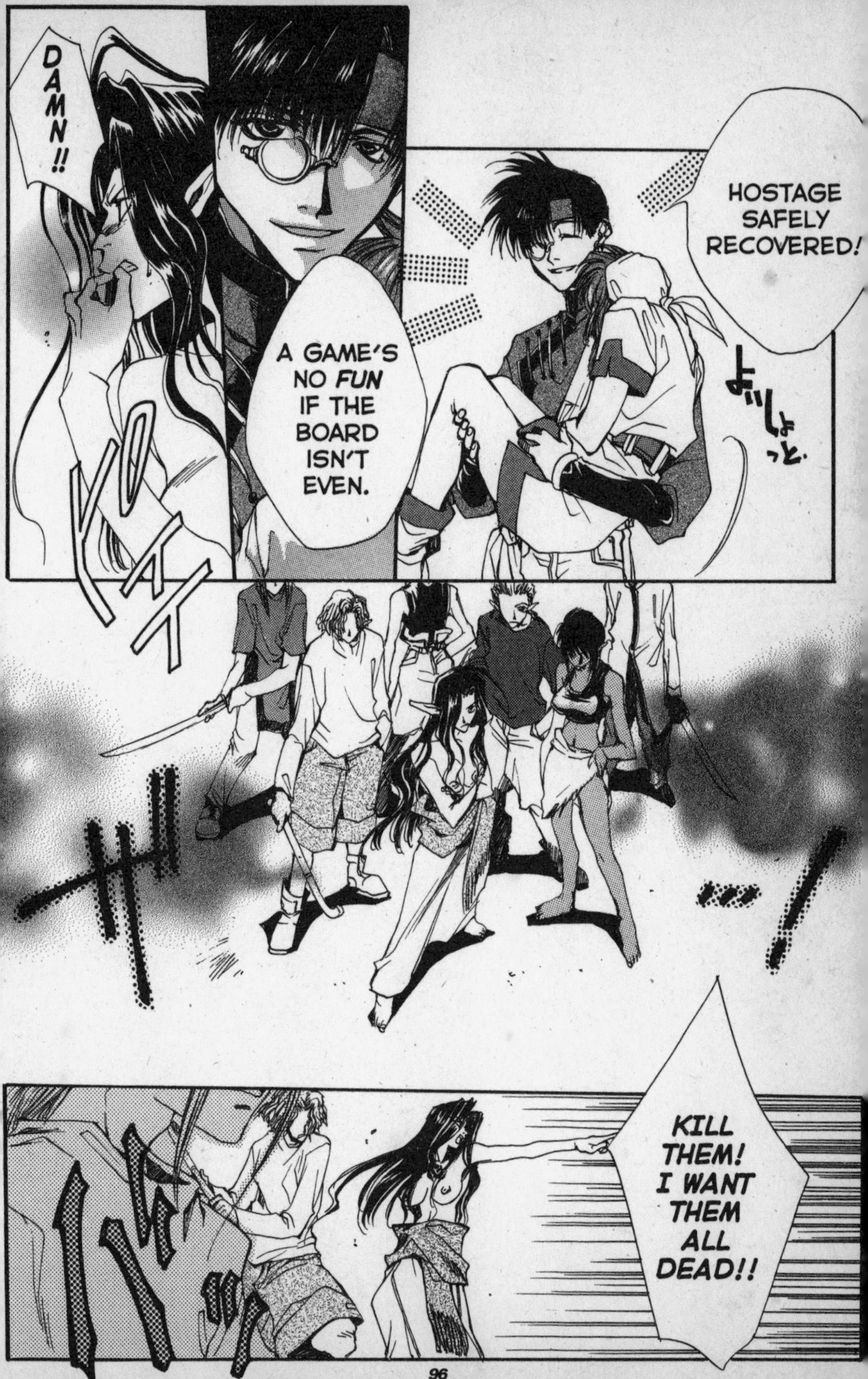
HOSTAGE SAFELY RECOVERED!
よいしょっと
A GAME'S NO *FUN* IF THE BOARD ISN'T EVEN.
DAMN!!
...!
KILL THEM! I WANT THEM ALL DEAD!!

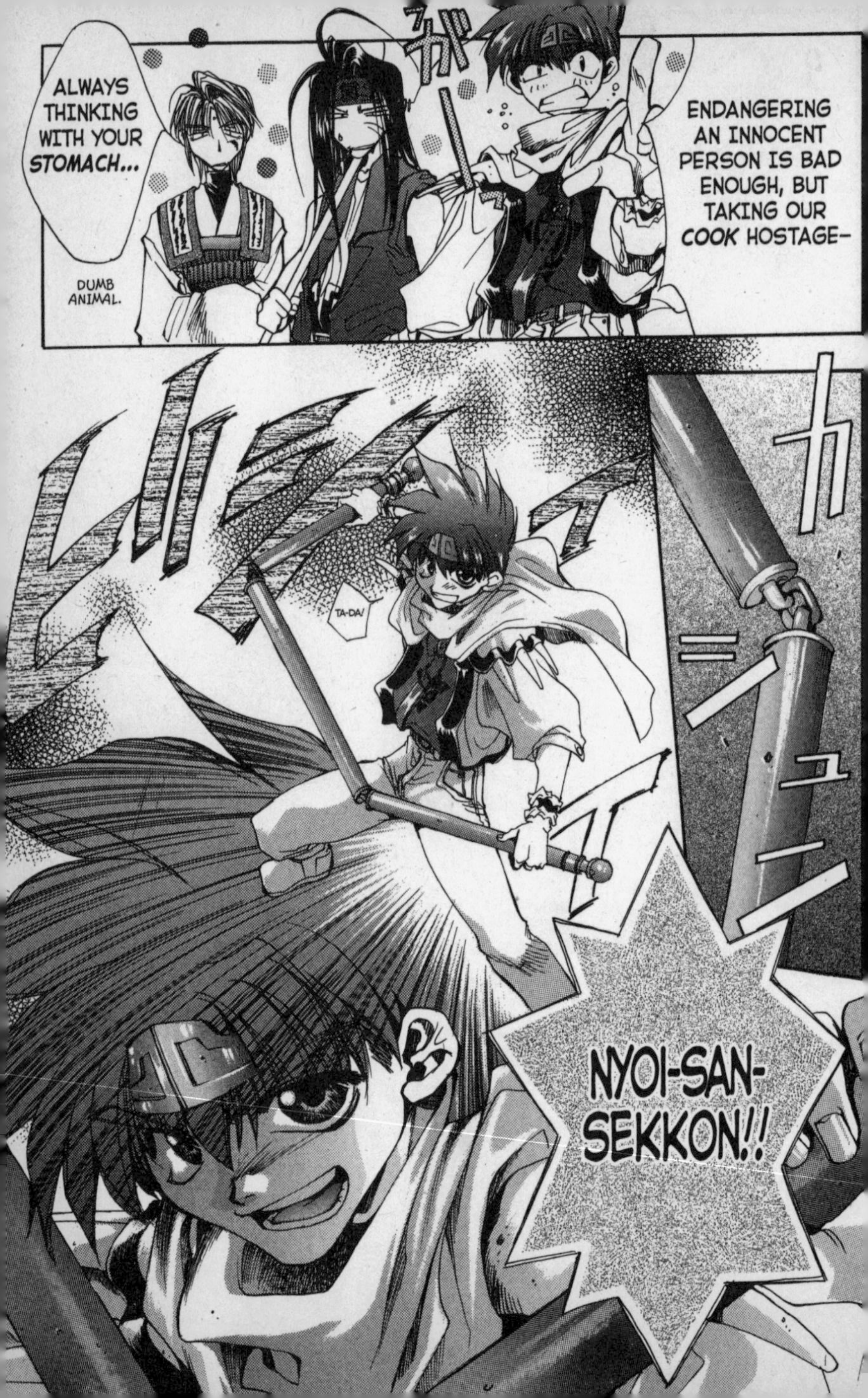
ENDANGERING AN INNOCENT PERSON IS BAD ENOUGH, BUT TAKING OUR *COOK* HOSTAGE–
ALWAYS THINKING WITH YOUR *STOMACH*...
DUMB ANIMAL.
TA-DA!
NYOI-SAN-SEKKON!!

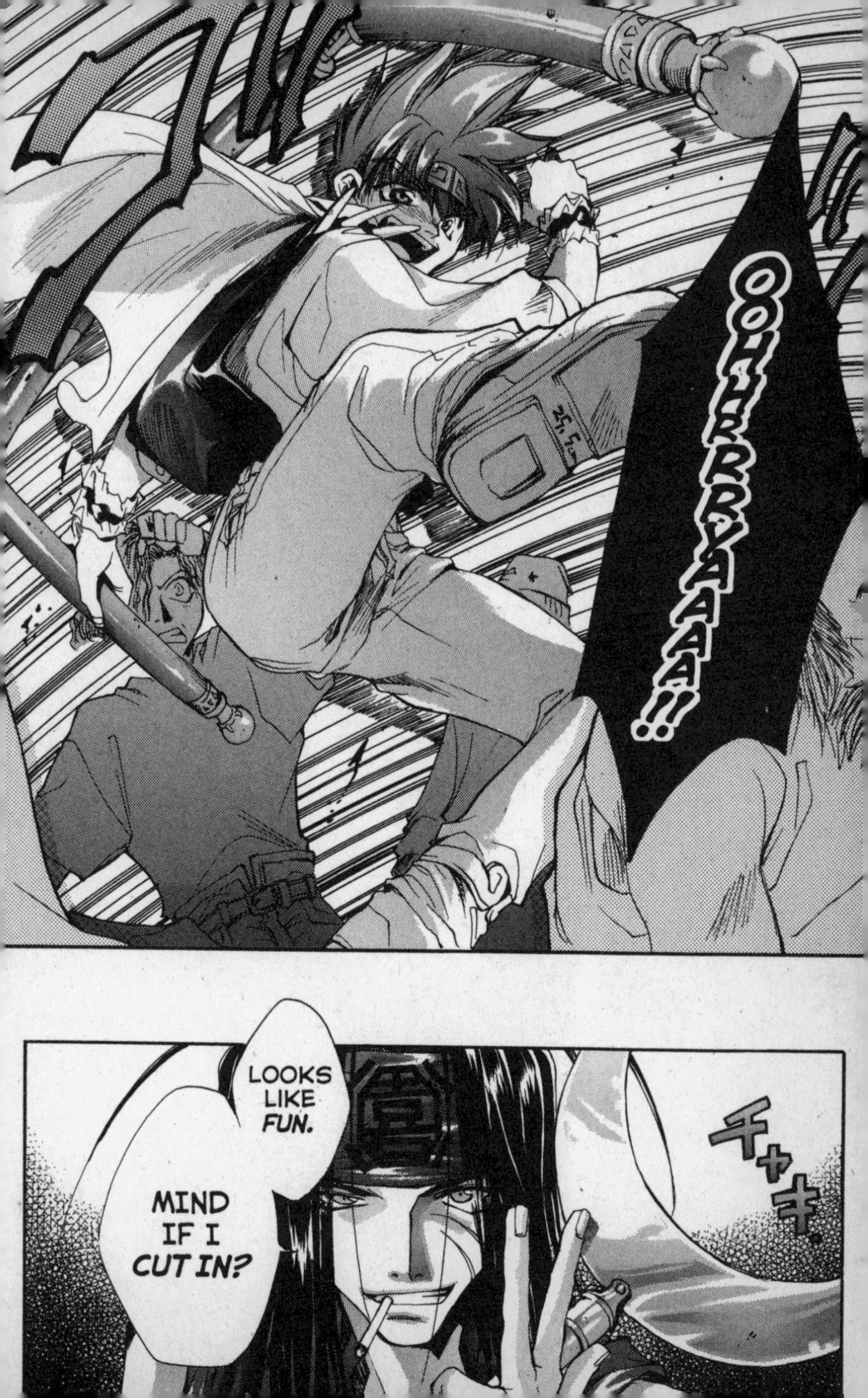
OOHRRRYAAAAA!!
LOOKS LIKE FUN.
MIND IF I CUT IN?
チャキ

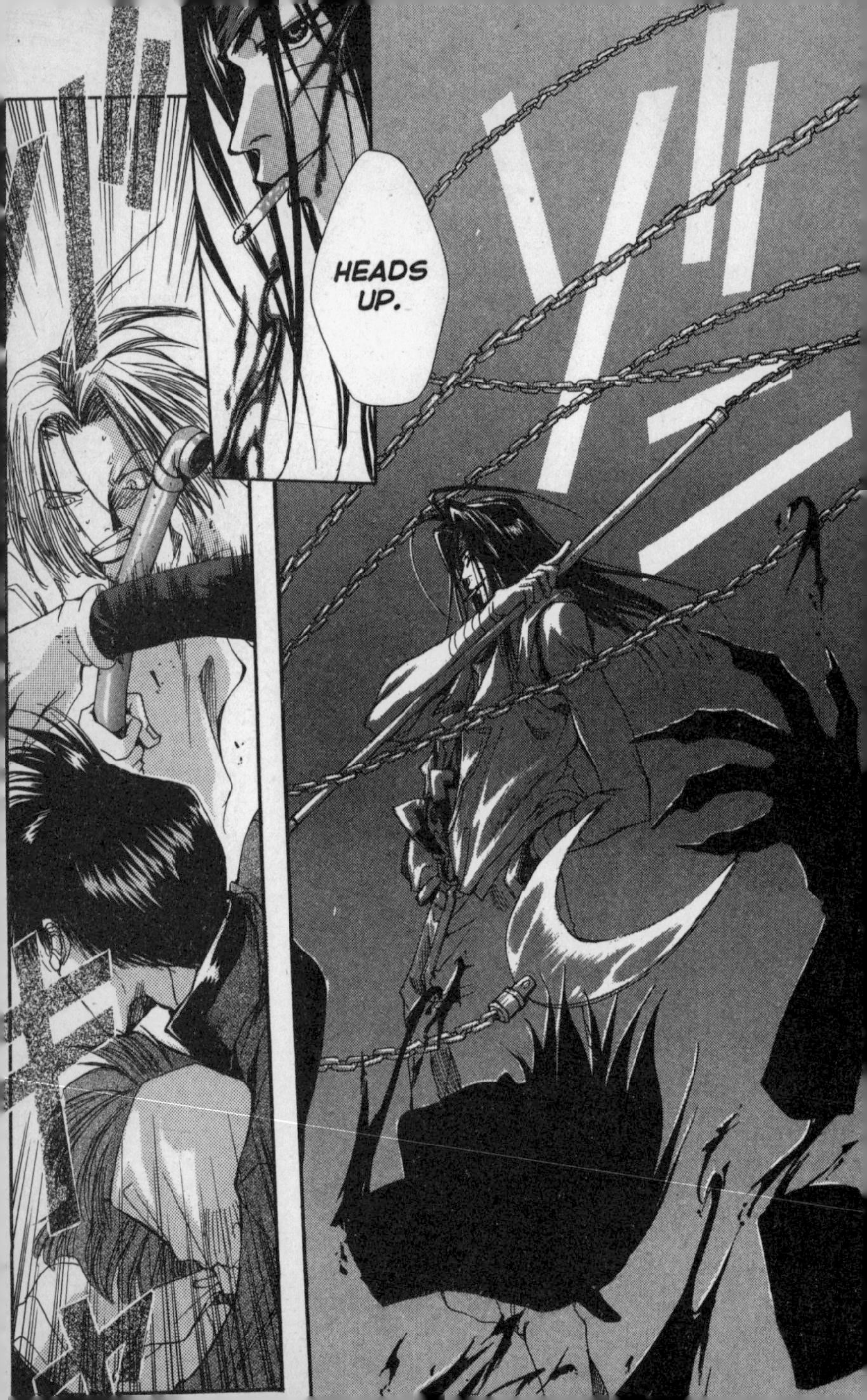
HEADS UP.

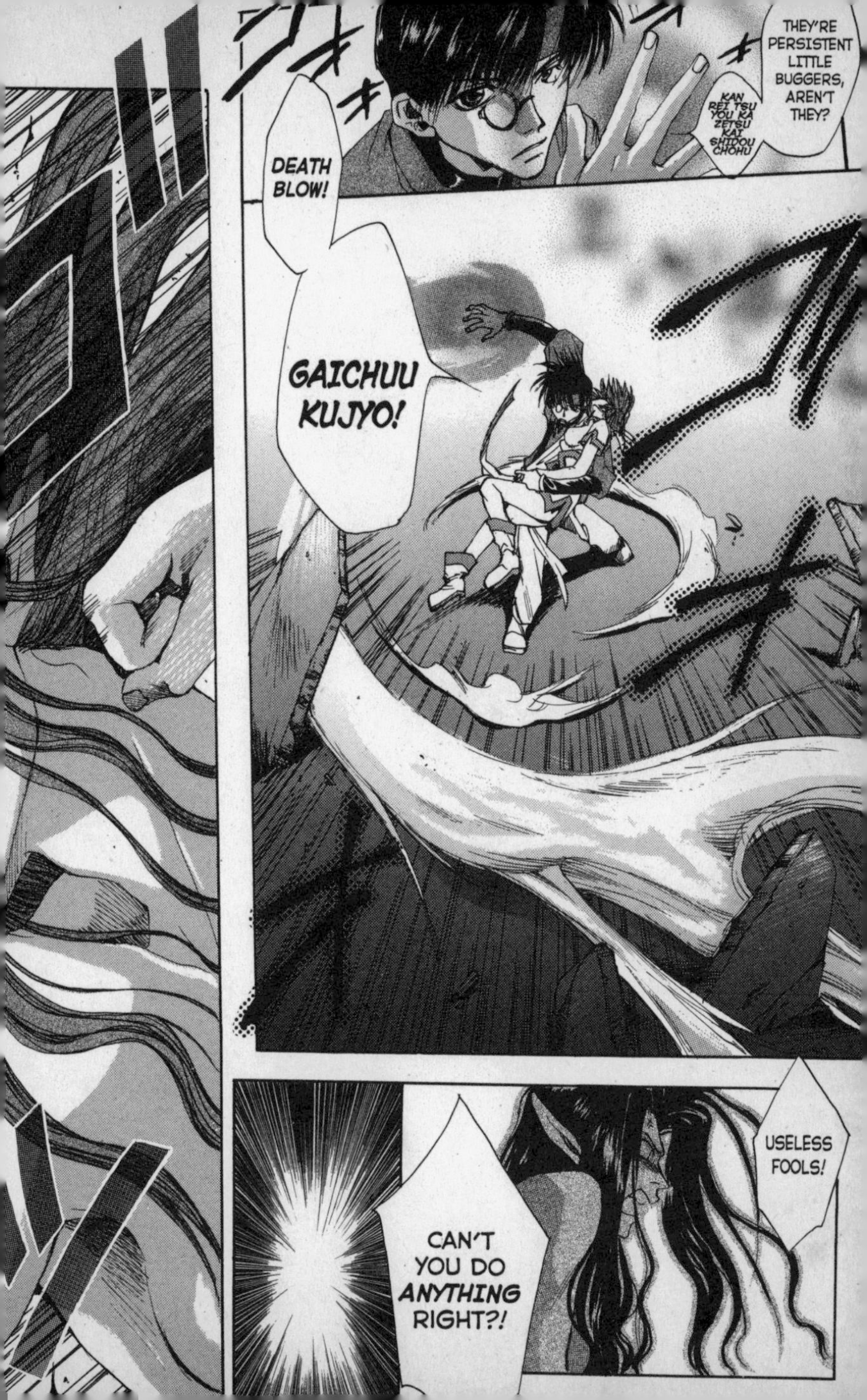
THEY'RE PERSISTENT LITTLE BUGGERS, AREN'T THEY?
KAN REI TSU YOU KA ZETSU KAI SHIDOU CHOHU
DEATH BLOW!
GAICHUU KUJYO!
USELESS FOOLS!
CAN'T YOU DO ANYTHING RIGHT?!

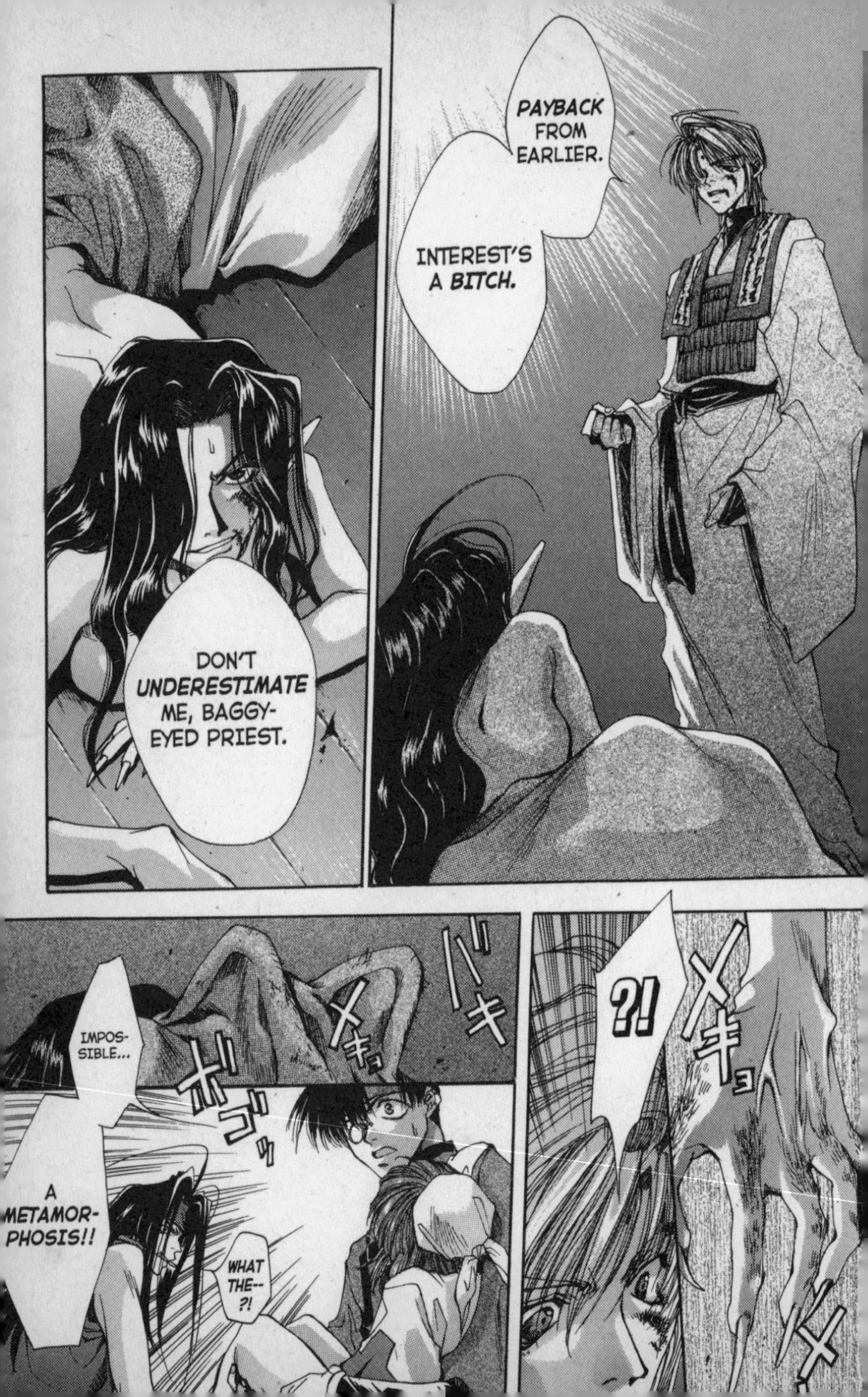
PAYBACK FROM EARLIER.
INTEREST'S A BITCH.
DON'T UNDERESTIMATE ME, BAGGY-EYED PRIEST.
?!
IMPOS-SIBLE...
A METAMOR-PHOSIS!!
WHAT THE--?!

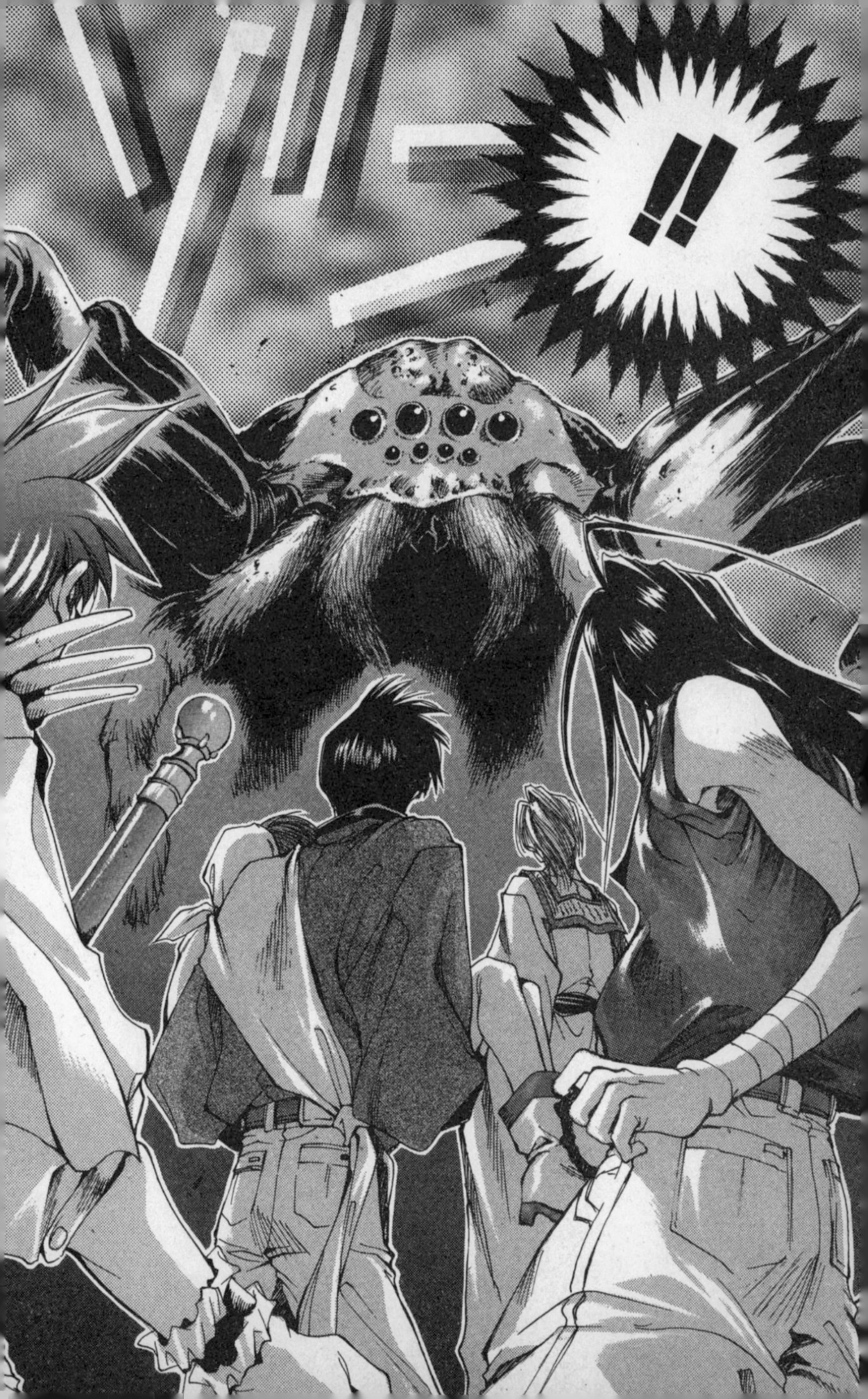
!!

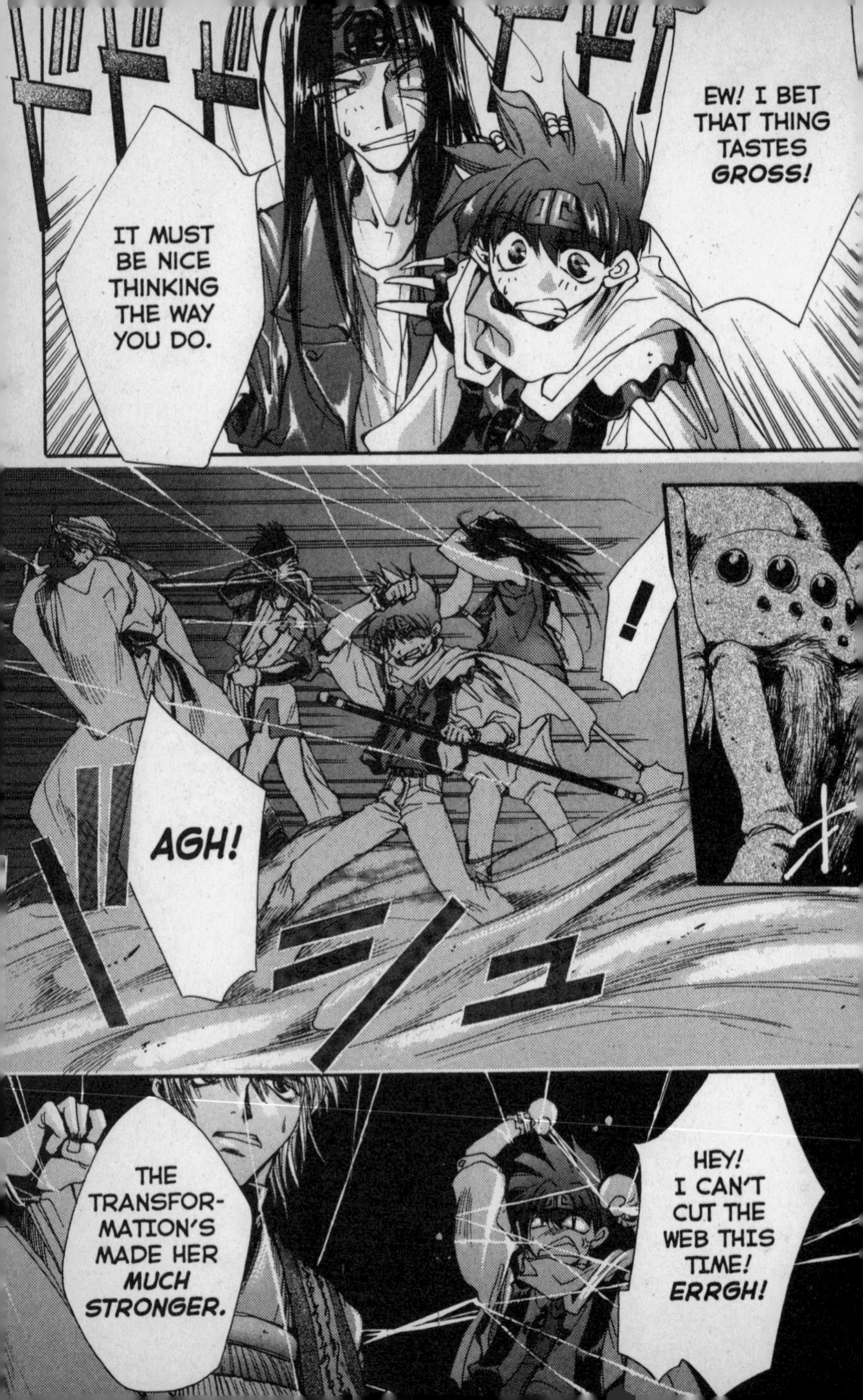
EW! I BET THAT THING TASTES GROSS!
IT MUST BE NICE THINKING THE WAY YOU DO.
!
AGH!
HEY! I CAN'T CUT THE WEB THIS TIME! ERRGH!
THE TRANSFOR-MATION'S MADE HER MUCH STRONGER.

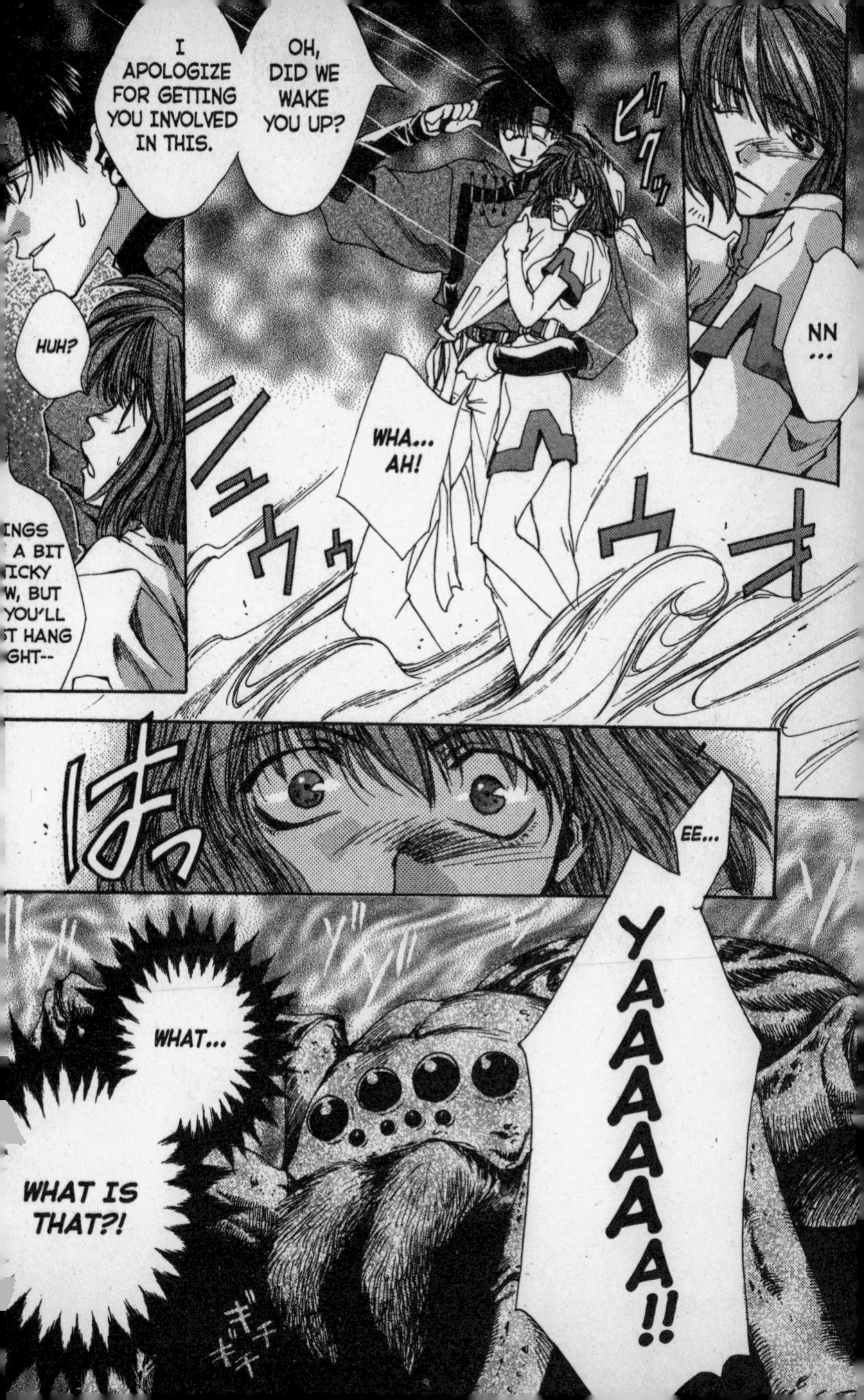
ビクッ
NN...
OH, DID WE WAKE YOU UP?
I APOLOGIZE FOR GETTING YOU INVOLVED IN THIS.
WHA... AH!
ウオ
ジュウゥ
HUH?
INGS A BIT ICKY W, BUT YOU'LL ST HANG GHT--
EE...
はっ
YAAAAAA!!
WHAT...
WHAT IS THAT?!
ギチギチ

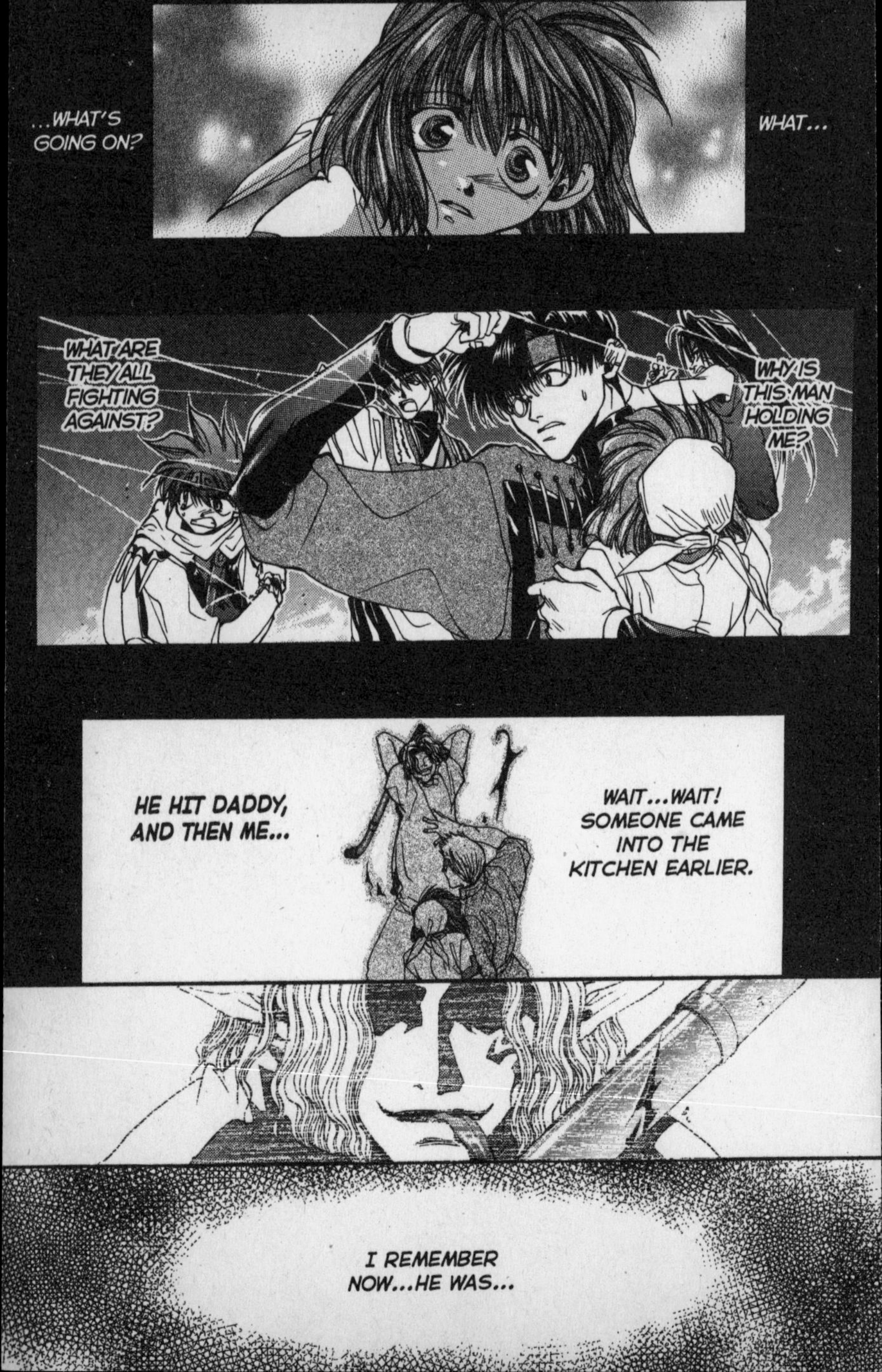
WHAT...
...WHAT'S GOING ON?
WHY IS THIS MAN HOLDING ME?
WHAT ARE THEY ALL FIGHTING AGAINST?
WAIT...WAIT! SOMEONE CAME INTO THE KITCHEN EARLIER.
HE HIT DADDY, AND THEN ME...
I REMEMBER NOW...HE WAS...

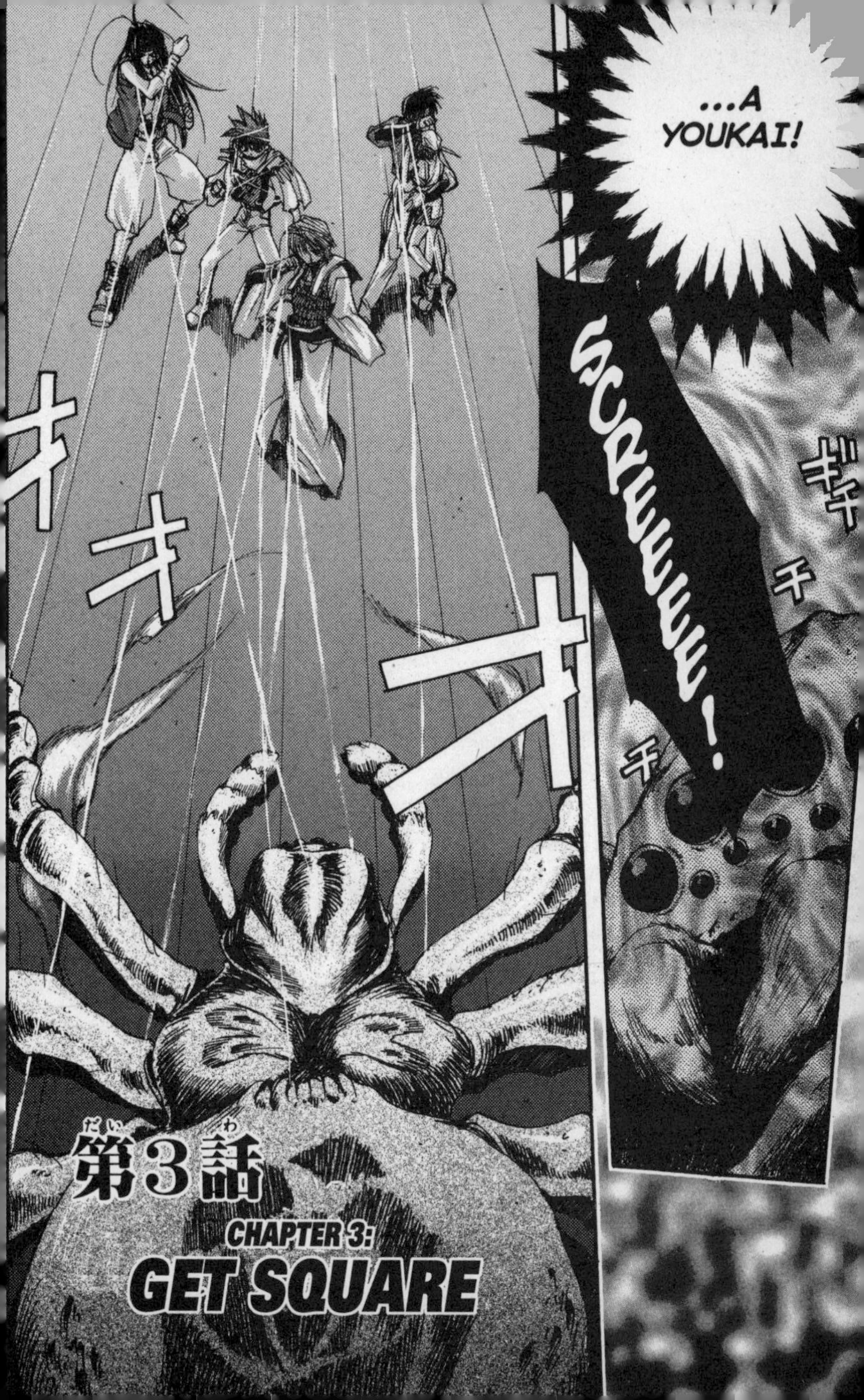
...A YOUKAI!
SCREEEEEE!
ギチチチ
オオオ
第3話
CHAPTER 3:
GET SQUARE

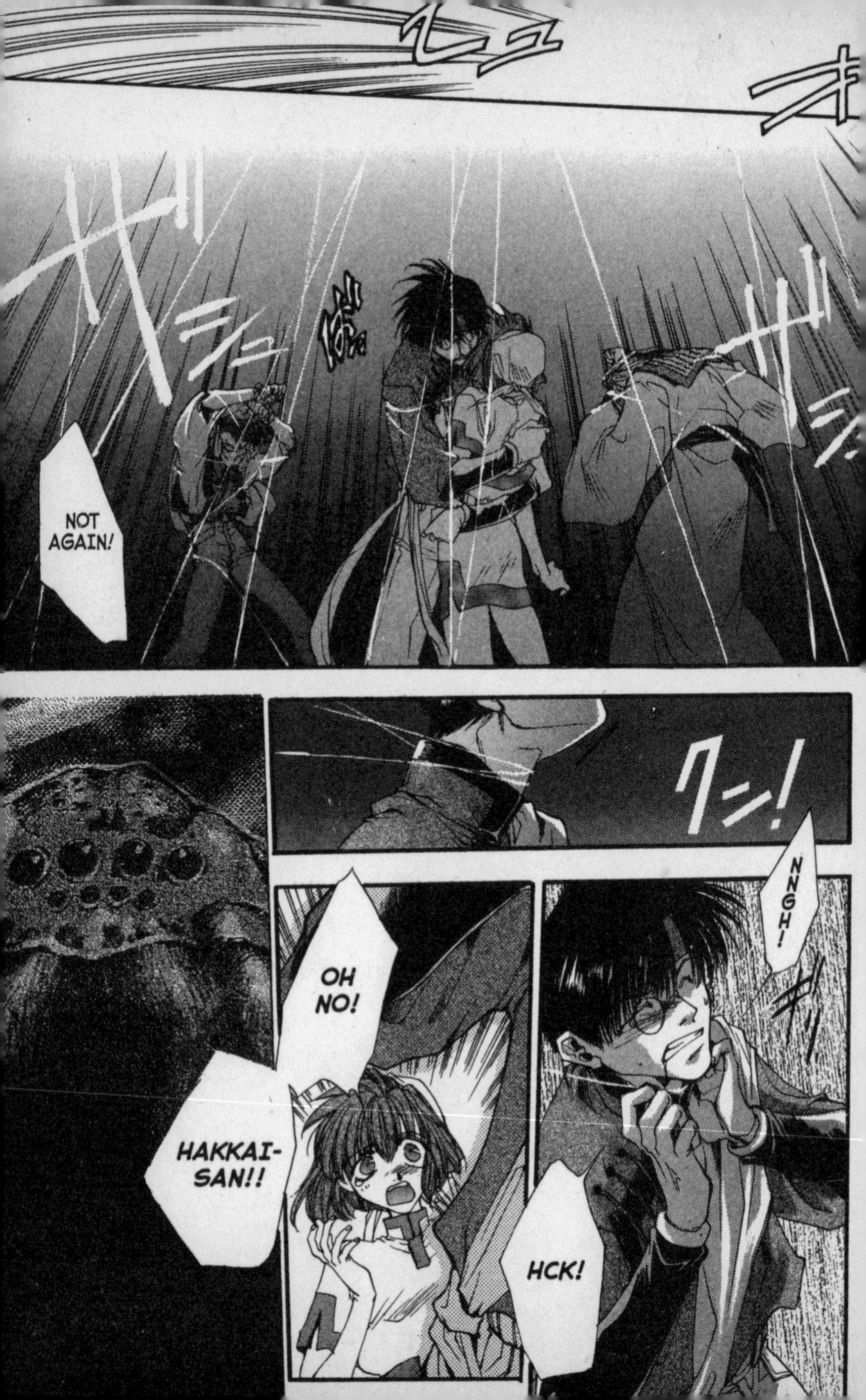

NOT AGAIN!
NNGH!
HCK!
OH NO!
HAKKAI-SAN!!

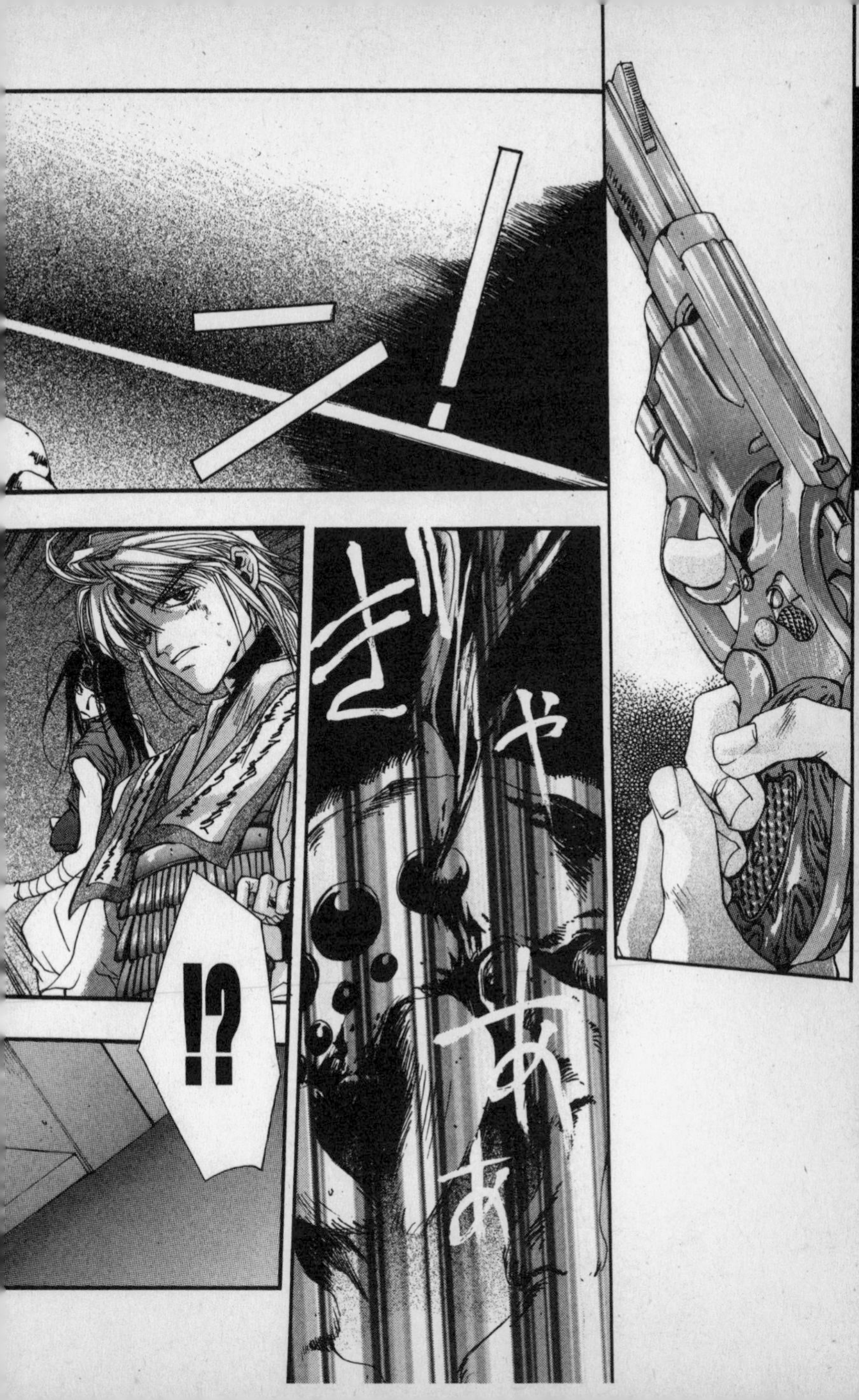
ぎゃああ
!?

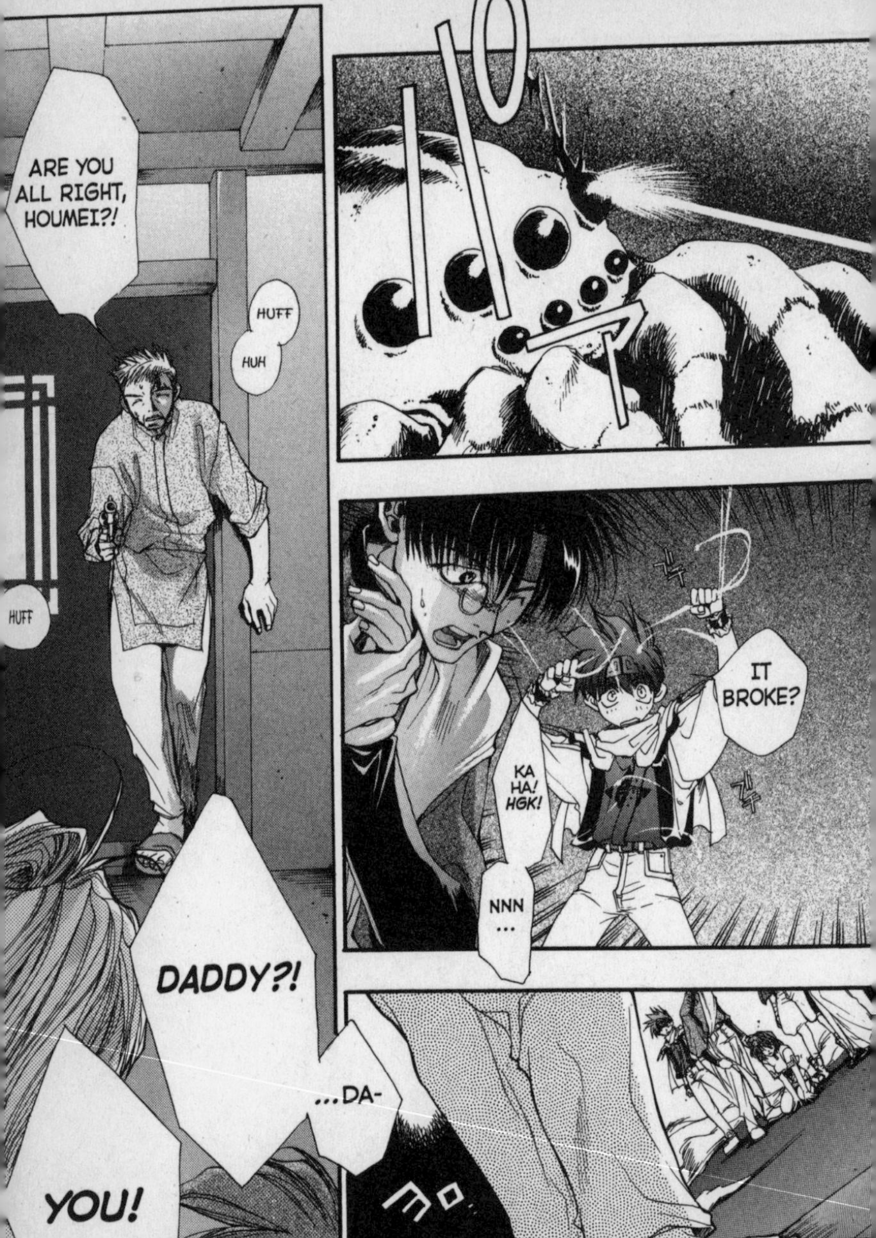
IT BROKE?
KA HA! HGK!
NNN ...
ARE YOU ALL RIGHT, HOUMEI?!
HUFF
HUH
HUFF
DADDY?!
...DA-
YOU!

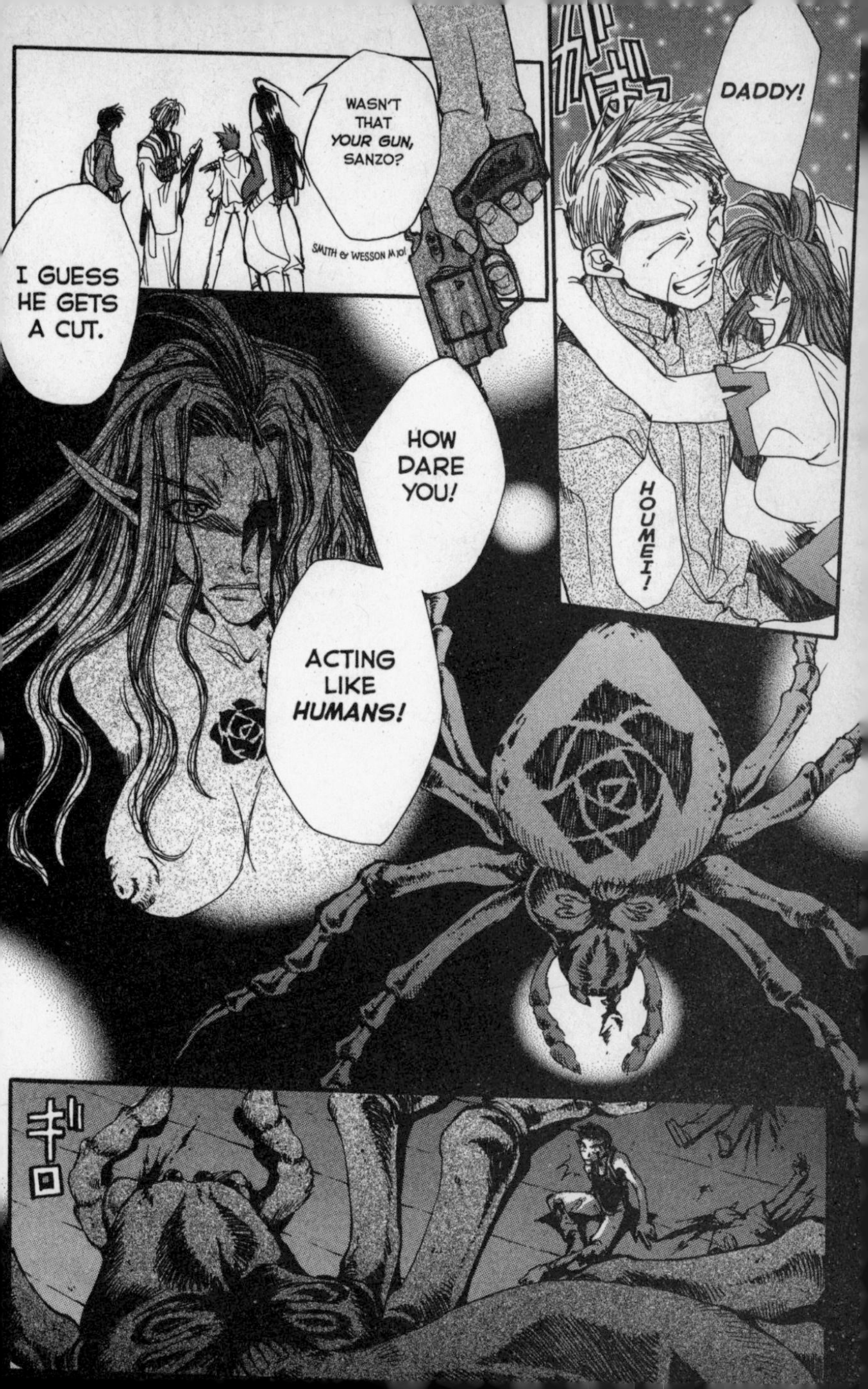
DADDY!
HOUMEI!
WASN'T THAT YOUR GUN, SANZO?
SMITH & WESSON M10!
I GUESS HE GETS A CUT.
HOW DARE YOU!
ACTING LIKE HUMANS!
ギロ

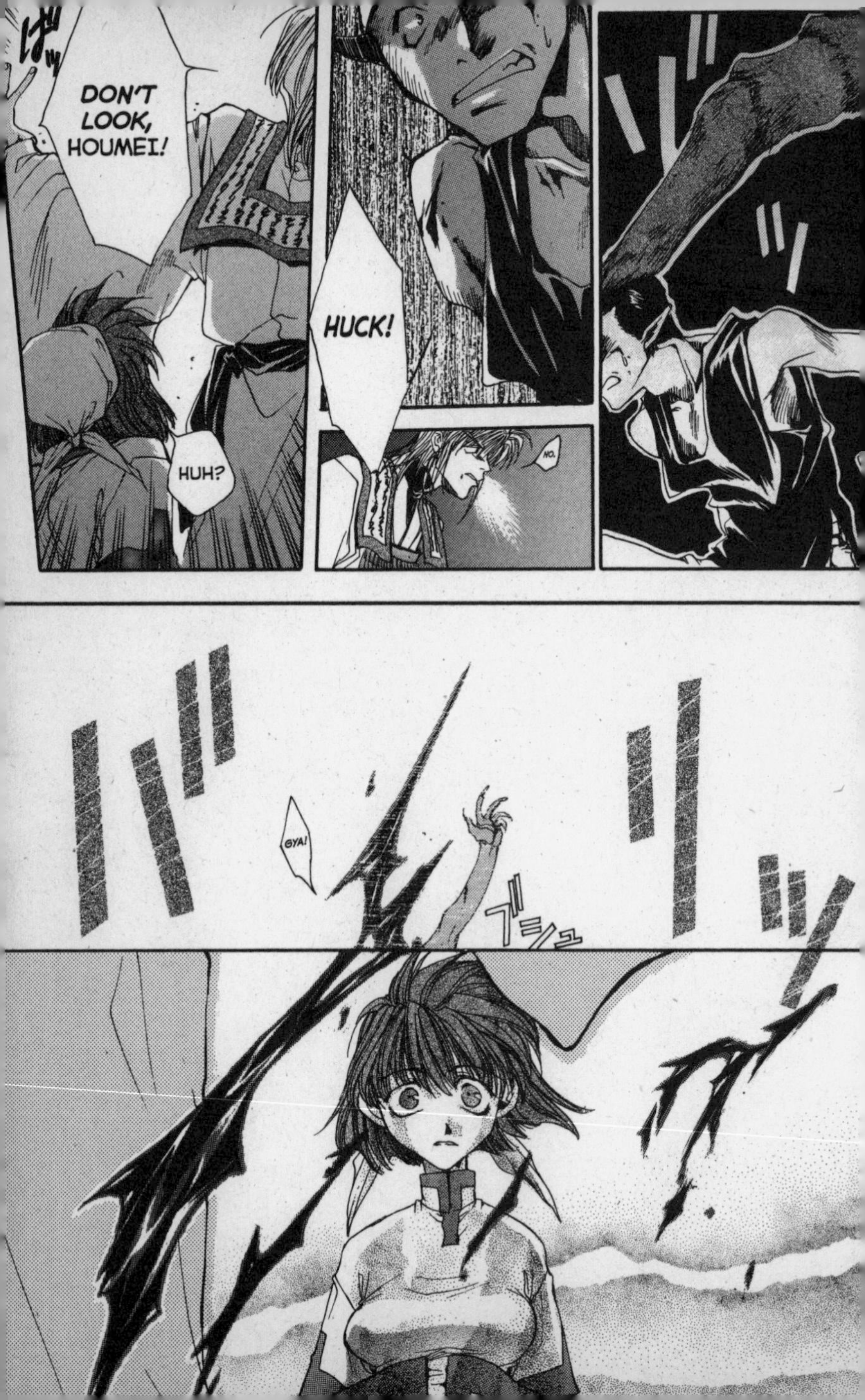
HUCK!
NO.
ばッ
DON'T LOOK, HOUMEI!
HUH?
GYA!
ブシュ

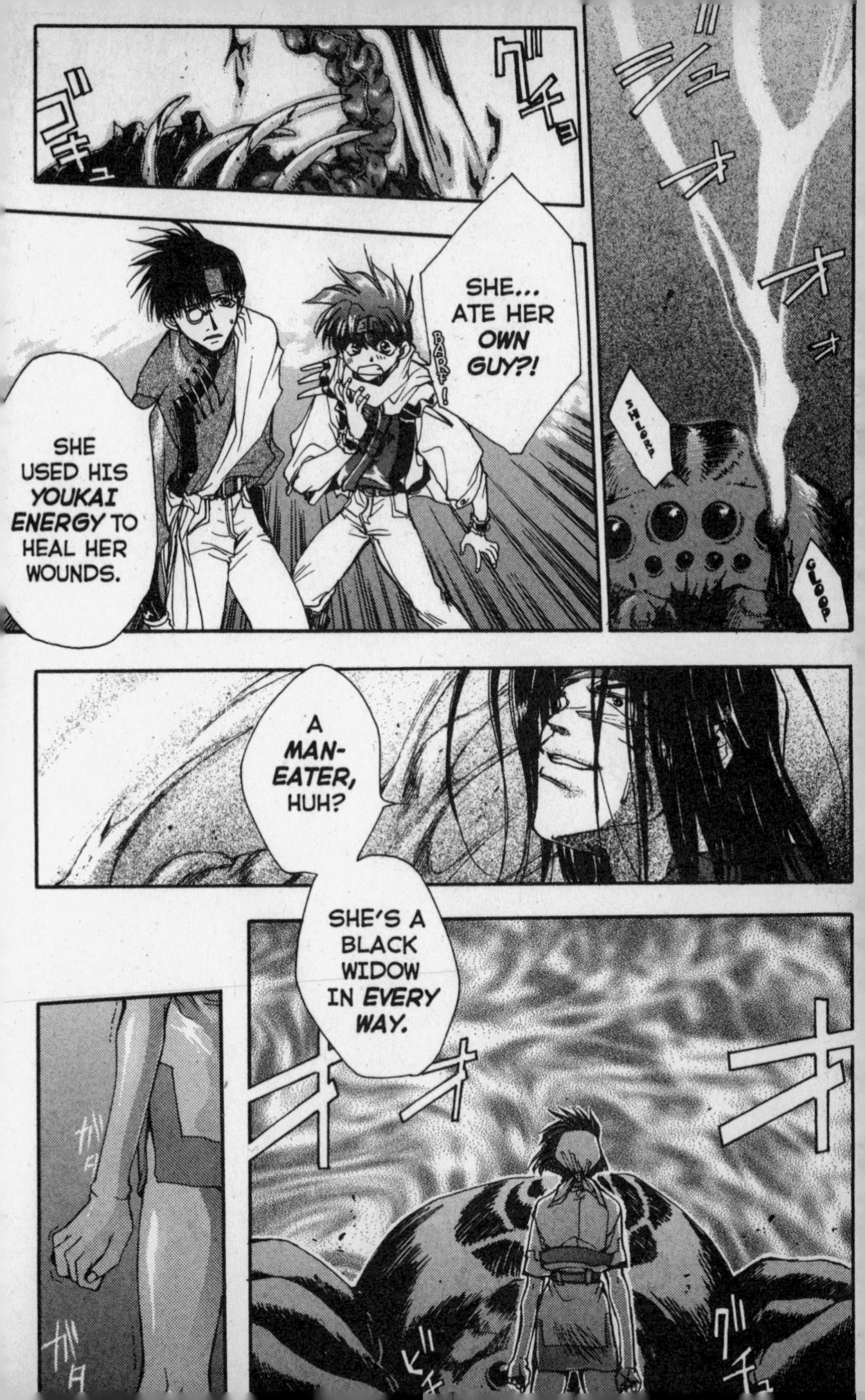
SHLORP
GLOOP
SHE... ATE HER OWN GUY?!
BARF!
SHE USED HIS YOUKAI ENERGY TO HEAL HER WOUNDS.
A MAN-EATER, HUH?
SHE'S A BLACK WIDOW IN EVERY WAY.

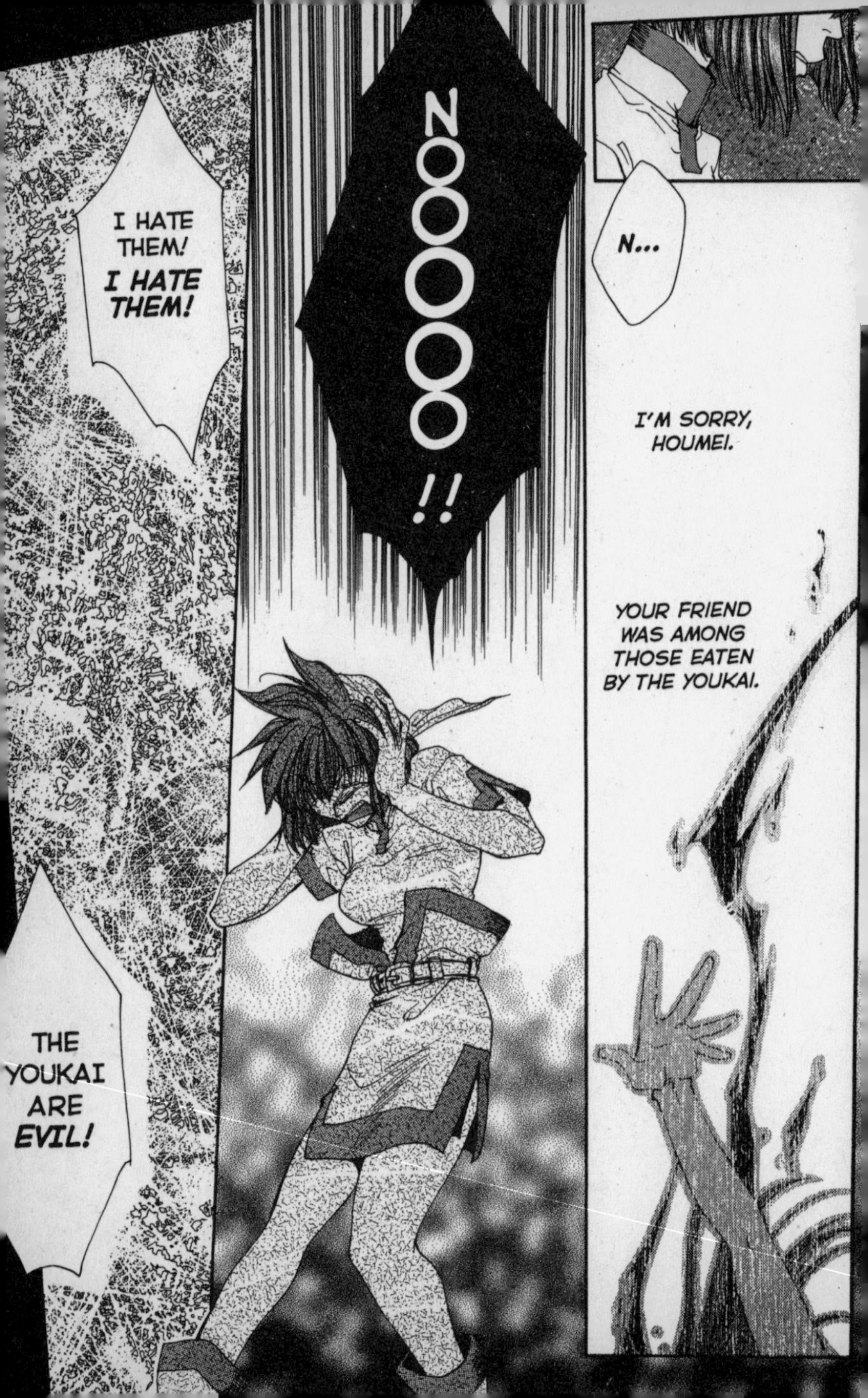
N...
I'M SORRY, HOUMEI.
YOUR FRIEND WAS AMONG THOSE EATEN BY THE YOUKAI.
NOOOOOO!!
I HATE THEM! *I HATE THEM!*
THE YOUKAI ARE *EVIL!*

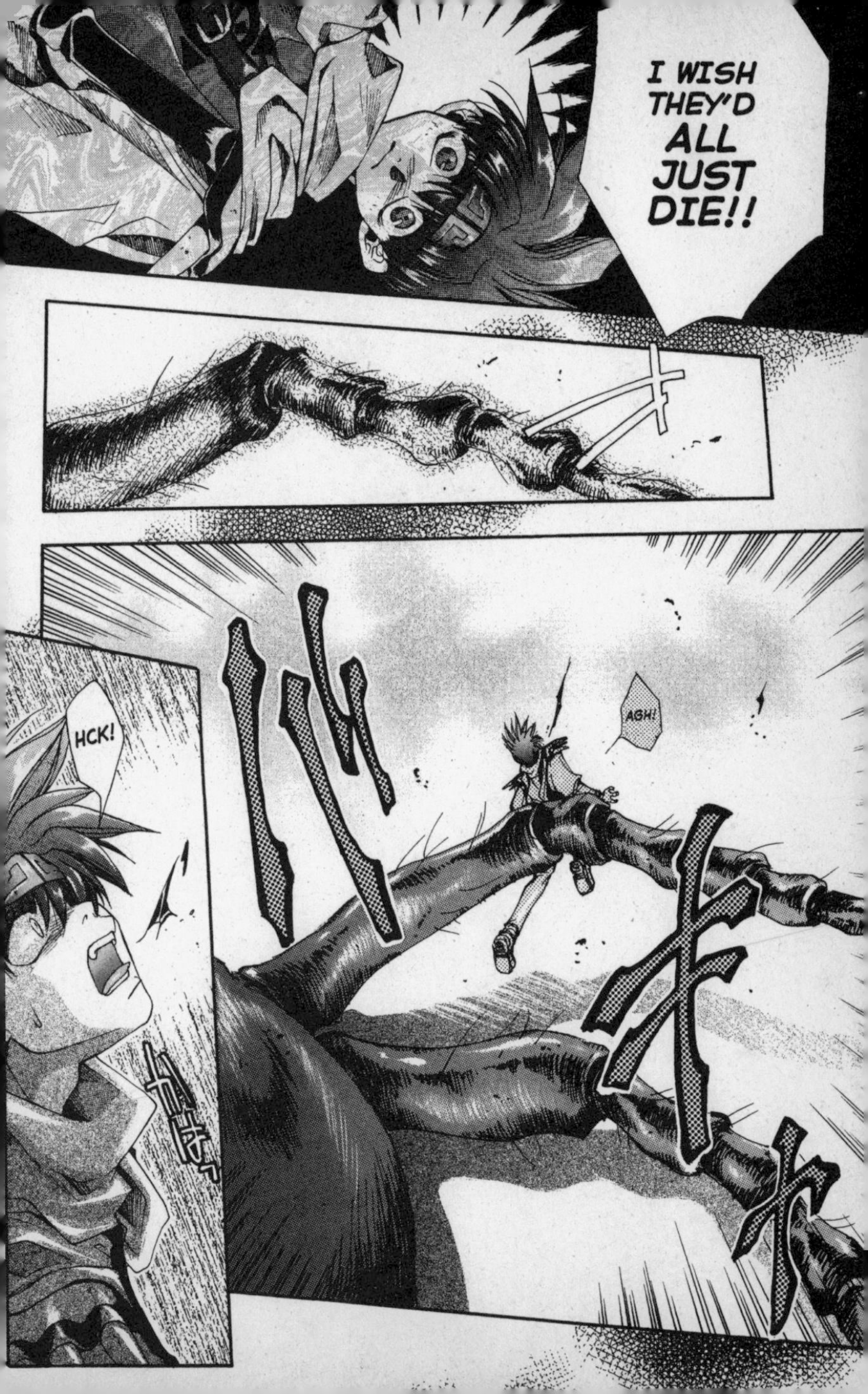
I WISH THEY'D ALL JUST DIE!!
AGH!
HCK!

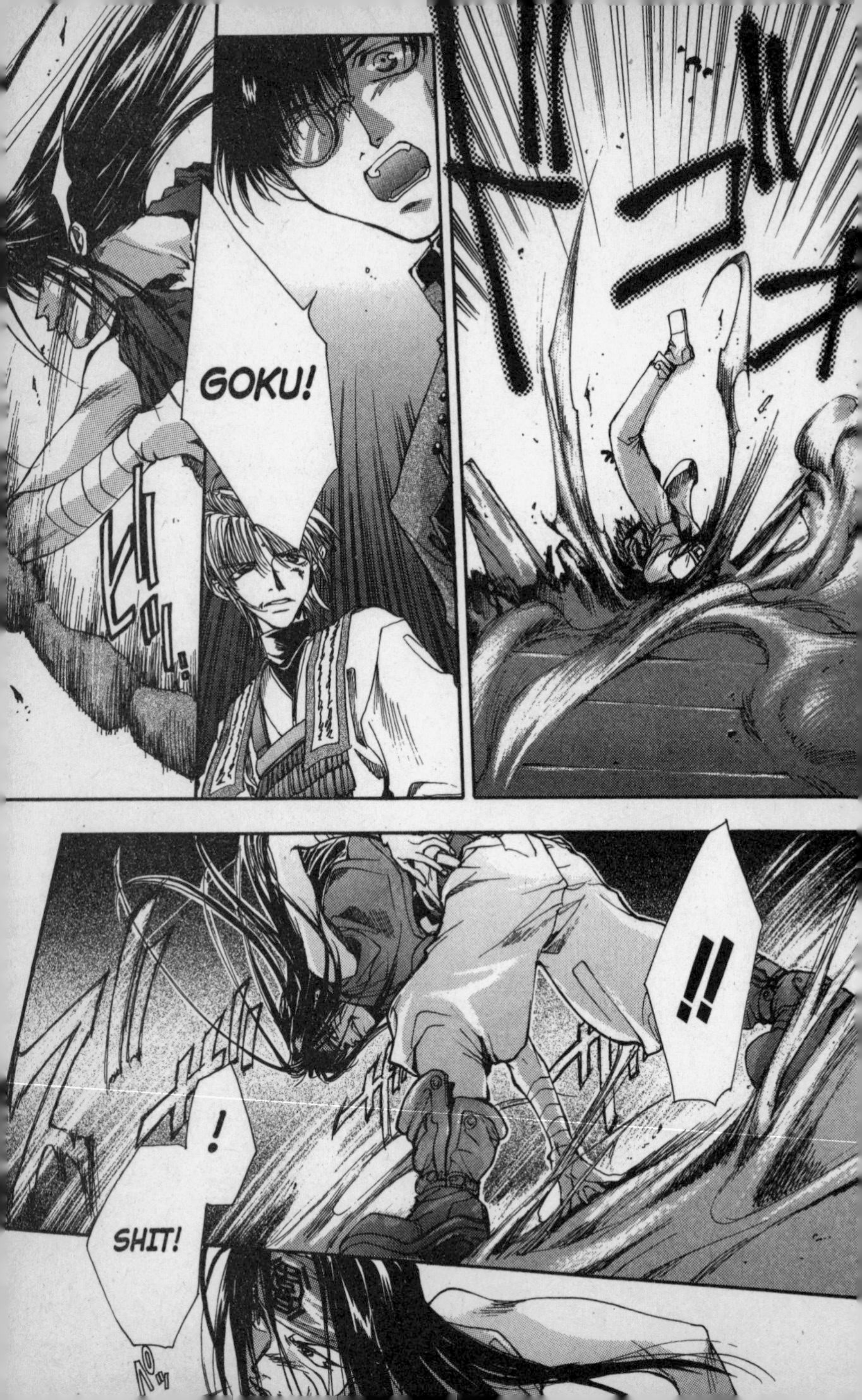
GOKU!
!!
!
SHIT!

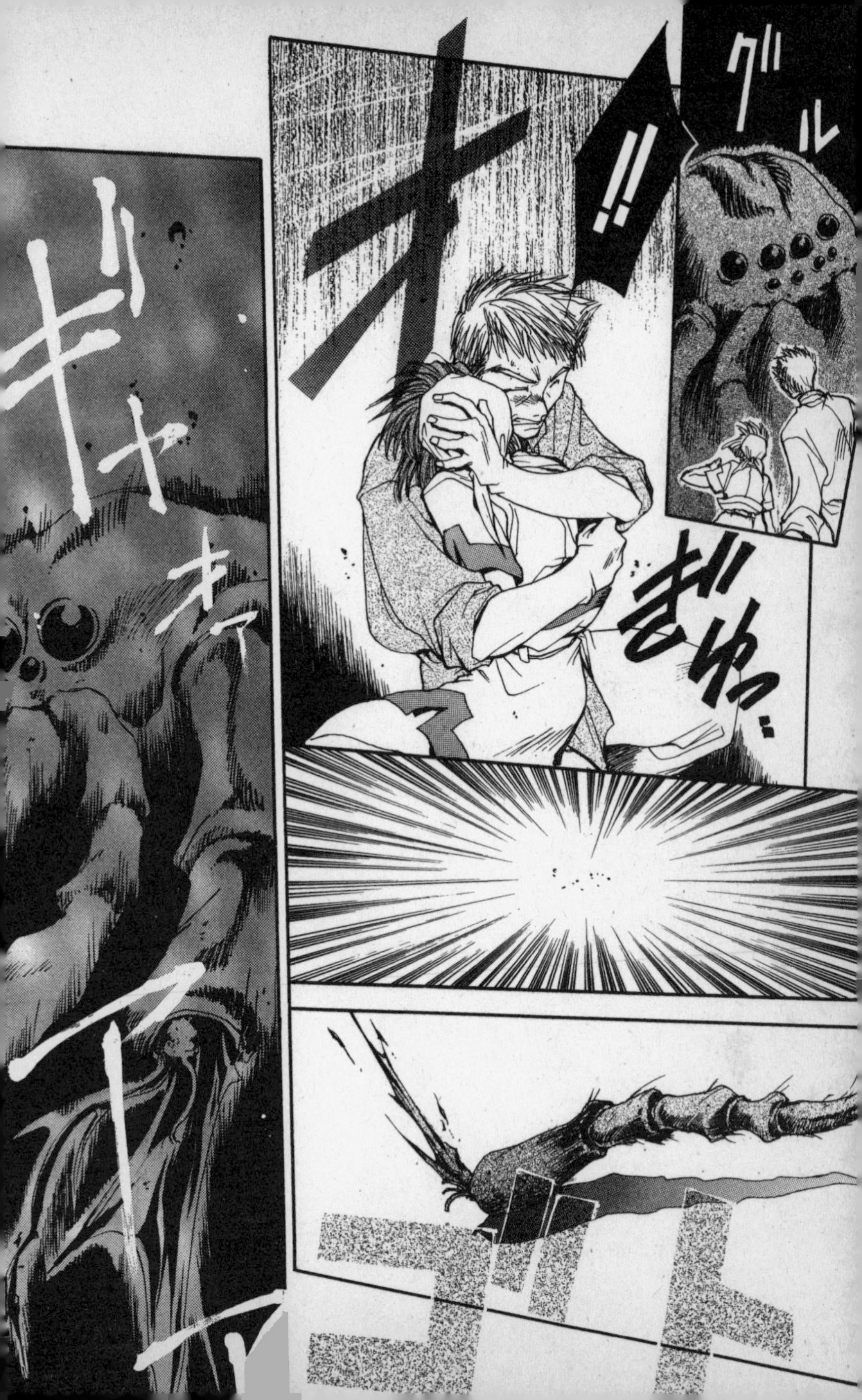
グル
オ!!
ぎゅっ
ゴト

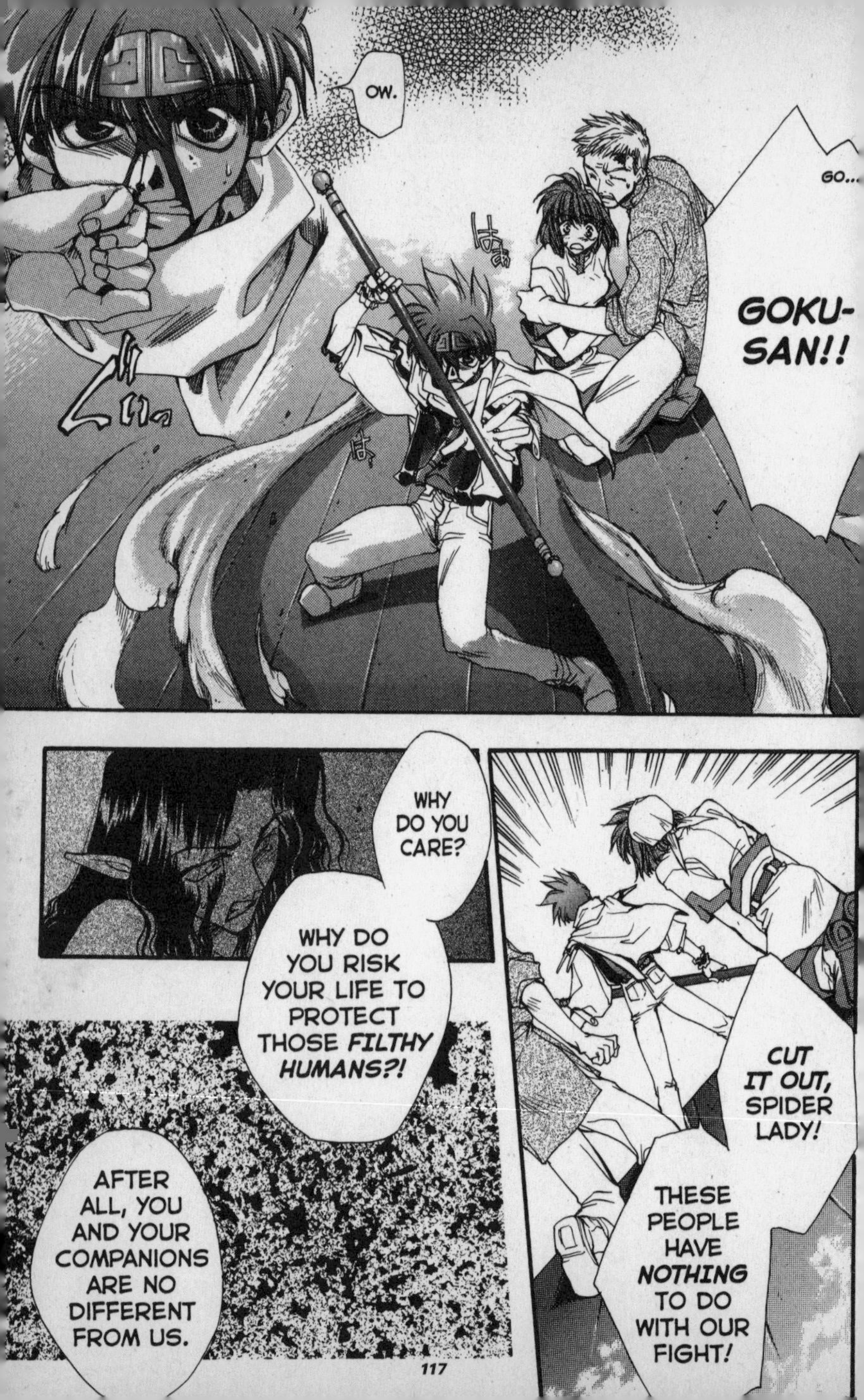
GO...
GOKU-SAN!!
OW.
CUT IT OUT, SPIDER LADY!
THESE PEOPLE HAVE NOTHING TO DO WITH OUR FIGHT!
WHY DO YOU CARE?
WHY DO YOU RISK YOUR LIFE TO PROTECT THOSE FILTHY HUMANS?!
AFTER ALL, YOU AND YOUR COMPANIONS ARE NO DIFFERENT FROM US.

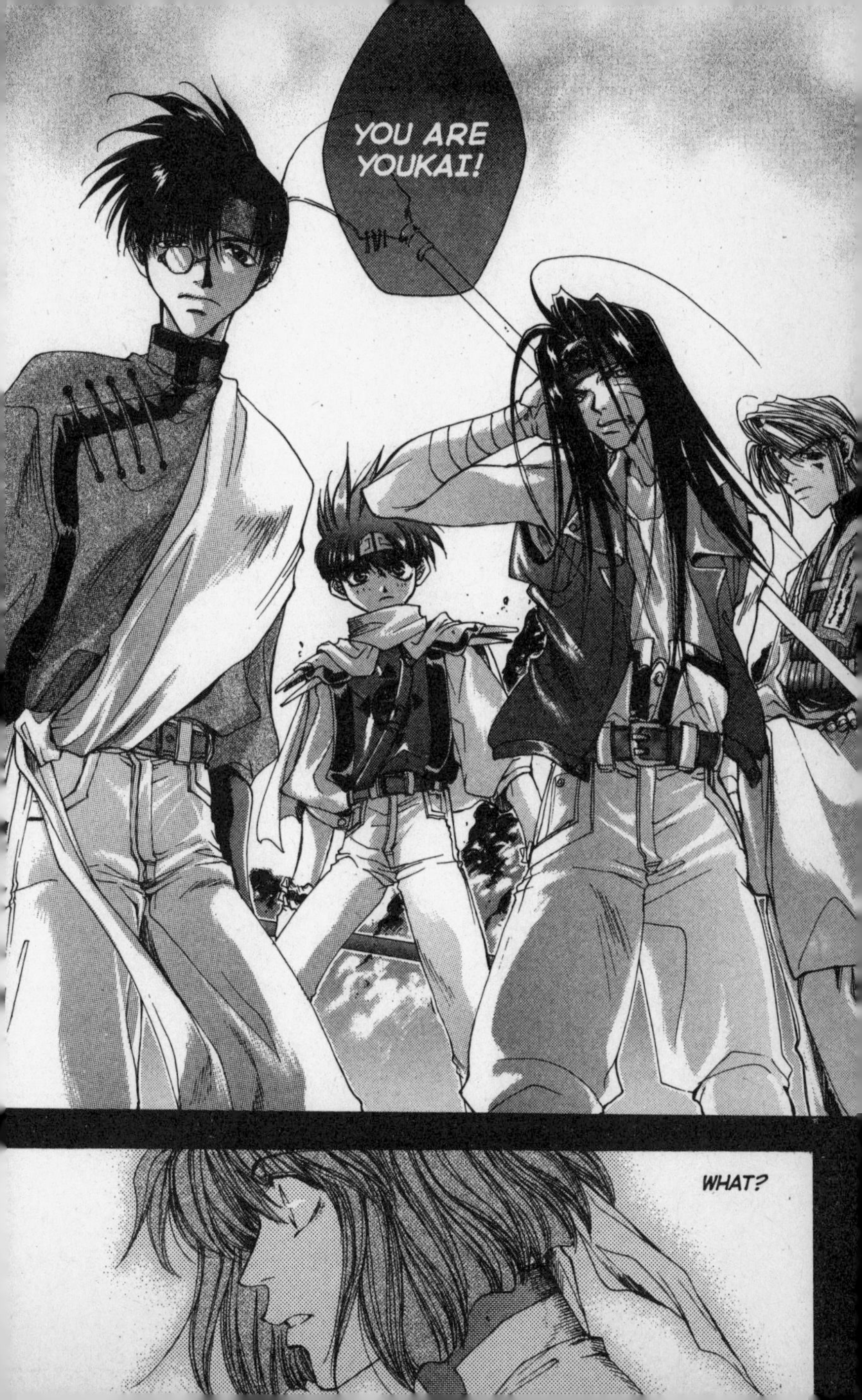
YOU ARE YOUKAI!
WHAT?

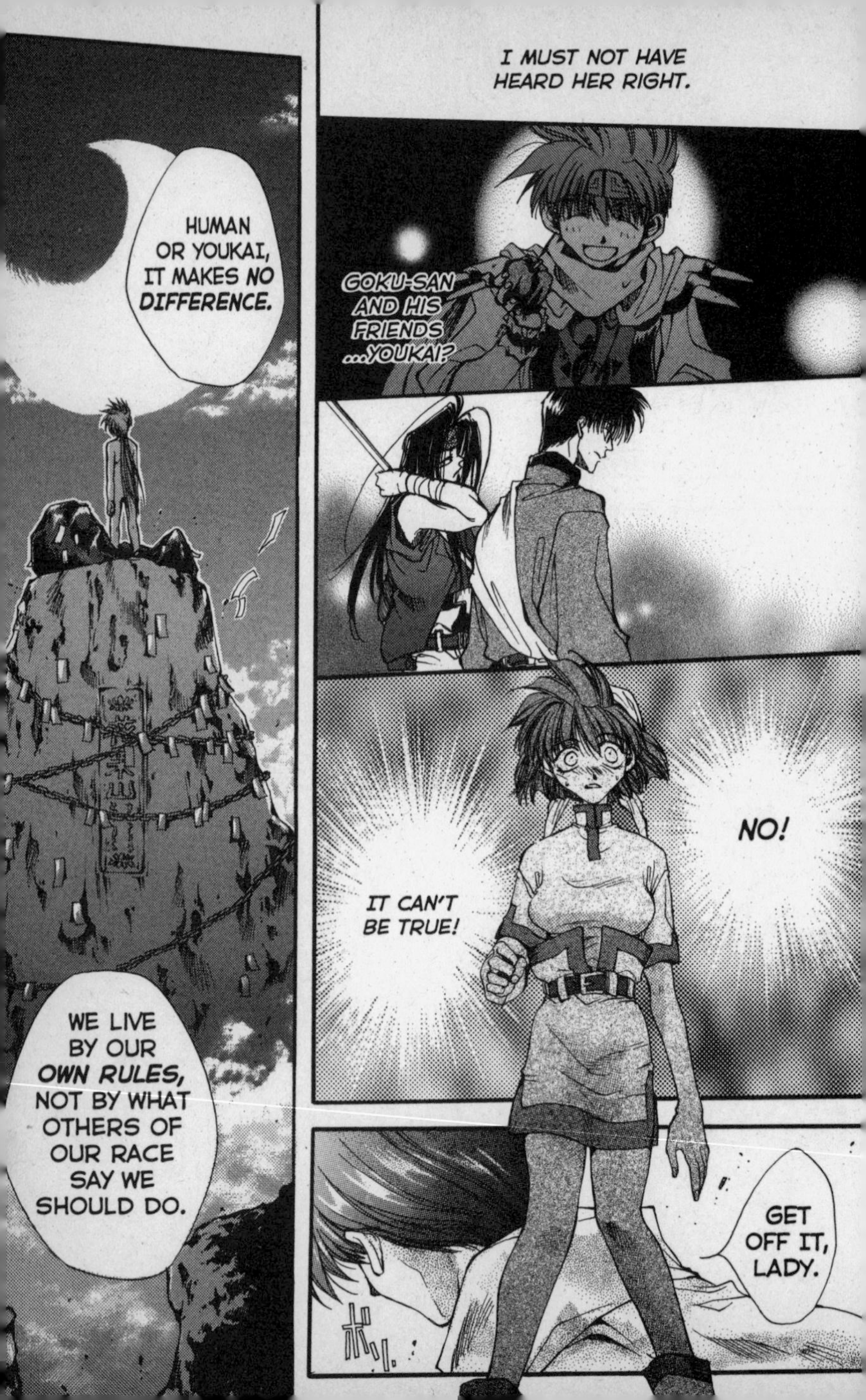
I MUST NOT HAVE HEARD HER RIGHT.
GOKU-SAN AND HIS FRIENDS ...YOUKAI?
NO!
IT CAN'T BE TRUE!
GET OFF IT, LADY.
HUMAN OR YOUKAI, IT MAKES NO DIFFERENCE.
WE LIVE BY OUR OWN RULES, NOT BY WHAT OTHERS OF OUR RACE SAY WE SHOULD DO.

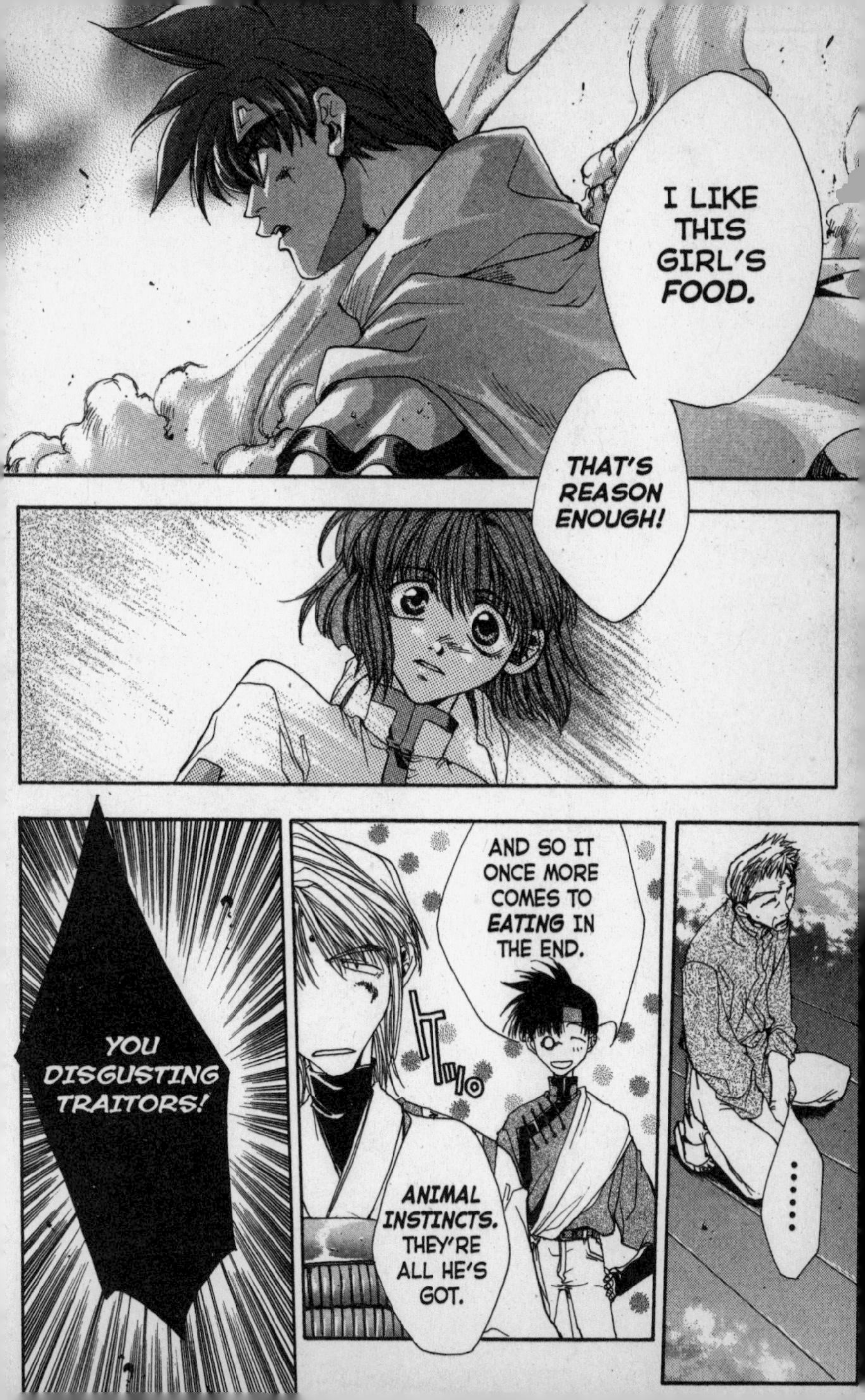
I LIKE THIS GIRL'S FOOD.
THAT'S REASON ENOUGH!
......
AND SO IT ONCE MORE COMES TO EATING IN THE END.
ANIMAL INSTINCTS. THEY'RE ALL HE'S GOT.
YOU DISGUSTING TRAITORS!

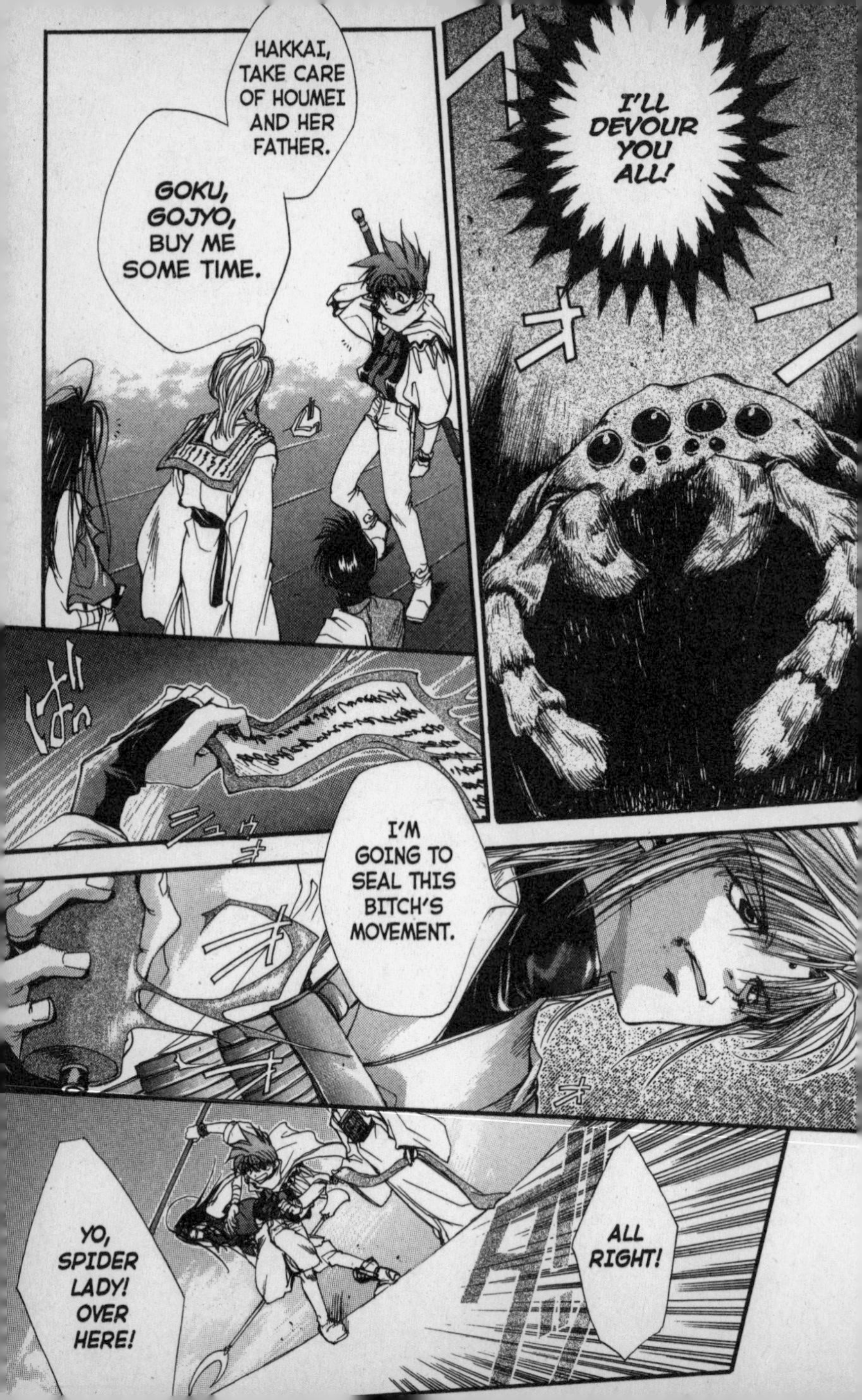

I'LL DEVOUR YOU ALL!
HAKKAI, TAKE CARE OF HOUMEI AND HER FATHER.
GOKU, GOJYO, BUY ME SOME TIME.
I'M GOING TO SEAL THIS BITCH'S MOVEMENT.
ALL RIGHT!
YO, SPIDER LADY! OVER HERE!

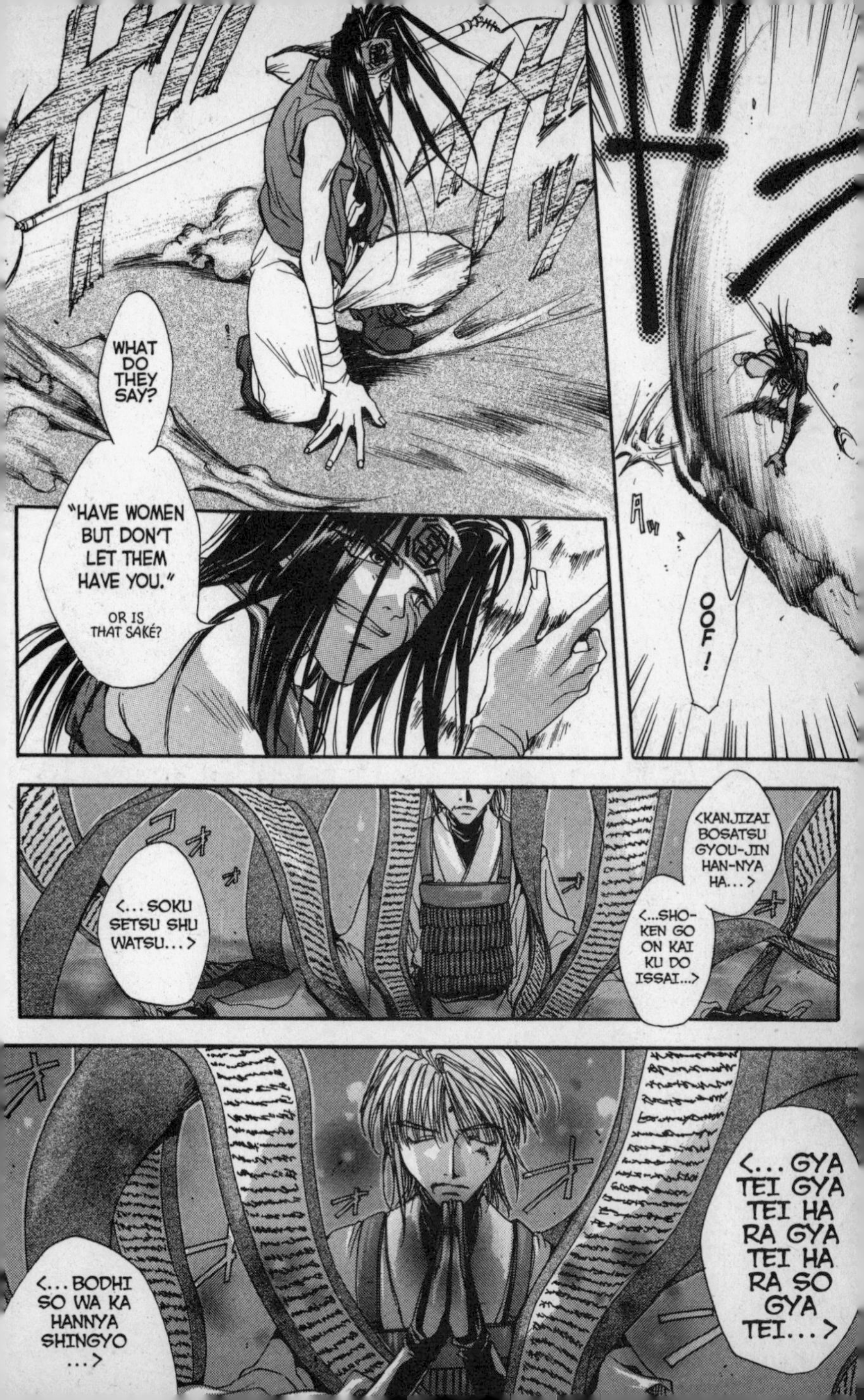
OOF!
WHAT DO THEY SAY?
"HAVE WOMEN BUT DON'T LET THEM HAVE YOU."
OR IS THAT SAKÉ?
<KANJIZAI BOSATSU GYOU-JIN HAN-NYA HA...>
<...SHO-KEN GO ON KAI KU DO ISSAI...>
<...SOKU SETSU SHU WATSU...>
<...GYA TEI GYA TEI HA RA GYA TEI HA RA SO GYA TEI...>
<...BODHI SO WA KA HANNYA SHINGYO ...>

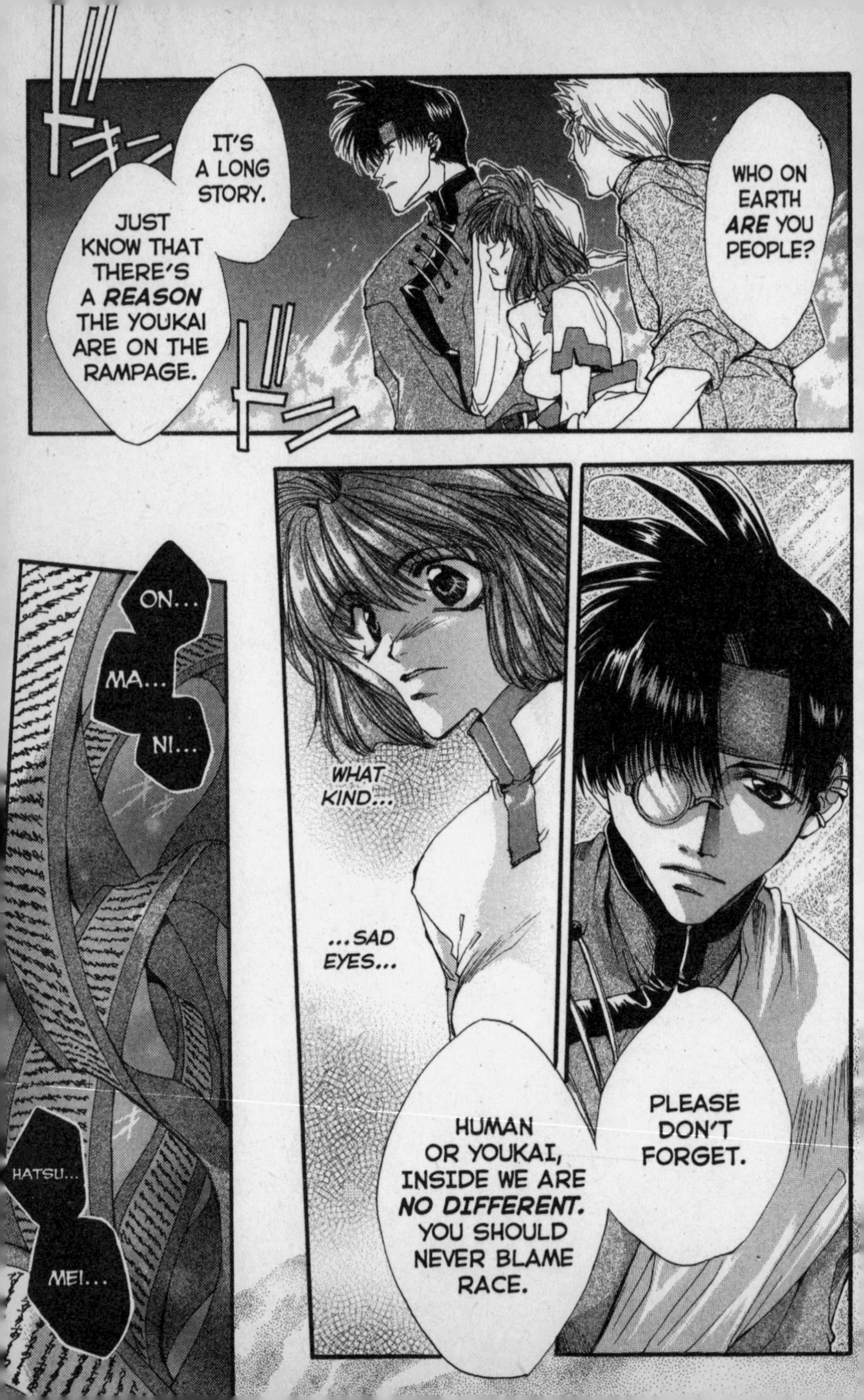
WHO ON EARTH ARE YOU PEOPLE?
IT'S A LONG STORY.
JUST KNOW THAT THERE'S A REASON THE YOUKAI ARE ON THE RAMPAGE.
WHAT KIND...
...SAD EYES...
PLEASE DON'T FORGET.
HUMAN OR YOUKAI, INSIDE WE ARE NO DIFFERENT. YOU SHOULD NEVER BLAME RACE.
ON...
MA...
NI...
HATSU...
MEI...

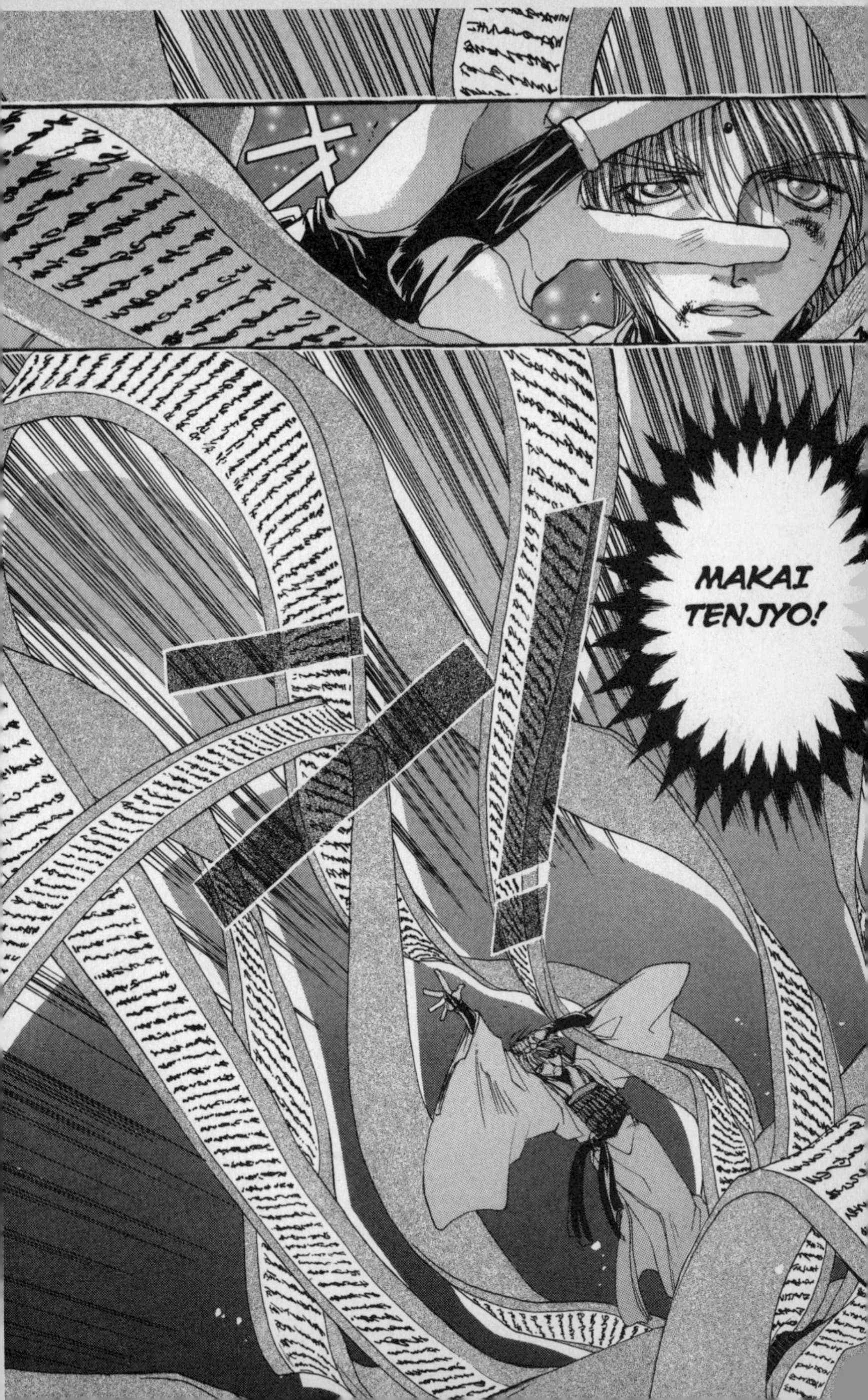
MAKAI
TENJYO!

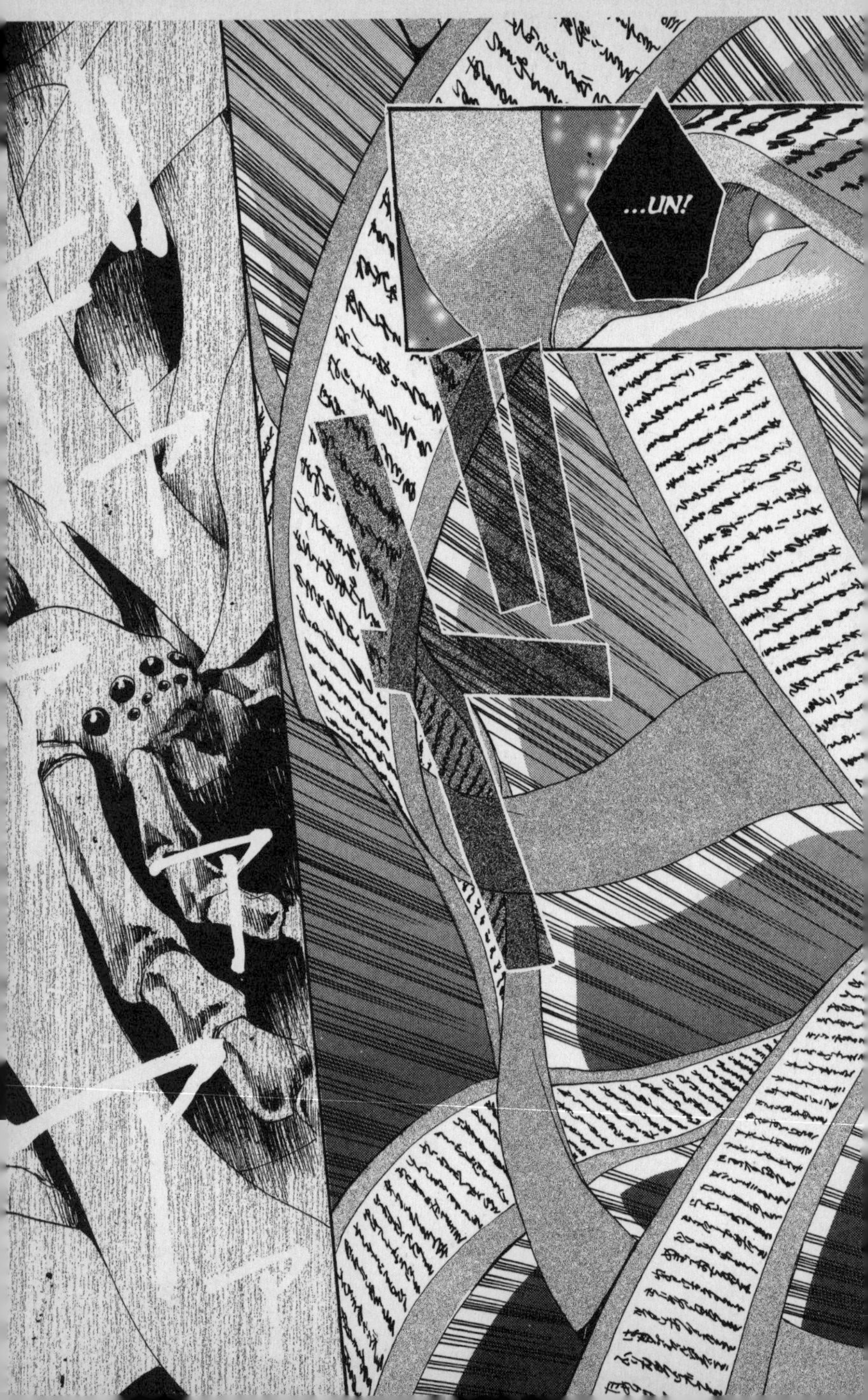
...UN!

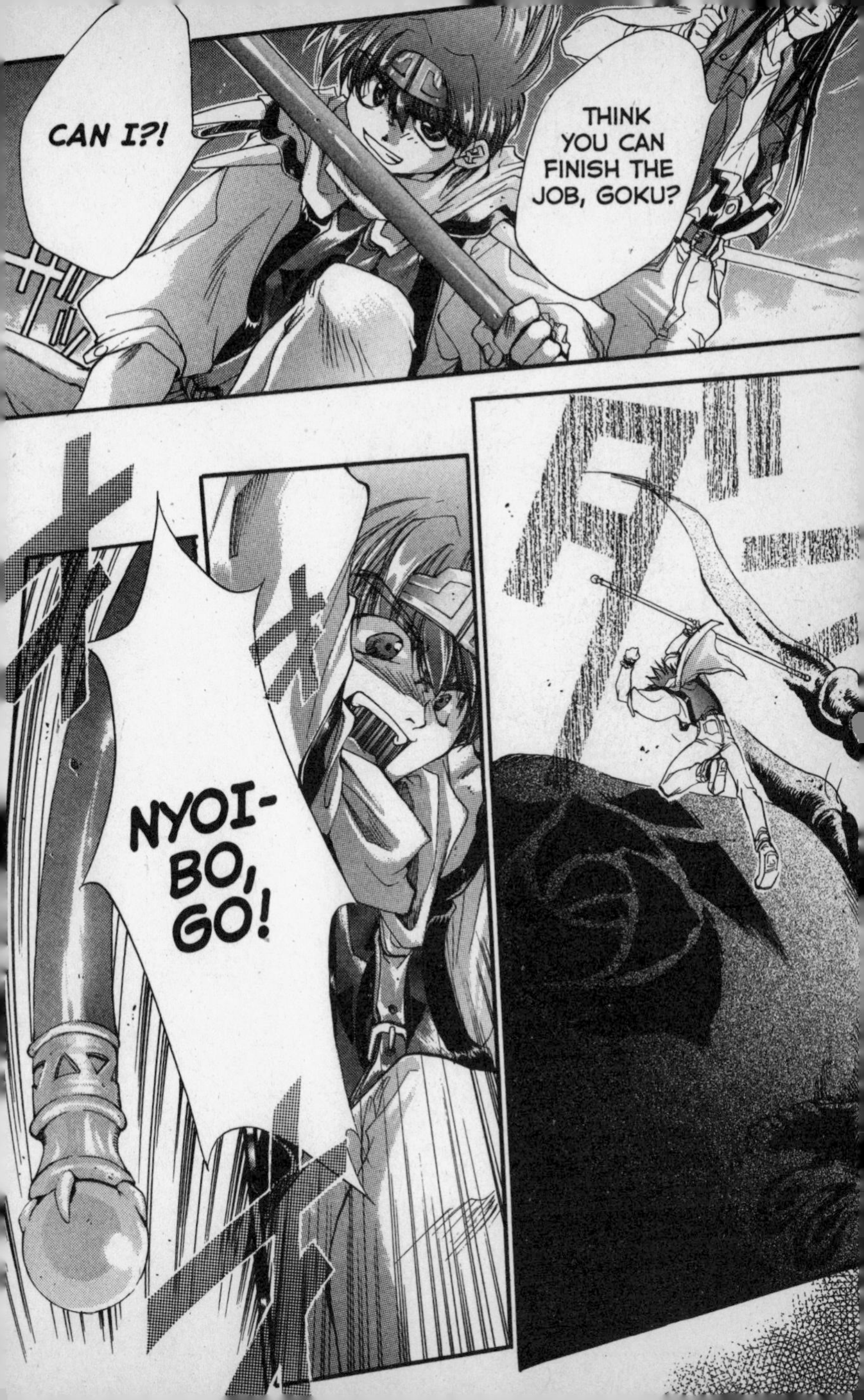
THINK YOU CAN FINISH THE JOB, GOKU?
CAN I?!
NYOI-BO, GO!

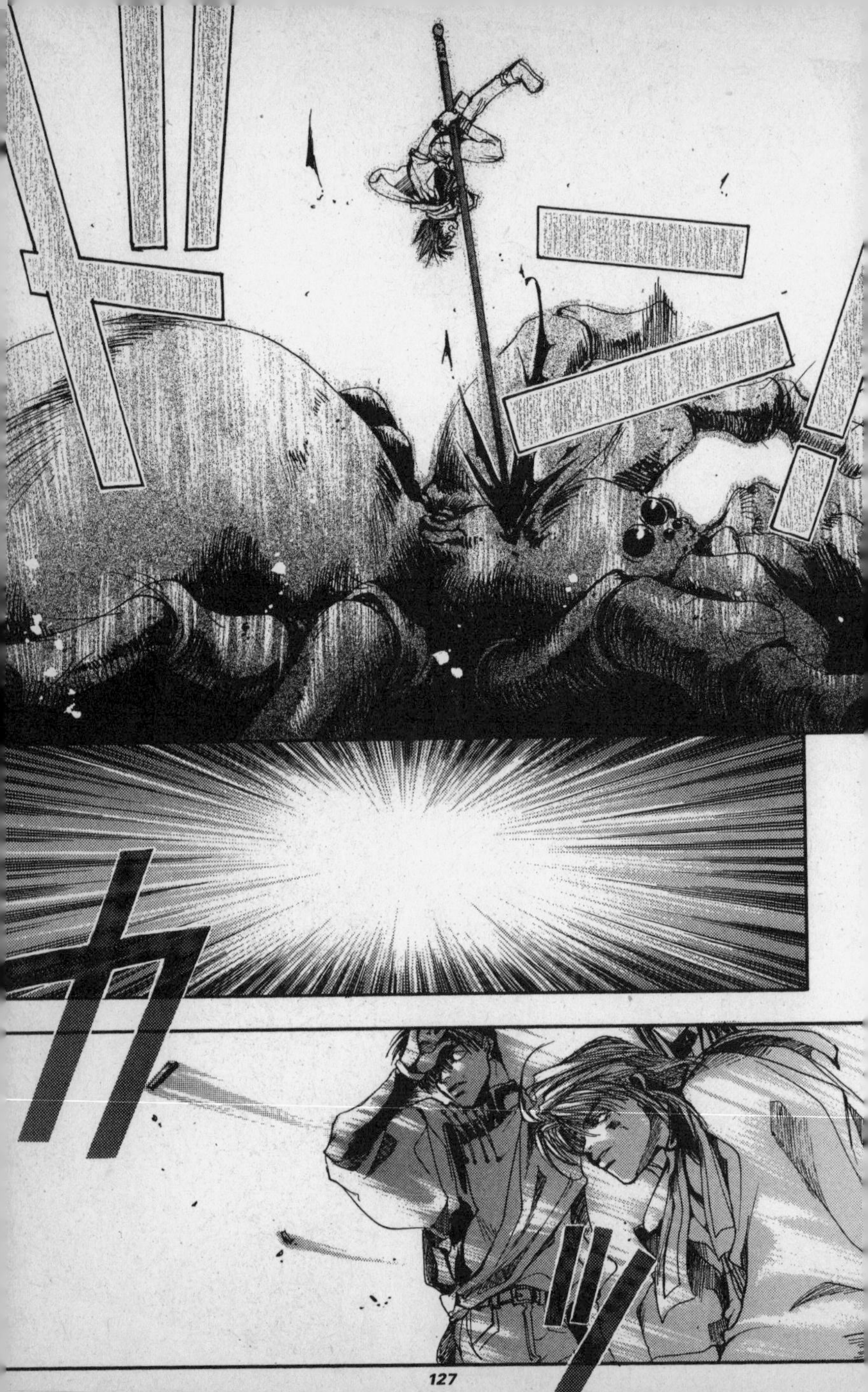

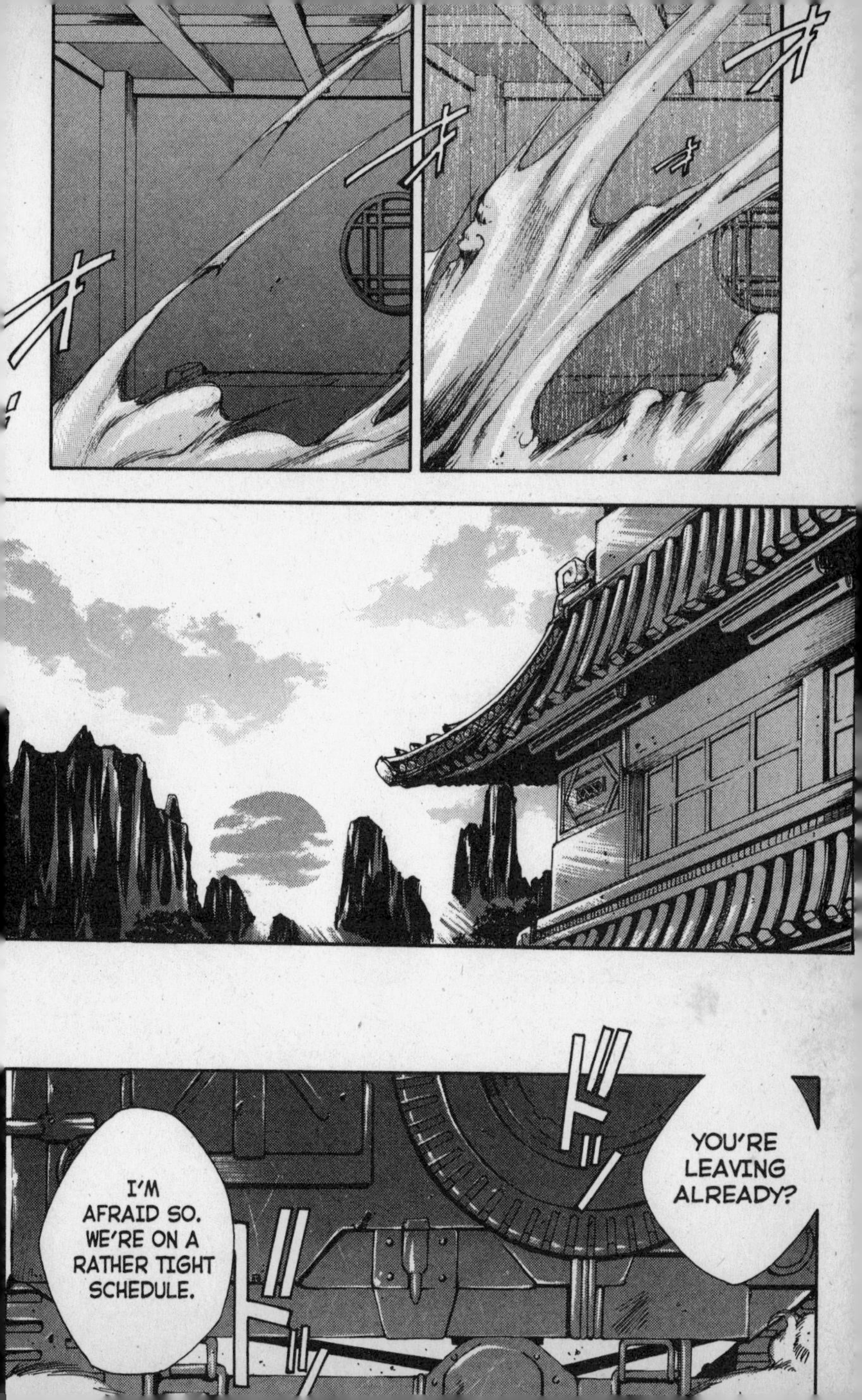
YOU'RE LEAVING ALREADY?
I'M AFRAID SO. WE'RE ON A RATHER TIGHT SCHEDULE.

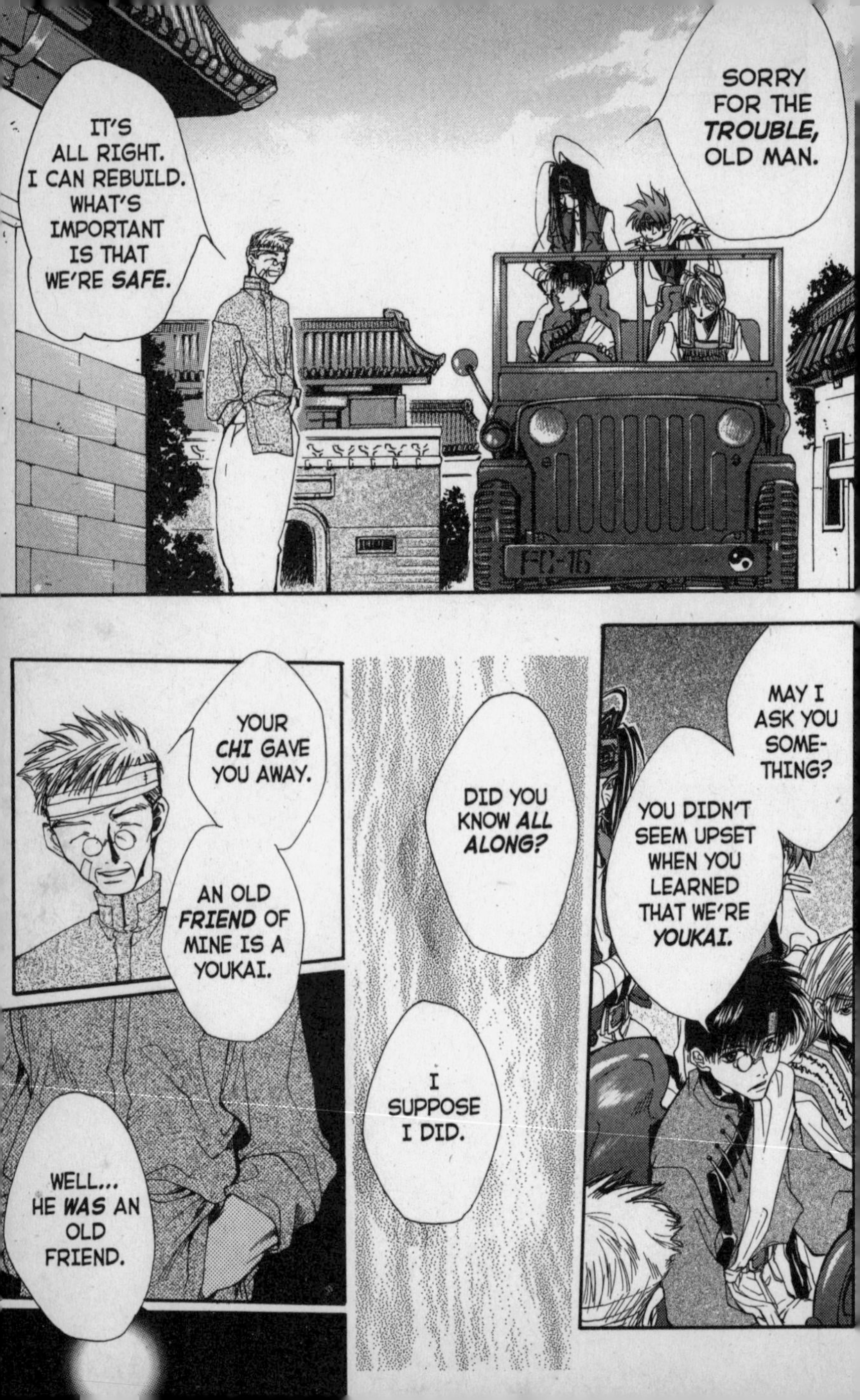
SORRY FOR THE TROUBLE, OLD MAN.
IT'S ALL RIGHT. I CAN REBUILD. WHAT'S IMPORTANT IS THAT WE'RE SAFE.
MAY I ASK YOU SOMETHING?
YOU DIDN'T SEEM UPSET WHEN YOU LEARNED THAT WE'RE YOUKAI.
DID YOU KNOW ALL ALONG?
I SUPPOSE I DID.
YOUR CHI GAVE YOU AWAY.
AN OLD FRIEND OF MINE IS A YOUKAI.
WELL... HE WAS AN OLD FRIEND.

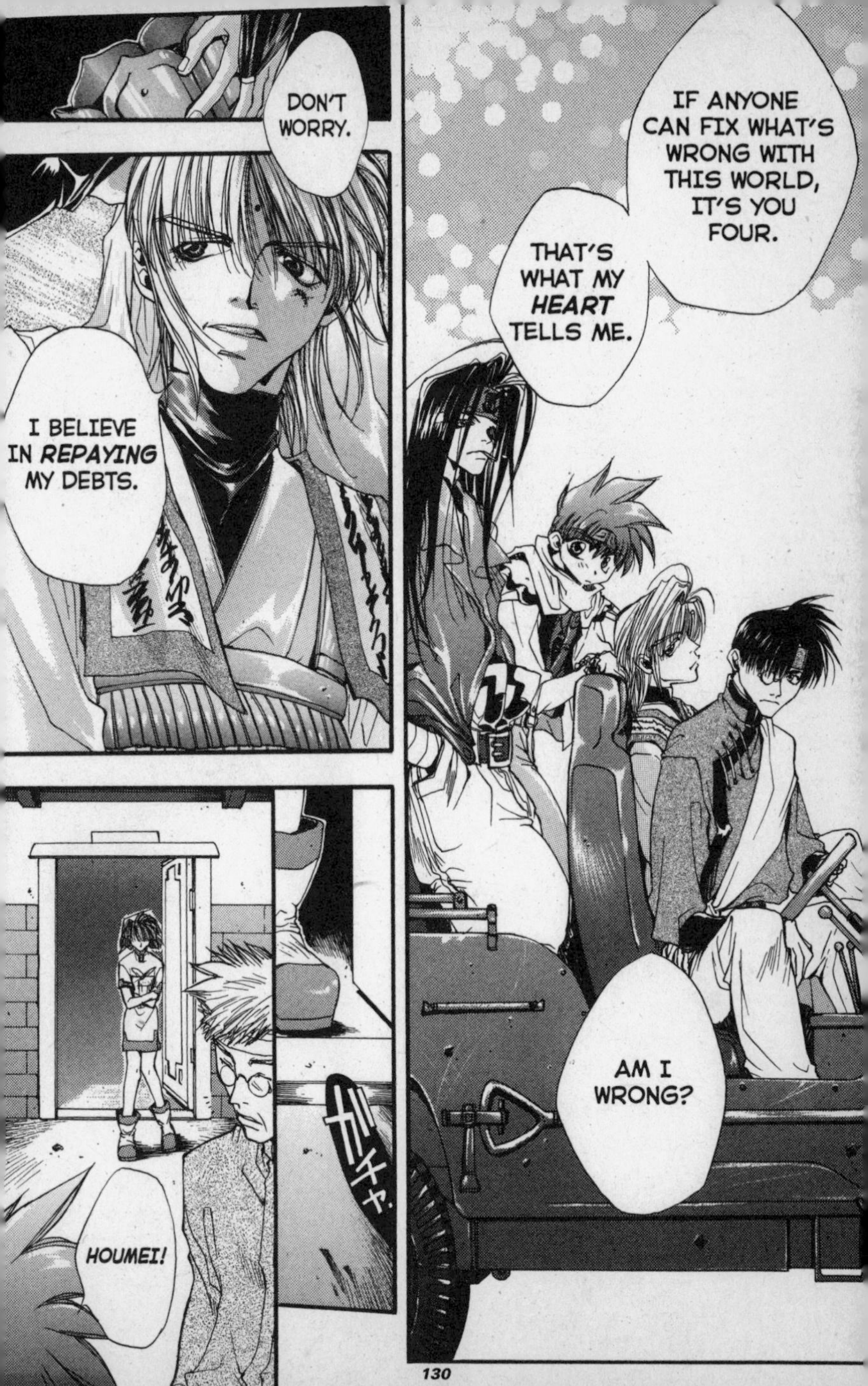
IF ANYONE CAN FIX WHAT'S WRONG WITH THIS WORLD, IT'S YOU FOUR.
THAT'S WHAT MY *HEART* TELLS ME.
AM I WRONG?
DON'T WORRY.
I BELIEVE IN *REPAYING* MY DEBTS.
ガチャ
HOUMEI!

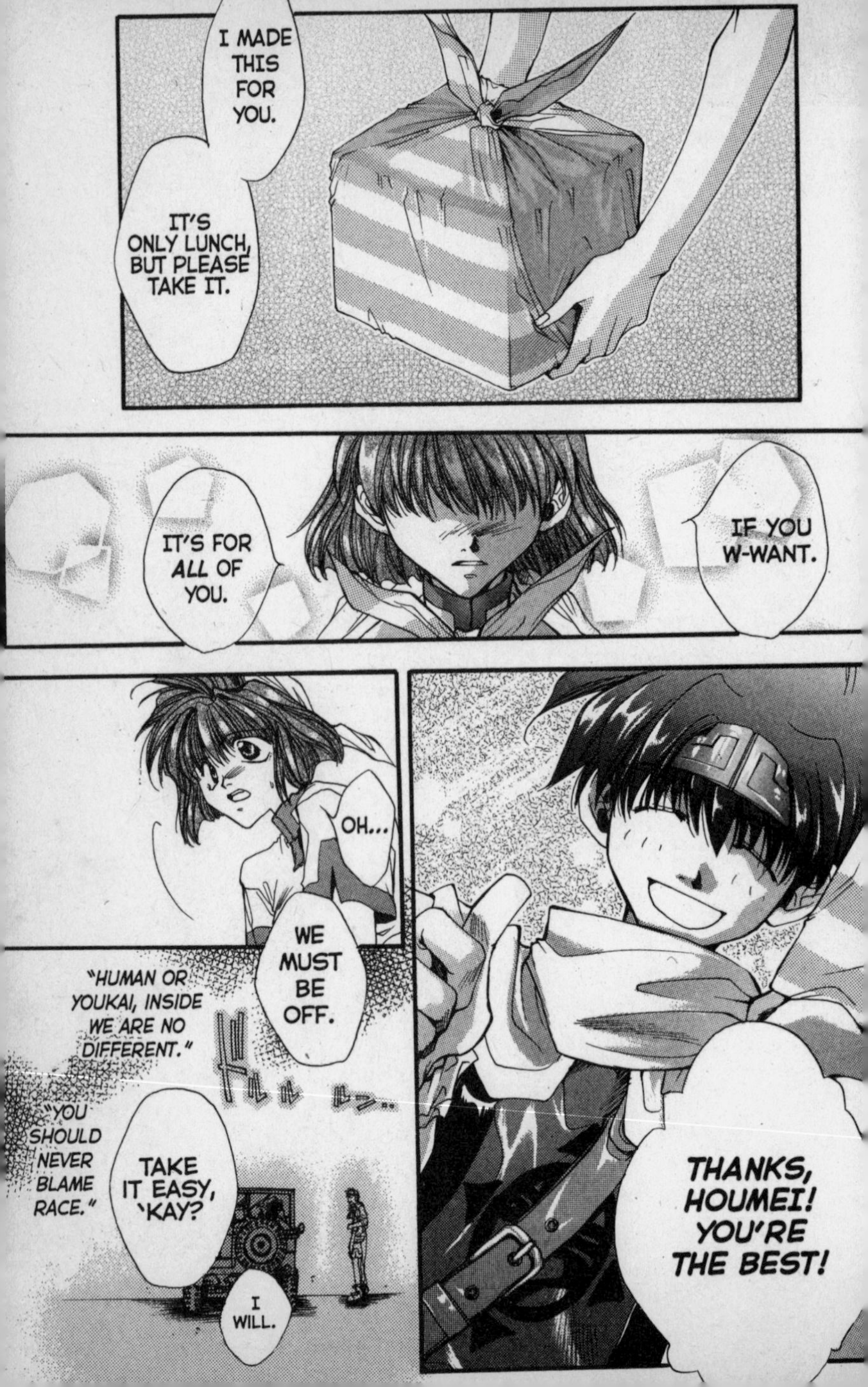
I MADE THIS FOR YOU.
IT'S ONLY LUNCH, BUT PLEASE TAKE IT.
IF YOU W-WANT.
IT'S FOR *ALL* OF YOU.
THANKS, HOUMEI! YOU'RE THE BEST!
OH...
WE MUST BE OFF.
"HUMAN OR YOUKAI, INSIDE WE ARE NO DIFFERENT."
TAKE IT EASY, 'KAY?
"YOU SHOULD NEVER BLAME RACE."
I WILL.

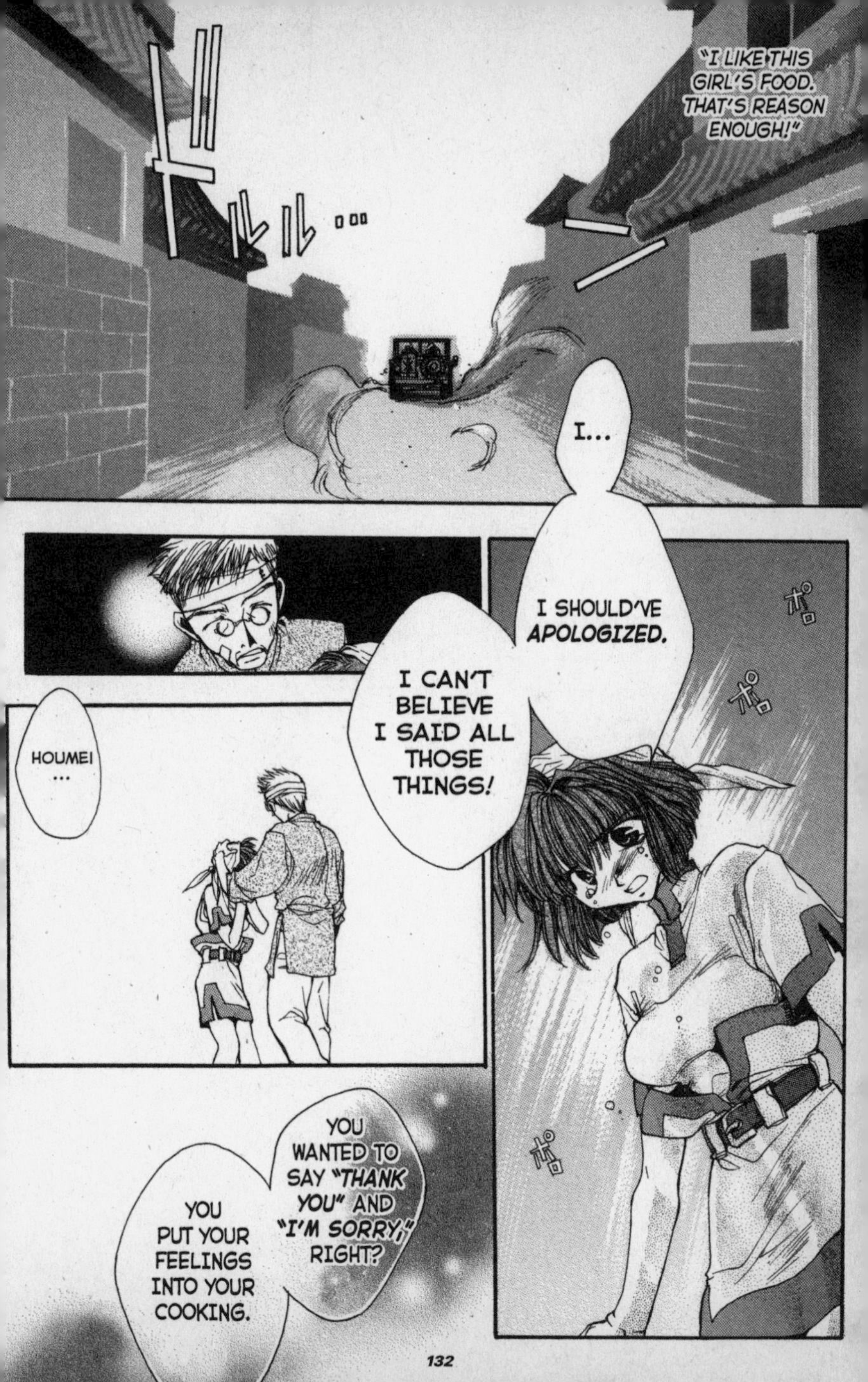
"I LIKE THIS GIRL'S FOOD. THAT'S REASON ENOUGH!"
I...
I SHOULD'VE *APOLOGIZED.*
I CAN'T BELIEVE I SAID ALL THOSE THINGS!
HOUMEI ...
YOU WANTED TO SAY "*THANK YOU*" AND "*I'M SORRY,*" RIGHT?
YOU PUT YOUR FEELINGS INTO YOUR COOKING.

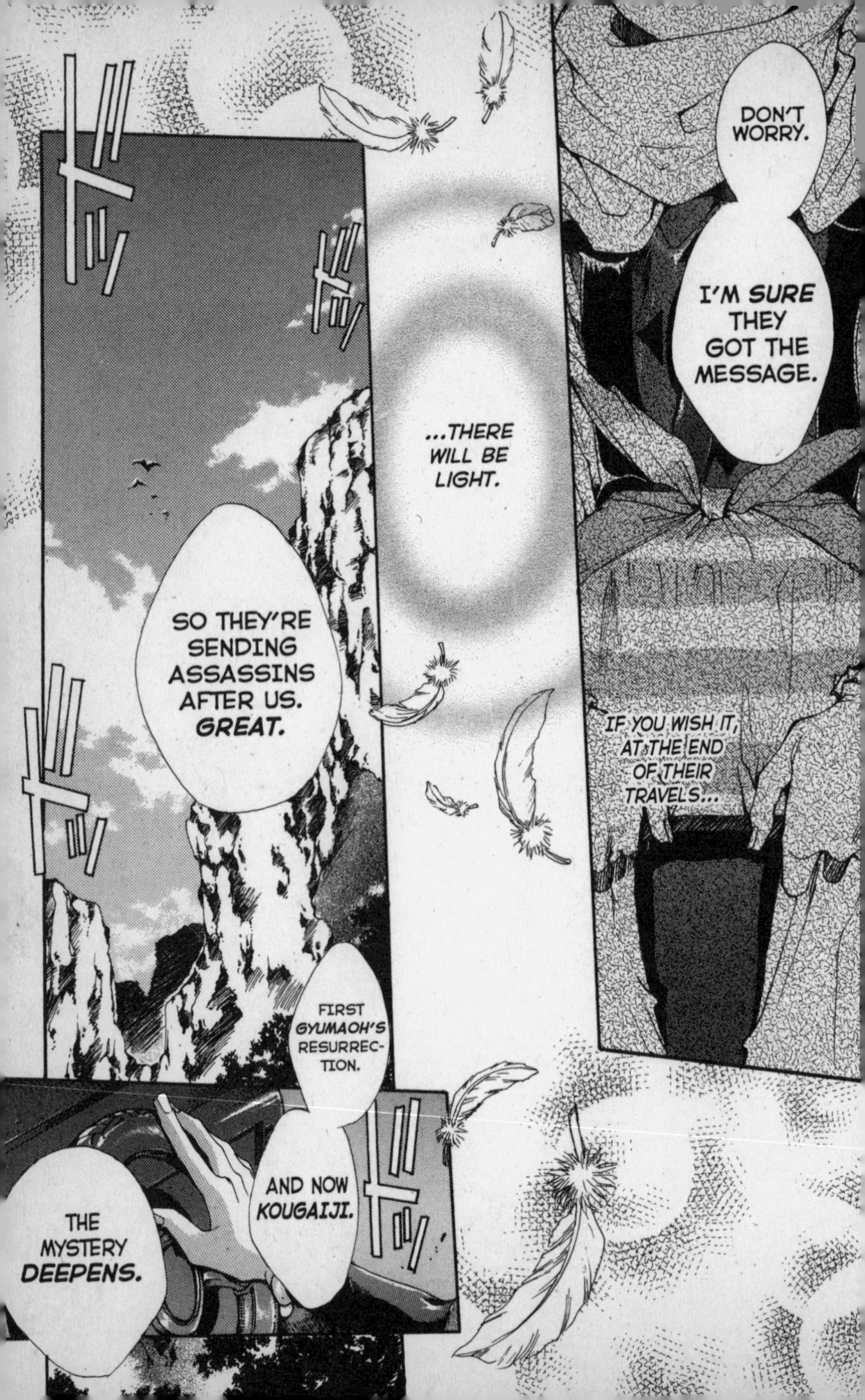
DON'T WORRY.
I'M *SURE* THEY GOT THE MESSAGE.
IF YOU WISH IT, AT THE END OF THEIR TRAVELS...
...THERE WILL BE LIGHT.
SO THEY'RE SENDING ASSASSINS AFTER US. *GREAT.*
FIRST *GYUMAOH'S* RESURREC-TION.
AND NOW *KOUGAIJI.*
THE MYSTERY *DEEPENS.*

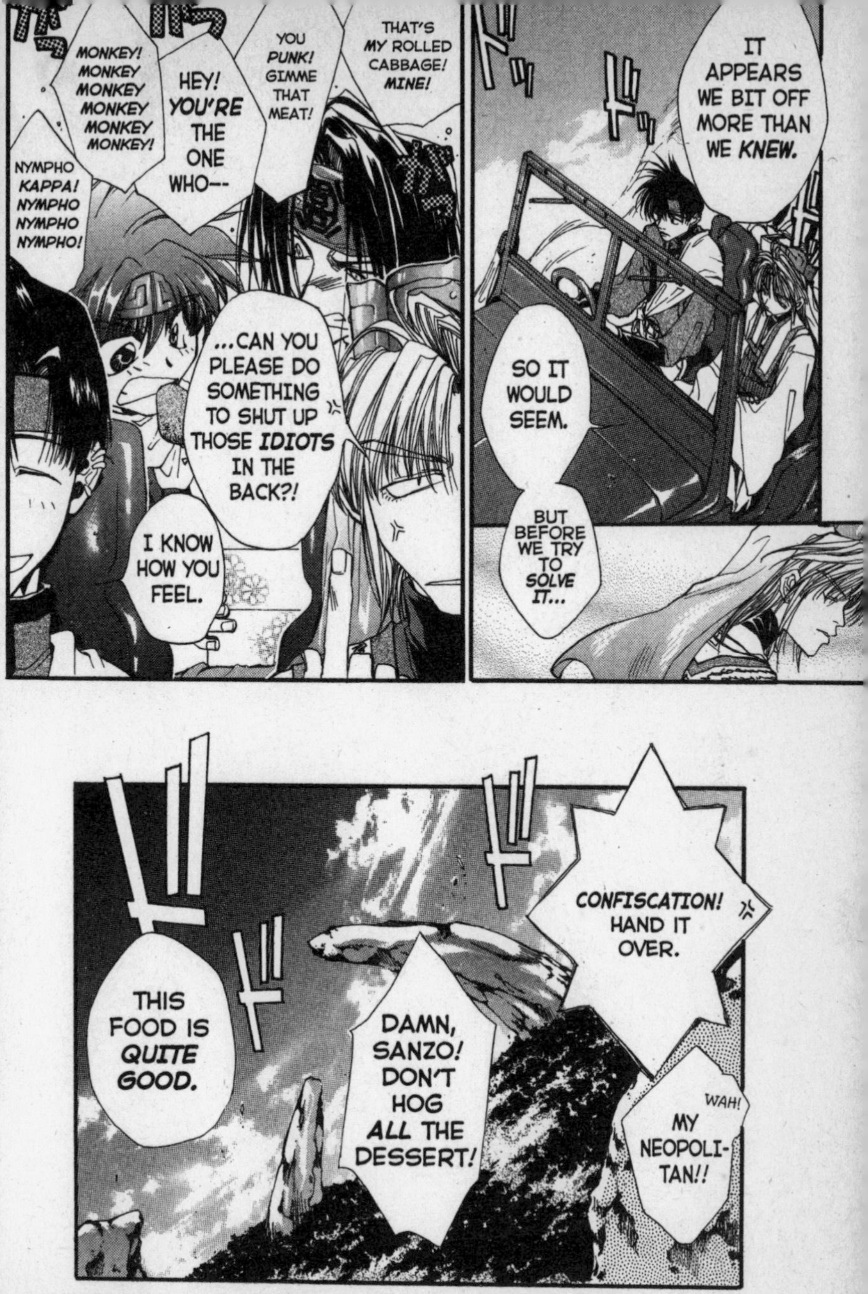
IT APPEARS WE BIT OFF MORE THAN WE KNEW.
SO IT WOULD SEEM.
BUT BEFORE WE TRY TO SOLVE IT...
THAT'S MY ROLLED CABBAGE! MINE!
YOU PUNK! GIMME THAT MEAT!
HEY! YOU'RE THE ONE WHO--
MONKEY! MONKEY MONKEY MONKEY MONKEY MONKEY!
NYMPHO KAPPA! NYMPHO NYMPHO NYMPHO!
...CAN YOU PLEASE DO SOMETHING TO SHUT UP THOSE IDIOTS IN THE BACK?!
I KNOW HOW YOU FEEL.
CONFISCATION! HAND IT OVER.
WAH!
MY NEOPOLITAN!!
DAMN, SANZO! DON'T HOG ALL THE DESSERT!
THIS FOOD IS QUITE GOOD.

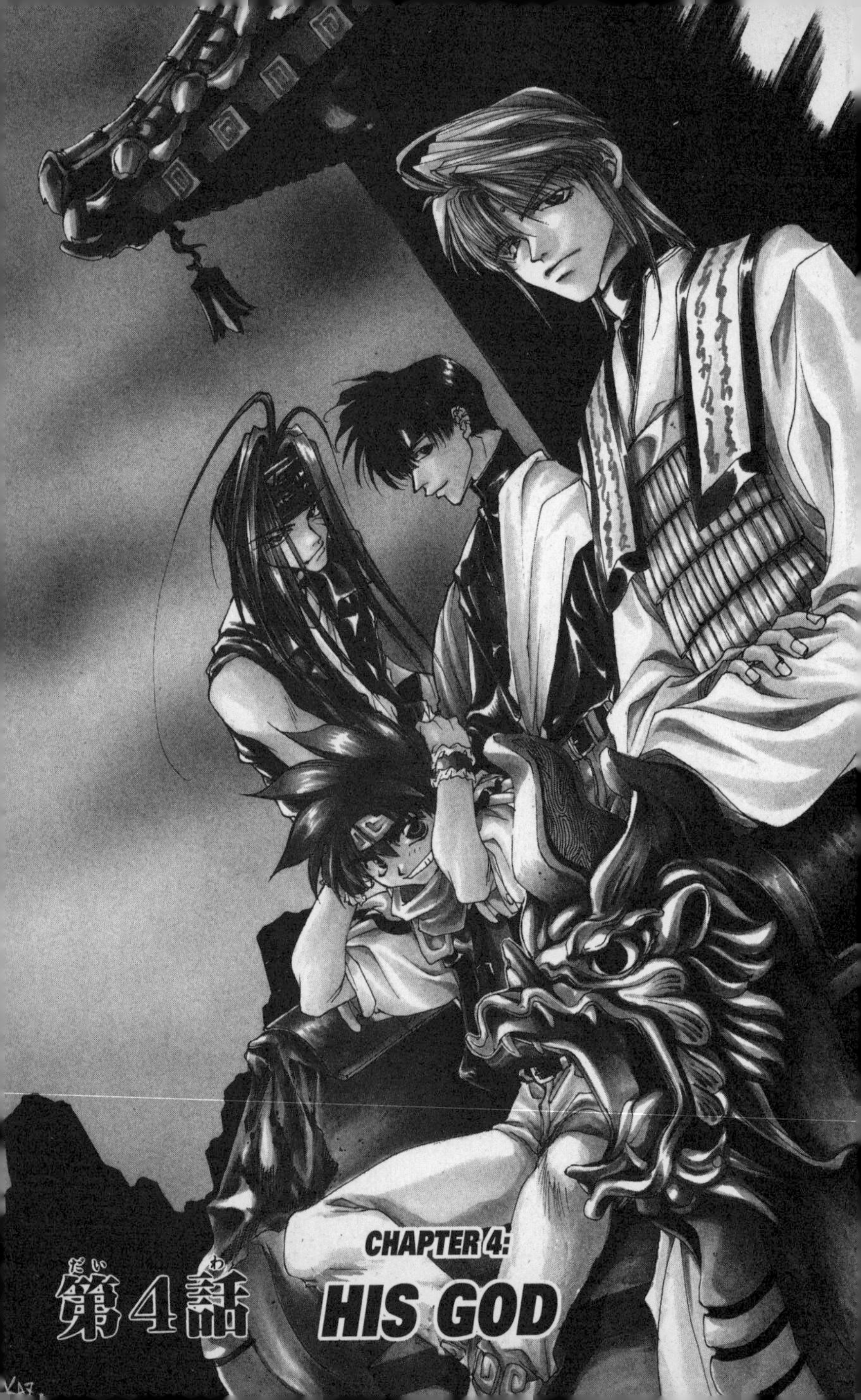
第4話
CHAPTER 4:
HIS GOD

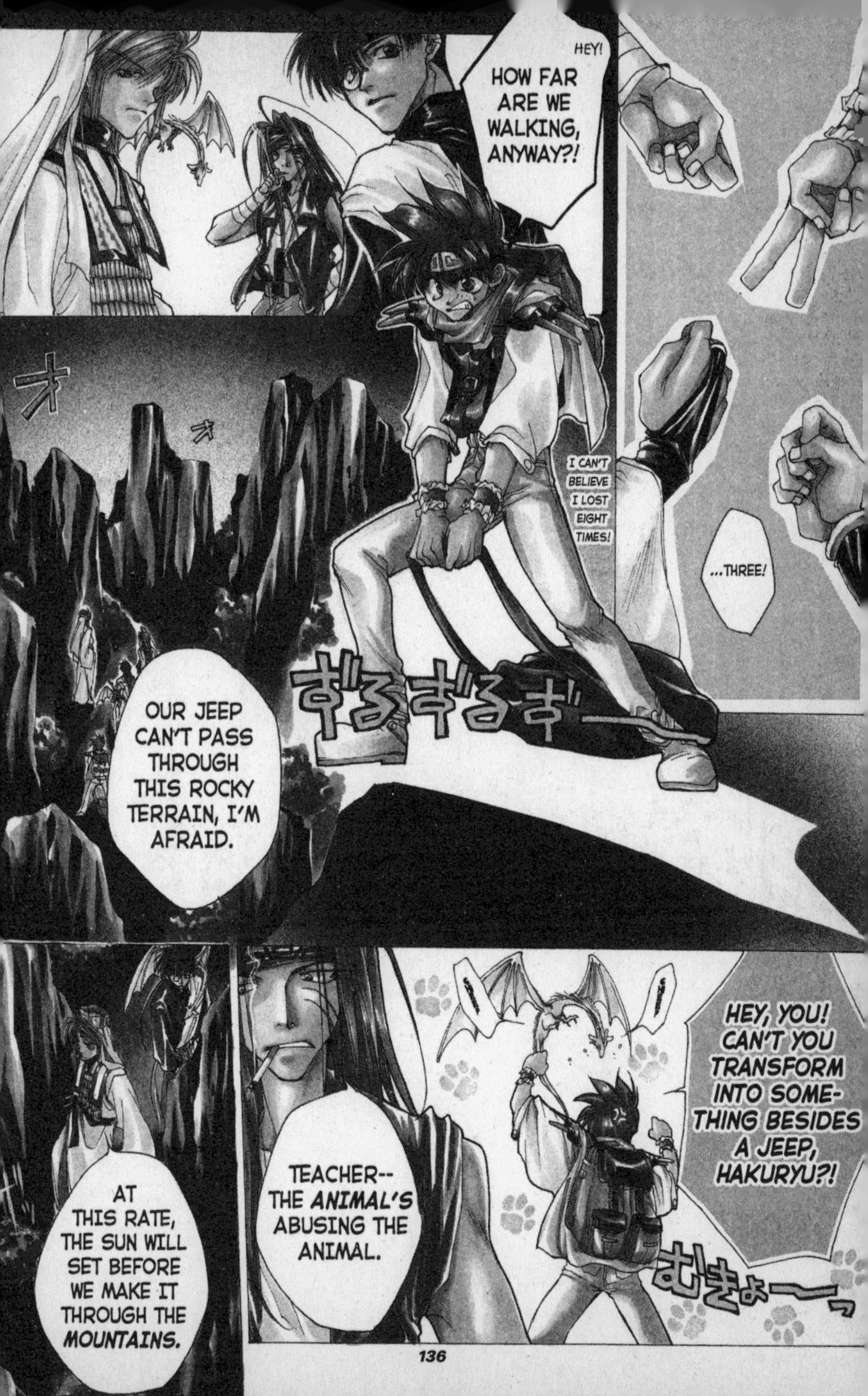
...THREE!
HEY!
HOW FAR ARE WE WALKING, ANYWAY?!
I CAN'T BELIEVE I LOST EIGHT TIMES!
ずるずるず—
OUR JEEP CAN'T PASS THROUGH THIS ROCKY TERRAIN, I'M AFRAID.
HEY, YOU! CAN'T YOU TRANSFORM INTO SOME-THING BESIDES A JEEP, HAKURYU?!
むきょー
TEACHER-- THE *ANIMAL'S* ABUSING THE ANIMAL.
AT THIS RATE, THE SUN WILL SET BEFORE WE MAKE IT THROUGH THE *MOUNTAINS.*

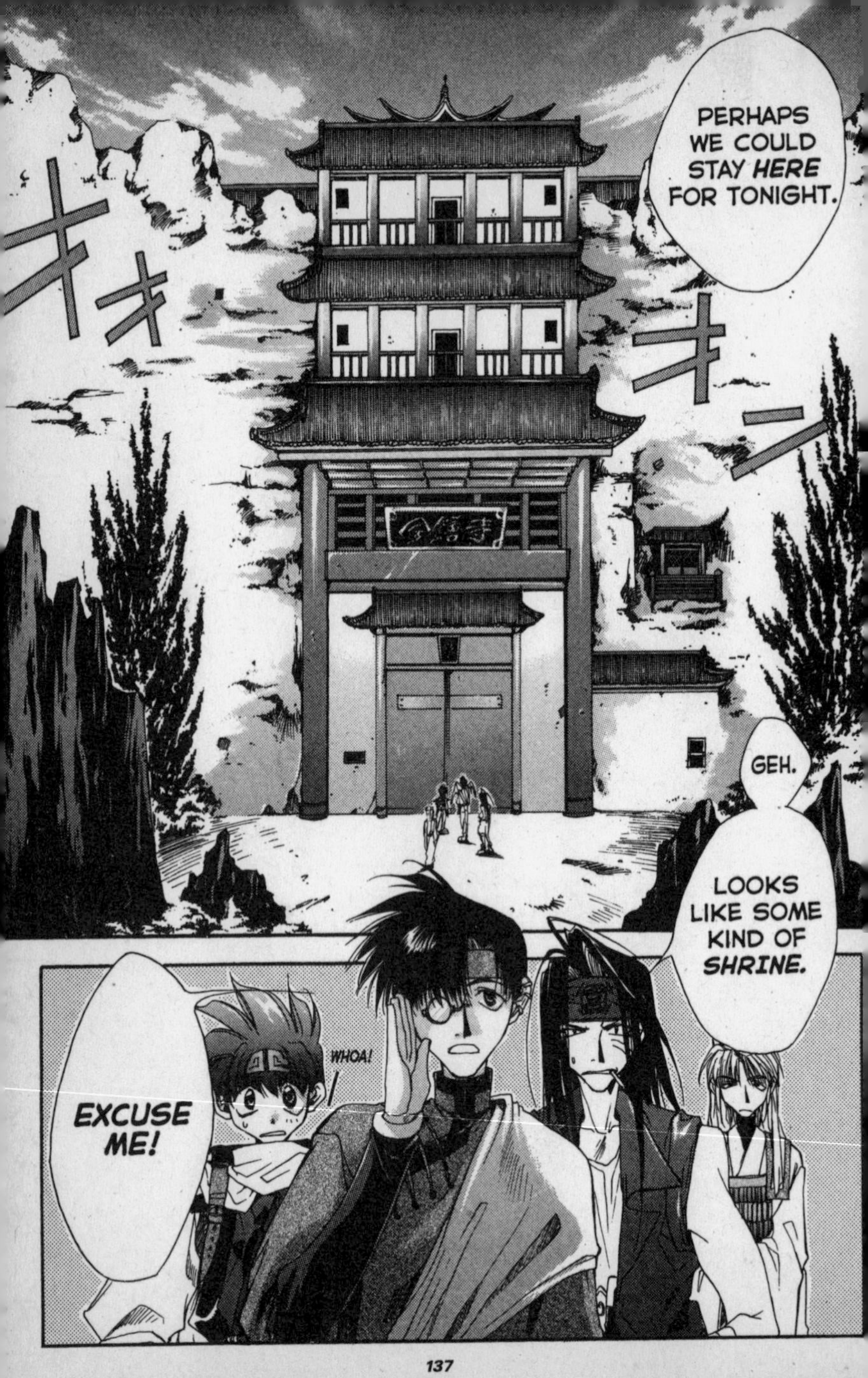

PERHAPS WE COULD STAY *HERE* FOR TONIGHT.
GEH.
LOOKS LIKE SOME KIND OF *SHRINE.*
WHOA!
EXCUSE ME!

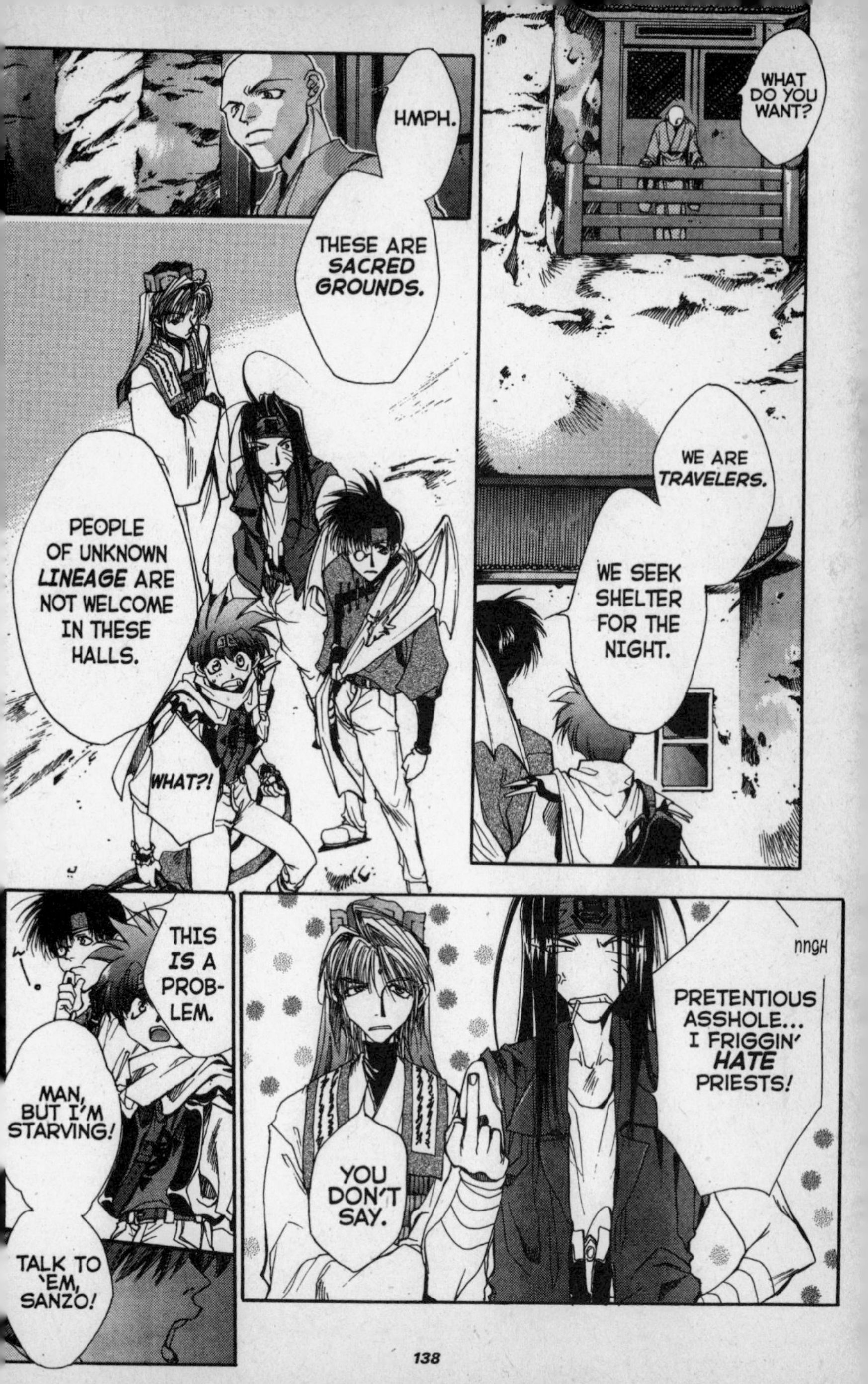
WHAT DO YOU WANT?
WE ARE *TRAVELERS.*
WE SEEK SHELTER FOR THE NIGHT.
HMPH.
THESE ARE *SACRED GROUNDS.*
PEOPLE OF UNKNOWN *LINEAGE* ARE NOT WELCOME IN THESE HALLS.
WHAT?!
nngh
PRETENTIOUS ASSHOLE... I FRIGGIN' *HATE* PRIESTS!
YOU DON'T SAY.
THIS *IS* A PROB-LEM.
MAN, BUT I'M STARVING!
TALK TO 'EM, SANZO!

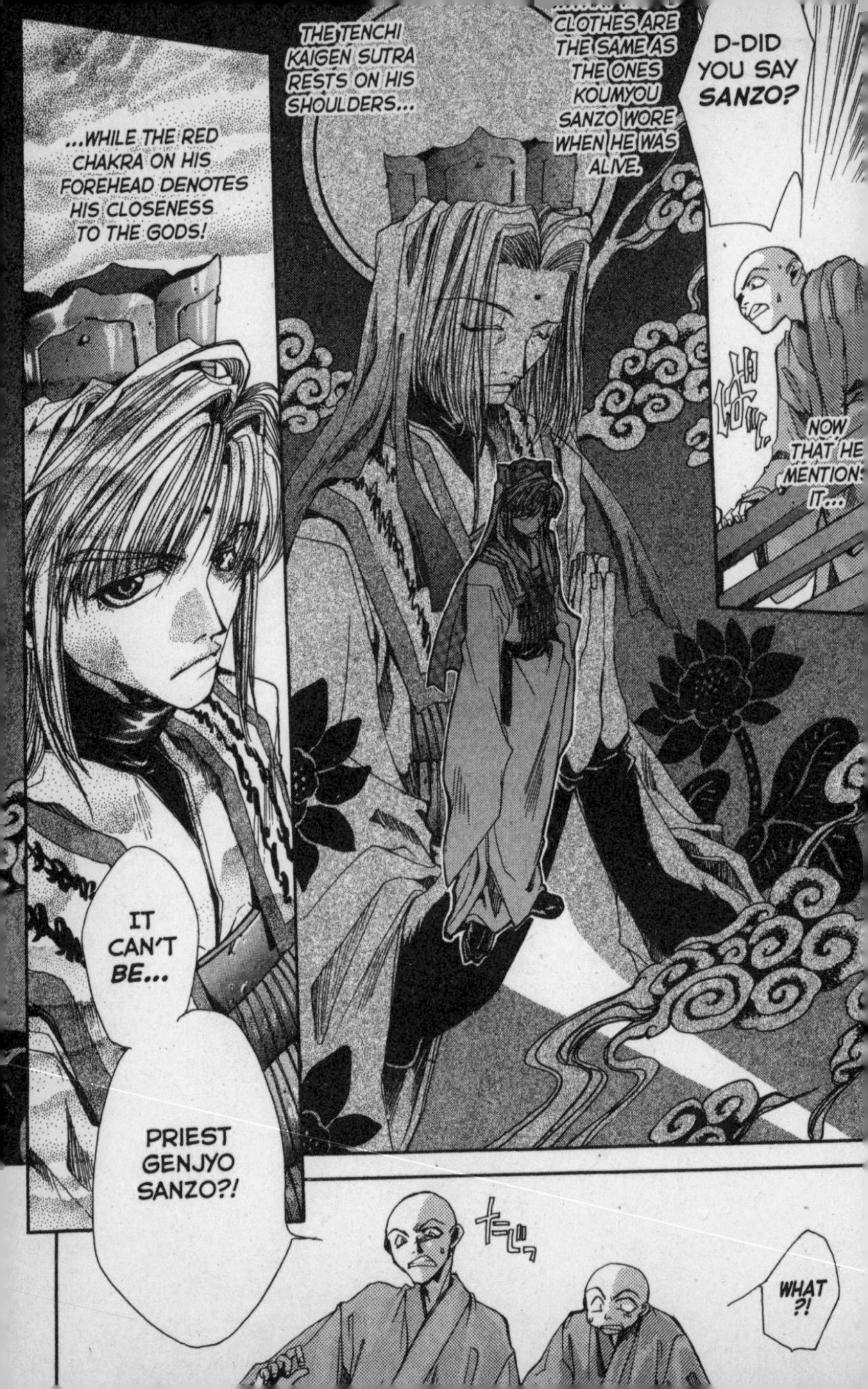
D-DID YOU SAY SANZO?
NOW THAT HE MENTIONS IT...
CLOTHES ARE THE SAME AS THE ONES KOUMYOU SANZO WORE WHEN HE WAS ALIVE.
THE TENCHI KAIGEN SUTRA RESTS ON HIS SHOULDERS...
...WHILE THE RED CHAKRA ON HIS FOREHEAD DENOTES HIS CLOSENESS TO THE GODS!
IT CAN'T BE...
PRIEST GENJYO SANZO?!
WHAT ?!

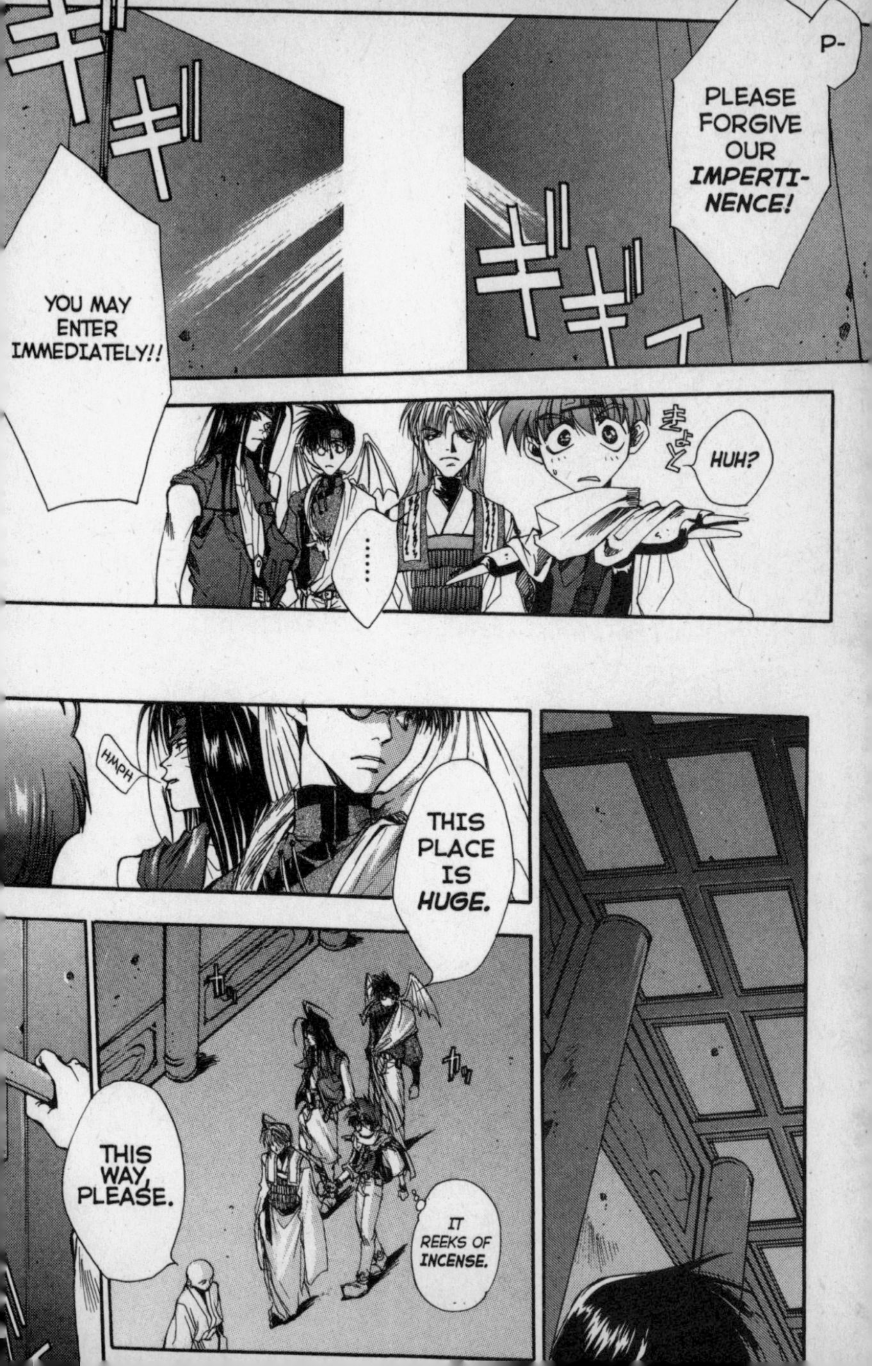
P-
PLEASE FORGIVE OUR IMPERTINENCE!
YOU MAY ENTER IMMEDIATELY!!
きょと
HUH?
......
HMPH
THIS PLACE IS HUGE.
THIS WAY, PLEASE.
IT REEKS OF INCENSE.

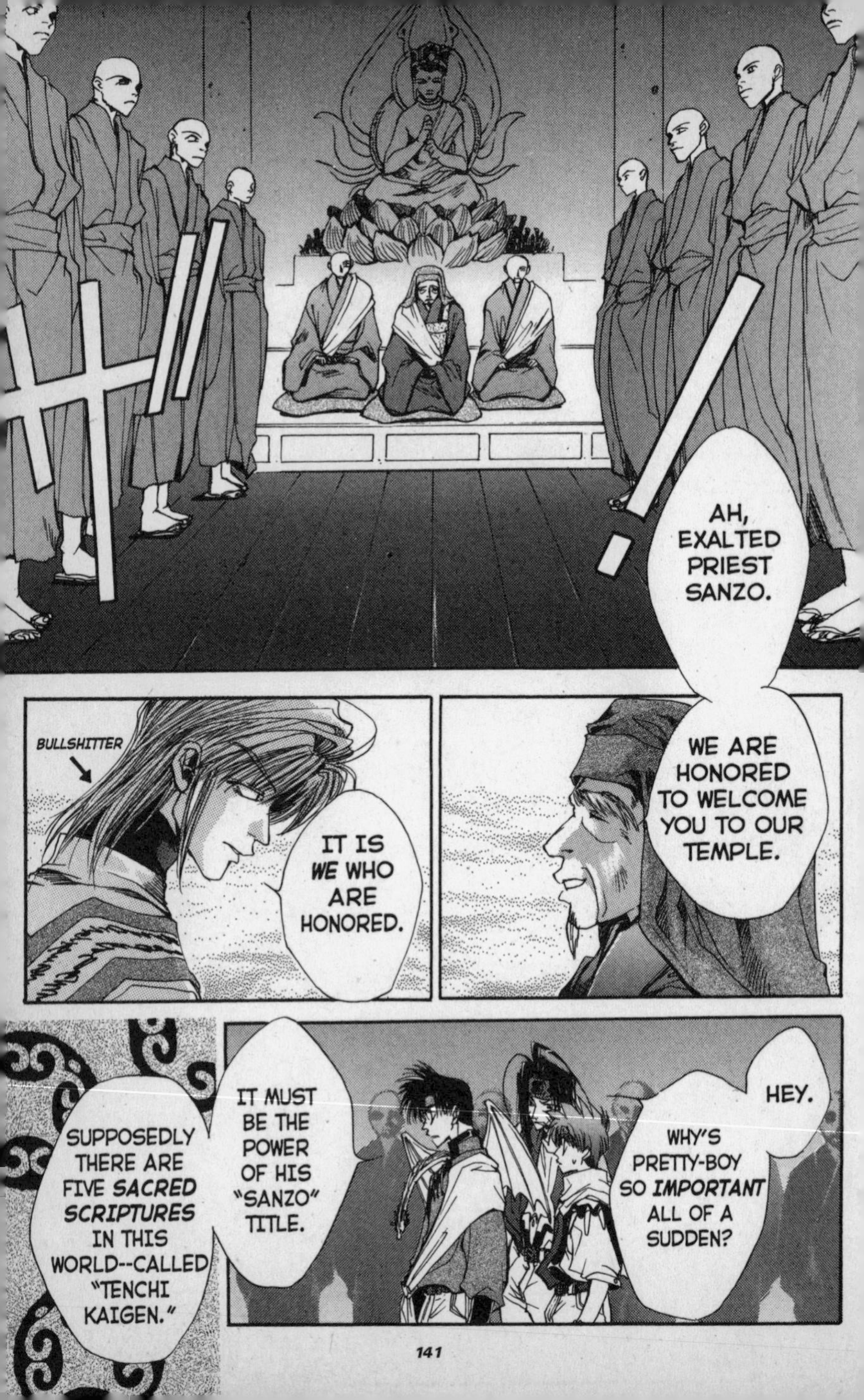
AH, EXALTED PRIEST SANZO.
WE ARE HONORED TO WELCOME YOU TO OUR TEMPLE.
IT IS *WE* WHO ARE HONORED.
BULLSHITTER
HEY.
WHY'S PRETTY-BOY SO *IMPORTANT* ALL OF A SUDDEN?
IT MUST BE THE POWER OF HIS "SANZO" TITLE.
SUPPOSEDLY THERE ARE FIVE *SACRED SCRIPTURES* IN THIS WORLD--CALLED "TENCHI KAIGEN."

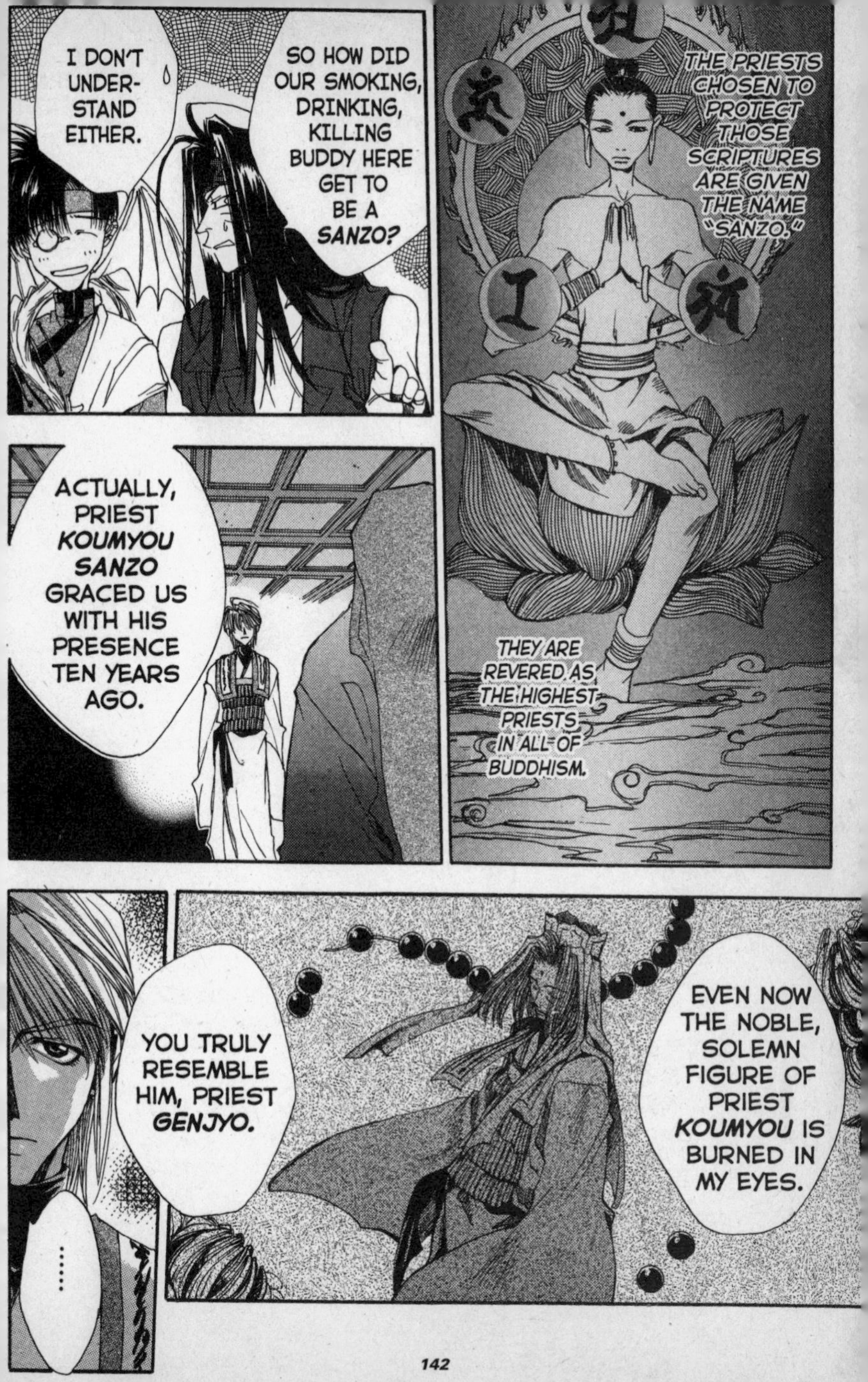
THE PRIESTS CHOSEN TO PROTECT THOSE SCRIPTURES ARE GIVEN THE NAME "SANZO."
THEY ARE REVERED AS THE HIGHEST PRIESTS IN ALL OF BUDDHISM.
SO HOW DID OUR SMOKING, DRINKING, KILLING BUDDY HERE GET TO BE A SANZO?
I DON'T UNDERSTAND EITHER.
ACTUALLY, PRIEST KOUMYOU SANZO GRACED US WITH HIS PRESENCE TEN YEARS AGO.
EVEN NOW THE NOBLE, SOLEMN FIGURE OF PRIEST KOUMYOU IS BURNED IN MY EYES.
YOU TRULY RESEMBLE HIM, PRIEST GENJYO.
......

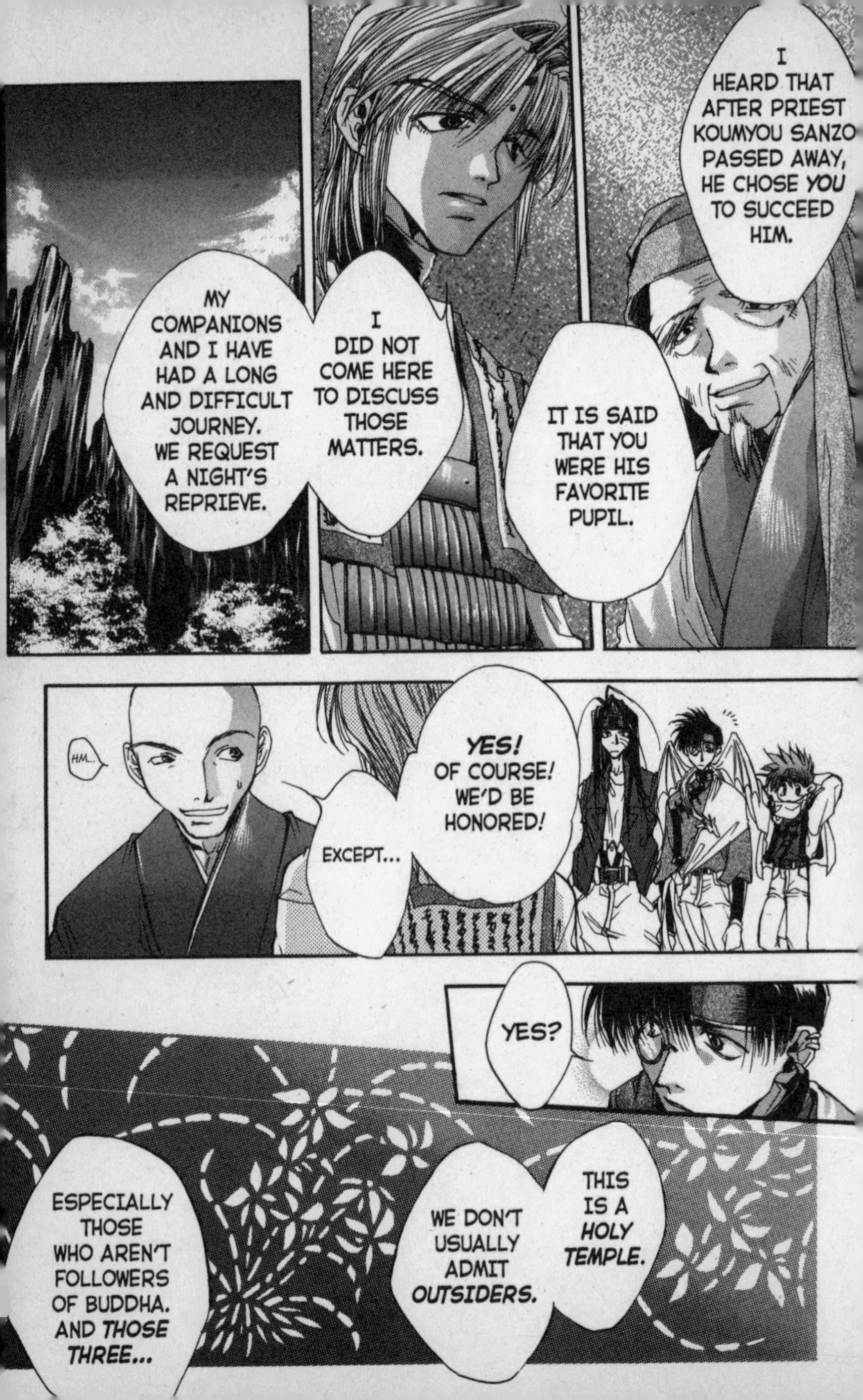
I HEARD THAT AFTER PRIEST KOUMYOU SANZO PASSED AWAY, HE CHOSE YOU TO SUCCEED HIM.
IT IS SAID THAT YOU WERE HIS FAVORITE PUPIL.
I DID NOT COME HERE TO DISCUSS THOSE MATTERS.
MY COMPANIONS AND I HAVE HAD A LONG AND DIFFICULT JOURNEY. WE REQUEST A NIGHT'S REPRIEVE.
YES! OF COURSE! WE'D BE HONORED!
EXCEPT...
HM...
YES?
THIS IS A HOLY TEMPLE.
WE DON'T USUALLY ADMIT OUTSIDERS.
ESPECIALLY THOSE WHO AREN'T FOLLOWERS OF BUDDHA. AND THOSE THREE...

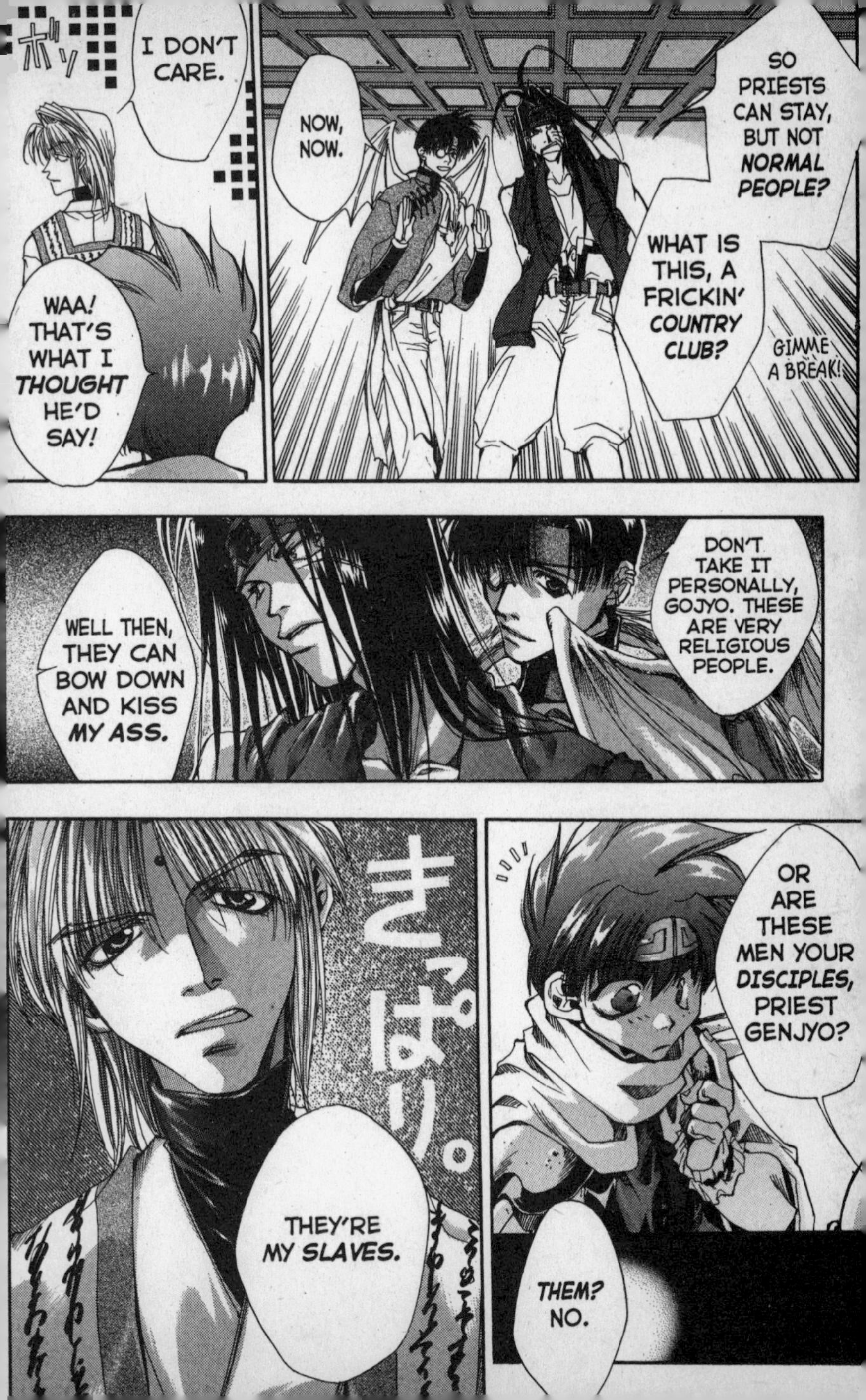
SO PRIESTS CAN STAY, BUT NOT *NORMAL PEOPLE?*
WHAT IS THIS, A FRICKIN' *COUNTRY CLUB?*
GIMME A BREAK!
NOW, NOW.
ボッ
I DON'T CARE.
WAA! THAT'S WHAT I *THOUGHT* HE'D SAY!
DON'T TAKE IT PERSONALLY, GOJYO. THESE ARE VERY RELIGIOUS PEOPLE.
WELL THEN, THEY CAN BOW DOWN AND KISS *MY ASS.*
OR ARE THESE MEN YOUR *DISCIPLES,* PRIEST GENJYO?
THEM? NO.
きっぱり。
THEY'RE MY *SLAVES.*

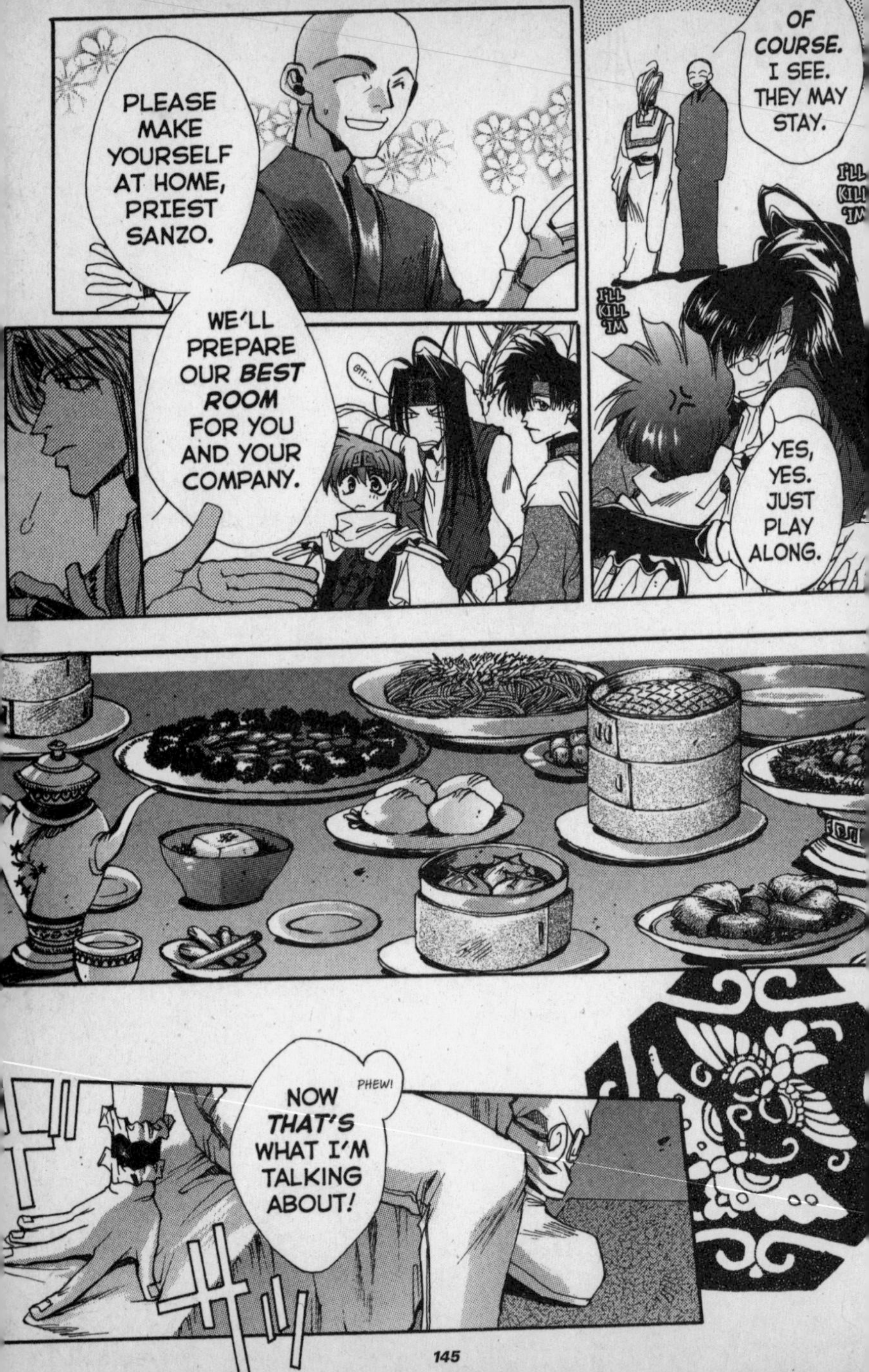

OF COURSE. I SEE. THEY MAY STAY.
I'LL KILL 'IM
I'LL KILL 'IM
YES, YES. JUST PLAY ALONG.
PLEASE MAKE YOURSELF AT HOME, PRIEST SANZO.
WE'LL PREPARE OUR *BEST ROOM* FOR YOU AND YOUR COMPANY.
GTT...
PHEW!
NOW *THAT'S* WHAT I'M TALKING ABOUT!

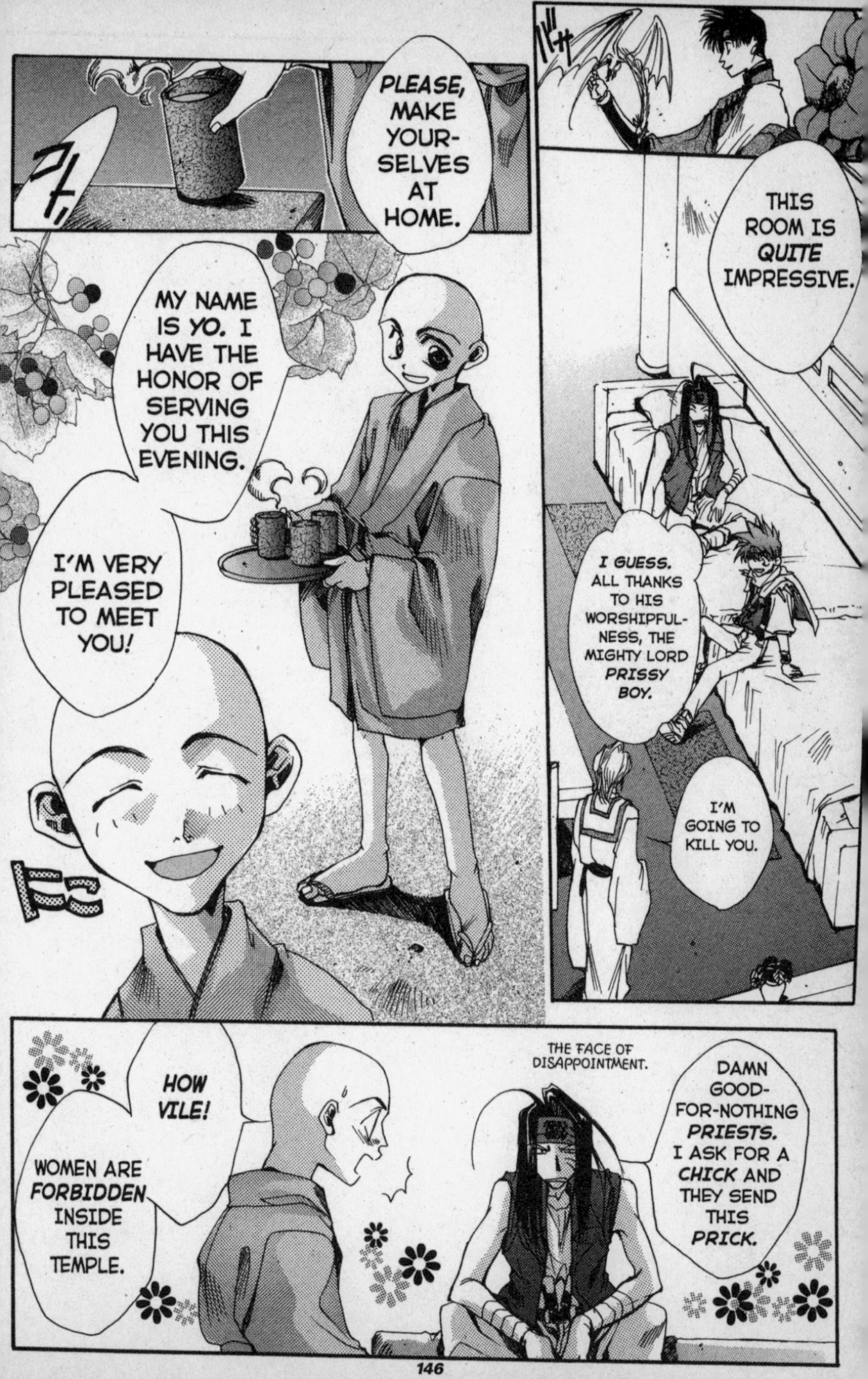
THIS ROOM IS QUITE IMPRESSIVE.
I GUESS. ALL THANKS TO HIS WORSHIPFUL-NESS, THE MIGHTY LORD PRISSY BOY.
I'M GOING TO KILL YOU.
PLEASE, MAKE YOUR-SELVES AT HOME.
MY NAME IS YO. I HAVE THE HONOR OF SERVING YOU THIS EVENING.
I'M VERY PLEASED TO MEET YOU!
THE FACE OF DISAPPOINTMENT.
DAMN GOOD-FOR-NOTHING PRIESTS. I ASK FOR A CHICK AND THEY SEND THIS PRICK.
HOW VILE!
WOMEN ARE FORBIDDEN INSIDE THIS TEMPLE.

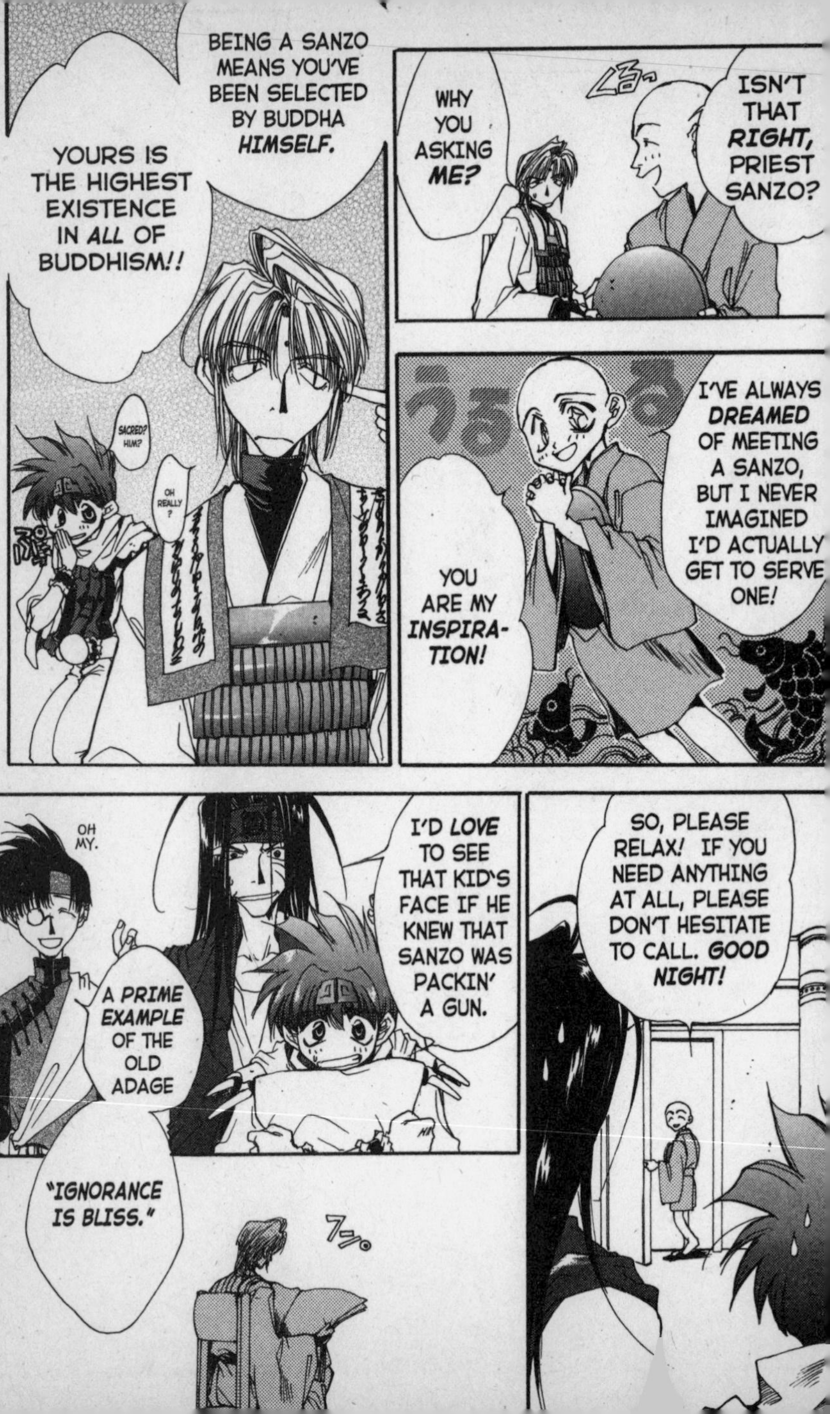
くるっ
ISN'T THAT RIGHT, PRIEST SANZO?
WHY YOU ASKING ME?
うるる
I'VE ALWAYS DREAMED OF MEETING A SANZO, BUT I NEVER IMAGINED I'D ACTUALLY GET TO SERVE ONE!
YOU ARE MY INSPIRATION!
BEING A SANZO MEANS YOU'VE BEEN SELECTED BY BUDDHA HIMSELF.
YOURS IS THE HIGHEST EXISTENCE IN ALL OF BUDDHISM!!
SACRED? HIM?
OH REALLY?
SO, PLEASE RELAX! IF YOU NEED ANYTHING AT ALL, PLEASE DON'T HESITATE TO CALL. GOOD NIGHT!
I'D LOVE TO SEE THAT KID'S FACE IF HE KNEW THAT SANZO WAS PACKIN' A GUN.
OH MY.
A PRIME EXAMPLE OF THE OLD ADAGE
"IGNORANCE IS BLISS."

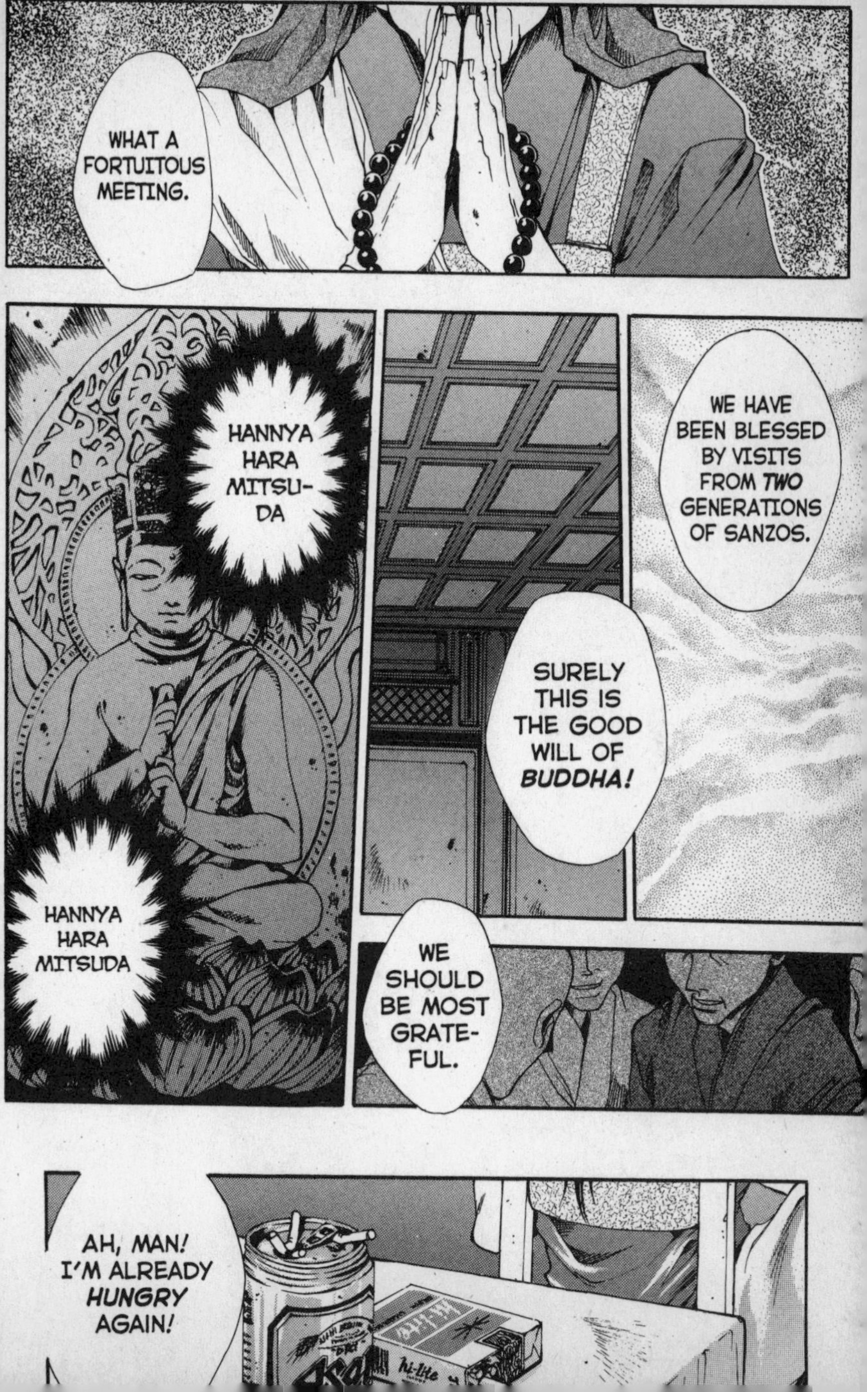
WHAT A FORTUITOUS MEETING.
WE HAVE BEEN BLESSED BY VISITS FROM *TWO* GENERATIONS OF SANZOS.
SURELY THIS IS THE GOOD WILL OF ***BUDDHA!***
WE SHOULD BE MOST GRATEFUL.
HANNYA HARA MITSU-DA
HANNYA HARA MITSUDA
AH, MAN! I'M ALREADY ***HUNGRY*** AGAIN!

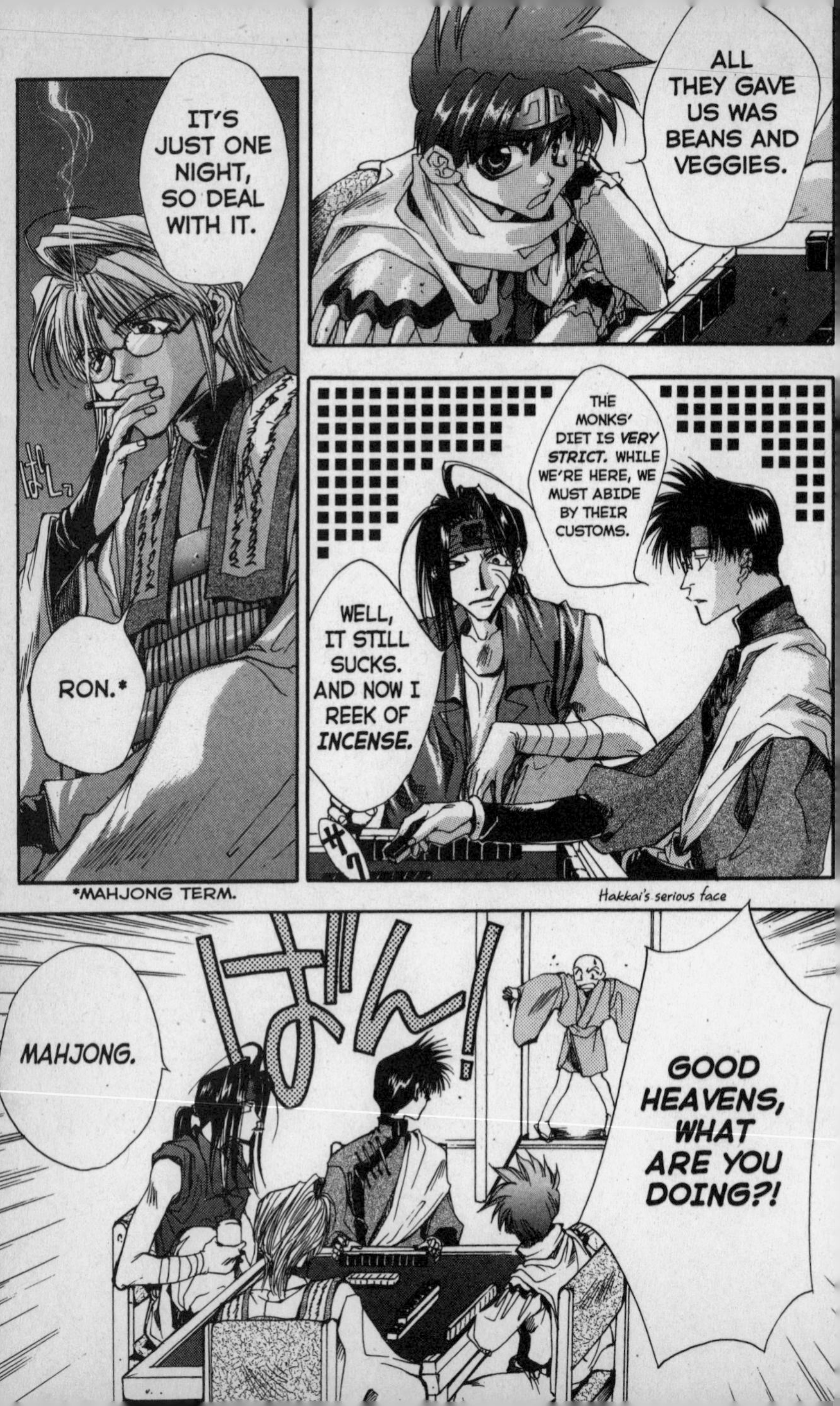
ALL THEY GAVE US WAS BEANS AND VEGGIES.
THE MONKS' DIET IS *VERY STRICT.* WHILE WE'RE HERE, WE MUST ABIDE BY THEIR CUSTOMS.
WELL, IT STILL SUCKS. AND NOW I REEK OF *INCENSE.*
Hakkai's serious face
IT'S JUST ONE NIGHT, SO DEAL WITH IT.
RON.*
*MAHJONG TERM.
ばん!
GOOD HEAVENS, WHAT ARE YOU DOING?!
MAHJONG.

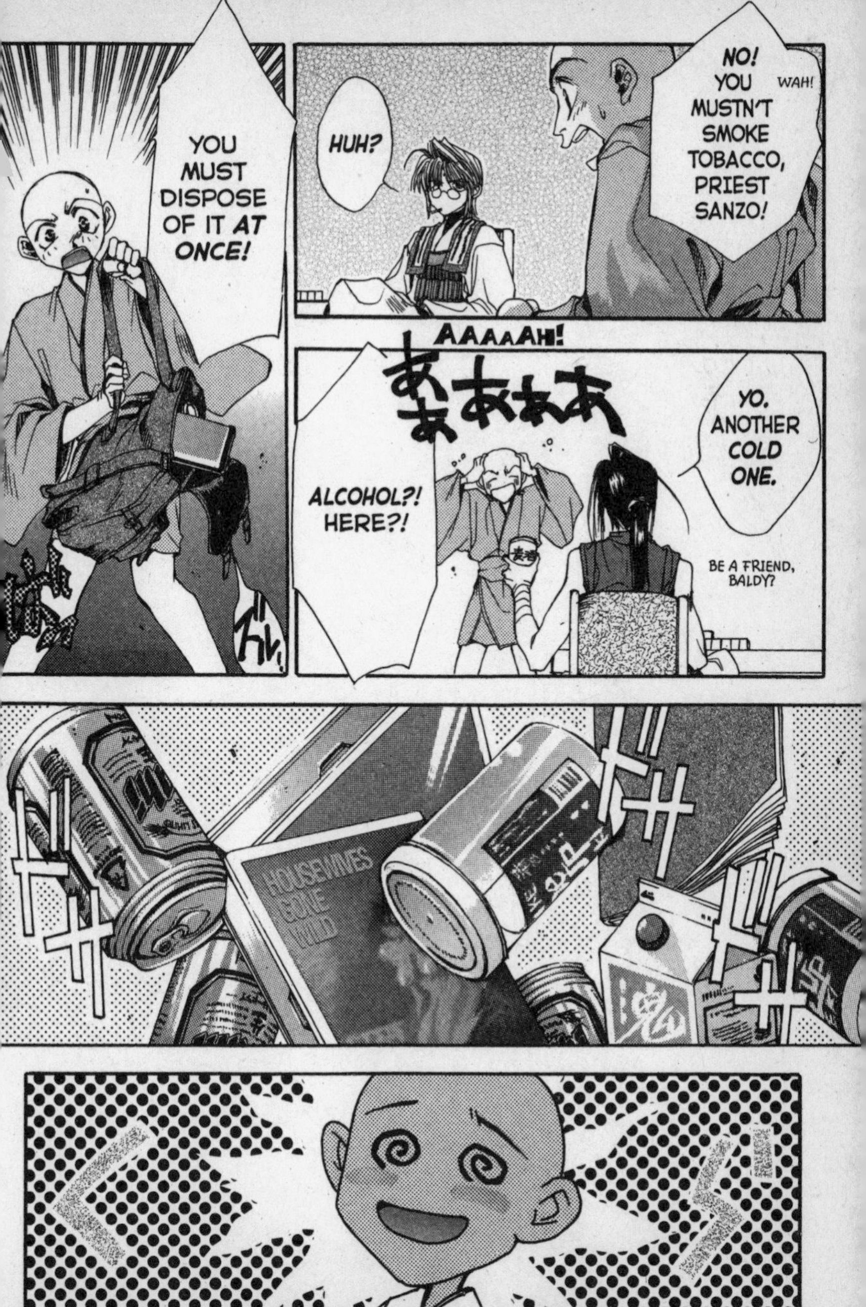
NO! YOU MUSTN'T SMOKE TOBACCO, PRIEST SANZO!
WAH!
HUH?
YO. ANOTHER COLD ONE.
BE A FRIEND, BALDY?
AAAAAH!
ALCOHOL?! HERE?!
YOU MUST DISPOSE OF IT AT ONCE!
HOUSEWIVES GONE WILD

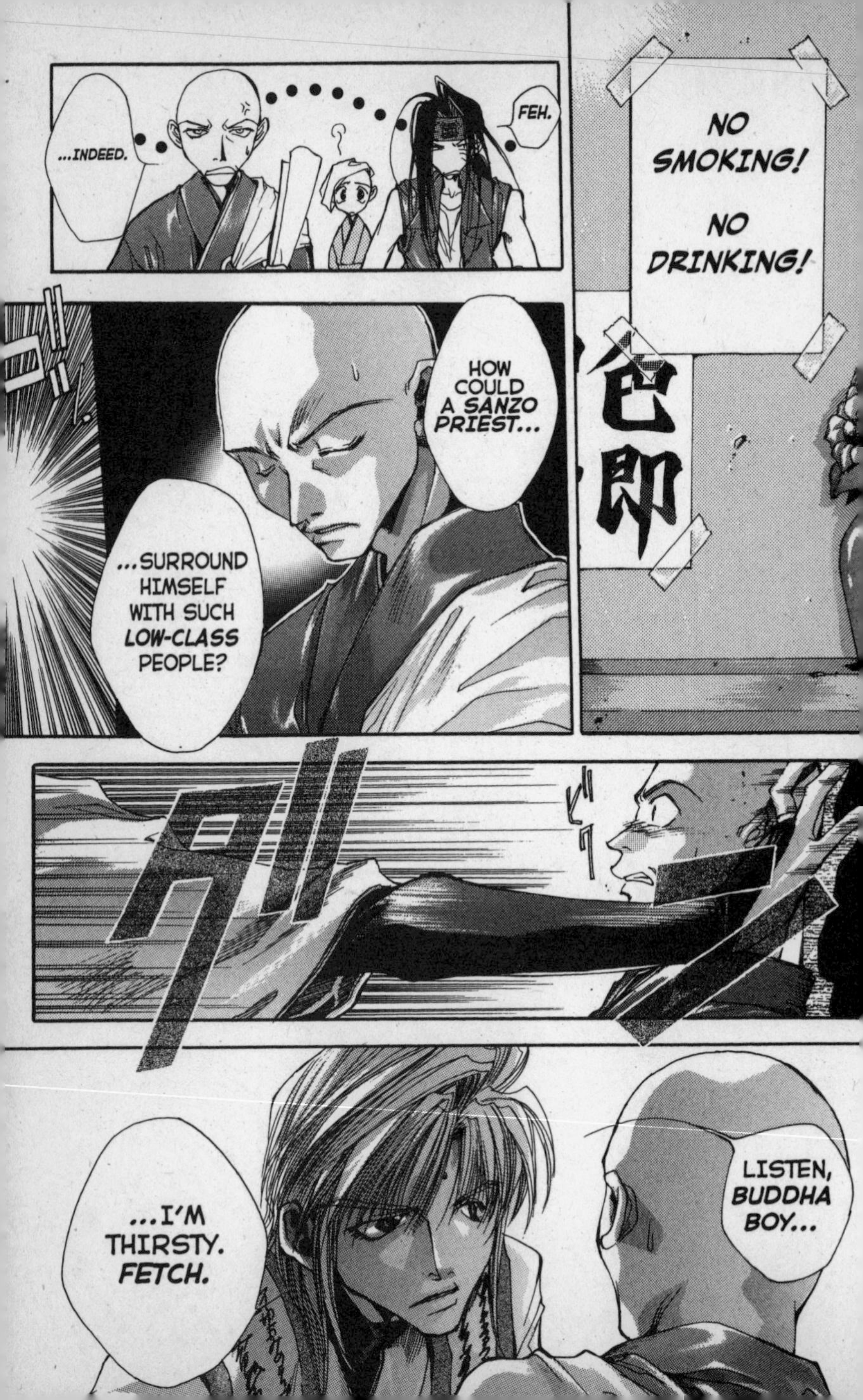
NO SMOKING!
NO DRINKING!
色即
FEH.
...INDEED.
HOW COULD A SANZO PRIEST...
...SURROUND HIMSELF WITH SUCH LOW-CLASS PEOPLE?
LISTEN, BUDDHA BOY...
...I'M THIRSTY. FETCH.

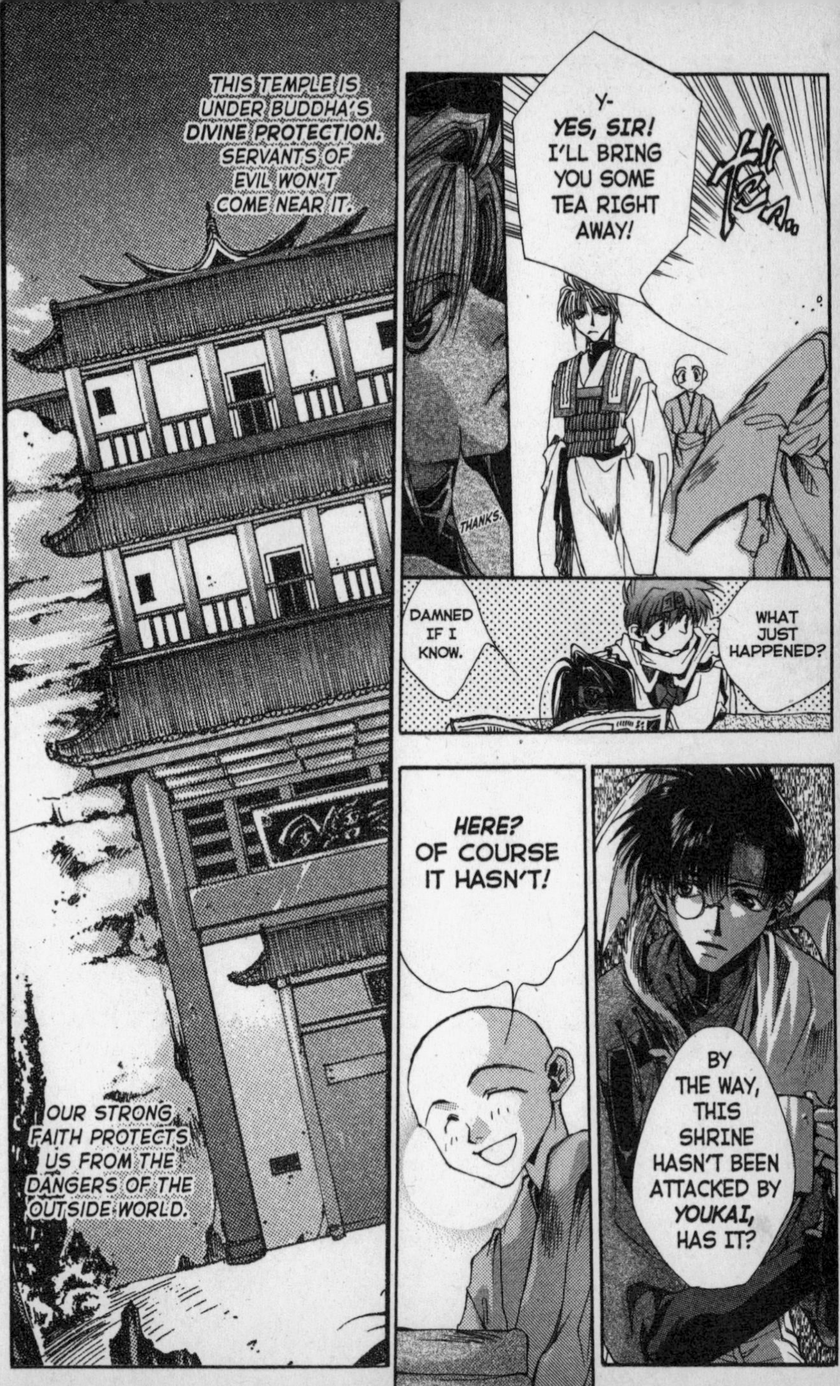
Y- YES, SIR! I'LL BRING YOU SOME TEA RIGHT AWAY!
THANKS.
WHAT JUST HAPPENED?
DAMNED IF I KNOW.
BY THE WAY, THIS SHRINE HASN'T BEEN ATTACKED BY YOUKAI, HAS IT?
HERE? OF COURSE IT HASN'T!
THIS TEMPLE IS UNDER BUDDHA'S DIVINE PROTECTION. SERVANTS OF EVIL WON'T COME NEAR IT.
OUR STRONG FAITH PROTECTS US FROM THE DANGERS OF THE OUTSIDE WORLD.

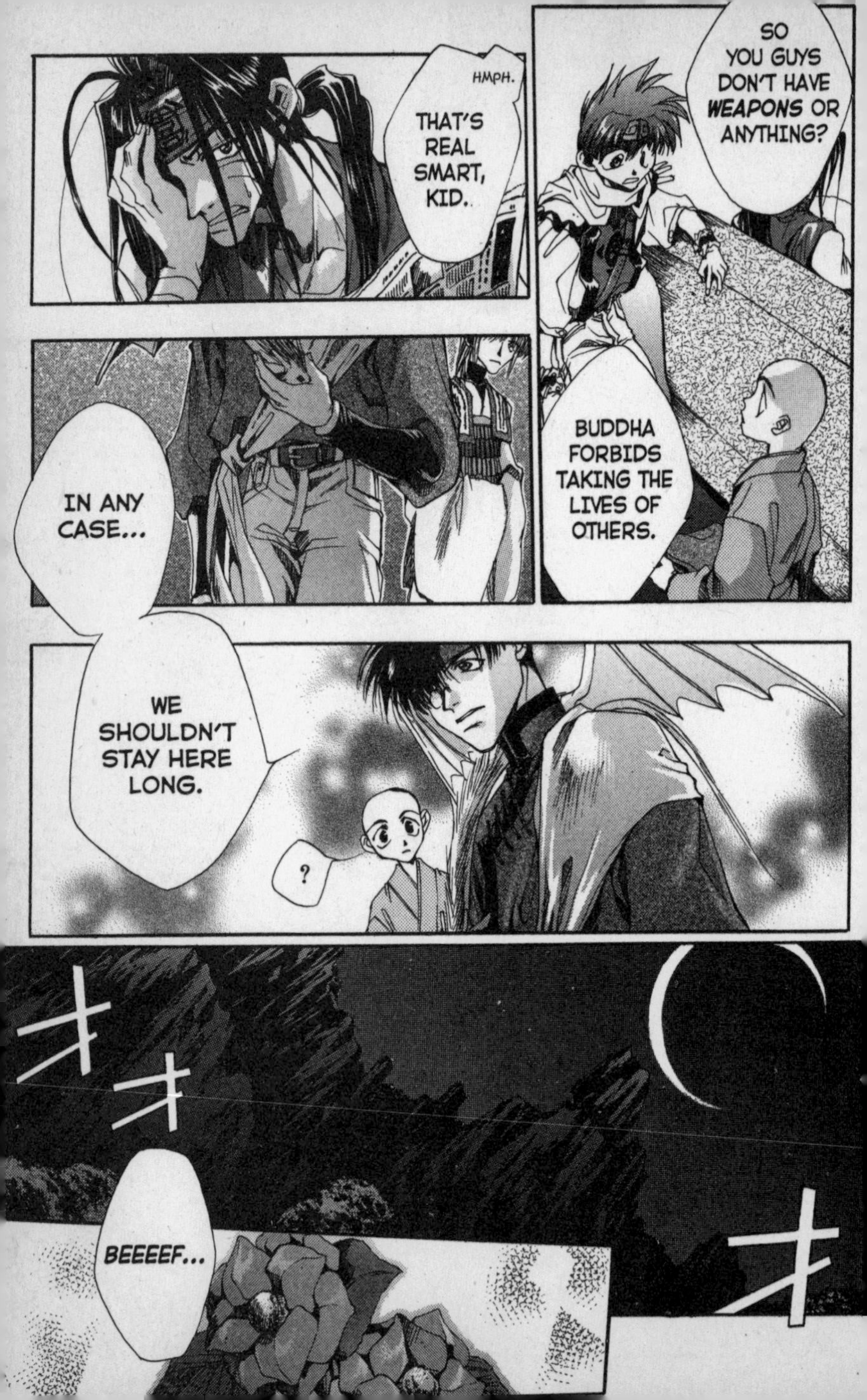
SO YOU GUYS DON'T HAVE WEAPONS OR ANYTHING?
BUDDHA FORBIDS TAKING THE LIVES OF OTHERS.
HMPH.
THAT'S REAL SMART, KID.
IN ANY CASE...
WE SHOULDN'T STAY HERE LONG.
?
BEEEEF...

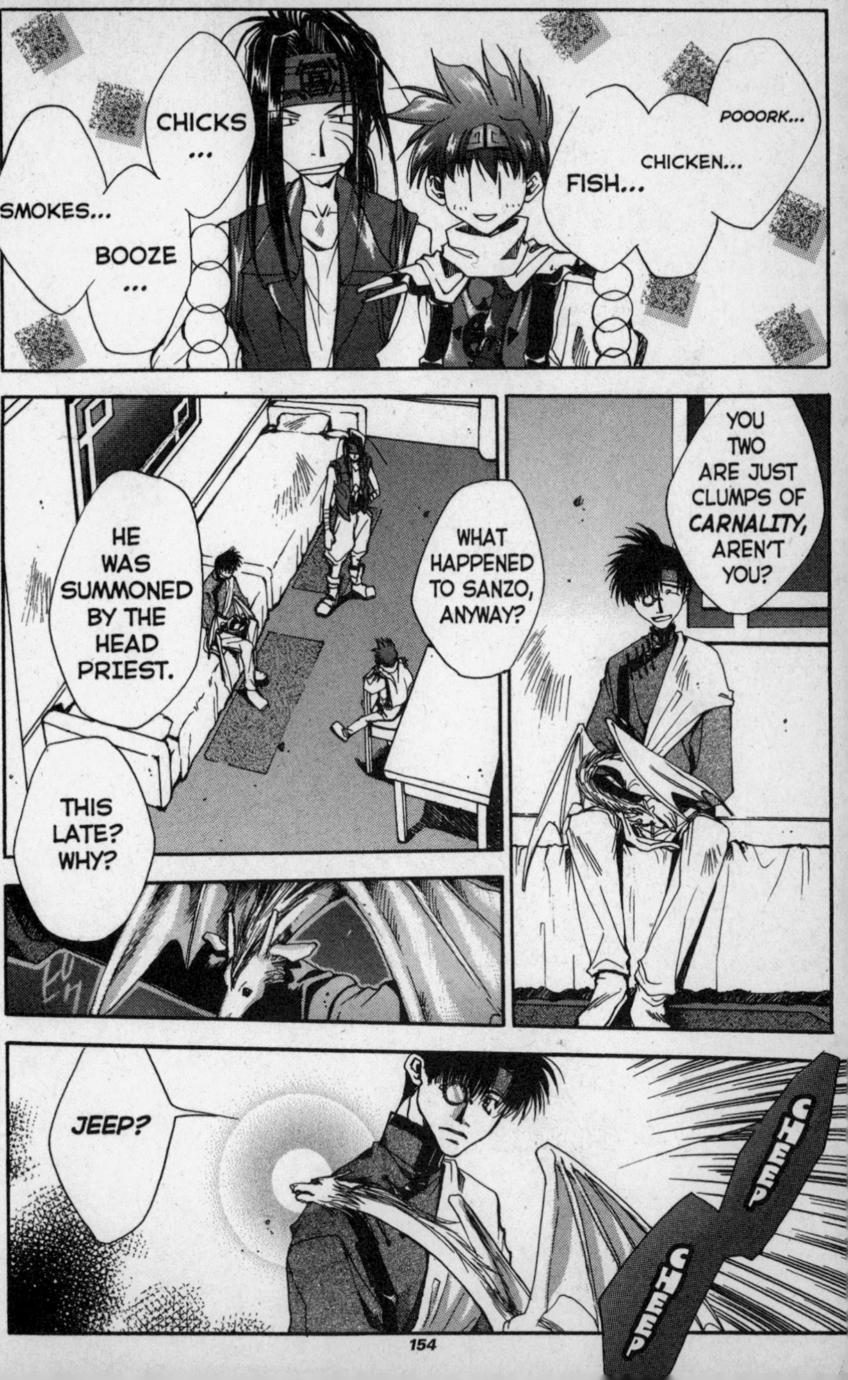
POOORK...
CHICKEN...
FISH...
CHICKS ...
SMOKES...
BOOZE ...
YOU TWO ARE JUST CLUMPS OF CARNALITY, AREN'T YOU?
WHAT HAPPENED TO SANZO, ANYWAY?
HE WAS SUMMONED BY THE HEAD PRIEST.
THIS LATE? WHY?
CHEEP
CHEEP
JEEP?

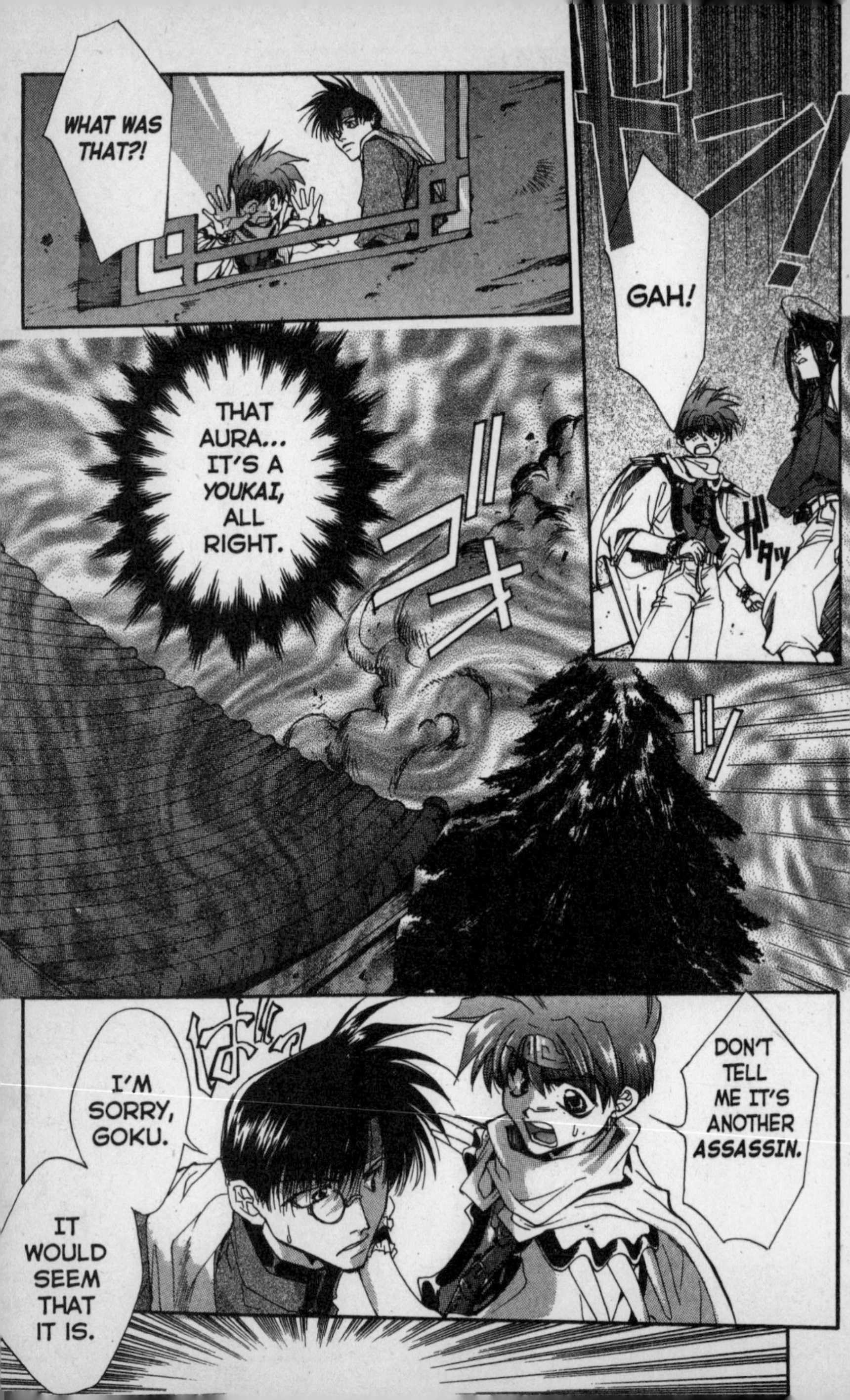
GAH!
WHAT WAS THAT?!
THAT AURA... IT'S A *YOUKAI,* ALL RIGHT.
DON'T TELL ME IT'S ANOTHER **ASSASSIN.**
I'M SORRY, GOKU.
IT WOULD SEEM THAT IT IS.

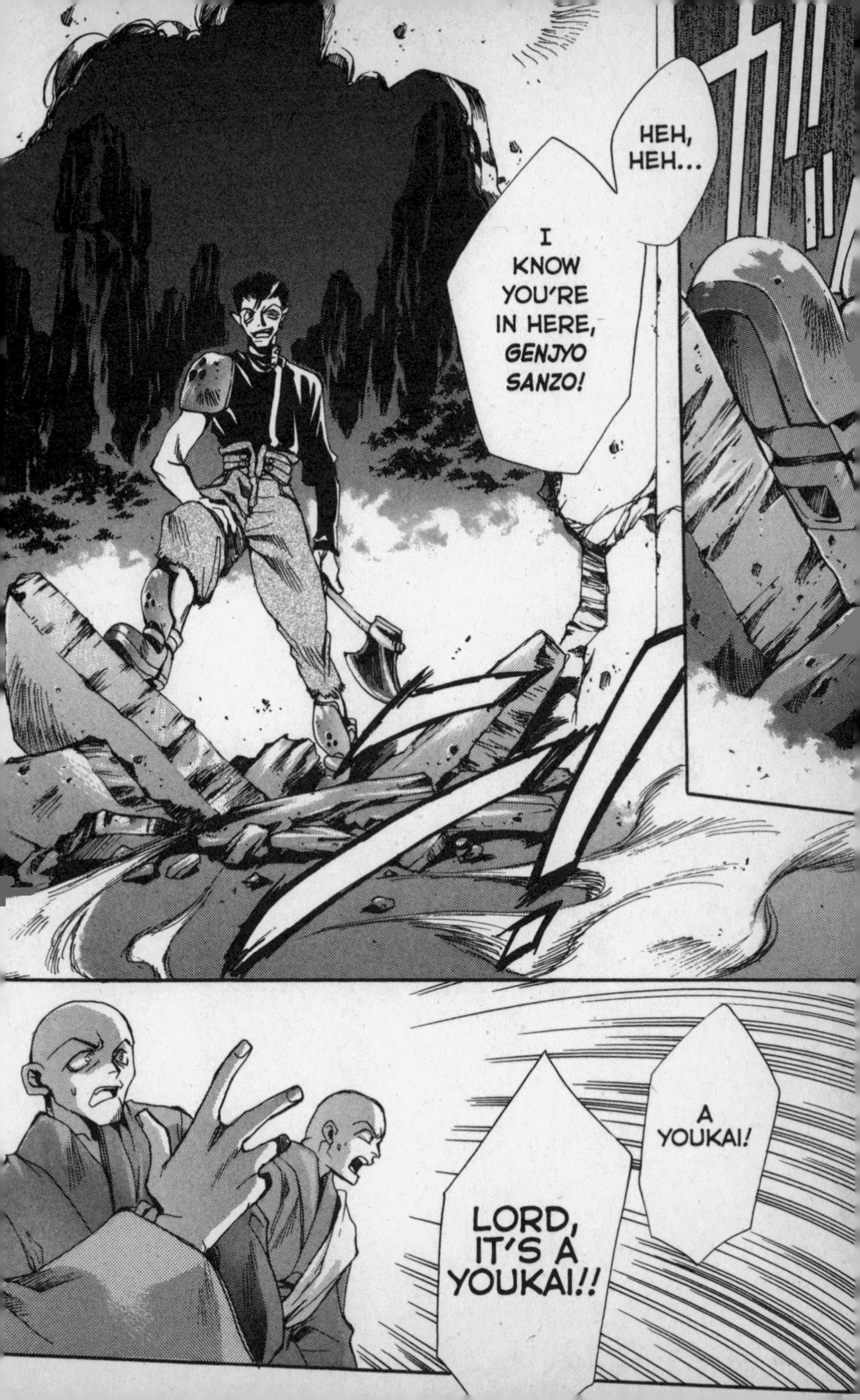
HEH, HEH...
I KNOW YOU'RE IN HERE, GENJYO SANZO!
A YOUKAI!
LORD, IT'S A YOUKAI!!

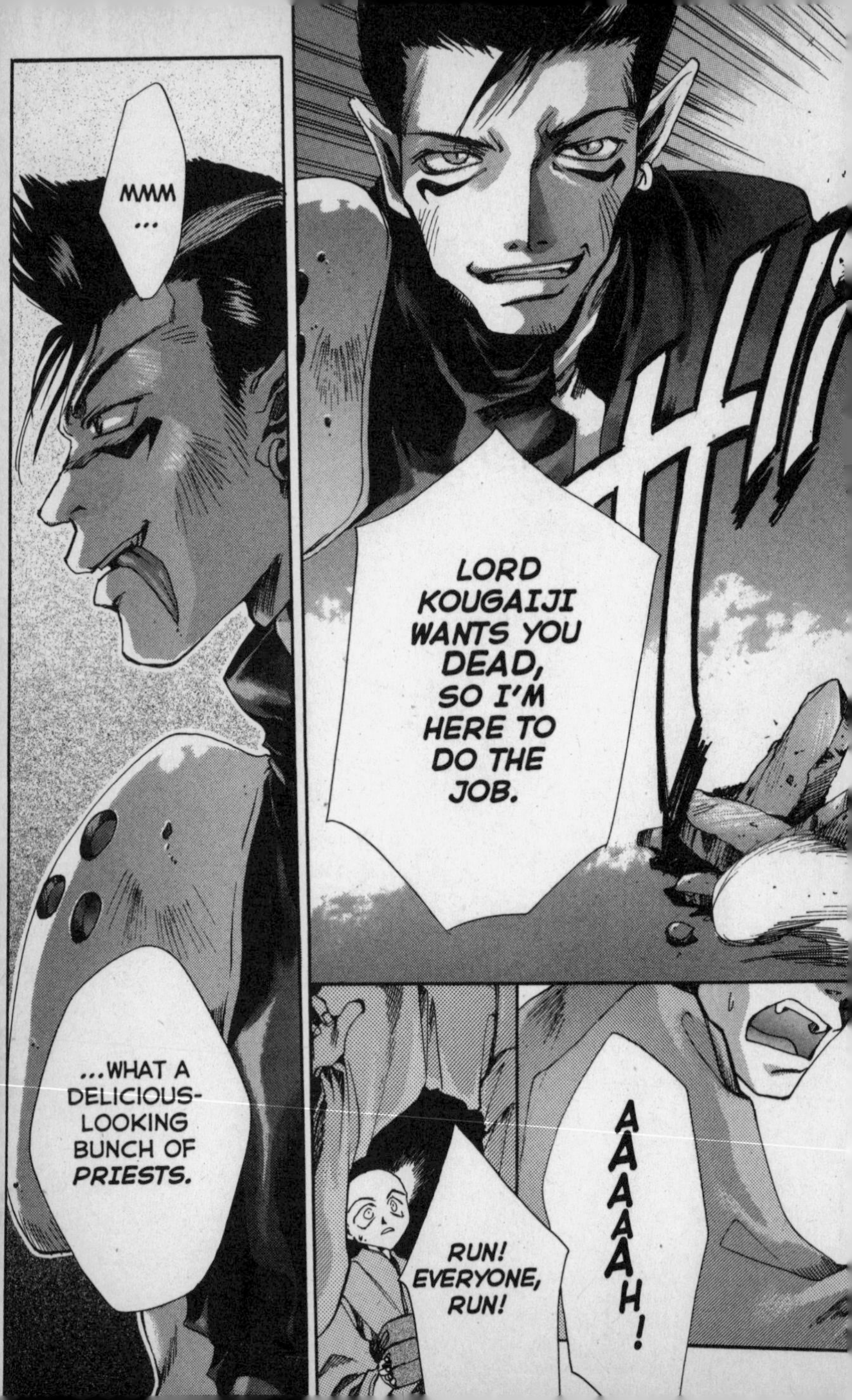
LORD KOUGAIJI WANTS YOU DEAD, SO I'M HERE TO DO THE JOB.
AAAAAH!
RUN! EVERYONE, RUN!
MMM ...
...WHAT A DELICIOUS-LOOKING BUNCH OF PRIESTS.

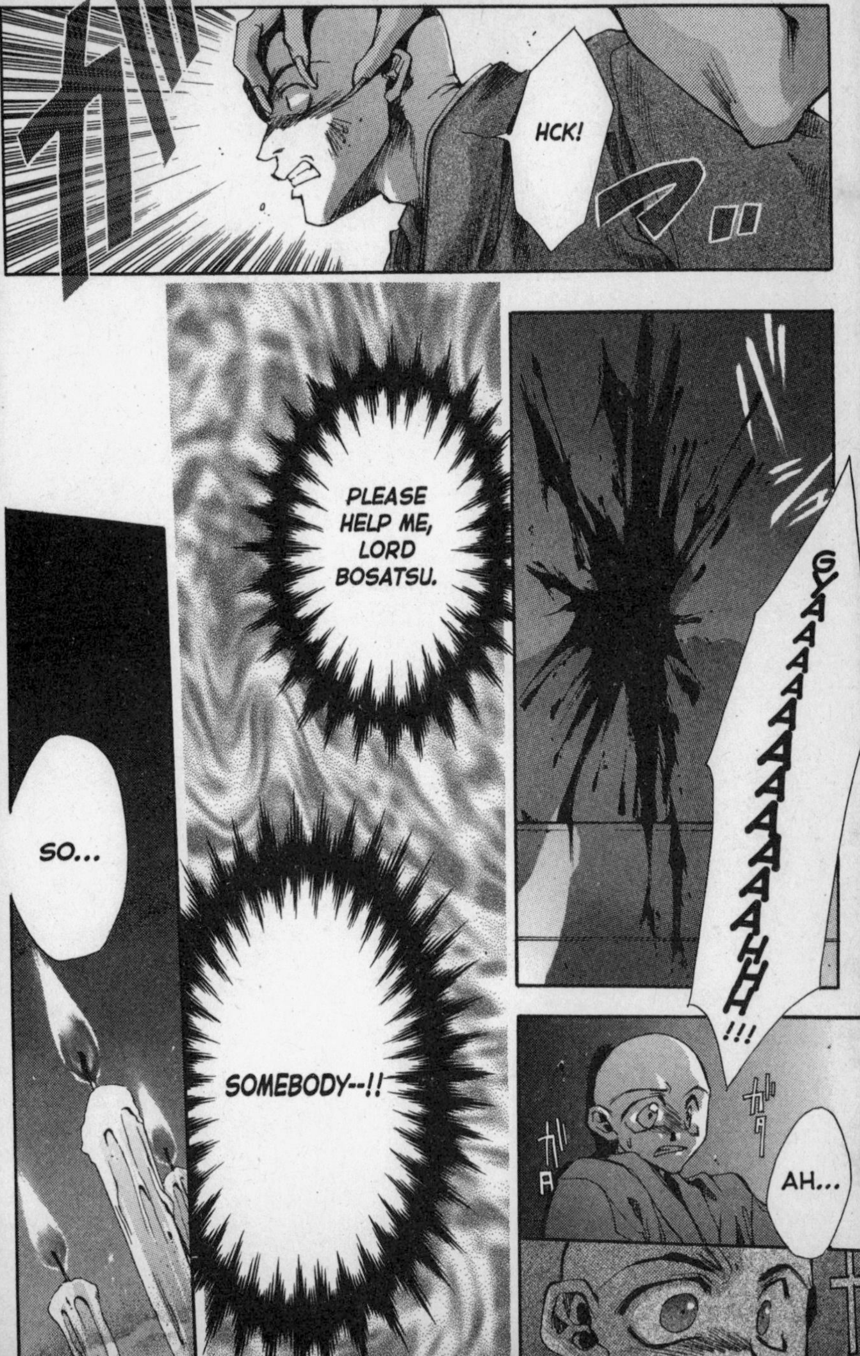
HCK!
GYAAAAAAAAAAAAAHH!!!
AH...
PLEASE HELP ME, LORD BOSATSU.
SOMEBODY--!!
SO...

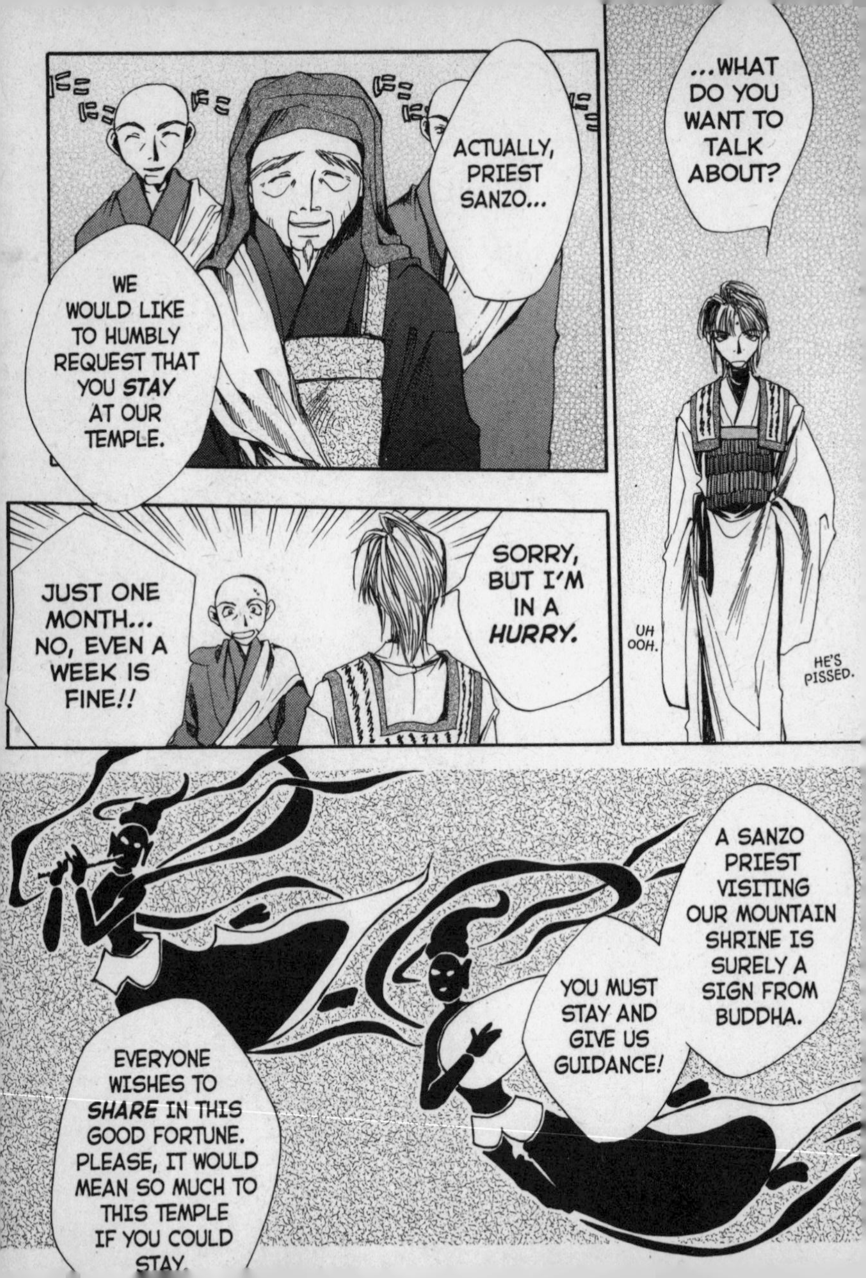
...WHAT DO YOU WANT TO TALK ABOUT?
UH OOH.
HE'S PISSED.
ACTUALLY, PRIEST SANZO...
WE WOULD LIKE TO HUMBLY REQUEST THAT YOU *STAY* AT OUR TEMPLE.
SORRY, BUT I'M IN A *HURRY.*
JUST ONE MONTH... NO, EVEN A WEEK IS FINE!!
A SANZO PRIEST VISITING OUR MOUNTAIN SHRINE IS SURELY A SIGN FROM BUDDHA.
YOU MUST STAY AND GIVE US GUIDANCE!
EVERYONE WISHES TO *SHARE* IN THIS GOOD FORTUNE. PLEASE, IT WOULD MEAN SO MUCH TO THIS TEMPLE IF YOU COULD STAY.

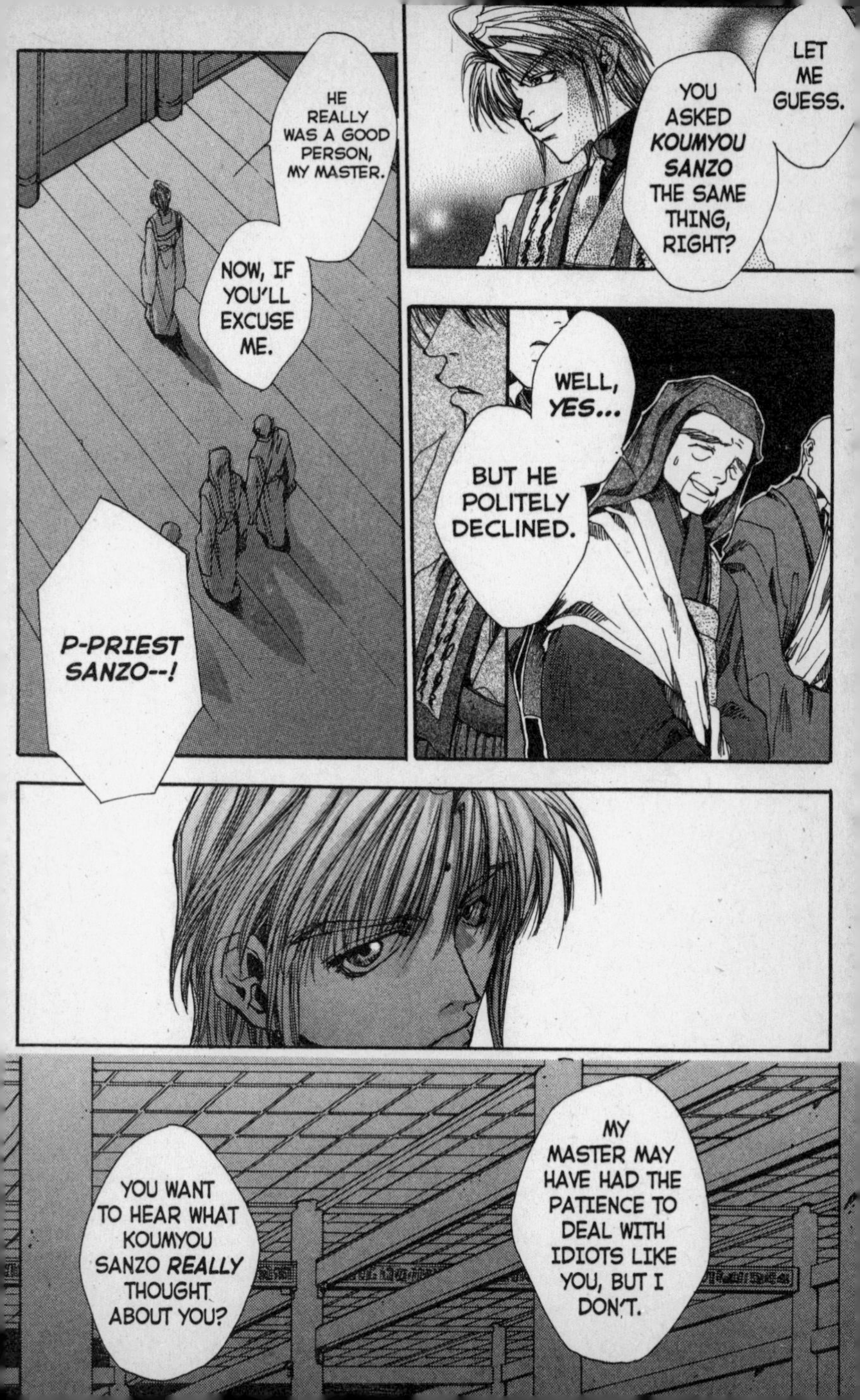
LET ME GUESS.
YOU ASKED *KOUMYOU SANZO* THE SAME THING, RIGHT?
WELL, *YES...*
BUT HE POLITELY DECLINED.
HE REALLY WAS A GOOD PERSON, MY MASTER.
NOW, IF YOU'LL EXCUSE ME.
P-PRIEST SANZO--!
MY MASTER MAY HAVE HAD THE PATIENCE TO DEAL WITH IDIOTS LIKE YOU, BUT I DON'T.
YOU WANT TO HEAR WHAT KOUMYOU SANZO *REALLY* THOUGHT ABOUT YOU?

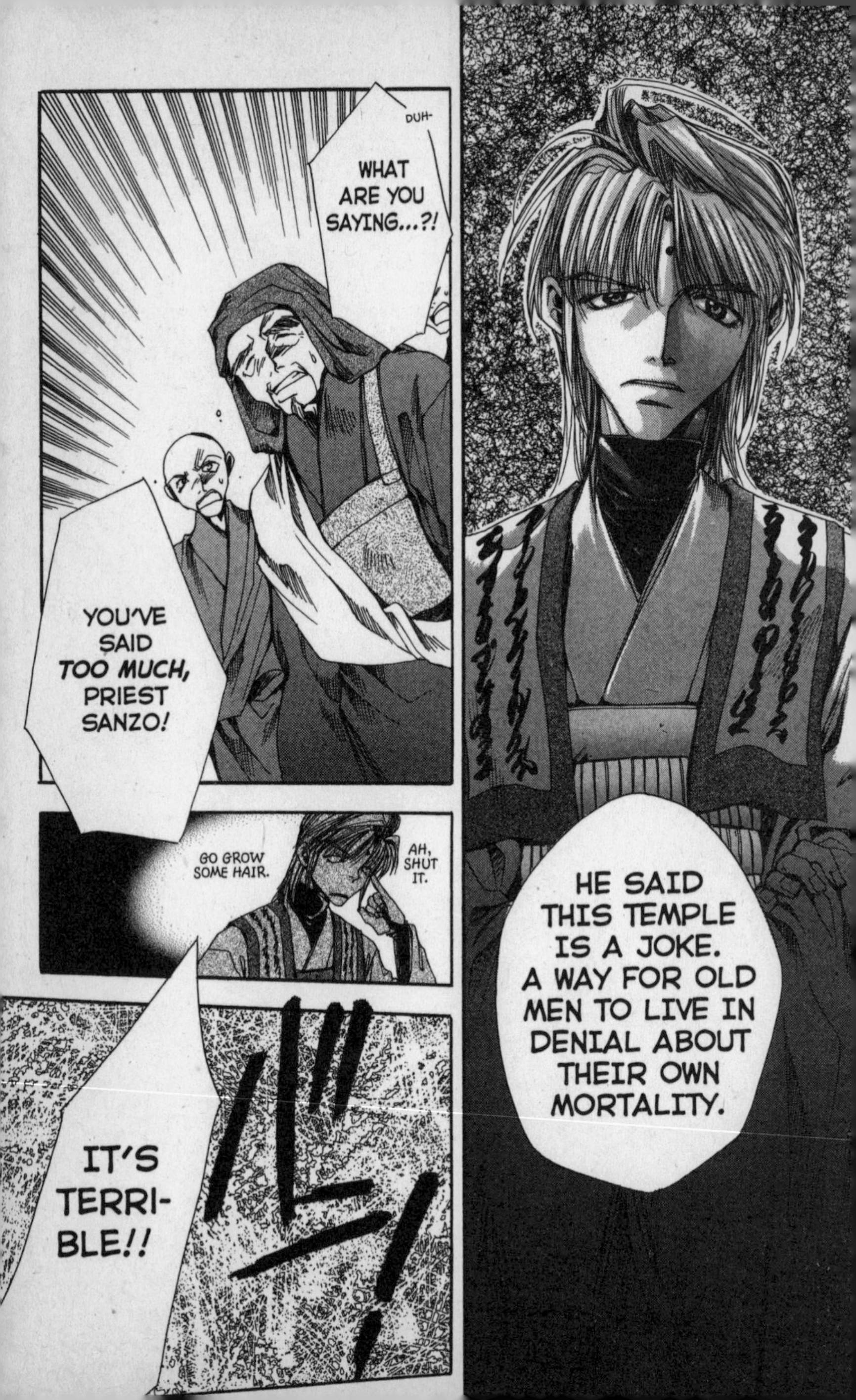
HE SAID THIS TEMPLE IS A JOKE. A WAY FOR OLD MEN TO LIVE IN DENIAL ABOUT THEIR OWN MORTALITY.
DUH-
WHAT ARE YOU SAYING...?!
YOU'VE SAID *TOO MUCH,* PRIEST SANZO!
AH, SHUT IT.
GO GROW SOME HAIR.
IT'S TERRI-BLE!!

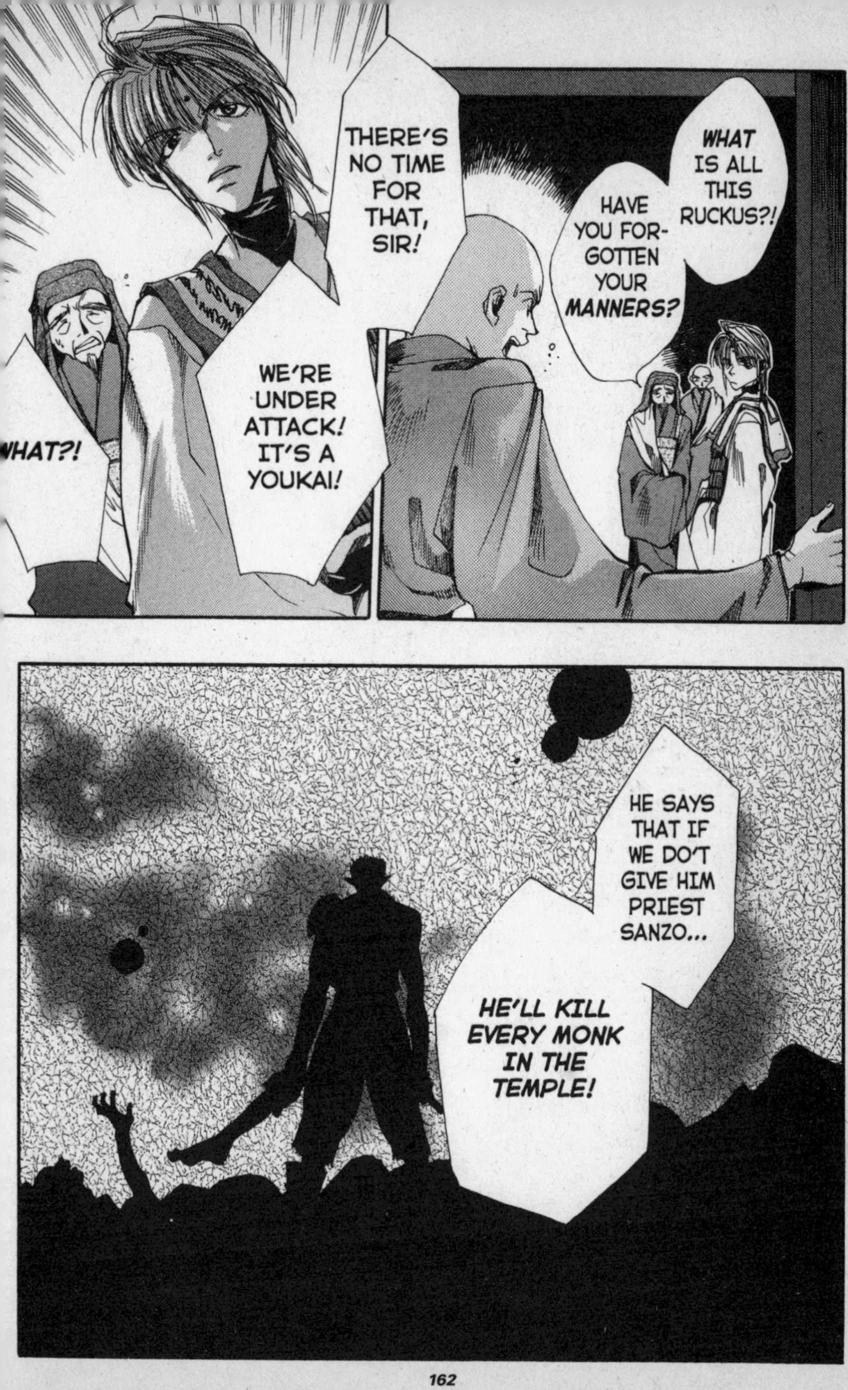
WHAT IS ALL THIS RUCKUS?!
HAVE YOU FOR-GOTTEN YOUR MANNERS?
THERE'S NO TIME FOR THAT, SIR!
WE'RE UNDER ATTACK! IT'S A YOUKAI!
WHAT?!
HE SAYS THAT IF WE DON'T GIVE HIM PRIEST SANZO...
HE'LL KILL EVERY MONK IN THE TEMPLE!

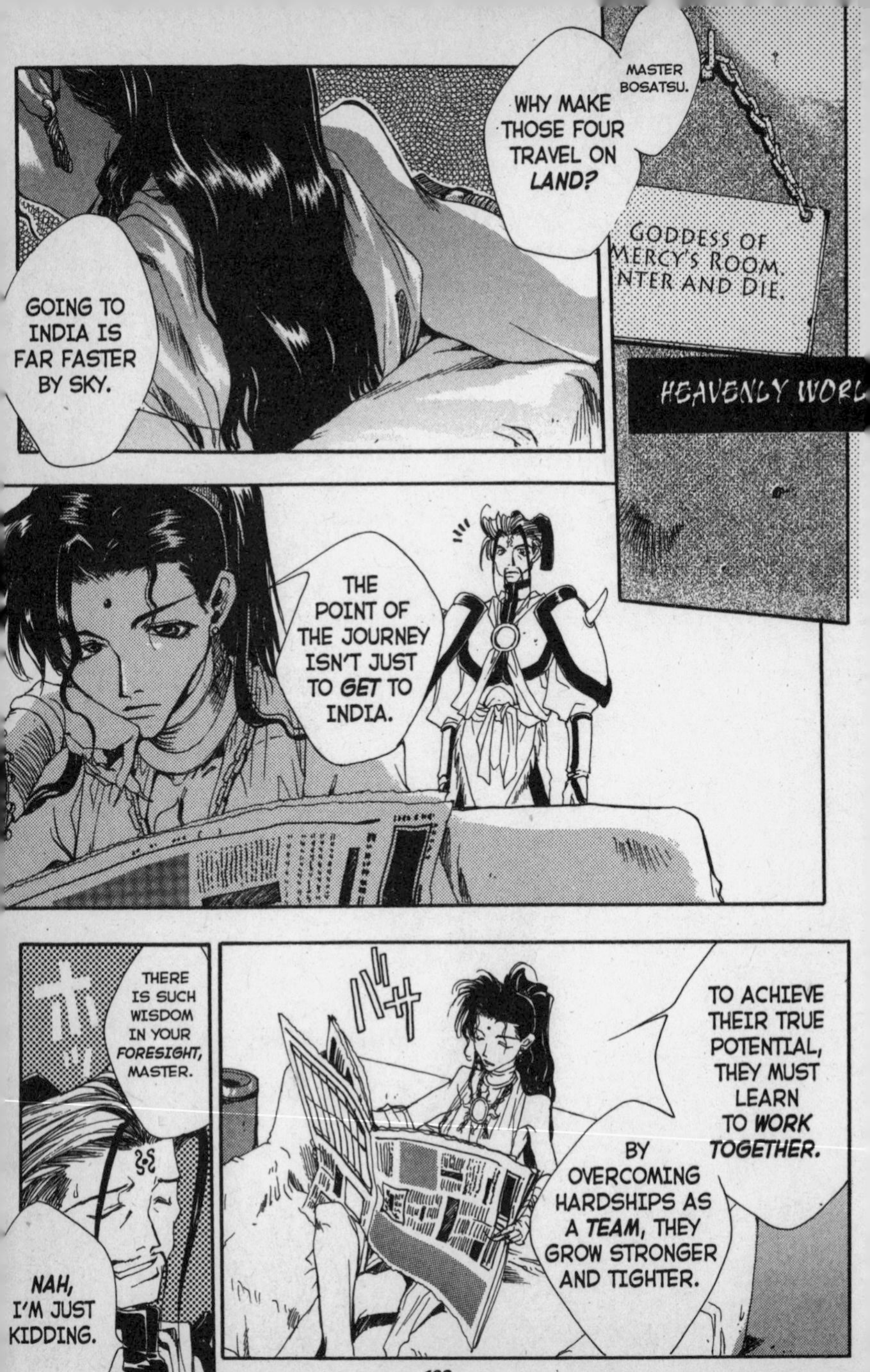
GODDESS OF
MERCY'S ROOM
NTER AND DIE.
HEAVENLY WORL
MASTER BOSATSU.
WHY MAKE THOSE FOUR TRAVEL ON *LAND?*
GOING TO INDIA IS FAR FASTER BY SKY.
THE POINT OF THE JOURNEY ISN'T JUST TO *GET* TO INDIA.
バサ
TO ACHIEVE THEIR TRUE POTENTIAL, THEY MUST LEARN TO *WORK TOGETHER.*
BY OVERCOMING HARDSHIPS AS A *TEAM*, THEY GROW STRONGER AND TIGHTER.
ホッ
THERE IS SUCH WISDOM IN YOUR *FORESIGHT*, MASTER.
NAH, I'M JUST KIDDING.

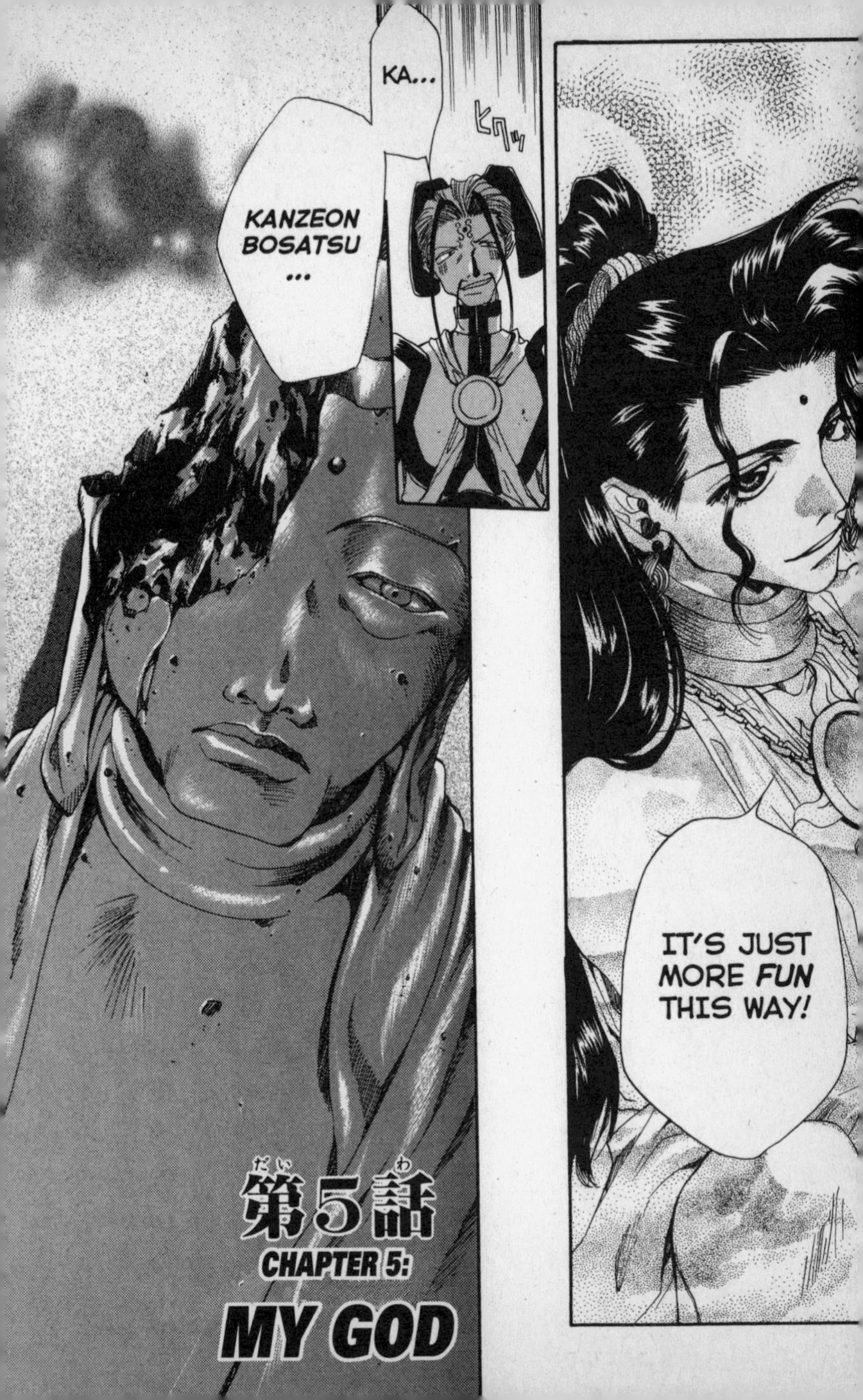
KA...
ヒクッ
KANZEON BOSATSU ...
IT'S JUST MORE FUN THIS WAY!
第5話
CHAPTER 5:
MY GOD

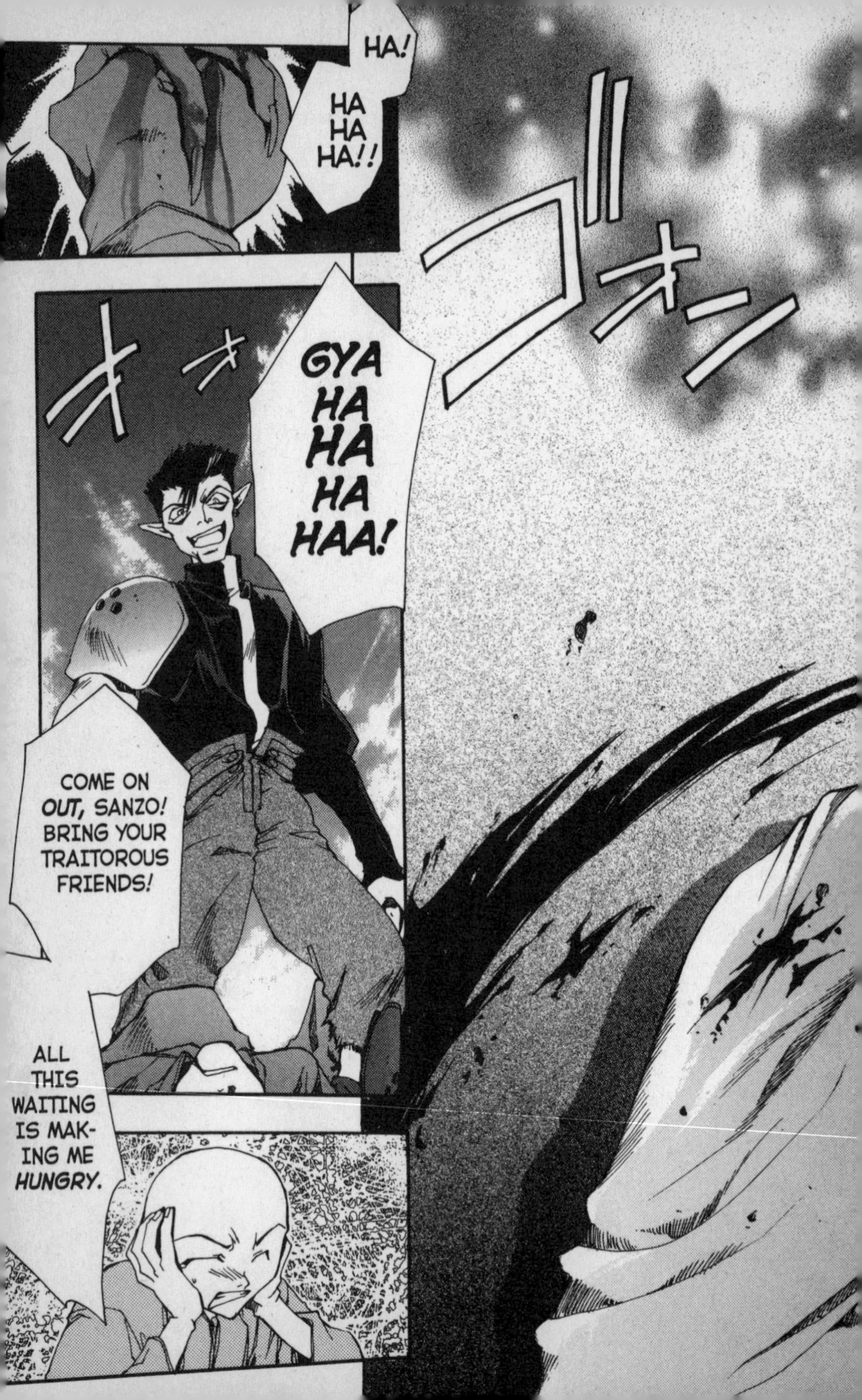
ゴオン
HA!
HA HA HA!!
GYA HA HA HA HAA!
オォ
COME ON OUT, SANZO! BRING YOUR TRAITOROUS FRIENDS!
ALL THIS WAITING IS MAKING ME HUNGRY.

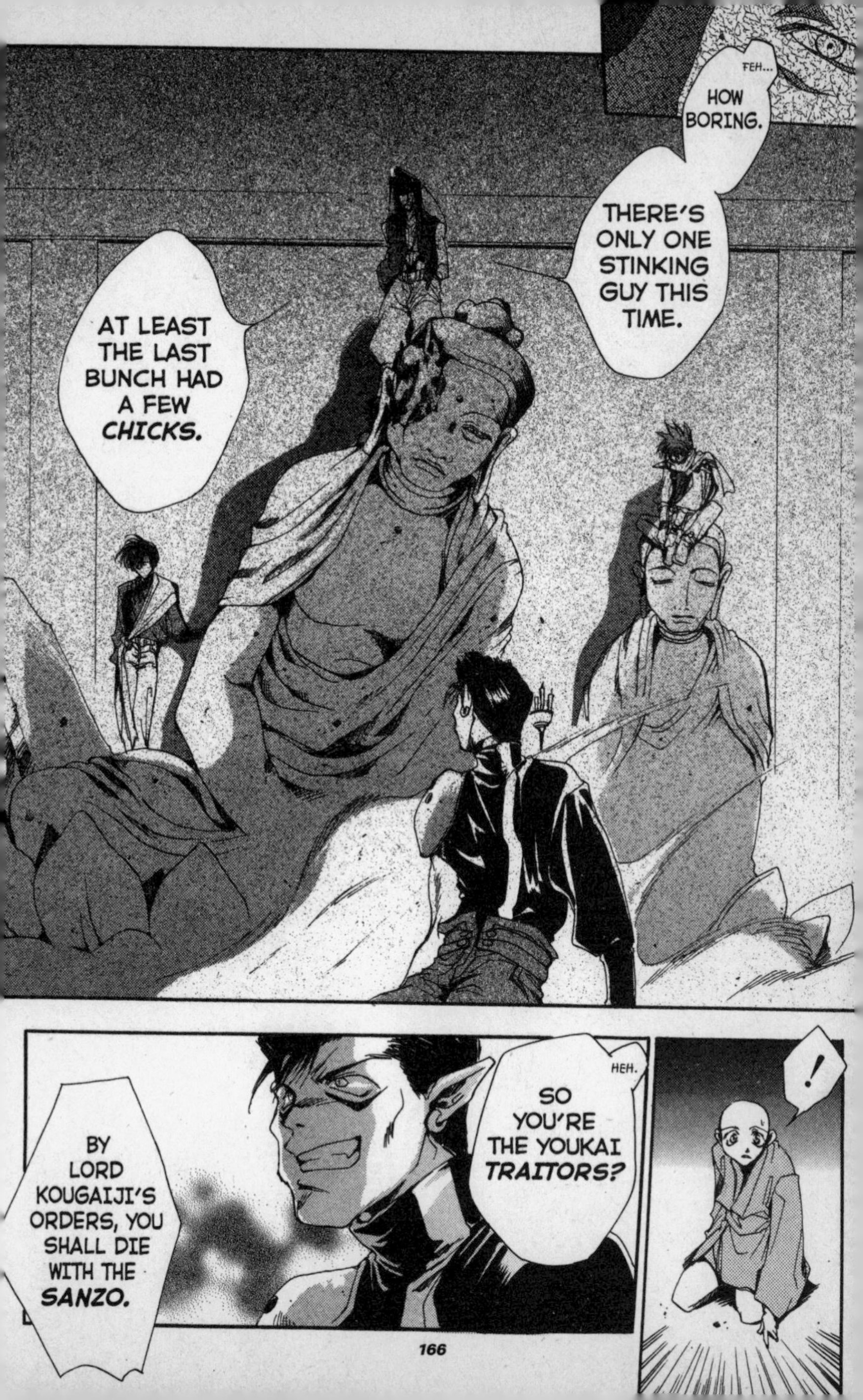
FEH... HOW BORING.
THERE'S ONLY ONE STINKING GUY THIS TIME.
AT LEAST THE LAST BUNCH HAD A FEW *CHICKS.*
!
HEH.
SO YOU'RE THE YOUKAI *TRAITORS?*
BY LORD KOUGAIJI'S ORDERS, YOU SHALL DIE WITH THE *SANZO.*

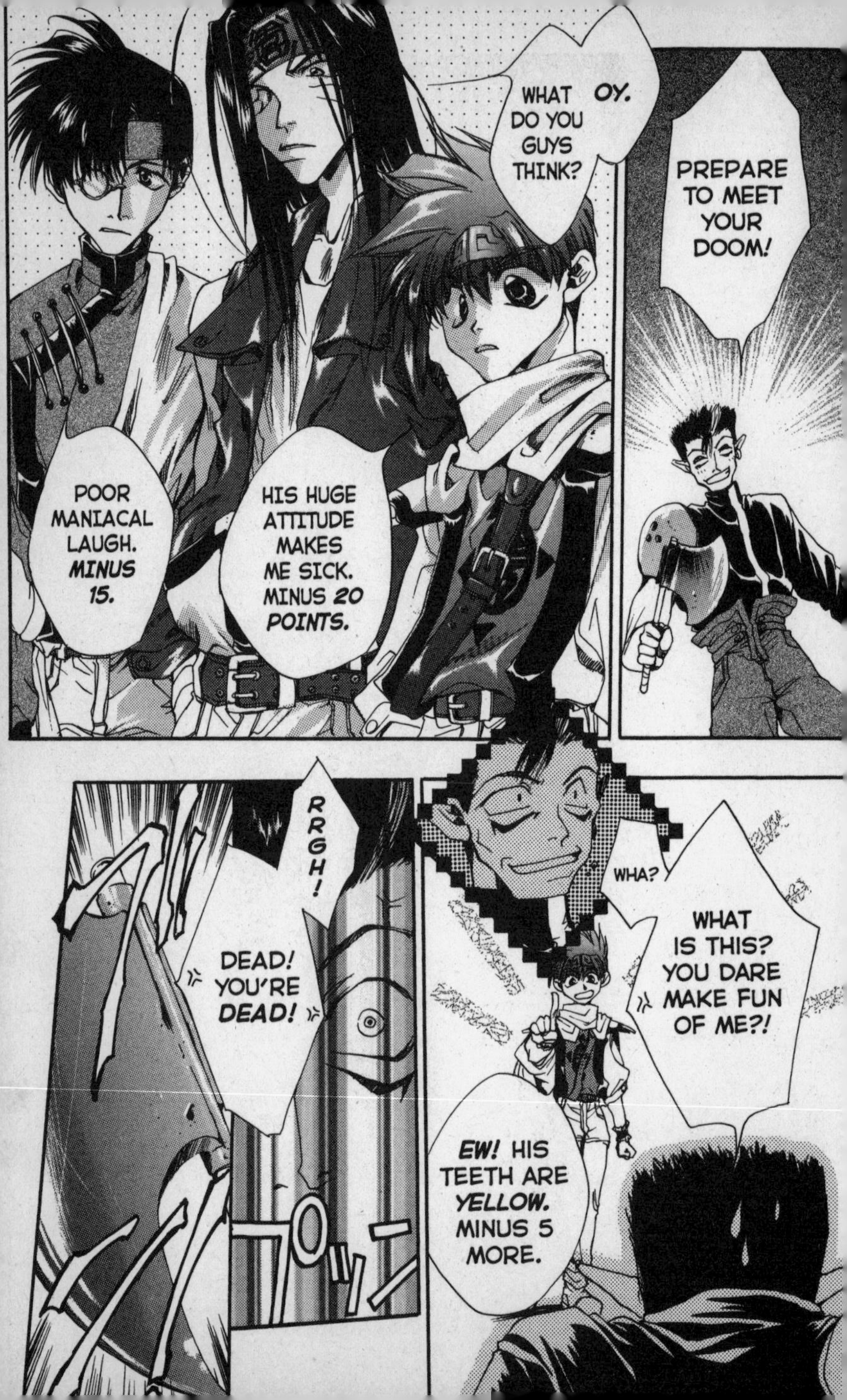
PREPARE TO MEET YOUR DOOM!
OY.
WHAT DO YOU GUYS THINK?
HIS HUGE ATTITUDE MAKES ME SICK. MINUS 20 POINTS.
POOR MANIACAL LAUGH. MINUS 15.
WHA?
WHAT IS THIS? YOU DARE MAKE FUN OF ME?!
EW! HIS TEETH ARE YELLOW. MINUS 5 MORE.
RRGH!
DEAD! YOU'RE DEAD!

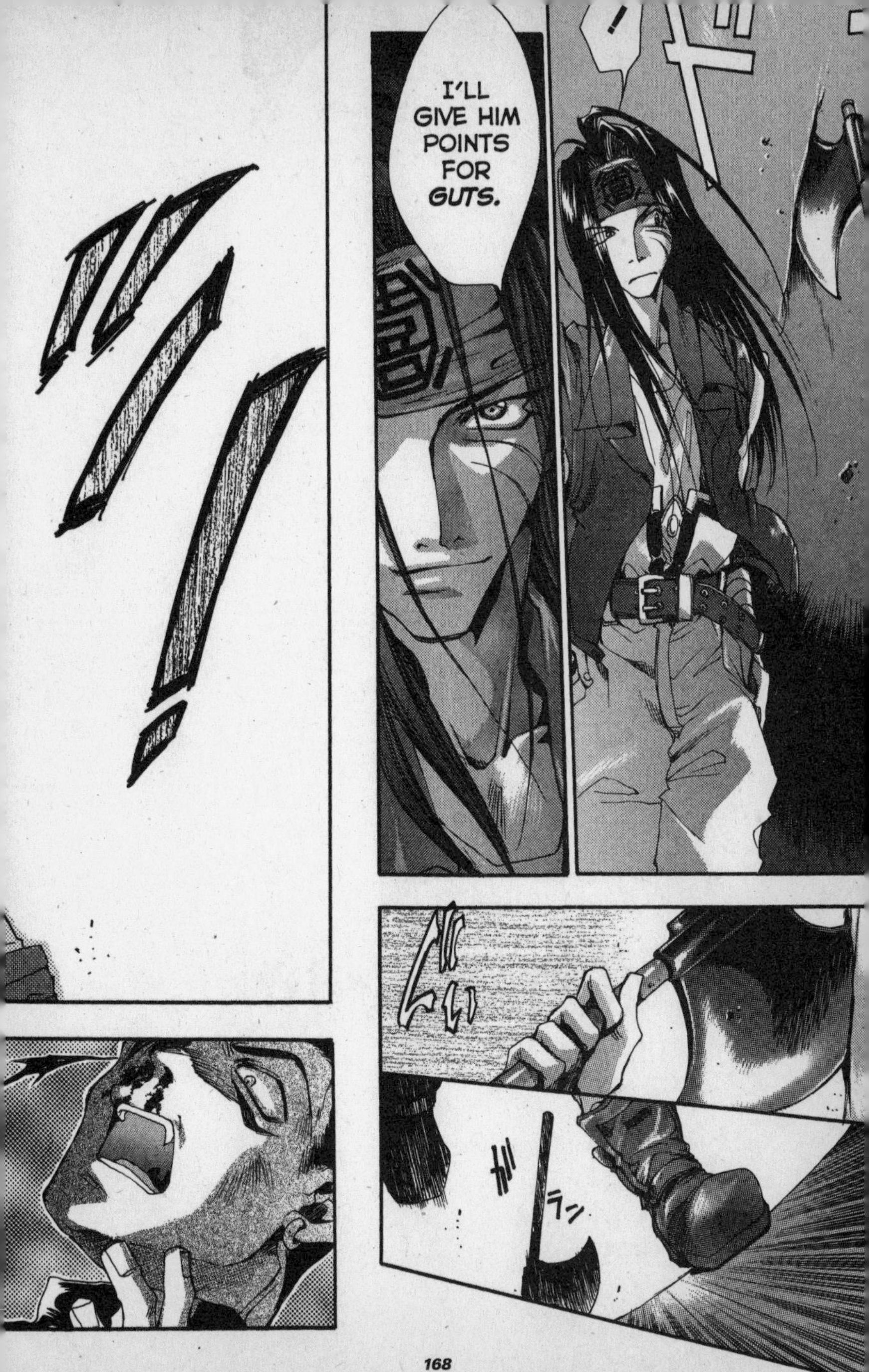
!
I'LL GIVE HIM POINTS FOR GUTS.

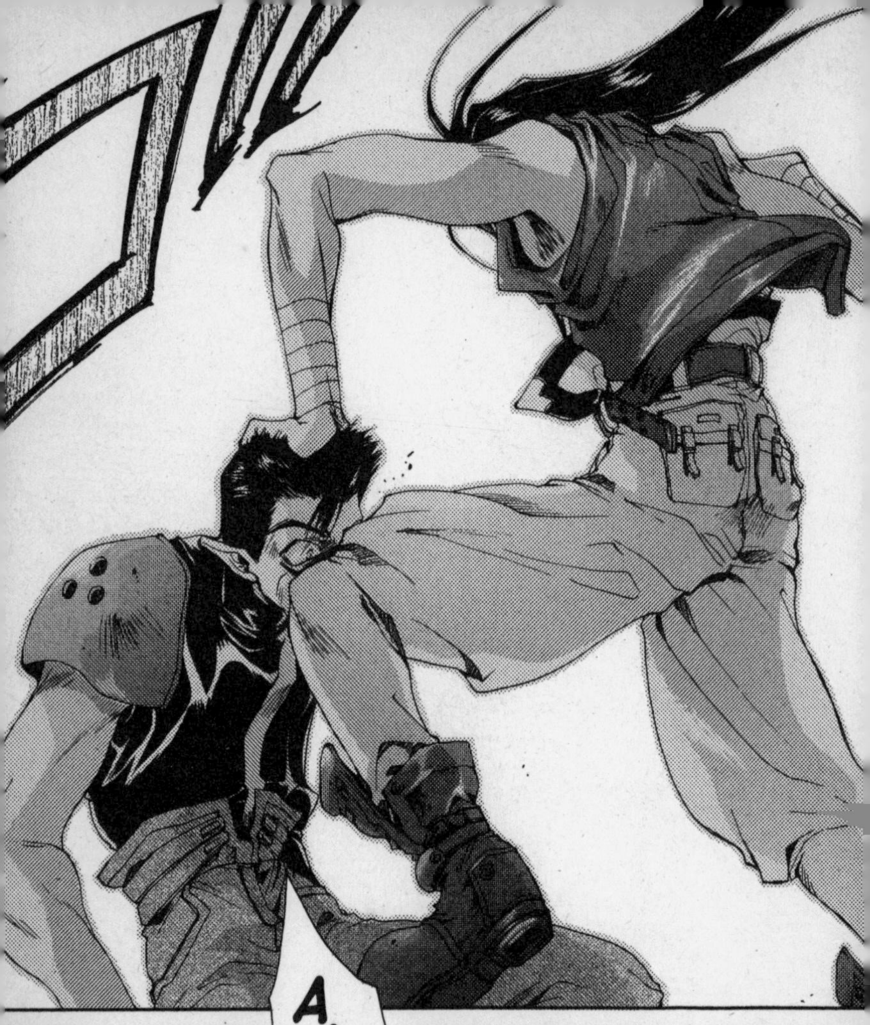
AAGH!
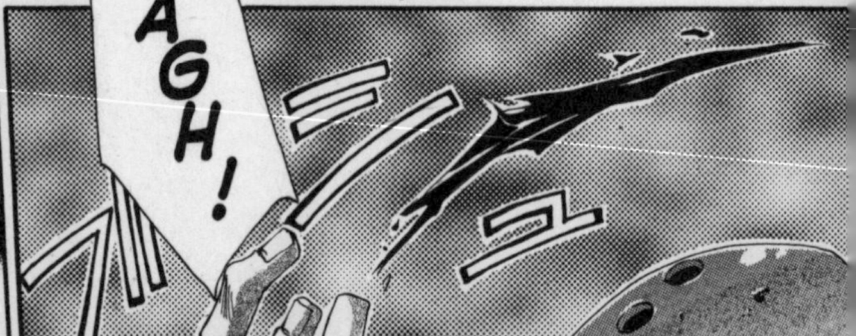
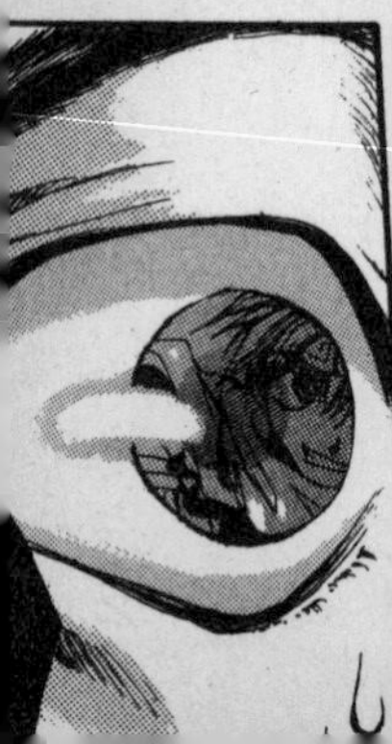

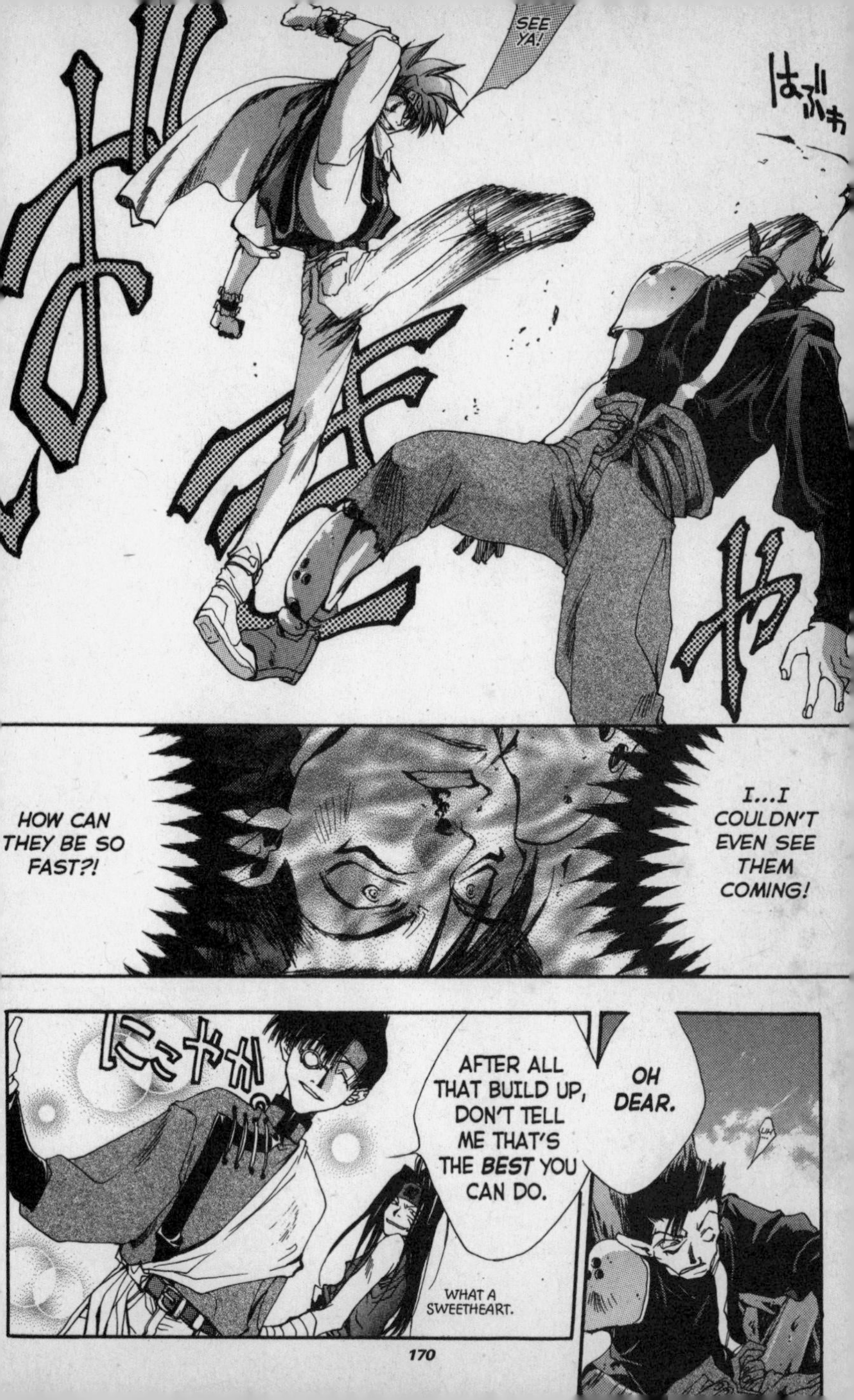
SEE YA!
I...I COULDN'T EVEN SEE THEM COMING!
HOW CAN THEY BE SO FAST?!
OH DEAR.
AFTER ALL THAT BUILD UP, DON'T TELL ME THAT'S THE BEST YOU CAN DO.
WHAT A SWEETHEART.

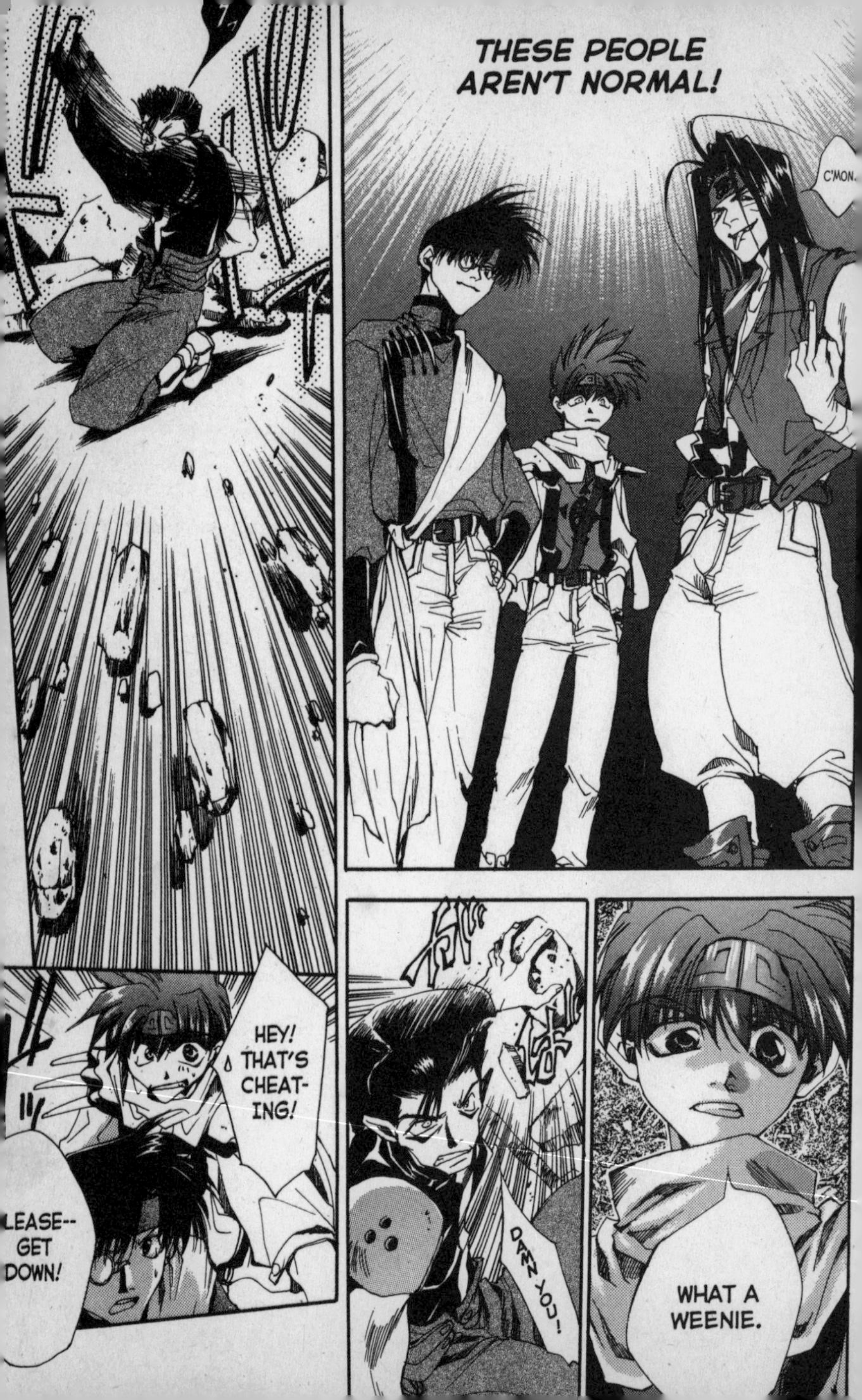
THESE PEOPLE AREN'T NORMAL!
C'MON.
WHAT A WEENIE.
DAMN YOU!
HEY! THAT'S CHEAT-ING!
LEASE-- GET DOWN!

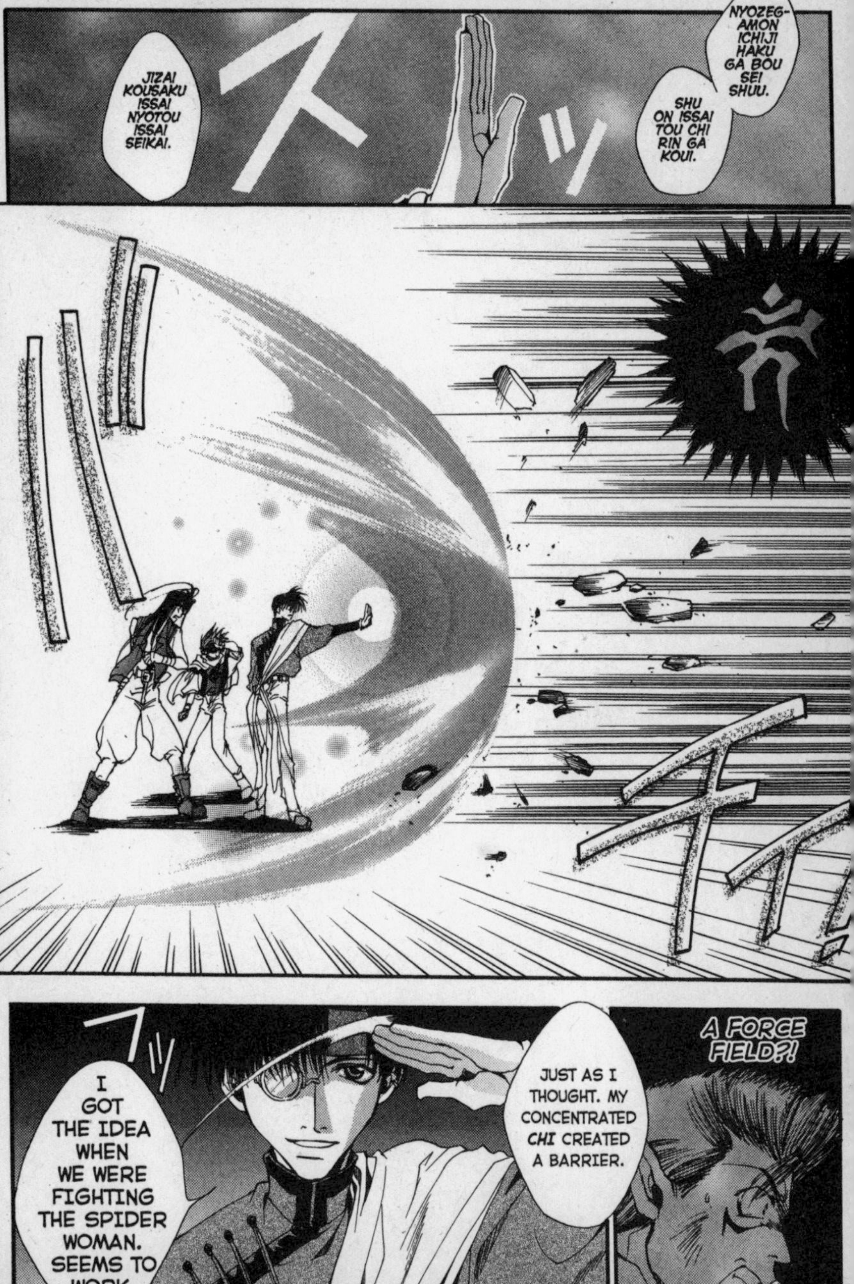
NYOZEG-AMON ICHIJI HAKU GA BOU SEI SHUU.
SHU ON ISSAI TOU CHI RIN GA KOUI.
JIZAI KOUSAKU ISSAI NYOTOU ISSAI SEIKAI.
A FORCE FIELD?!
JUST AS I THOUGHT. MY CONCENTRATED *CHI* CREATED A BARRIER.
I GOT THE IDEA WHEN WE WERE FIGHTING THE SPIDER WOMAN. SEEMS TO WORK.

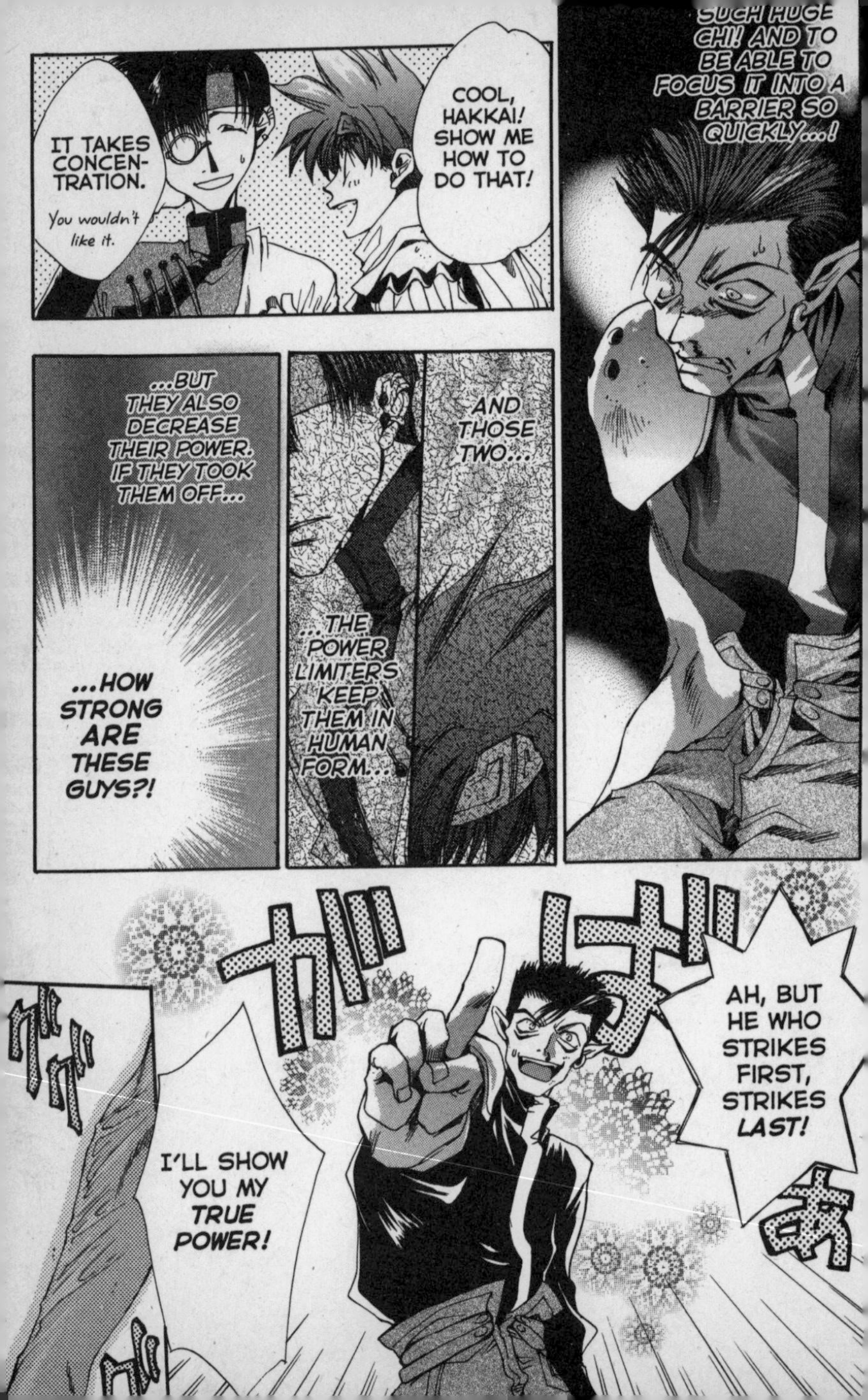
SUCH HUGE CHI! AND TO BE ABLE TO FOCUS IT INTO A BARRIER SO QUICKLY...!
COOL, HAKKAI! SHOW ME HOW TO DO THAT!
IT TAKES CONCENTRATION.
You wouldn't like it.
AND THOSE TWO...
...THE POWER LIMITERS KEEP THEM IN HUMAN FORM...
...BUT THEY ALSO DECREASE THEIR POWER. IF THEY TOOK THEM OFF...
...HOW STRONG ARE THESE GUYS?!
AH, BUT HE WHO STRIKES FIRST, STRIKES LAST!
I'LL SHOW YOU MY TRUE POWER!

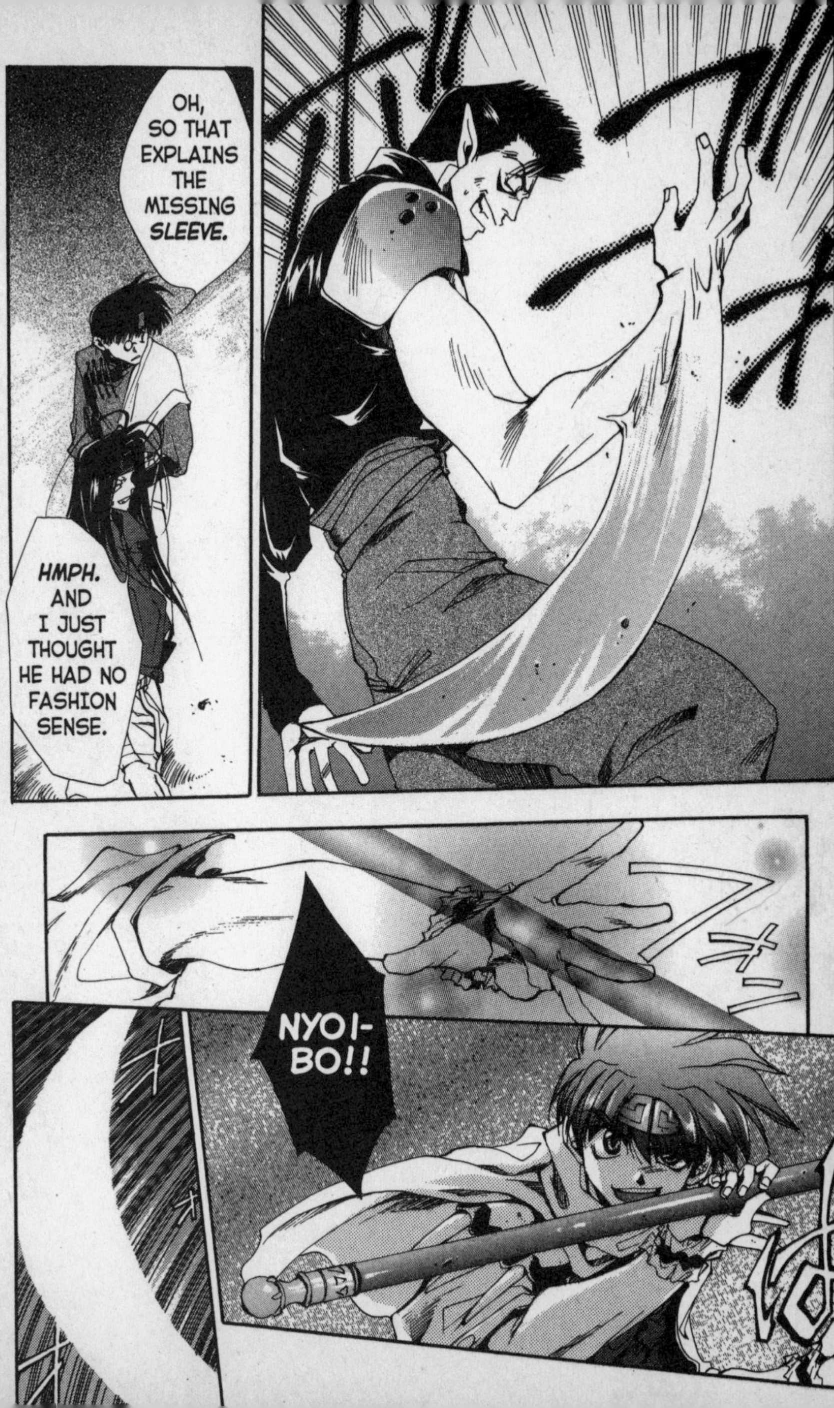
OH, SO THAT EXPLAINS THE MISSING *SLEEVE.*
HMPH. AND I JUST THOUGHT HE HAD NO FASHION SENSE.
NYOI-BO!!

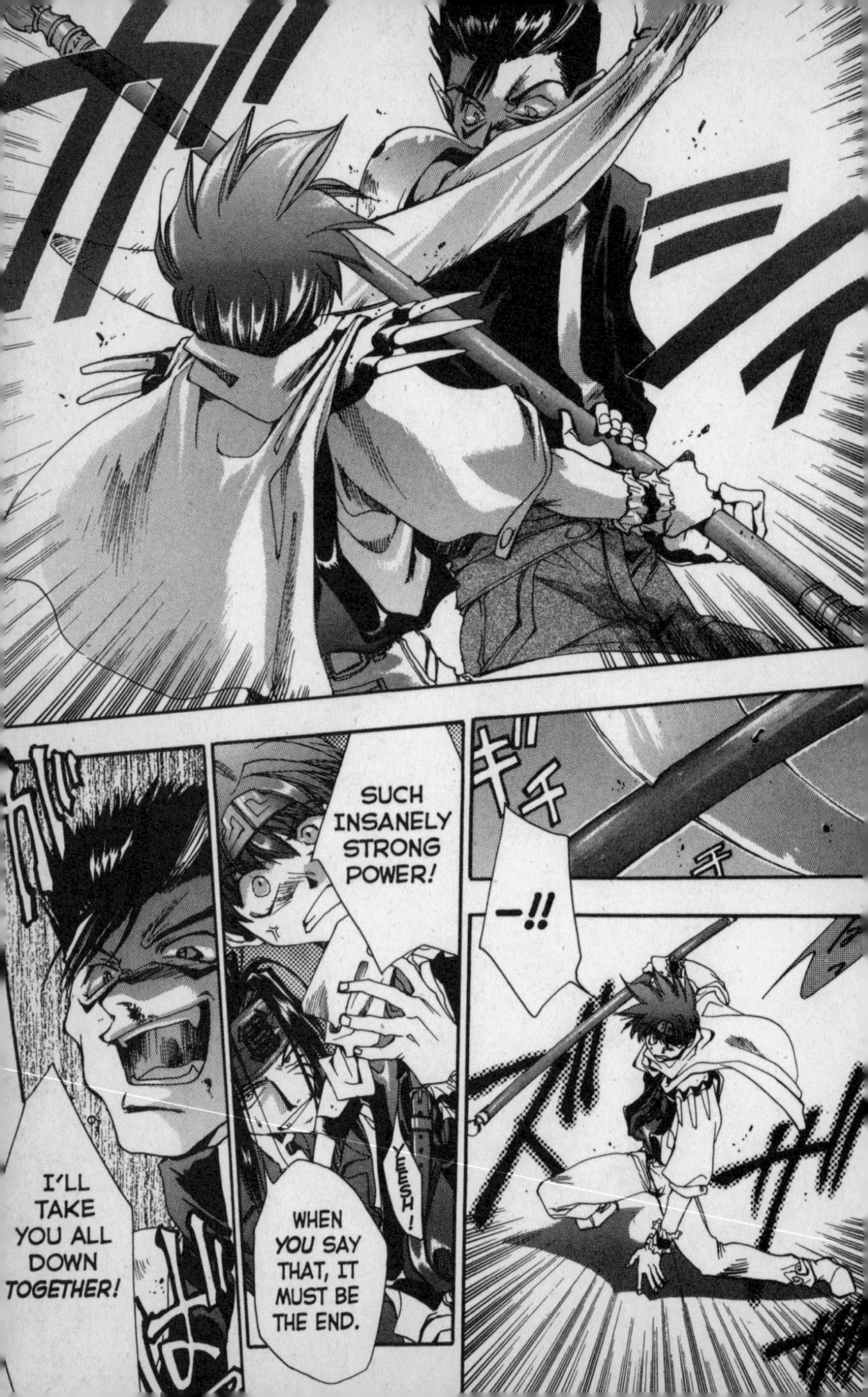
—!!
SUCH INSANELY STRONG POWER!
YEESH!
WHEN *YOU* SAY THAT, IT MUST BE THE END.
I'LL TAKE YOU ALL DOWN *TOGETHER!*

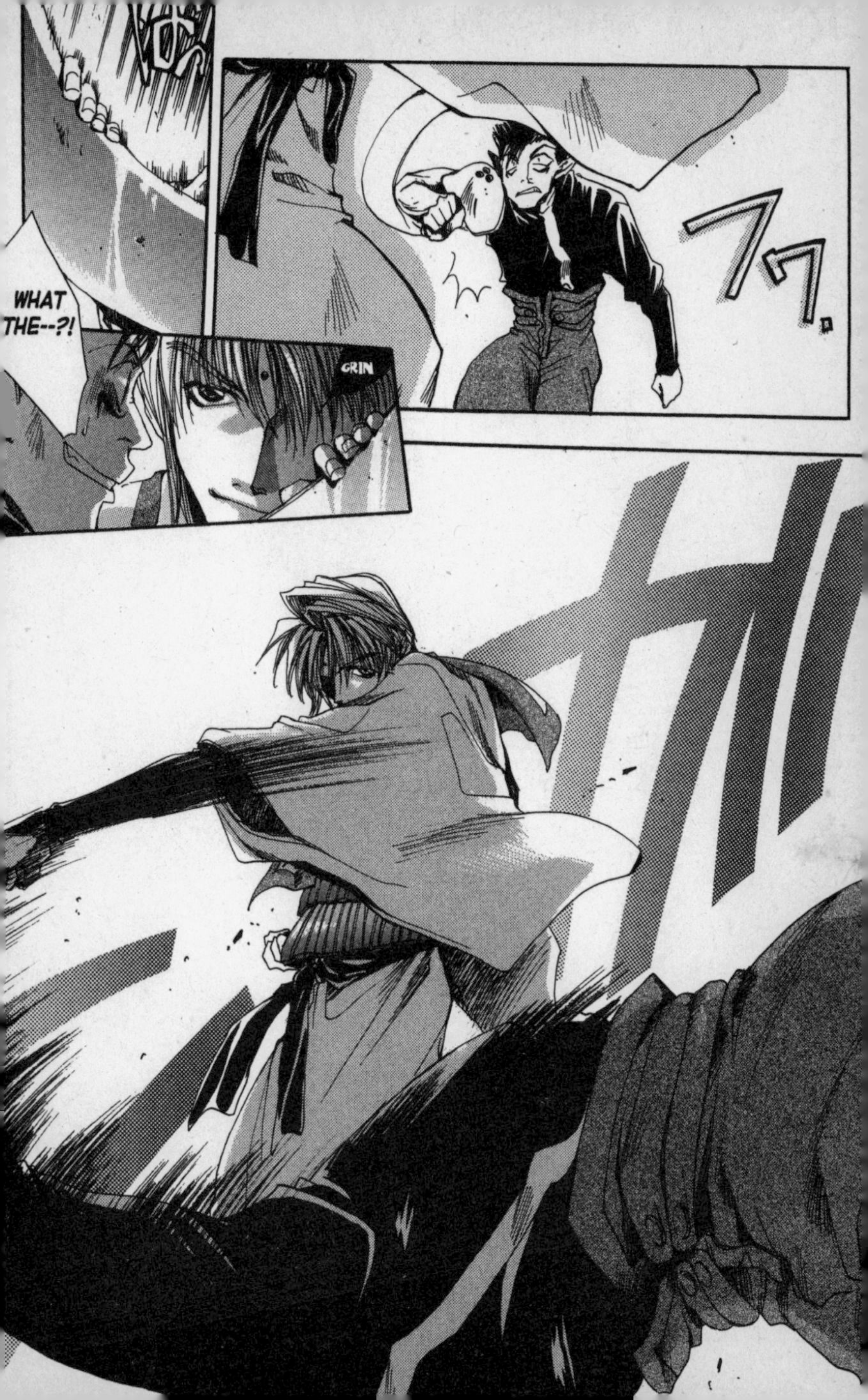
GRIN
WHAT THE--?!

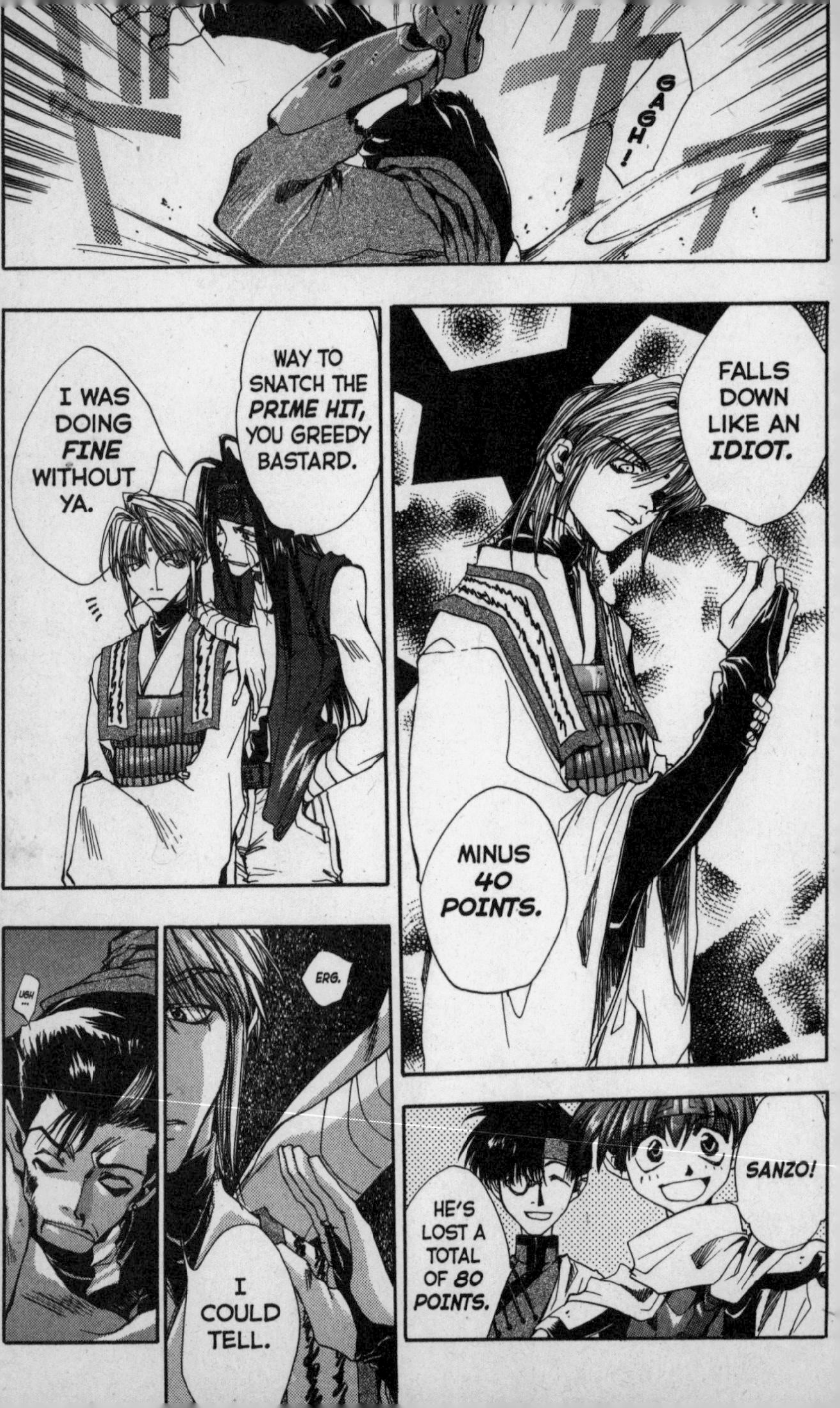
GAGH!
FALLS DOWN LIKE AN *IDIOT.*
MINUS *40* POINTS.
WAY TO SNATCH THE *PRIME HIT,* YOU GREEDY BASTARD.
I WAS DOING *FINE* WITHOUT YA.
ERG.
I COULD TELL.
UGH...
SANZO!
HE'S LOST A TOTAL OF *80* POINTS.

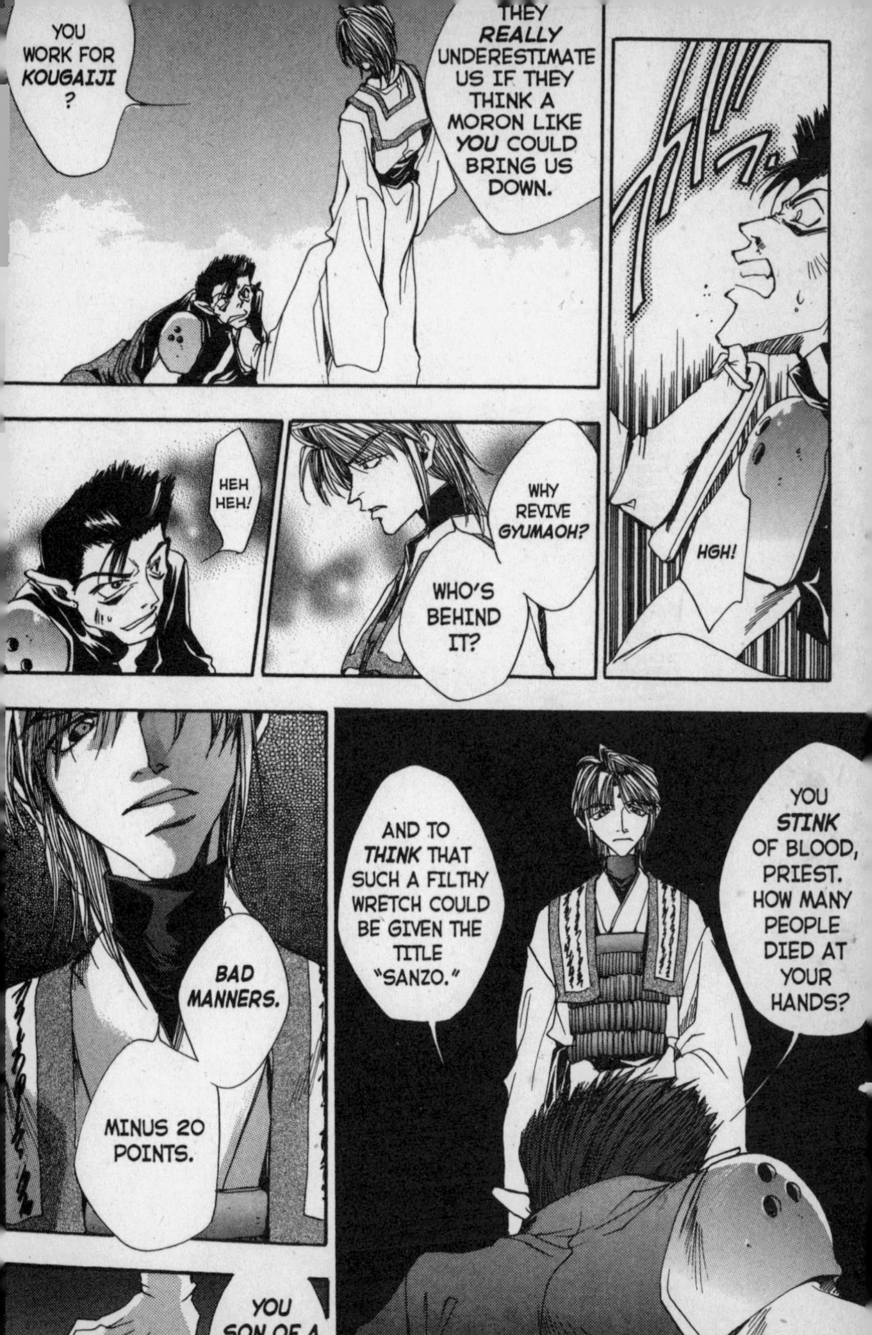
HGH!
THEY *REALLY* UNDERESTIMATE US IF THEY THINK A MORON LIKE *YOU* COULD BRING US DOWN.
YOU WORK FOR *KOUGAIJI* ?
WHY REVIVE *GYUMAOH?*
WHO'S BEHIND IT?
HEH HEH!
YOU *STINK* OF BLOOD, PRIEST. HOW MANY PEOPLE DIED AT YOUR HANDS?
AND TO *THINK* THAT SUCH A FILTHY WRETCH COULD BE GIVEN THE TITLE "SANZO."
BAD MANNERS.
MINUS 20 POINTS.
YOU SON OF A BITCH.

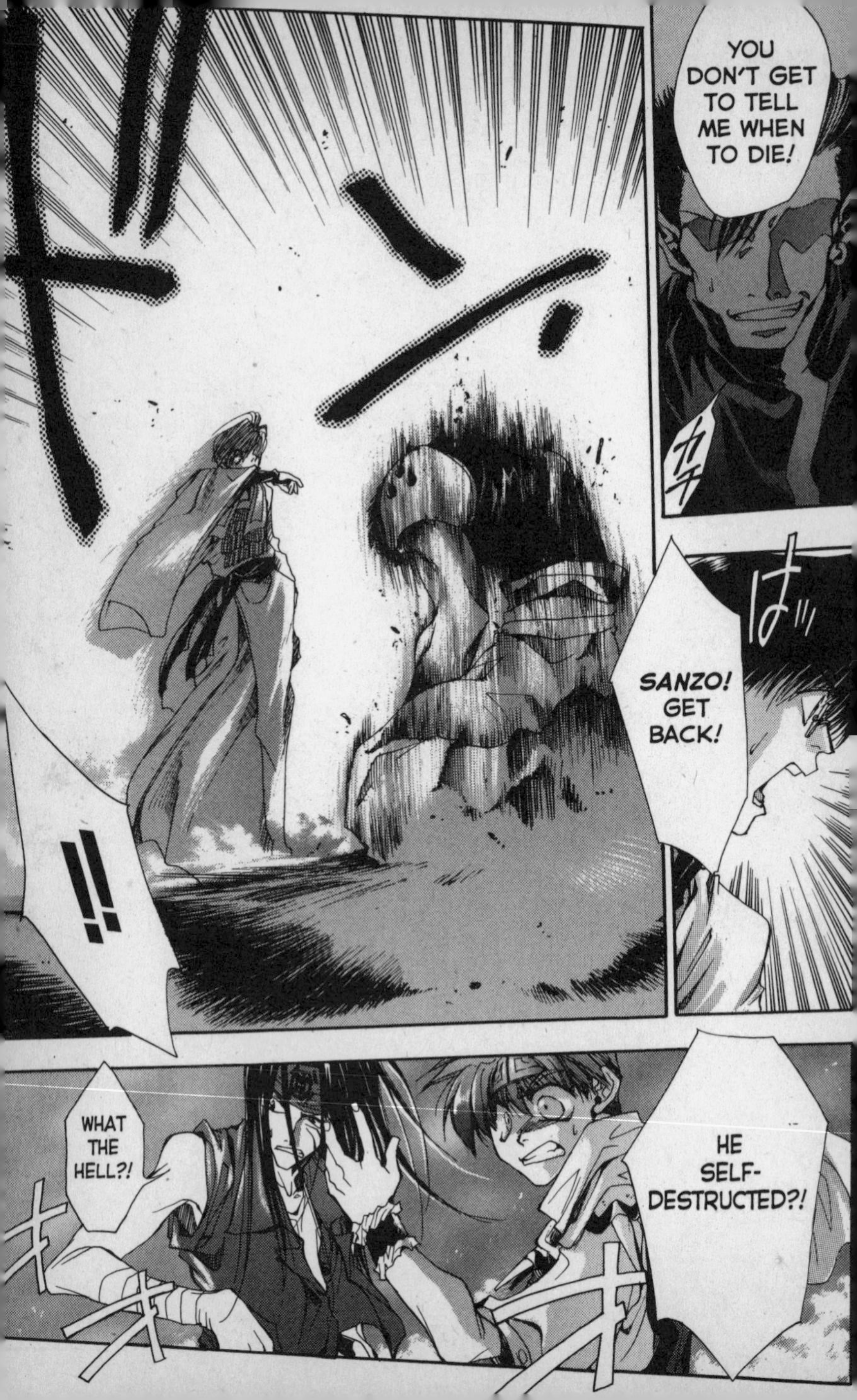
YOU DON'T GET TO TELL ME WHEN TO DIE!
SANZO! GET BACK!
!!
HE SELF-DESTRUCTED?!
WHAT THE HELL?!

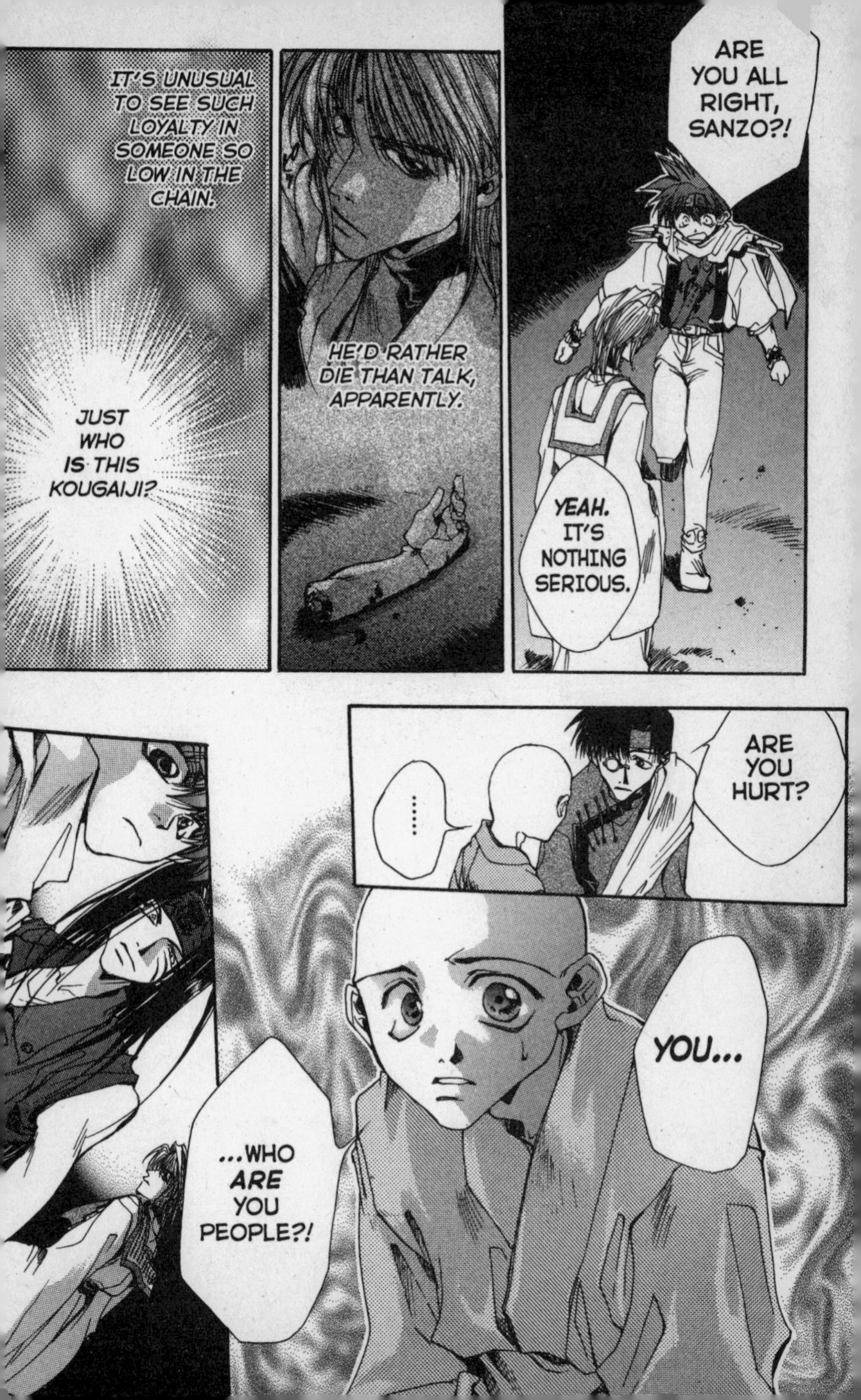
ARE YOU ALL RIGHT, SANZO?!
YEAH. IT'S NOTHING SERIOUS.
HE'D RATHER DIE THAN TALK, APPARENTLY.
IT'S UNUSUAL TO SEE SUCH LOYALTY IN SOMEONE SO LOW IN THE CHAIN.
JUST WHO IS THIS KOUGAIJI?
ARE YOU HURT?
......
YOU...
...WHO ARE YOU PEOPLE?!

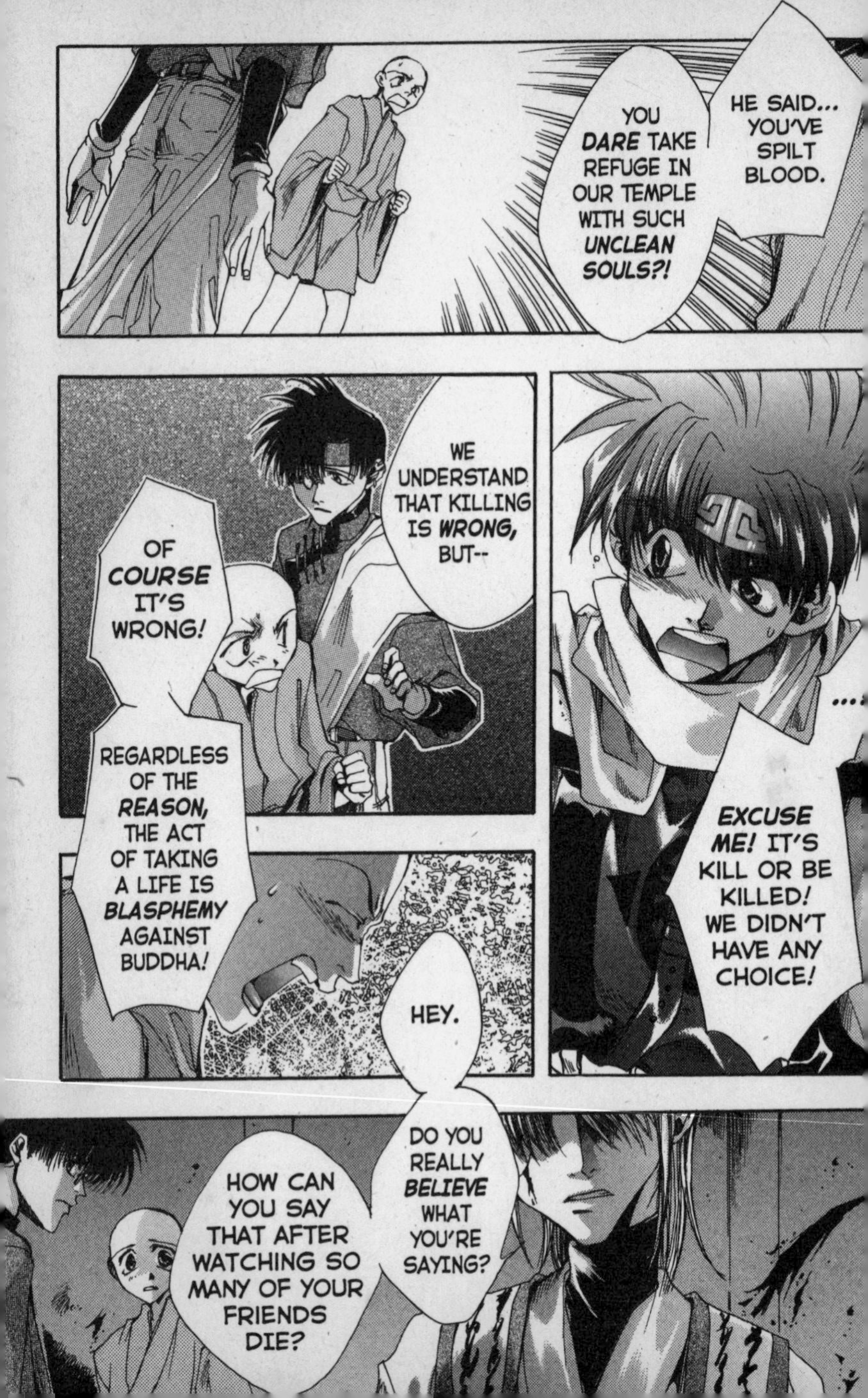
HE SAID... YOU'VE SPILT BLOOD.
YOU DARE TAKE REFUGE IN OUR TEMPLE WITH SUCH UNCLEAN SOULS?!
....
EXCUSE ME! IT'S KILL OR BE KILLED! WE DIDN'T HAVE ANY CHOICE!
WE UNDERSTAND THAT KILLING IS WRONG, BUT--
OF COURSE IT'S WRONG!
REGARDLESS OF THE REASON, THE ACT OF TAKING A LIFE IS BLASPHEMY AGAINST BUDDHA!
HEY.
DO YOU REALLY BELIEVE WHAT YOU'RE SAYING?
HOW CAN YOU SAY THAT AFTER WATCHING SO MANY OF YOUR FRIENDS DIE?

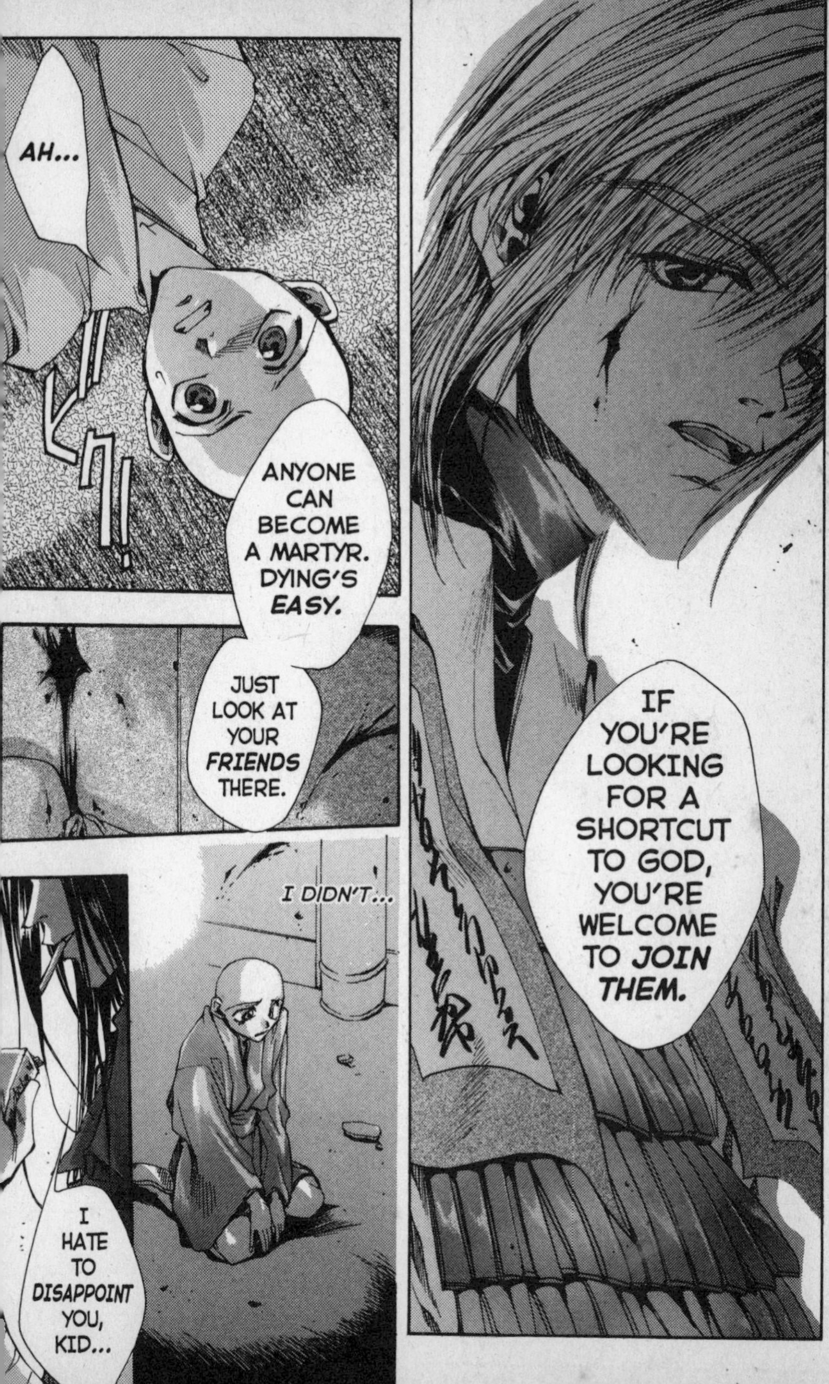
AH...
ANYONE CAN BECOME A MARTYR. DYING'S *EASY.*
JUST LOOK AT YOUR *FRIENDS* THERE.
IF YOU'RE LOOKING FOR A SHORTCUT TO GOD, YOU'RE WELCOME TO *JOIN THEM.*
I DIDN'T...
I HATE TO *DISAPPOINT* YOU, KID...

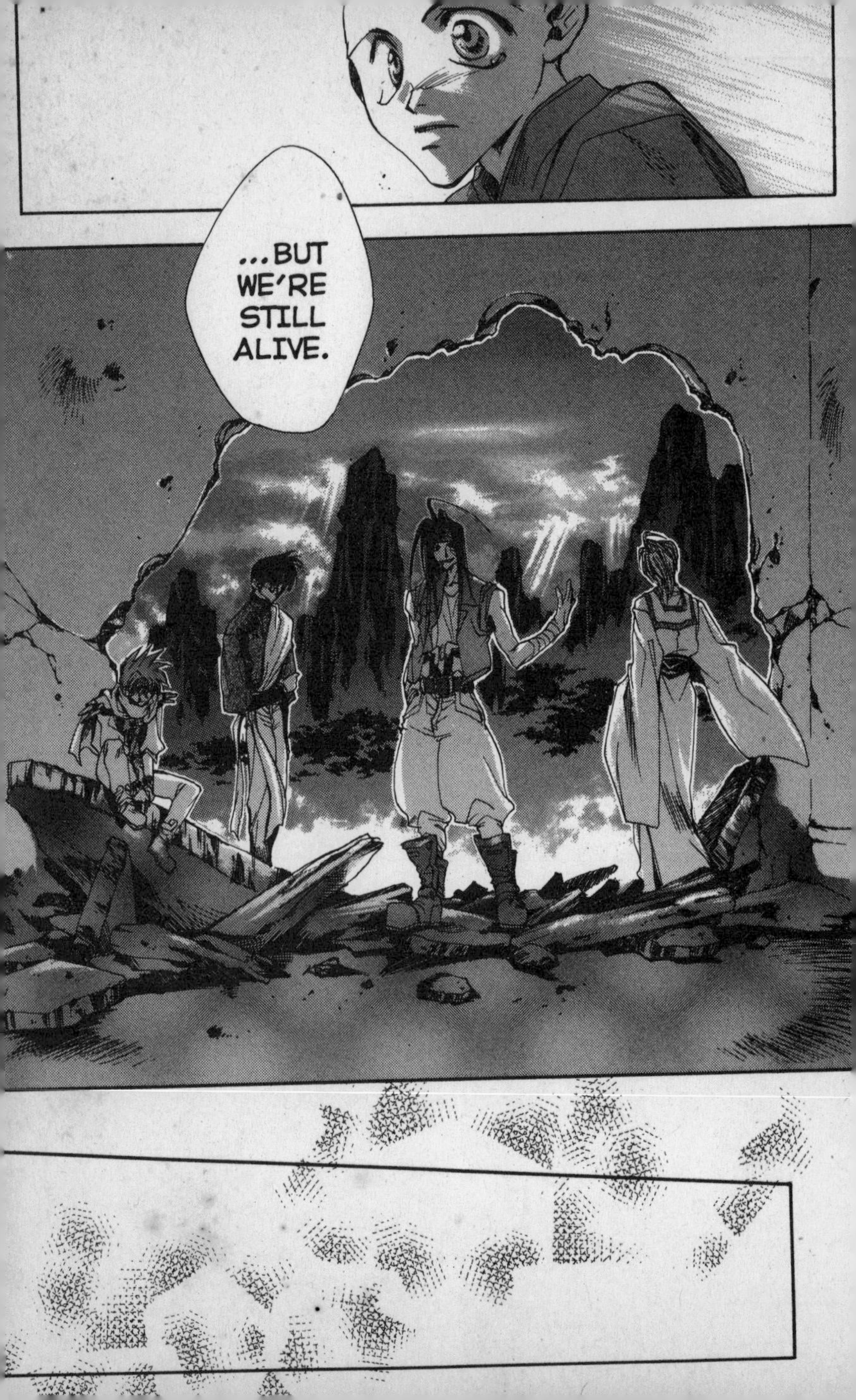
...BUT WE'RE STILL ALIVE.

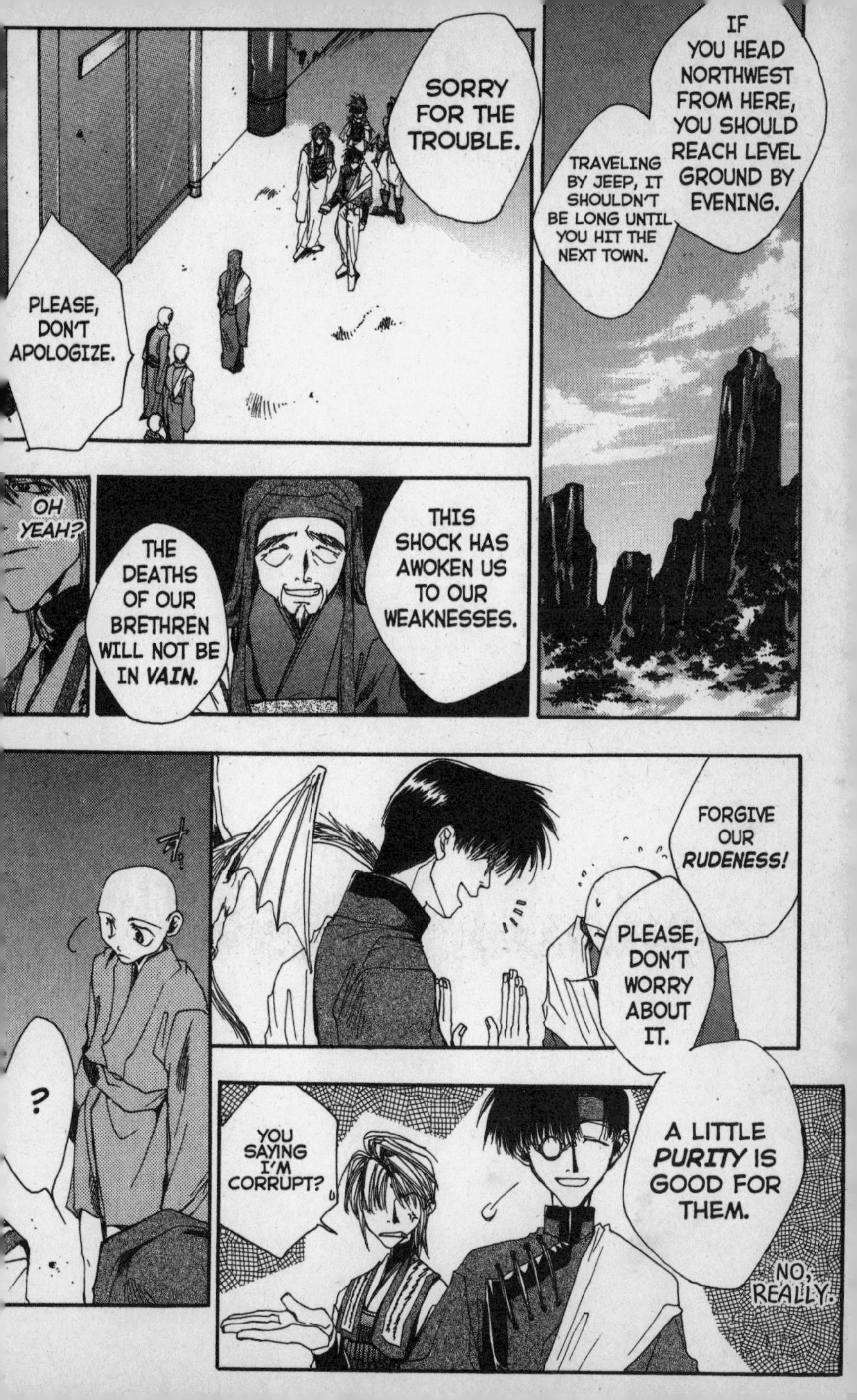
IF YOU HEAD NORTHWEST FROM HERE, YOU SHOULD REACH LEVEL GROUND BY EVENING.
TRAVELING BY JEEP, IT SHOULDN'T BE LONG UNTIL YOU HIT THE NEXT TOWN.
SORRY FOR THE TROUBLE.
PLEASE, DON'T APOLOGIZE.
THIS SHOCK HAS AWOKEN US TO OUR WEAKNESSES.
THE DEATHS OF OUR BRETHREN WILL NOT BE IN *VAIN.*
OH YEAH?
FORGIVE OUR *RUDENESS!*
PLEASE, DON'T WORRY ABOUT IT.
A LITTLE *PURITY* IS GOOD FOR THEM.
YOU SAYING I'M CORRUPT?
NO, REALLY.
?

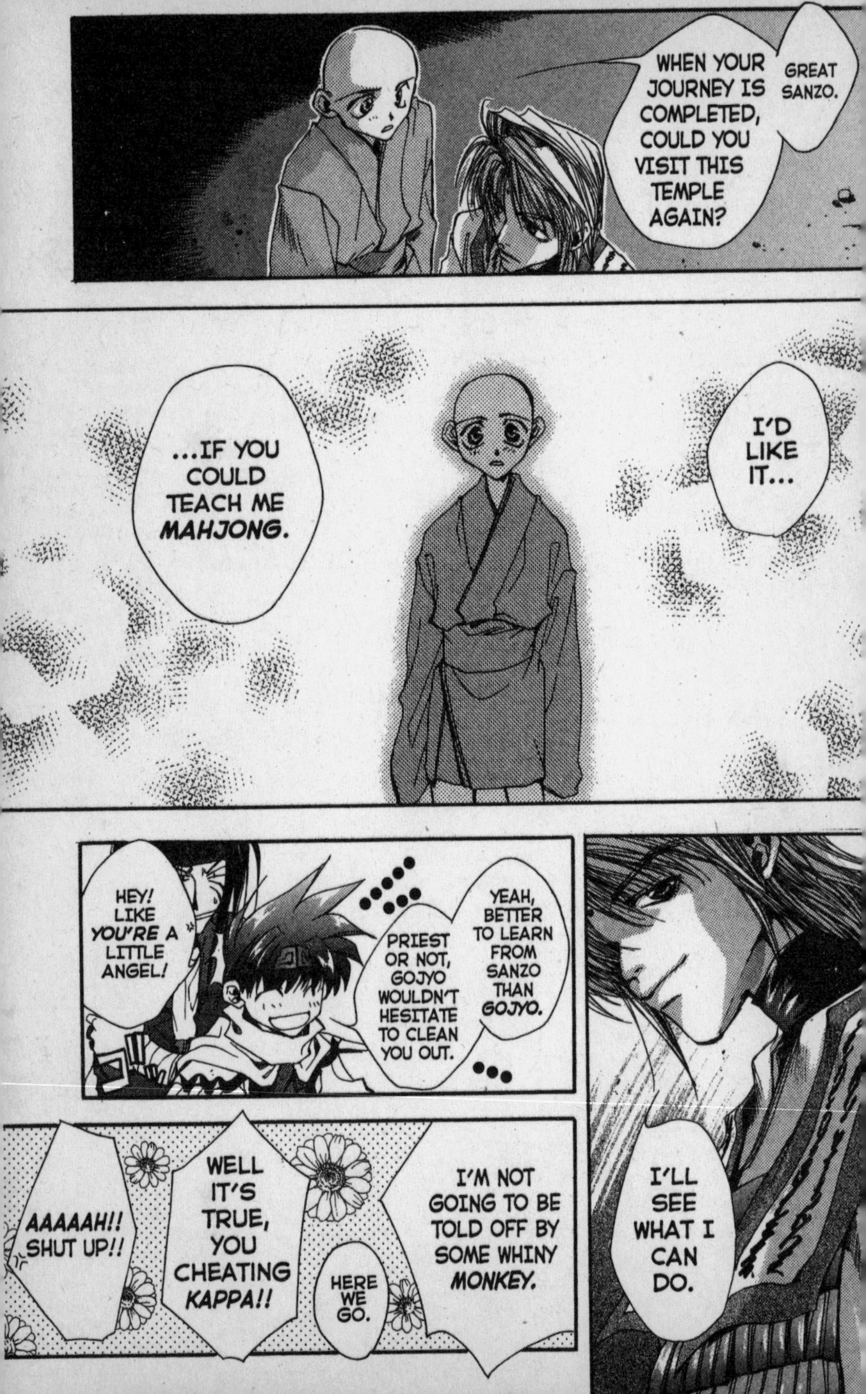
GREAT SANZO.
WHEN YOUR JOURNEY IS COMPLETED, COULD YOU VISIT THIS TEMPLE AGAIN?
I'D LIKE IT...
...IF YOU COULD TEACH ME *MAHJONG*.
I'LL SEE WHAT I CAN DO.
YEAH, BETTER TO LEARN FROM SANZO THAN *GOJYO*.
PRIEST OR NOT, GOJYO WOULDN'T HESITATE TO CLEAN YOU OUT.
HEY! LIKE *YOU'RE* A LITTLE ANGEL!
I'M NOT GOING TO BE TOLD OFF BY SOME WHINY *MONKEY*.
HERE WE GO.
WELL IT'S TRUE, YOU CHEATING *KAPPA!!*
AAAAAH!! SHUT UP!!

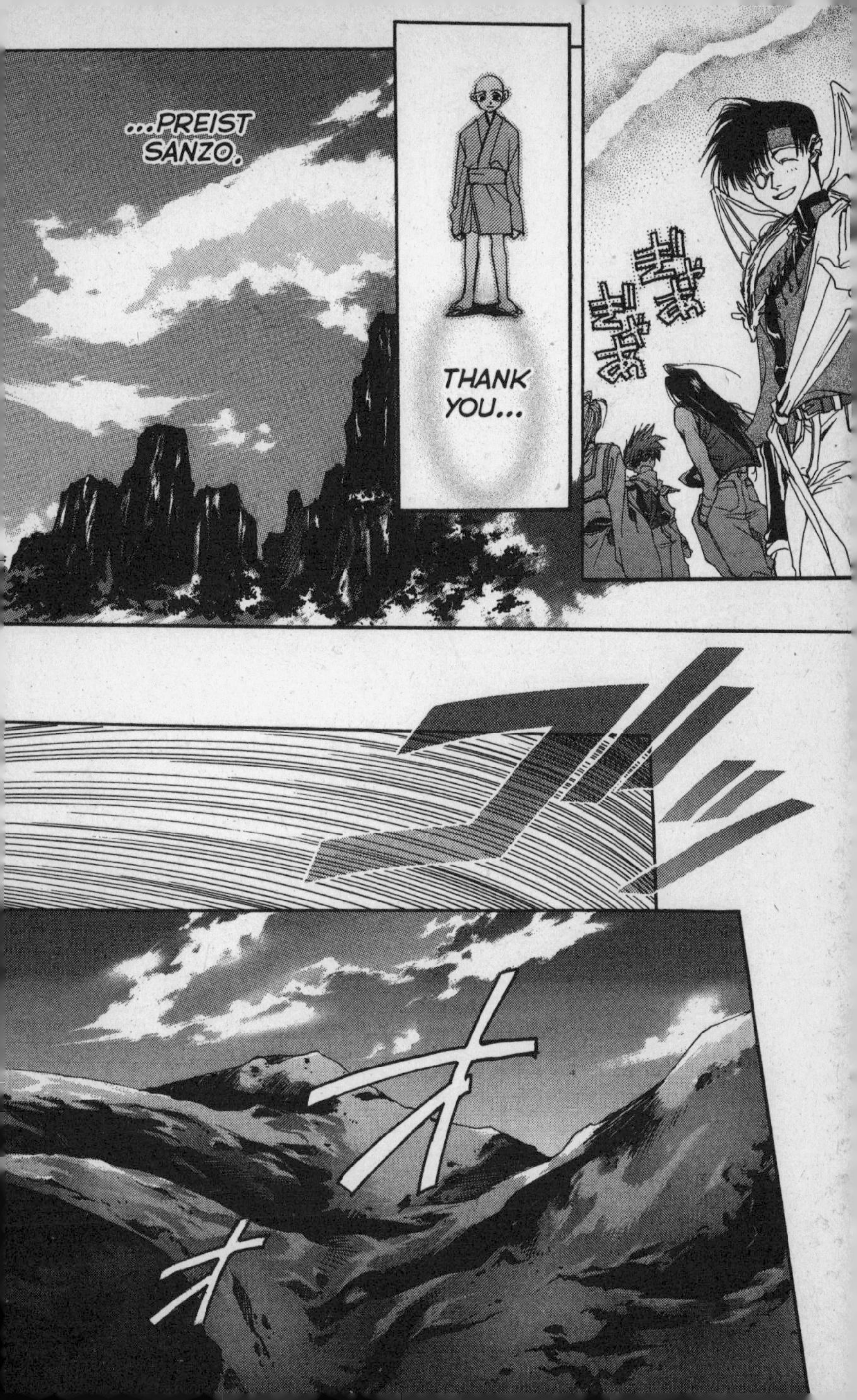

THANK YOU...
...PREIST SANZO.

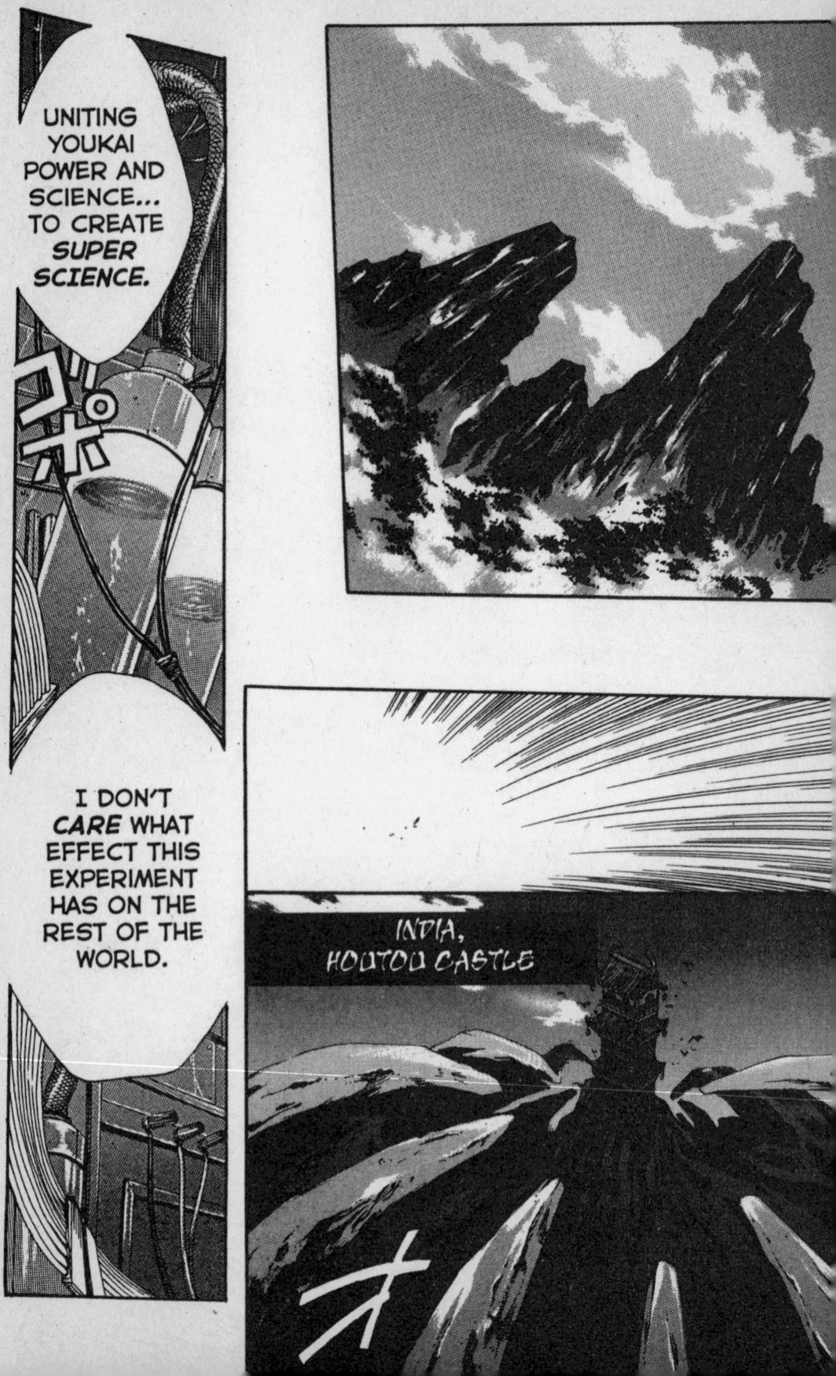
INDIA, HOUTOU CASTLE
UNITING YOUKAI POWER AND SCIENCE... TO CREATE *SUPER SCIENCE.*
I DON'T *CARE* WHAT EFFECT THIS EXPERIMENT HAS ON THE REST OF THE WORLD.

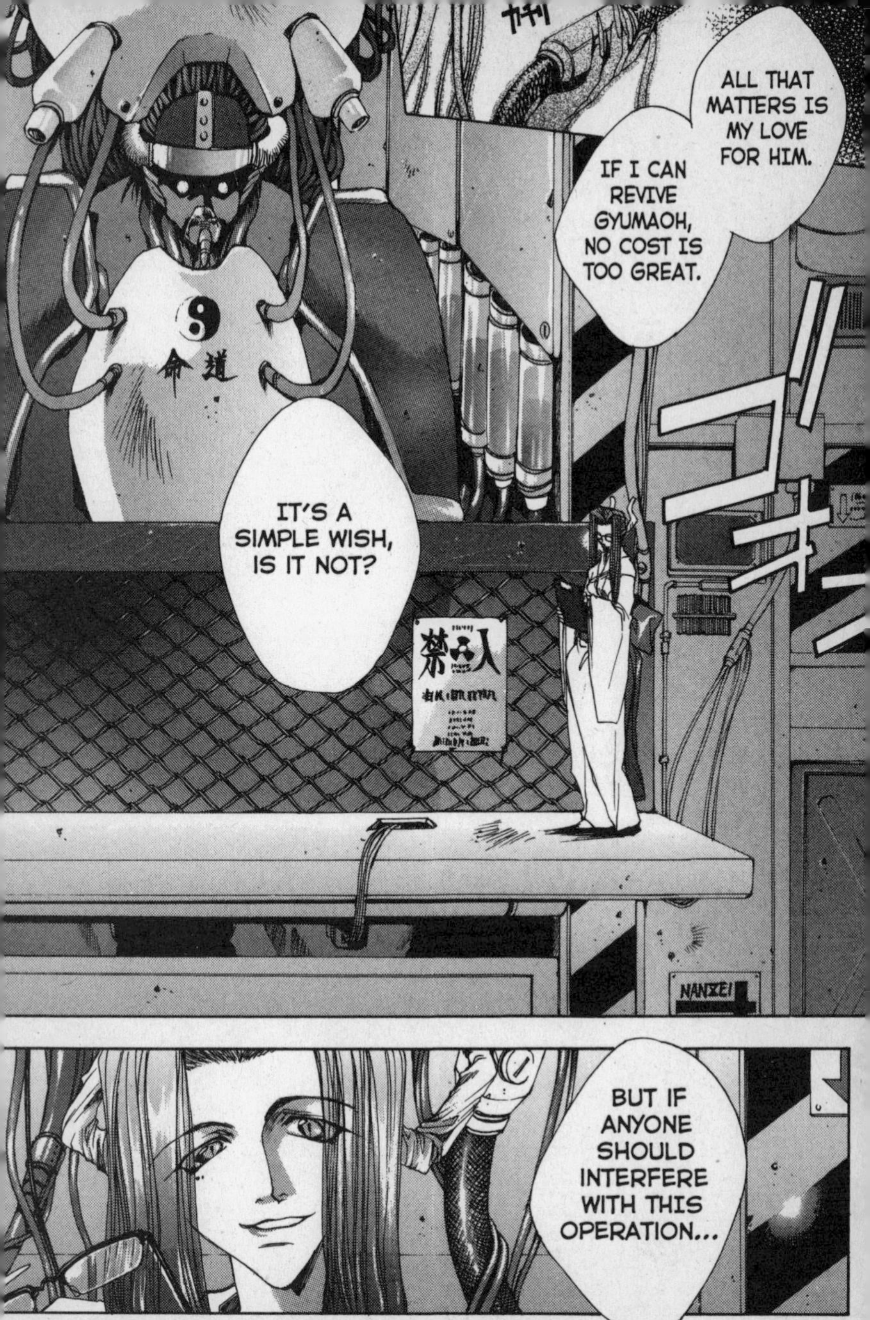
ALL THAT MATTERS IS MY LOVE FOR HIM.
IF I CAN REVIVE GYUMAOH, NO COST IS TOO GREAT.
IT'S A SIMPLE WISH, IS IT NOT?
NANZEI
BUT IF ANYONE SHOULD INTERFERE WITH THIS OPERATION...

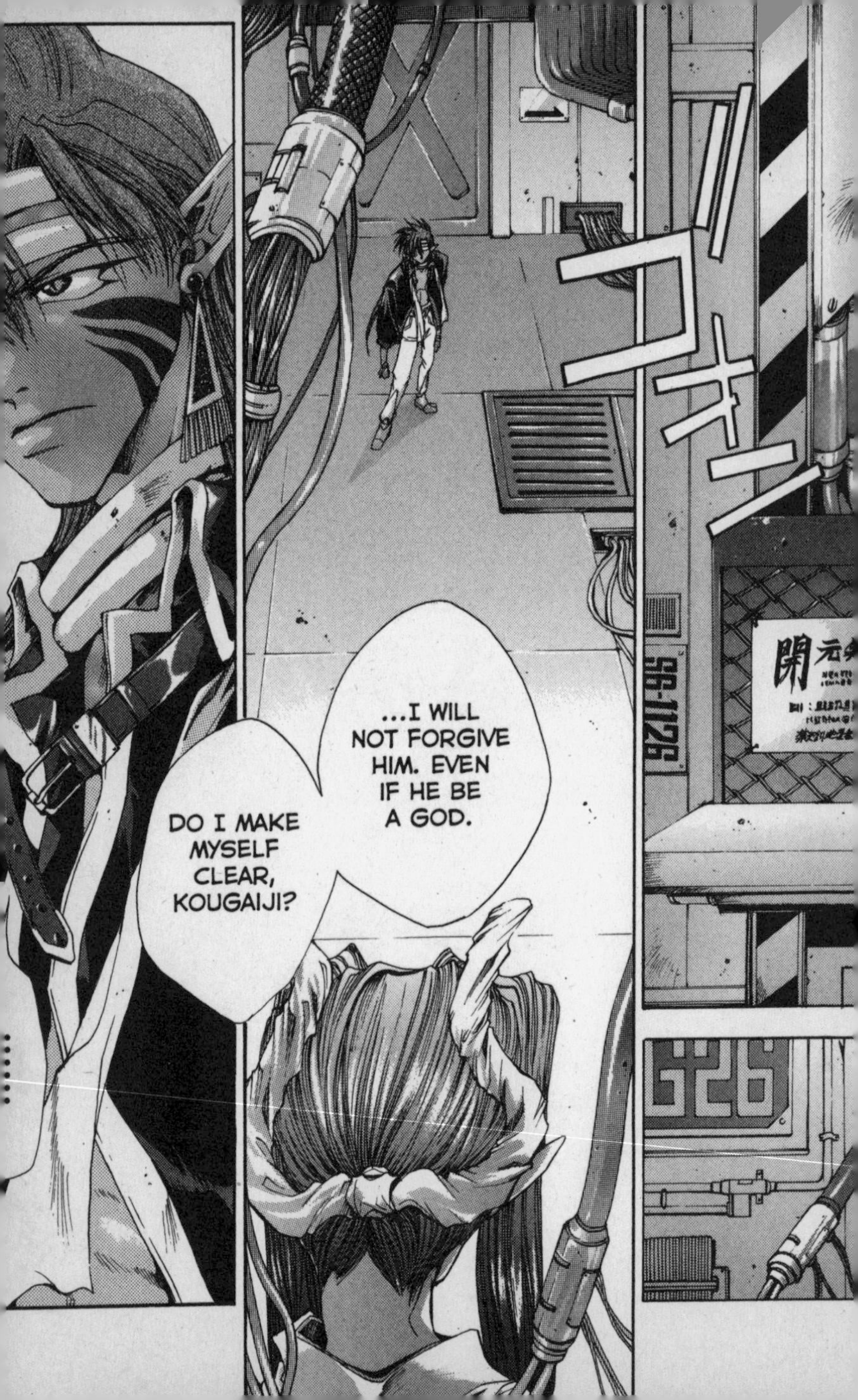
...I WILL NOT FORGIVE HIM. EVEN IF HE BE A GOD.
DO I MAKE MYSELF CLEAR, KOUGAIJI?

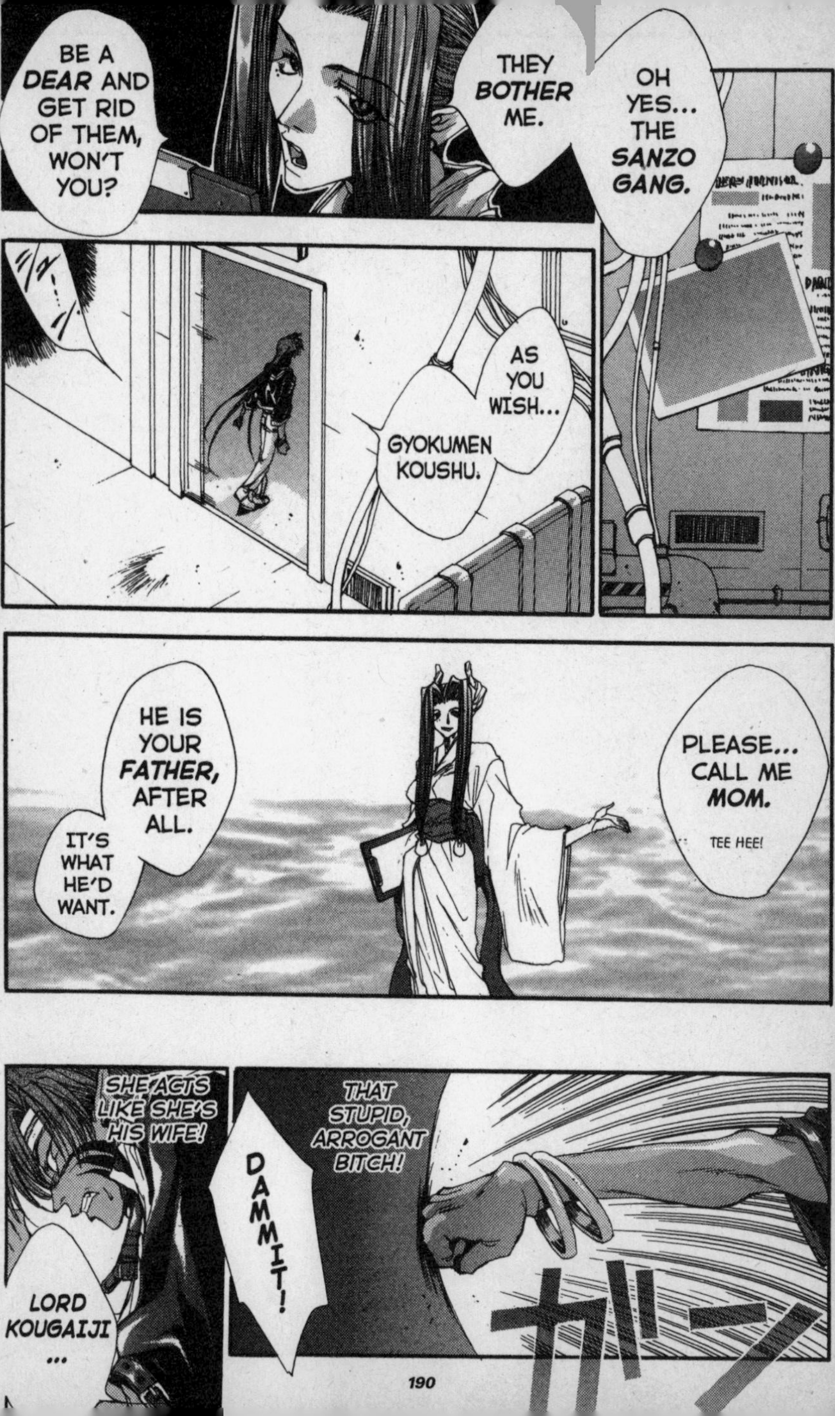
OH YES... THE SANZO GANG.
THEY BOTHER ME.
BE A DEAR AND GET RID OF THEM, WON'T YOU?
AS YOU WISH...
GYOKUMEN KOUSHU.
...!
PLEASE... CALL ME MOM.
TEE HEE!
HE IS YOUR FATHER, AFTER ALL.
IT'S WHAT HE'D WANT.
THAT STUPID, ARROGANT BITCH!
DAMMIT!
SHE ACTS LIKE SHE'S HIS WIFE!
LORD KOUGAIJI...

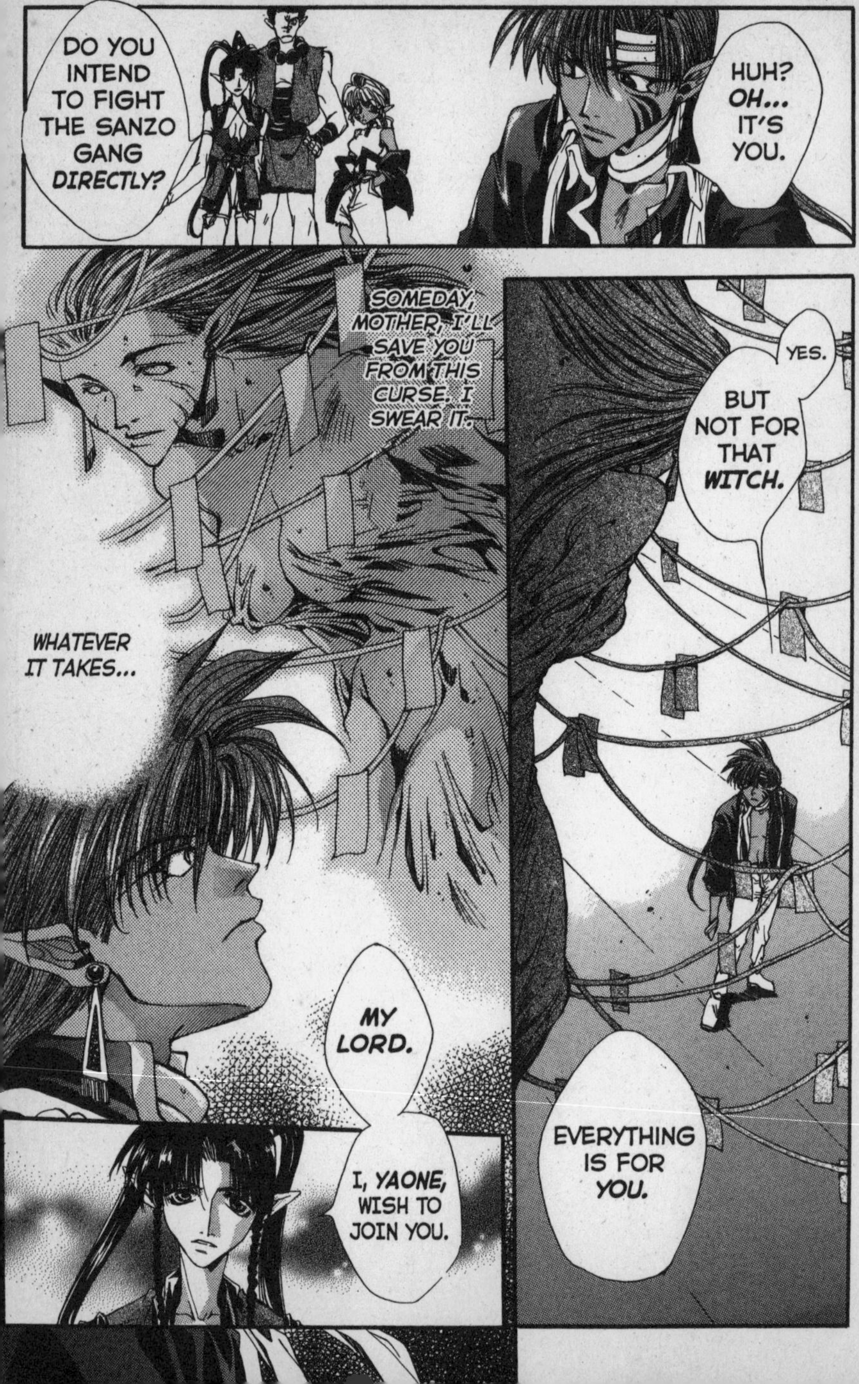

HUH? OH... IT'S YOU.
DO YOU INTEND TO FIGHT THE SANZO GANG DIRECTLY?
YES.
BUT NOT FOR THAT WITCH.
EVERYTHING IS FOR YOU.
SOMEDAY, MOTHER, I'LL SAVE YOU FROM THIS CURSE. I SWEAR IT.
WHATEVER IT TAKES...
MY LORD.
I, YAONE, WISH TO JOIN YOU.

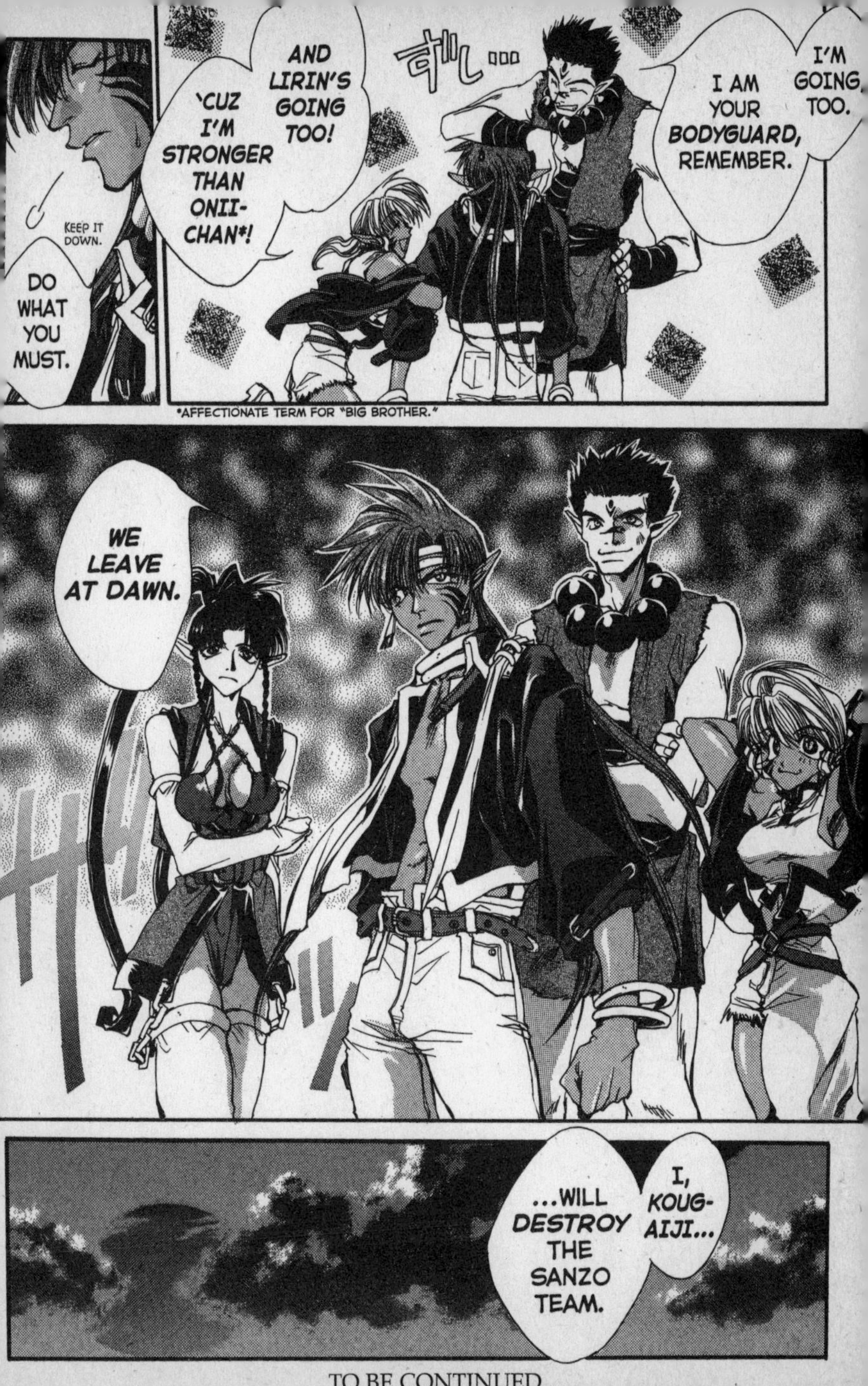
I'M GOING TOO.
I AM YOUR BODYGUARD, REMEMBER.
ずし...
AND LIRIN'S GOING TOO!
'CUZ I'M STRONGER THAN ONII-CHAN*!
KEEP IT DOWN.
DO WHAT YOU MUST.
*AFFECTIONATE TERM FOR "BIG BROTHER."
WE LEAVE AT DAWN.
I, KOUG-AIJI...
...WILL DESTROY THE SANZO TEAM.

TO BE CONTINUED...

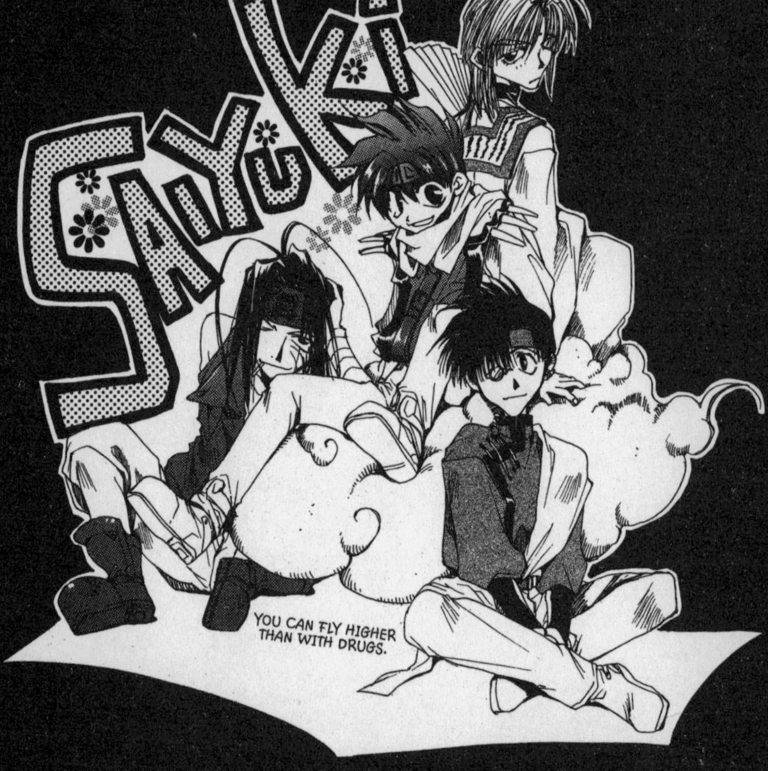
SAIYUKI
YOU CAN FLY HIGHER THAN WITH DRUGS.

CHARACTER INTRODUCTIONS

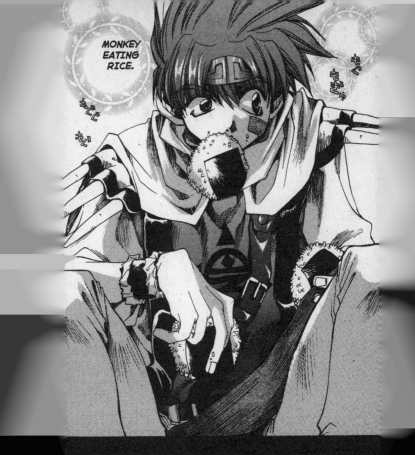

MONKEY EATING RICE.

Son Goku

...erful little monkey...or an unholy child born from the rocks where the a... Earth was gathered. As his brain is full of thoughts of food and games... seem there's not much room for deep thought. To pay for crimes... ...itted when he was young, he was imprisoned in the rocks for five h... ...years without aging. Because of his optimistic personality, he's beco... ...ascot character of the group; this healthy eighteen-year-old is made... ...Gojyo, yelled at by Sanzo, and watched over by Hakkai. He's 162cm... ...ox. 5'4"]. His main weapon is the Nyoi-Bo, which can also become... ...kkon.

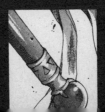

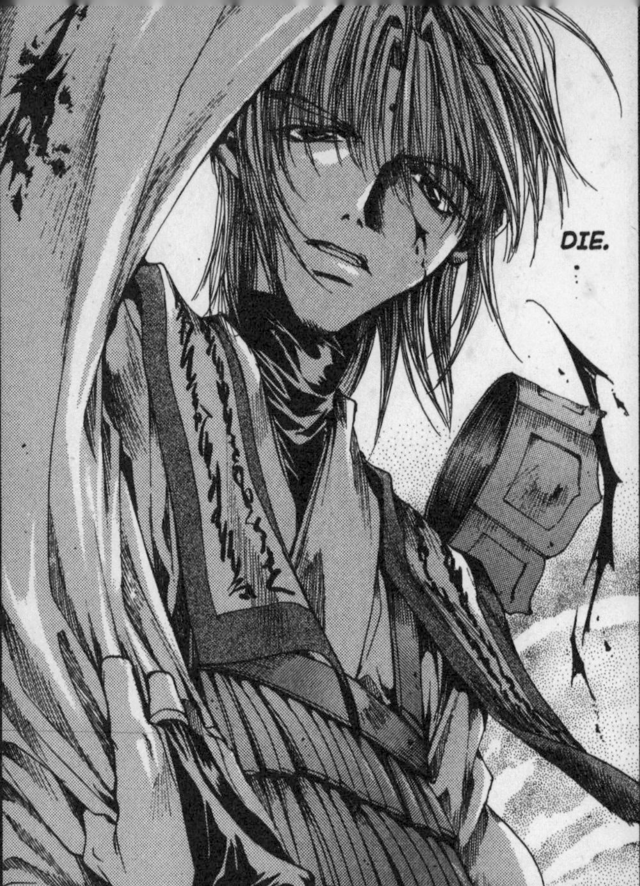
DIE.

Genjyo Sanzo

A very brutal, worldly priest. He drinks, smokes, gambles, and carries a gun, which is pushing it even for normal people (let alone Buddhist monks). He's searching for the stolen Sutra of his mentor and father figure, Priest Koumyou Sanzo, who was killed in Sanzo's youth by a mob of murderous Youkai. Sanzo is egotistical, haughty, and can be very cruel, yet our 23-year-old hero also has calm judgment, unwavering intensity, and surprising charisma. His favorite phrases, incidentally, are "Die," and "I'll kill you." His weapons of choice are the magical Maten Sutra, a handgun, and a paper fan for idiots. He's 177 cm tall (approx. 5'10"), and is often noted for his good looks and drooping purple eyes.

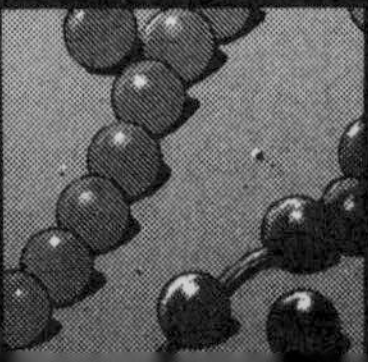

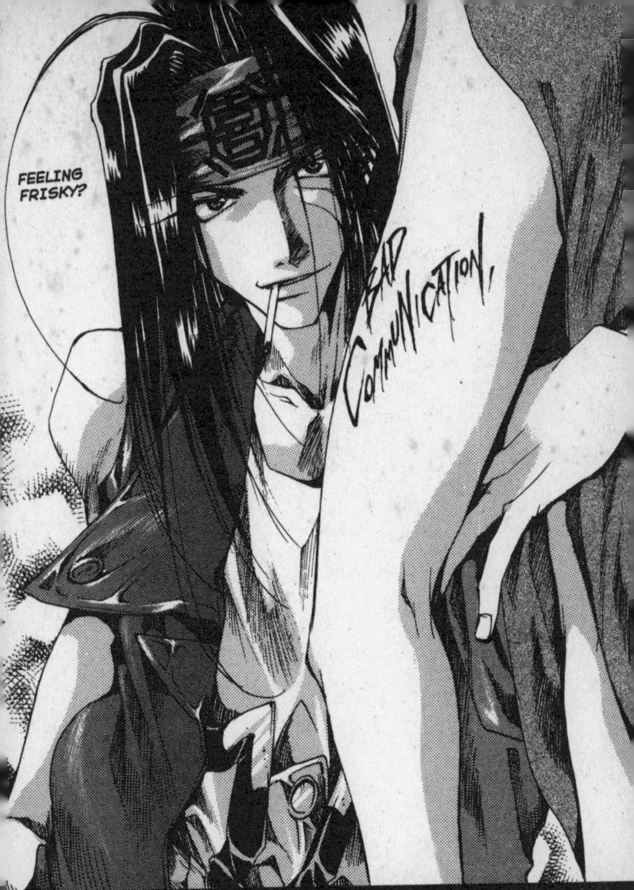
FEELING FRISKY?
BAD COMMUNICATION,

Sha Gojyo

s a flirtatious, sly, and (let's face it) flat-out horny rogue. His behavior
and vulgar at first (and it is), but to the friends who know him, he's the d
rother. He's best friends with Hakkai, sparring partners with Goku, and
ntances with Sanzo. Although his love for the ladies sometimes leads to
ms to be searching for someone in particular, and it's not necessarily
sn't need a power limiter to blend in with humans because of his unusua
orite weapon is his shakujou staff that uses a chain to control its blade
battle to be sure. He's 184 cm tall (approx. 6'0"), has scarlet hair and
smokes like a chimney with a burning lust for cancer.

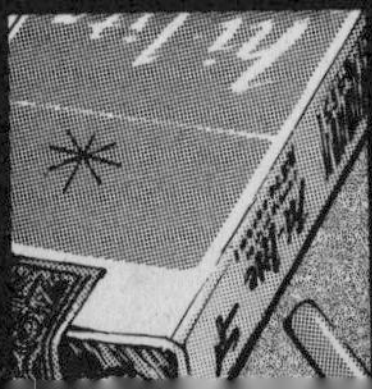

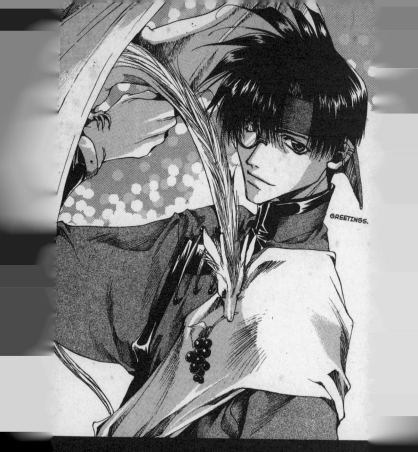

GREETINGS.

Cho Hakkai

...er perplexing young man. Hakkai is usually quite pleasant and polite and is...
...smile, but he can be so off-putting it's hard to tell when he's serious...t...
...e he's the straight man, but that's open to debate. His occasionally shar...
...ly in contrast with his warm expressions–is symbolic of his dark, close...
...ep belongs to him, he often drives when the group is riding. He uses ch...
...manipulation as his weapon in battle. He, like Gojyo, is 22 years old, but...
...lightly shorter 181 cm tall (approx. 5'11"). His eyes are deep green...
...s nearly blind. The cuffs he wears on his left ear are Youkai power limit...
...an also be appreciated as an ancient Chinese fashion statement.

TRANSLATORS' NOTES

GENJYO SANZO.
IN THE ORIGINAL LEGEND, GENJYO (SANZANG IN CHINESE) IS A T'ANG PRIEST, SENT TO INDIA TO BRING THE BUDDHIST SCRIPTURES BACK TO CHINA. ALONG THE WAY HE IS JOINED BY THE MONKEY KING, A RIVER IMP, AND A PIG.

SON GOKU.
IN THE ORIGINAL LEGEND, SON GOKU (*SUN WUKONG* IN CHINESE) IS KNOWN AS THE "MONKEY KING." GOJYO'S INCESSANT INSULTS ARE A REFERENCE TO THIS FACT. AND YES, THIS IS THE SAME GOKU WHO STARS IN *DRAGONBALL* MANGA AND ANIME. IN CHINA, THE MONKEY KING IS STILL THE MOST WELL-KNOWN AND LOVED CHARACTER IN POP CULTURE.

SHA GOJYO.
IN THE ORIGINAL LEGEND, GOJYO (*SHA WUJING* IN CHINESE) IS KNOWN AS "FRIAR SAND." HE'S A KAPPA, A MONSTER IN JAPANESE MYTHOLOGY THAT INHABITS RIVERS AND SUCKS BLOOD OR LIFE ESSENCE FROM ITS VICTIMS. IT'S OFTEN TRANSLATED TO "WATER SPRITE." (TRIVIA NOTE: KAPPA HAVE A SOFT SPOT FOR CUCUMBERS AND APPRECIATE AN OFFERING OF THE VEGGIE. THAT'S WHY A CUCUMBER ROLL AT A SUSHI BAR IS NOW CALLED KAPPA *MAKI*.)

CHO HAKKAI.
IN THE ORIGINAL LEGEND, HAKKAI (*ZHU BAJIE* IN CHINESE) WAS A LECHEROUS PIG. HIS TRAGIC ORIGINS ARE SOMEWHAT DIFFERENT HERE.

YOUKAI.
A GENERAL TERM FOR SUPERNATURAL BEINGS. THE WORD *YOUKAI* IS OFTEN TRANSLATED TO "DEMON," HOWEVER THE JAPANESE WORD DOESN'T CARRY WITH IT THAT NEGATIVE CONNOTATION, AS YOUKAI AREN'T INHERENTLY EVIL.

PG. 25
NYOI-BO. THIS IS GOKU'S WEAPON FROM THE ORIGINAL LEGEND, SOMETIMES TRANSLATED TO "AS-YOU-WILL CUDGEL." IT CAN CHANGE LENGTH AT THE USER'S WILL, AND IN THIS MANGA IT CHANGES INTO THE LONGER, THREE-JOINTED NYOI-SANSEKKON.

PG. 32
HADOUKEN. "WAVE FIST." THE FAMOUS ATTACK OF RYU IN *STREET FIGHTER*.

PG. 45
KANZEON BOSATSU. THE MERCIFUL GODDESS, ALSO KNOWN AS *KANNON,* OR *KUAN YIN.* IN MOST VERSIONS OF THE LEGEND, SHE'S PURELY FEMALE, BUT IN THIS VERSION SHE'S A HER-MAPHRODITE. A *BOSATSU* IS A *BODHISATTVA*— SOMEONE WHO HAS ACHIEVED ENLIGHTENMENT BUT DECIDED TO STAY ON EARTH TO HELP HUMANITY RATHER THAN GO ON TO NIRVANA.

PG. 45
MT. KAKA. IN THE ORIGINAL LEGEND, IT WAS KNOWN AS THE "MOUNTAIN OF FLOWERS AND FRUIT" AND WAS WHERE GOKU HAD HIS MONKEY KINGDOM.

PG. 64
SEITEN LITERALLY MEANS HOLY HEAVEN, AND IS OFTEN TRANS-LATED AS CELESTIAL LAND. *MATEN* LITERALLY MEANS YOUKAI HEAVEN, OR INFERNAL LAND, HENCE THE POWERS OF "LIGHT" AND "DARKNESS" EACH CONTAIN.

PG. 75
RASESTSUNYO. IN BUDDHIST MYTHOLOGY, A *RASETSU* IS A YOUKAI OF HELL WHO ASSISTS WITH PUNISHING THE DAMNED AND TORMENTING THE LIVING. THE SUFFIX *NYO* MEANS FEMALE. HERE IT COULD BE A NAME, OR A TITLE.

PG. 125
SANZO'S CHANT. THIS IS TAKEN DIRECTLY FROM THE BUDDHIST HEART SUTRA; HOWEVER, THERE ARE CERTAIN SYLLABLES TAKEN OUT.

PG. 125-126
ON MA NI HATSU MEI UN. THIS IS THE JAPANESE READING OF THE MANTRA *OM MANI PADME HUM,* OR "THE JEWEL IS IN THE LOTUS." THE MOST COMMON MANTRA OF TIBETAN BUDDHISM.

PG. 126
MAKAI TENJYO. A MANTRA THAT TRANSLATES AS "DIVINE PURIFICATION FROM EVIL."

PG. 150
HANNYA HARA MITSUDA. ANOTHER LINE FROM THE HEART SUTRA.

PG. 174
HAKKAI'S CHANT. WE COULDN'T FIND ANY REFERENCE TO A KNOWN SUTRA, AND AS HAKKAI ISN'T A PRIEST, WE SUSPECT THIS CHANT IS MADE UP.

PG. 176
GAICHUU KUJYO. TRANSLATES TO "PEST EXTERMINATION."

PG. 198
SHAKUJOU. A BISHOP'S STAFF, IN REFERENCE TO GOJYO'S HERITAGE AS FRIAR SAND.

SOUND EFFECT CHART

THE FOLLOWING IS A LIST OF THE SOUND EFFECTS USED IN *SAIYUKI*. EACH SOUND IS LABELED BY PAGE AND PANEL NUMBER, SEPARATED BY A PERIOD. THE FIRST DESCRIPTION (IN BOLD) IS THE PHONETIC READING OF THE JAPANESE, AND IS FOLLOWED BY THE EQUIVALENT ENGLISH SOUND OR A DESCRIPTION.

13.2 ***BUU:*** (STOMACH GRUMBLE)
13.3 ***OO:*** (BLOWING WIND)
14.1 ***PAN!:*** WHAP!
14.3 ***GESHI GESHI:*** STOMP STOMP
15.4 ***O-O-O:*** (BLOWING WIND)
15.6 ***GI-GI-GI-GI:*** CREEEEAK
16.2 ***GOUU:*** FOOM (ROARING FIRE)
16.3 ***GOPO GOPO:*** GLUB GLUB (WATER)
22.2 ***HAAAAA:*** SIGH!
22.4 ***GASA:*** RUSTLE
23.1 ***ZAA!:*** (SUDDEN APPEARANCE!)
23.2 ***GIIII:*** (MONKEY GROWL)

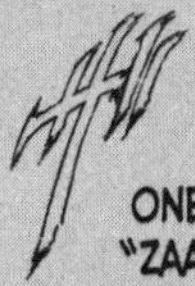

ZAA!

YOU'LL SEE THIS ONE A LOT IN *SAIYUKI*. "ZAA" INDICATES A DRAMATIC APPEARANCE. IF YOU WANT TO MAKE A LASTING IMPRESSION, ALWAYS COME IN WITH A COOL POSE AND A BIG "ZAA!"

23.3 ***SHUU:*** SHOOM
23.4 ***GAA:*** CLASH
23.6 ***GA:*** BURST
24.1 ***KIIN:*** WHAM
24.2 ***ZYAA!!:*** LUNGE
24.3 ***KARAN:*** CLANK
24.6 ***GOKI!:*** WHAM

25.2 ***ZAA!:*** (SUDDEN APPEARANCE!)
25.3 ***CHI:*** TCH!
25.5 ***RAGE:*** GULP
26.1 ***ZOPAN:*** SLICE
26.3 ***GO:*** THUD
26.4 ***TSU:*** SPLAT
26.5 ***HYUN:*** SWISH
27.1A ***ZAN!:*** (SUDDEN APPEARANCE!)
27.1B ***CHIIN:*** SHING
29.1 ***BAA:*** (SURPRISE)
29.2 ***NII:*** GRIN
29.3 ***GUWA:*** (SUDDEN ACTION)
29.5 ***GOH:*** WHAM
29.6 ***DOCHA:*** SPLAT
30.1 ***DAH:*** DASH!
30.2 ***TOH:*** TAP
30.4 ***KO-O-O-O-O:*** (CHARGING UP)
30.5 ***DON!:*** BOOM
31.3 ***BEH:*** NYA! (TONGUE STICKING OUT)
32.5 ***BAN!:*** ATTACK!
33.1 ***GOH:*** WHAM
36.2 ***PAN!:*** SLAP!
36.4 ***GAH:*** GRAB
37.2 ***GAHAA!***
37.3 ***GUSHA:*** SQUISH
40.2 ***GO-O:*** (HOWLING WIND)
42.1A ***BU-RO-RO-RO:*** (ENGINE RUMBLE)
42.1B ***GASA-GON:*** RUMMAGE
42.2 ***BU-RO-RO-RO:*** (ENGINE RUMBLE)
46 ***TATTOO:*** "DEATH FLOWER"
47.1 ***BU-RO-RO-RO:*** (ENGINE RUMBLE)
48.2 ***DOH-DOH-DOH:*** (ENGINE RUMBLE)

48.4 GOH: (SUN BEATING DOWN)
49.1 O-O-O-O: (BLOWING WIND)
50.2 ZAWA-ZAWA: CHATTER CHATTER
50.3 JYARI: CRUNCH
50.6 GO: WHAM
51.1 GAN: SLAM
51.2 KYON: (REALIZATION)
51.3 JYARI: CRUNCH
51.4 ZA: (SUDDEN APPEARANCE)
51.5 GURI: GRIND
52.1A POKAAN: (SHOCK)
52.1B PACHIN: KACHINK
52.3 GO: WHAM
52.4 DOSA DOSAA: THUD THUD
53.1 KII: SKREETCH (BRAKE)

はっ **HAH!**
THIS IS ONE OF THE MOST COMMON SOUNDS YOU'LL SEE IN MANGA. IT'S USED TO INDICATE SURPRISE AND IS USUALLY EQUIVALENT TO "GASP!" "H" ISN'T NECESSARILY VOCALIZED, THOUGH.

53.2A DOH DO: (ENGINE RUMBLE)
53.2B ZAWA-ZAWA: CHATTER CHATTER
53.5 HYOI: YOINK
53.6 HAH: GASP
54.4 GAH-GAH-GAH: GOBBLE GOBBLE
55.1 GATAH: CLATTER
55.2 PA-PAN: WHAP WHAP
55.3 GACHA: (DOOR OPENING)
55.5 GOTO: CLINK
56.1 KACHA: CLICK (CHOPSTICKS BREAK)
56.3 GIKU: GULP
57.2 GAGOH!!: GAGH!
58.7 GUSU: SNIFFLE
59.1 KACHA: CLACK
59.6 PATA: SLAP
60.4 GOH: FOOSH (ROARING FIRE)
61.1 O-O-O-O: (IMPOSING HUM)
61.3 ZAH: BOW
62.4 GIRI: CLENCH
63.1 HAH: GASP
63.3 KOTO: CLACK
66.1 GU GU GU: PUSH SHOVE PUSH
66.2 ZAWA-ZAWA: CHATTER CHATTER
66.4 PIIII: (WHISTLE)
67.2 PEKO: NOD
68.1 ZORO ZORO: SHUFFLE SHUFFLE
68.2 ZAWA: RUSTLE
69.1 GIII: CREEEEAK
69.4 NYA: SMIRK
70.1 PASHII: GRAB
70.3 BAH: LEAP (AS IN TO ACTION)
70.4 GIRI: TWIST
70.5 GAN: SLAM
70.6 ZURU: SLIDE
71.1 JA-KII: SHING
71.2 JA: SWIPE
71.3 SUH: (SHOOP)
71.4 GOH: THUD
71.5 KEH: GRUNT
71.6 GABAA: LUNGE
72.1 GO: (IMPACT)
72.2 ZAA: (ASS KICKING POSE!)
72.4 GACHA: CLICK
73.3 GIRI: GRIND
73.4A IRA-IRA: (ANNOYED)
73.4B PAN!: BANG!
74.2 CHIRA...: GLANCE
74.3 POU: GLOW
74.4 KYU: TWIP (THREAD)
74.7 HYU: WHOOSH
74.8 PASHII: GRAB
75.1 BAH: FWAP (QUICK MOVEMENT)
75.2 GASHA: CLACK
75.3 PERO: LICK
75.4 O-O-O: (MENACING)
75.5 O: (MENACING)
76.3 KU KU: (EVIL LAUGH)
76.4 PIKU: TWITCH
77.6 KUSU: GIGGLE
78-79 O-O-O: (MENACING)
79.4 KAH: STEP
80.2 MOZO: SCRATCH
80.3 GII...: CREEEAK

DON!

FOR NORMAL SLAMS, BAMS AND BASHES, A SIMPLE "BAN!" SOUND WILL SUFFICE, BUT WHEN A CHARACTER PULLS OUT THE BIG GUNS, A "DON!" INDICATES AN IMPACT OF THE NEXT ORDER.

122.4 KO-O-O-O-O: (CHARGING UP)
122.5 **KO-O-O-O-O:** (CHARGING UP)
123.1 **DOON-DON:** BOOM BOOM
124.1 **O:** (CHARGE)
124-125 **DON!:** POWER RELEASE
125.2 **GYAAAAA:** (MONSTER SCREAM)
126.1 **ZAA:** (COOL POSE!)
126.2 **DAN:** LEAP
126.3 **O-O-O:** WHOOSH!
127.1 **DON!:** SLAM
127.3 **KAH:** (BLOWN AWAY)
128.1 **O-O-O-O:** WHOOSH
128.4 **DOH-DOH** (ENGINE RUMBLE)
131.5 **DO-RU-RU-RUH...** (ENGINE RUMBLE)
132.1 **DO-RU-RU-N:** (ENGINE RUMBLE)
132.2 **PORO-PORO-PORO:** DRIP DRIP DRIP (OF TEARS)
132.3 **DOH-DOH-DOH:** (ENGINE RUMBLE)
133.4 **DOH:** (ENGINE RUMBLE)
134.1 **DOH-DOH-DOH:** (ENGINE RUMBLE)
134.2 **GAH-GAH-GAH:** GOBBLE GOBBLE
134.3 **DO-DO-DO:** (ENGINE RUMBLE)
136.3A **O-O:** (WIND)
136.3B **ZURUZURUZUUU:** DRAG
136.4 **MUKYOOH:** GRR!
136.5 **ZAH:** SHUFFLE
137.1 **O-O-O-N:** (HOWLING WIND)
139.1 **BAH:** GRAB
139.4 **TAJII:** (SHOCK)
140.1 **GI-GI-GI-GI:** CREEEEAK
140.2 **KYOTO BLINK:** (DUMBSTRUCK)
140.5 **KAH-KAH:** STEP STEP
140.6 **GACHA:** CLICK
141.1 **ZA!:** (APPEARANCE OF CROWD)
144.2 **BON:** TURN
145.7 **DOSAH:** SIT
146.1 **BASA:** FLAP
146.3 **KOTO:** CLACK
146.4 **NIKO-CHAN:** CUTE LITTLE SMILE
147.1 **KURU:** TURN
147.2 **U-RU-RU:** GIDDY
147.3 **PUH:** PFF! (HOLDING IN LAUGH)
147.6 **FUN:** HMPH
149.3 **PASHI:** PUFF
149.4 **BAN!:** BAM!
150.2 AAAAAAAH!

111.5B BUSHU: SQUOOOSH
112.1 **JU-O-O-O:** FIZZZZ
112.2 **GUCHO-GOCHU:** GLOOP GLOOP
112.5A **O-O-O:** (MENACING)
112.5B **GUCHU-BICHA:** GLOOP, SHLORP
112.6 **GATA-GATA:** TREMBLE
114.2 **O:** (MENACING)
114.3 **BAKYA:** SLAM
114.4 **KAHAH:** KOFF
115.1 **DOGOO:** WHAM
115.3 **BII:** HIT
115.4 **ZU-ZA-ZA-ZA:** SKID

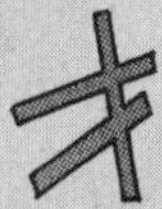

O-O-O!

CAN YOU HEAR IT, THE SOUND OF THE DIVINE WIND? OH SORRY, WRONG MANGA. ANYWAY, THE KATAKANA FOR "O" IS A MANGA-KA'S BEST TOOL FOR INDICATING WIND. JUST DRAW A FEW CURLY LINES IN THE SKY AND SCATTER SOME "O"S AND, 'VOILÀ!' INSTANT WIND. "O"S CAN ALSO BE USED TO INDICATE A CREEPY PRESENCE. AS IN OOOOO...SPOOOOKY!

115.5 **PEH:** PTOOI (SPIT)
116.1 **GU-RA...:** GROWL
116.2A **O:** (MENACING)
116.2B **GYUU:** HUG
116.4 **GOTO:** THUNK
116.5 **GYOAAA:** (MONSTER SCREAM)
117.1A **HAA-HA:** PANT PANT
117.1B **GUII:** WIPE
119.5 **BOSO:** RUSTLE
120.4 **KEH:** GRUNT
121.1 **O-OON:** (MENACING)
121.3 **BAH:** FWAP
121.4 **SHU-U-O-O-O:** (CHARGING)
121.5 **DAH:** DASH!
122.1A **DON!:** WHAM!
122.1B **TAH:** TAP
122.2 ZA-ZAH: SKID

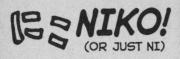

174.1 **BOGOO:** SHWING
174.3 **FUON:** SHIMMER
174.4 **BAH:** GRAB
174.5 **O-O-O:** WHOOSH!
175.1 **GASHI:** CLASH
175.2 **GICH-CHI:** GRIND
175.3 **ZU-ZA-ZA:** SKID
175.5 **GABAA:** FWOOM
176.1 **FUWA:** FLUTTER
176.2 **BAH:** GRAB
176.4 **GAN:** POW
177.1 **DOZAA:** SLAM
178.1 **GAH:** SHOVE

ニコ NIKO!
(OR JUST NI)

IT TAKES 26 MUSCLES TO SMILE, OR JUST TWO KATAKANA! "NIKO," REPEATED AS MUCH AS YOU WANT FOR EMPHASIS, GIVES THE READER AN INDICATION OF JUST HOW BIG A SMILE IS.

179.2 **HAH:** GASP
179.3 **DON:** BOOM
179.4 **O-O-O:** WHOOSH
182.2 **BIKU!:** SURPRISE!
184.7 **SU:** STEP
185.4 **GOH:** WHAP
186.1 **GYAA-GYAA:** BICKER BICKER
186-187.1 **GOH:** VOOM
186-187.2 **O-O-O:** (WIND)
187.3 **GOPO:** GLUB
188.1 **KACHIRI:** CLINK
188-189 **GO-ON GO-ON:** HMMM
188-189 SIGNS: "NO ADMITTANCE" "ROAD TO LIFE"
190.5 **GAN:** SLAM
192.1 **ZUSHI:** NUDGE
192.3 **ZAA:** (BAD-ASS POSE)
194 **MOGUGU-MOGU:** MUNCH MUNCH

150.3 **BAH:** FLAP
150.4 **DOSA-DOSA-DOSA:** THUD THUD THUD
150.5 **KURA:** DIZZY (OVERWHELMED)
151.4 **GOH:** WHOOSH
151.5A **BIKU:** (SURPRISE)
151.5B **DAN:** SLAM
152.1 **DAH:** DASH!
153.5 **O-O-O:** (WIND)
154.4 **PIKU:** BINK (REALIZATION)
155.1A **DON:** BOOM
155.1B **GATAH:** CLATTER
155.3 **GO-OH:** (EVIL AURA)
155.4 **BAH:** RUSH
156.1 **GAH:** STOMP
156-157 **ZAN!:** (DRAMATIC ENTRANCE)
158.1 **GAH:** GRAB
158.2 **BASHU:** SPLAT
158.3 **GATA-GATA:** TREMBLE
158.4 **GA:** TREMBLE
159.2 **NIKO-NIKO-NIKO:** SMILE SMILE
159.5 **FUH:** HMPH
161.4 **BAN!:** BAM!
163.4 **BASA:** FWAP
163.5 **HOH:** HUFF
164.2 **HIKUH:** TWITCH
165.1 **GO-ON:** (MENACING)
165.3 **O-O:** (MENACING)
167.4 **PUUN:** (FURY)
167.5 **BUN!:** SHOOM
168.1 **DOKA:** THUNK
168.3 **GUI:** GRAB
168.4 **GARAN:** CLANK
168-169 **GOH!:** SLAM!
169.2 **BUSHU:** GUSH
170.1A **BUSHU:** GUSH
170.1B **BAKYA:** WHACK
170.4 **NIKOYAKA:** GENTLE SMILE
171.3 **GABA:** GRAB
171.4 **DOPAA:** FLING
171.5 **ZAH:** DASH
172.1 **SUH:** FWISH
172.2 **BACHII:** SMASH
172.4 **FUH:** SWISH
173.6 **GABAA:** THRUST
173.7 **GU-GU-GU:** GURGLE RUMBLE (METAMORPHOSIS)

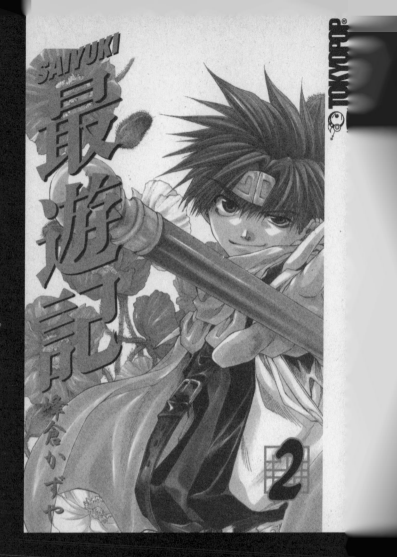

SAIYUKI

TOKYOPOP®

Continuing their journey west, Genjyo Sanzo and company c
upon a young woman with a tragic tale. Her long lost lover, a Yo
succumbed to the Minus Wave and she's been waiting pati
ever since for his return. Something about the woman's des
tion strikes a chord with Gojyo—could it be a clue to the mys
In the next volume of *Saiyuki*, the battle become

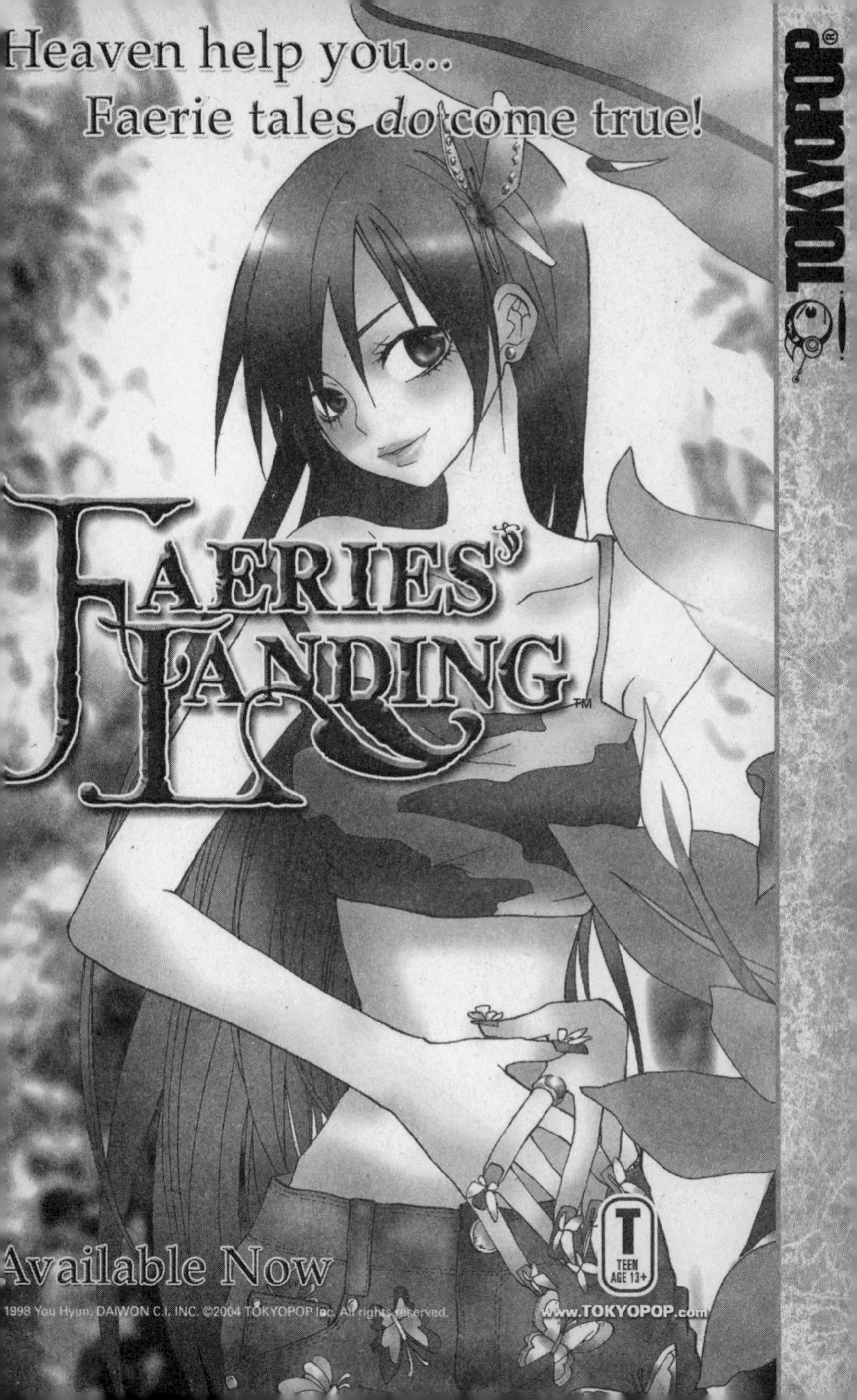

Heaven help you...
Faerie tales *do* come true!

FAERIES' LANDING™

Available Now

TOKYOPOP®

T TEEN AGE 13+

www.TOKYOPOP.com

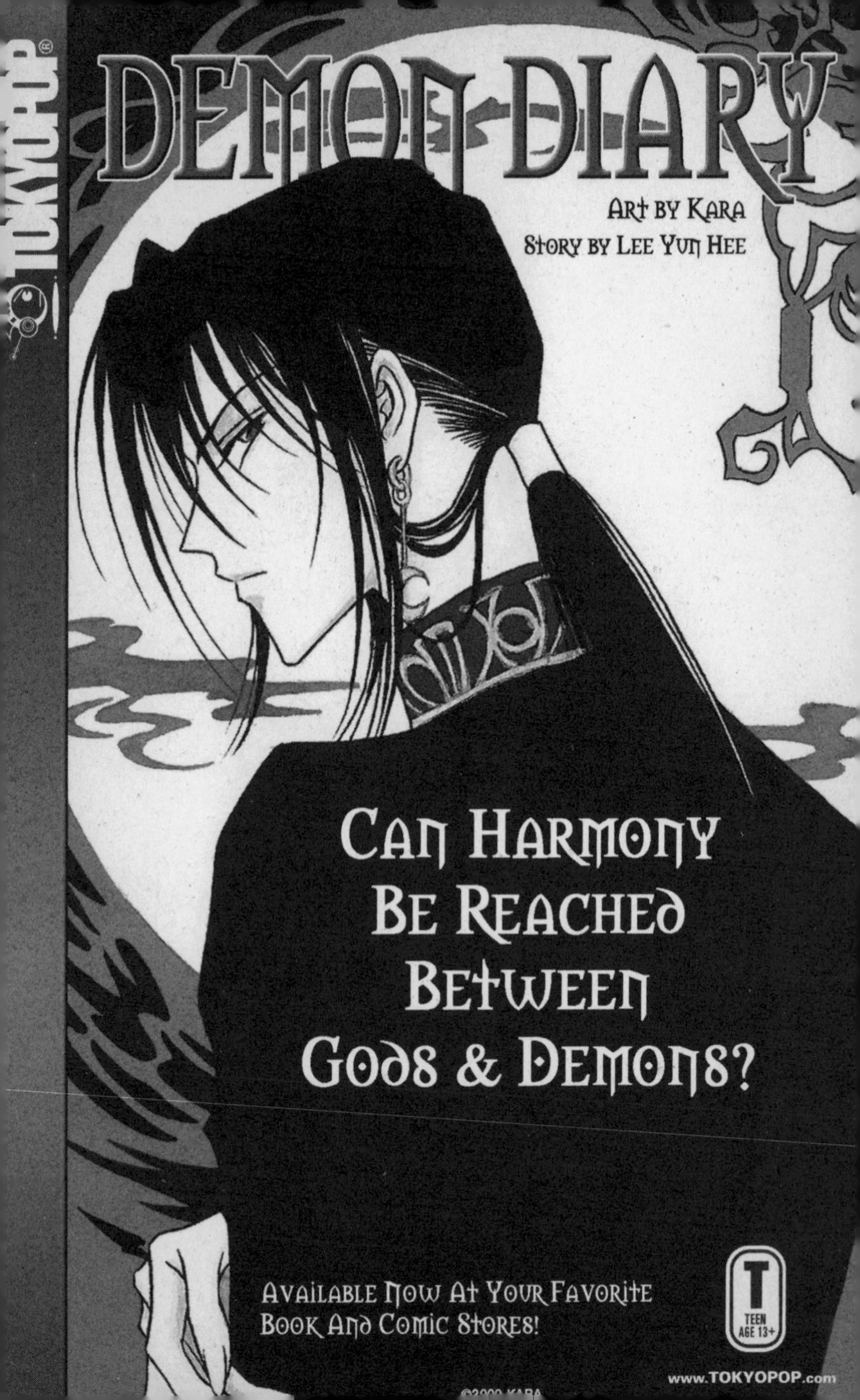
TOKYOPOP
DEMON DIARY
Art by Kara
Story by Lee Yun Hee
Can Harmony Be Reached Between Gods & Demons?
Available Now At Your Favorite Book And Comic Stores!
T
TEEN AGE 13+
www.TOKYOPOP.com

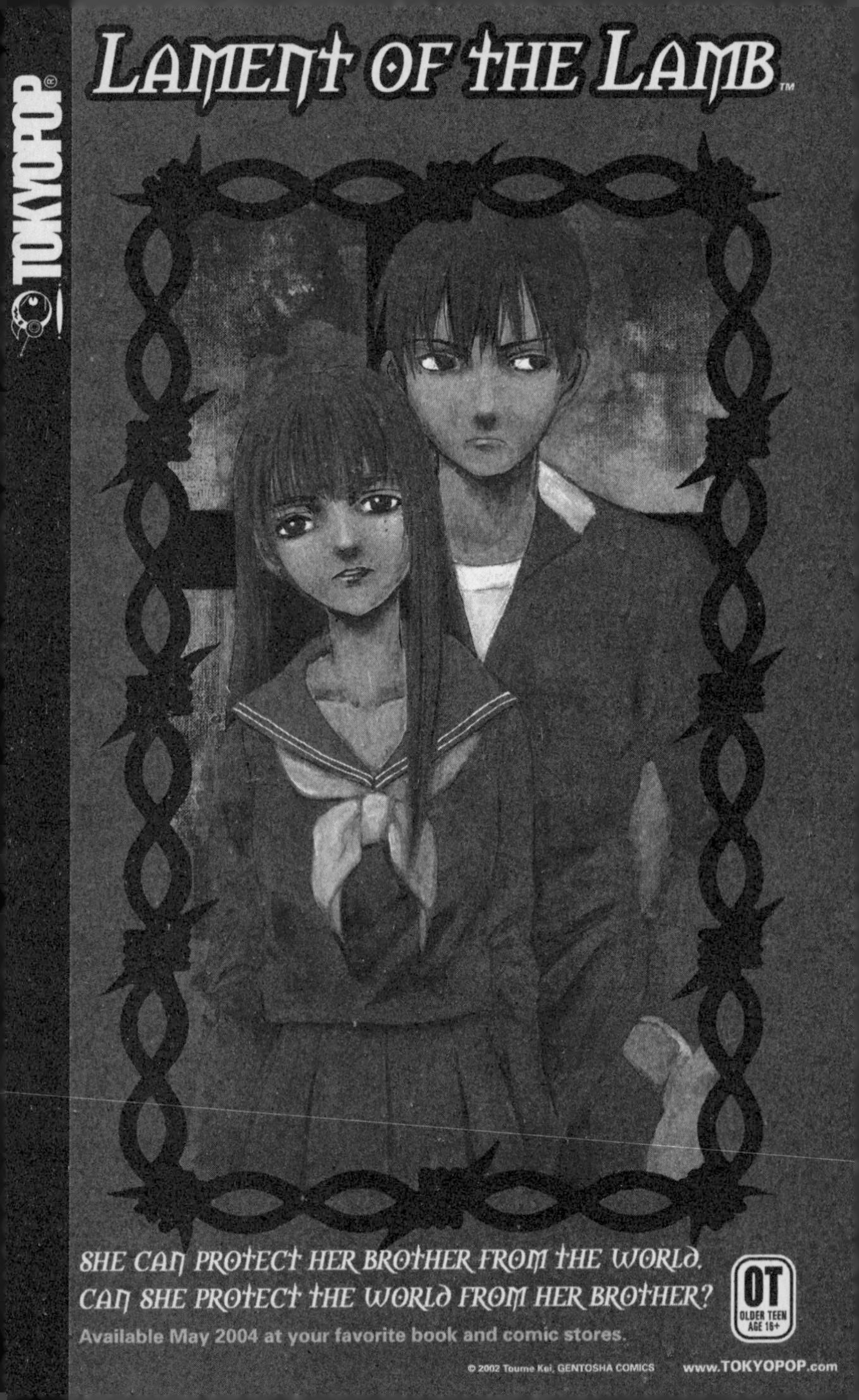
TOKYOPOP
LAMENT OF THE LAMB™
SHE CAN PROTECT HER BROTHER FROM THE WORLD.
CAN SHE PROTECT THE WORLD FROM HER BROTHER?
Available May 2004 at your favorite book and comic stores.
OT
OLDER TEEN AGE 16+
© 2002 Toume Kei, GENTOSHA COMICS
www.TOKYOPOP.com

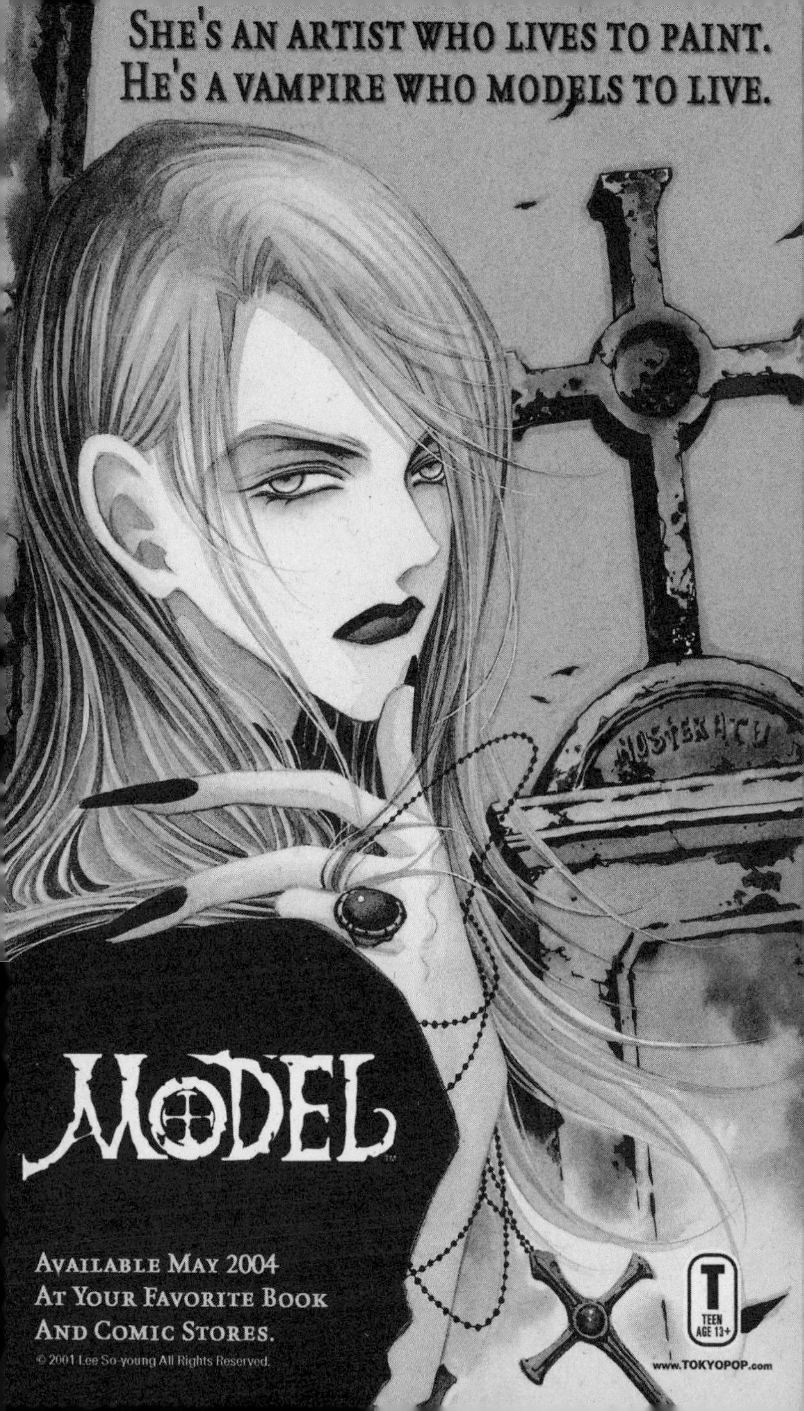

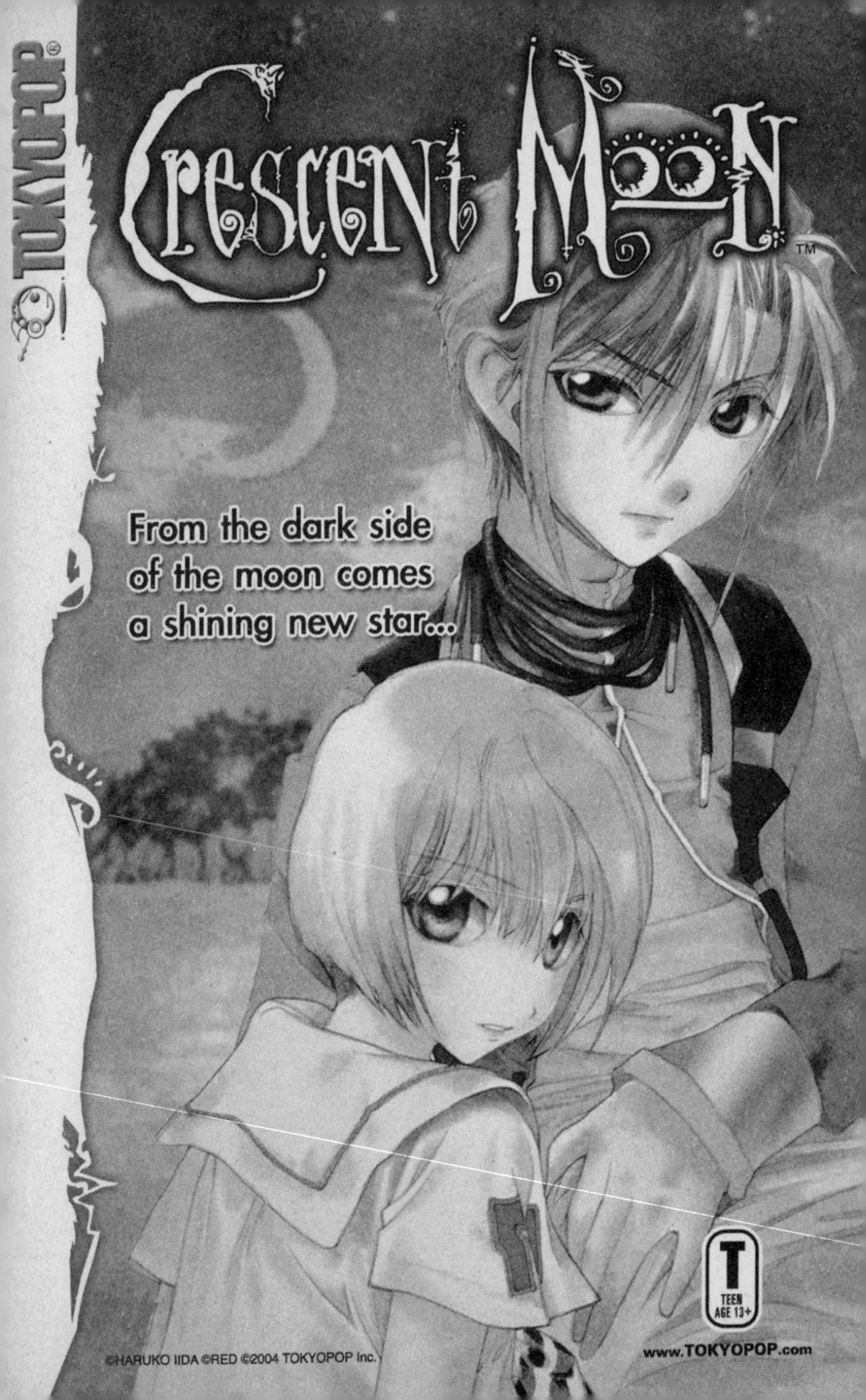
TOKYOPOP
Crescent Moon™
From the dark side of the moon comes a shining new star...
T TEEN AGE 13+
©HARUKO IIDA ©RED ©2004 TOKYOPOP Inc.
www.TOKYOPOP.com

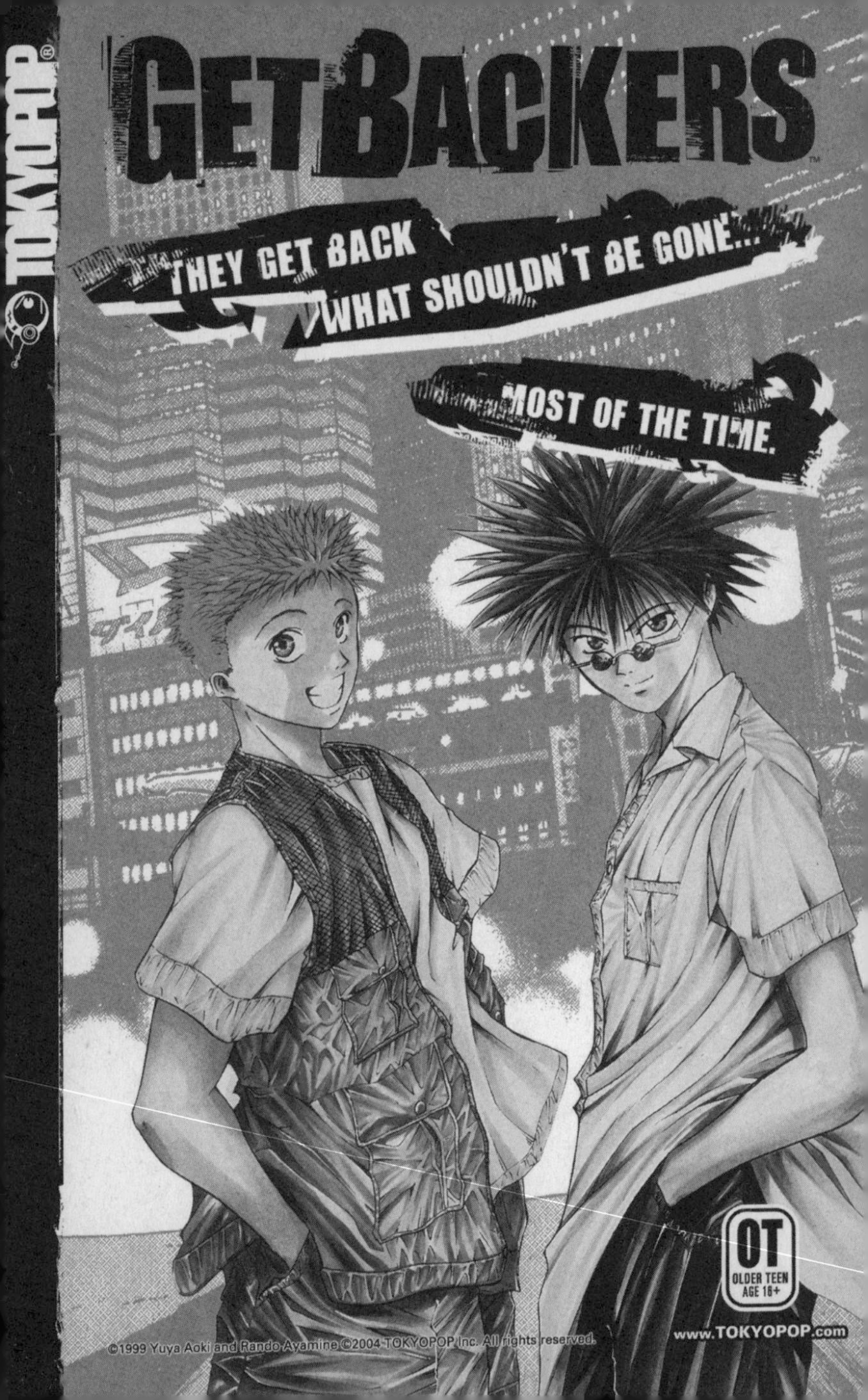
TOKYOPOP
GETBACKERS™
THEY GET BACK WHAT SHOULDN'T BE GONE...
MOST OF THE TIME.
OT
OLDER TEEN AGE 16+
www.TOKYOPOP.com
©1999 Yuya Aoki and Rando Ayamine ©2004 TOKYOPOP Inc. All rights reserved.

ALSO AVAILABLE FROM TOKYOPOP

MANGA

.HACK//LEGEND OF THE TWILIGHT
@LARGE
ABENOBASHI
A.I. LOVE YOU
AI YORI AOSHI
ANGELIC LAYER
ARM OF KANNON
BABY BIRTH
BATTLE ROYALE
BATTLE VIXENS
BRAIN POWERED
BRIGADOON
B'TX
CANDIDATE FOR GODDESS, THE
CARDCAPTOR SAKURA
CARDCAPTOR SAKURA - MASTER OF THE CLOW
CHOBITS
CHRONICLES OF THE CURSED SWORD
CLAMP SCHOOL DETECTIVES
CLOVER
COMIC PARTY
CONFIDENTIAL CONFESSIONS
CORRECTOR YUI
COWBOY BEBOP
COWBOY BEBOP: SHOOTING STAR
CRESCENT MOON
CULDCEPT
CYBORG 009
D.N. ANGEL
DEMON DIARY
DEMON ORORON, THE
DEUS VITAE
DIGIMON
DIGIMON ZERO TWO
DIGIMON TAMERS
DOLL
DRAGON HUNTER
DRAGON KNIGHTS
DREAM SAGA
DUKLYON: CLAMP SCHOOL DEFENDERS
ERICA SAKURAZAWA COLLECTED WORKS
EERIE QUEERIE!
ET CETERA
ETERNITY
EVIL'S RETURN
FAERIES' LANDING
FAKE
FLCL
FORBIDDEN DANCE
FRUITS BASKET
G GUNDAM
GATE KEEPERS

GETBACKERS
GIRL GOT GAME
GRAVITATION
GTO
GUNDAM SEED ASTRAY
GUNDAM WING
GUNDAM WING: BATTLEFIELD OF PACIFISTS
GUNDAM WING: ENDLESS WALTZ
GUNDAM WING: THE LAST OUTPOST (G-UNIT)
HAPPY MANIA
HARLEM BEAT
I.N.V.U.
IMMORTAL RAIN
INITIAL D
ISLAND
JING: KING OF BANDITS
JULINE
KARE KANO
KILL ME, KISS ME
KINDAICHI CASE FILES, THE
KING OF HELL
KODOCHA: SANA'S STAGE
LAMENT OF THE LAMB
LES BIJOUX
LEGEND OF CHUN HYANG, THE
LOVE HINA
LUPIN III
MAGIC KNIGHT RAYEARTH I
MAGIC KNIGHT RAYEARTH II
MAHOROMATIC: AUTOMATIC MAIDEN
MAN OF MANY FACES
MARMALADE BOY
MARS
MINK
MIRACLE GIRLS
MIYUKI-CHAN IN WONDERLAND
MODEL
ONE
PARADISE KISS
PARASYTE
PEACH GIRL
PEACH GIRL: CHANGE OF HEART
PET SHOP OF HORRORS
PITA-TEN
PLANET LADDER
PLANETES
PRIEST
PRINCESS AI
PSYCHIC ACADEMY
RAGNAROK
RAVE MASTER
REALITY CHECK
REBIRTH

12.20.03T

STOP!

This is the back of the book. You wouldn't want to spoil a great ending!

This book is printed "manga-style," in the authentic Japanese right-to-left format. Since none of the artwork has been flipped or altered, readers get to experience the story just as the creator intended. You've been asking for it, so TOKYOPOP® delivered: authentic, hot-off-the-press, and far more fun!

DIRECTIONS

If this is your first time reading manga-style, here's a quick guide to help you understand how it works.

It's easy... just start in the top right panel and follow the numbers. Have fun, and look for more 100% authentic manga from TOKYOPOP®!

1
2
3
4
5
6
7
8
9
10

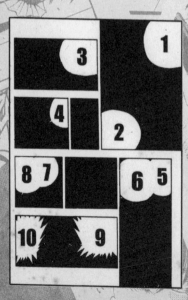

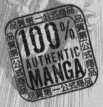